Get the eBook FREE!
(PDF, ePub, Kindle, and liveBook all included)

We believe that once you buy a book from us, you should be able to read it in any format we have available. To get electronic versions of this book at no additional cost to you, purchase and then register this book at the Manning website.

Go to https://www.manning.com/freebook and follow the instructions to complete your pBook registration.

That's it!
Thanks from Manning!

Quantum Programming in Depth

Solving problems with Q# and Qiskit

MARIIA MYKHAILOVA

MANNING
SHELTER ISLAND

For online information and ordering of this and other Manning books, please visit www.manning.com. The publisher offers discounts on this book when ordered in quantity.

For more information, please contact

    Special Sales Department
    Manning Publications Co.
    20 Baldwin Road
    PO Box 761
    Shelter Island, NY 11964
    Email: orders@manning.com

© 2025 Manning Publications Co. All rights reserved.

No part of this publication may be reproduced, stored in a retrieval system, or transmitted, in any form or by means electronic, mechanical, photocopying, or otherwise, without prior written permission of the publisher.

Many of the designations used by manufacturers and sellers to distinguish their products are claimed as trademarks. Where those designations appear in the book, and Manning Publications was aware of a trademark claim, the designations have been printed in initial caps or all caps.

♾ Recognizing the importance of preserving what has been written, it is Manning's policy to have the books we publish printed on acid-free paper, and we exert our best efforts to that end. Recognizing also our responsibility to conserve the resources of our planet, Manning books are printed on paper that is at least 15 percent recycled and processed without the use of elemental chlorine.

The author and publisher have made every effort to ensure that the information in this book was correct at press time. The author and publisher do not assume and hereby disclaim any liability to any party for any loss, damage, or disruption caused by errors or omissions, whether such errors or omissions result from negligence, accident, or any other cause, or from any usage of the information herein.

Manning Publications Co.	Development editor: Dustin Archibald
20 Baldwin Road	Technical editor: Guenevere E. Prawiroatmodjo
PO Box 761	Review editor: Dunja Nikitovic
Shelter Island, NY 11964	Production editor: Keri Hales
	Copy editor: Alisa Larson
	Proofreader: Jason Everett
	Technical proofreader: Edoardo Altamura
	Typesetter: Ammar Taha Mohamedy
	Cover designer: Marija Tudor

ISBN 9781633436909
Printed in the United States of America

brief contents

    1 ■ Quantum computing: The hype and the promise 1

PART 1 BUILDING YOUR OWN LIBRARY 17

    2 ■ Preparing quantum states 19
    3 ■ Implementing quantum operations 51

PART 2 LEARNING INFORMATION ABOUT A QUANTUM SYSTEM 87

    4 ■ Analyzing quantum states 89
    5 ■ Analyzing quantum operations 121

PART 3 SOLVING A CLASSICAL PROBLEM USING A QUANTUM ALGORITHM 153

    6 ■ Evaluating classical functions on a quantum computer 155
    7 ■ Grover's search algorithm 190
    8 ■ Solving N queens puzzle using Grover's algorithm 215
    9 ■ Evaluating the performance of quantum algorithms 241

contents

preface ix
acknowledgments xi
about this book xiii
about the author xvii
about the cover illustration xviii

1 Quantum computing: The hype and the promise 1

1.1 Your second book on quantum computing: The prerequisites 2

1.2 The hype and the promise: What kinds of problems can quantum computing solve? 3

1.3 A peek inside the fridge: How does quantum computing work? 5

Algorithms 5 ▪ Hardware 7 ▪ Software 9 ▪ Quantum application software development workflow 11

1.4 Why learn quantum computing? 12

1.5 Learning quantum computing through quantum programming 13

1.6 Further reading 14

PART 1 BUILDING YOUR OWN LIBRARY 17

2 Preparing quantum states 19

2.1 Preparing a single-qubit state 21

Math 22 ▪ Qiskit 24 ▪ Q# 25

- 2.2 What does your solution do? 27
  - *Qiskit* 28 ▪ *Q#* 29
- 2.3 Preparing a two-qubit state 30
  - *Refresher: Controlled gates in Dirac notation* 31 ▪ *Math* 33
  - *Qiskit* 34 ▪ *Q#* 36
- 2.4 Testing your solution 39
  - *Qiskit* 40 ▪ *Q#* 42
- 2.5 Preparing a multiqubit state 43
  - *Math* 44 ▪ *Qiskit* 46 ▪ *Q#* 47
- 2.6 Further reading 48
- 2.7 Going beyond 49

3 *Implementing quantum operations* 51

- 3.1 Implementing a single-qubit gate 55
  - *Math* 56 ▪ *Qiskit* 58 ▪ *Q#* 58
- 3.2 What does your solution do? 59
  - *Qiskit* 59 ▪ *Q#* 60
- 3.3 Testing your solution 62
  - *Qiskit* 62 ▪ *Q#* 63
- 3.4 Matrix decomposition 64
- 3.5 Implementing a two-qubit block-diagonal unitary with 2×2 blocks 66
  - *Refresher: Controlled gates in matrix notation* 66 ▪ *Math* 68
  - *Qiskit* 69 ▪ *Q#* 70
- 3.6 Implementing a two-qubit CS unitary 71
  - *Math* 71 ▪ *Qiskit* 72 ▪ *Q#* 72
- 3.7 Implementing a two-qubit block-antidiagonal unitary with 2×2 blocks 73
  - *Math* 73 ▪ *Qiskit* 74 ▪ *Q#* 74
- 3.8 Implementing a two-block block-diagonal unitary of arbitrary size 75
  - *Math* 76 ▪ *Qiskit* 78 ▪ *Q#* 79
- 3.9 Implementing a CS unitary of arbitrary size 80
  - *Math* 80 ▪ *Qiskit* 82 ▪ *Q#* 82
- 3.10 Implementing an arbitrary unitary of arbitrary size 83
  - *Math* 83 ▪ *Qiskit* 84
- 3.11 Further reading 84
- 3.12 Going beyond 85

Part 2 Learning information about a quantum system 87

4 Analyzing quantum states 89

4.1 Reading out information from a quantum system 91
    Math 91 ▪ Qiskit 93 ▪ Q# 95

4.2 Distinguishing superposition states consisting of distinct basis states 98
    Math 99 ▪ Qiskit 101 ▪ Q# 102

4.3 Distinguishing superposition states consisting of overlapping basis states 102
    Math 103 ▪ Qiskit 105 ▪ Q# 106

4.4 Distinguishing nonorthogonal states with minimum error 106
    Math 106 ▪ Qiskit 109 ▪ Q# 109

4.5 Reconstructing the state from multiple copies 109
    Math 110 ▪ Qiskit 111 ▪ Q# 112

4.6 Joint/parity measurements: Extracting partial information from a state 113
    Math 114 ▪ Qiskit 116 ▪ Q# 117

4.7 Further reading 118

4.8 Going beyond 118

5 Analyzing quantum operations 121

5.1 Distinguishing unitaries 123
    Math 123 ▪ Qiskit 127 ▪ Q# 128

5.2 Reconstructing the unitary 129
    Math 130 ▪ Qiskit 131 ▪ Q# 132

5.3 Finding eigenvalue of the given eigenvector: The phase estimation problem 133
    Phase kickback 136 ▪ Iterative phase estimation 137 Adaptive phase estimation 139 ▪ Quantum Fourier transform 142 ▪ Quantum phase estimation 144 Qiskit 146 ▪ Q# 148

5.4 Going beyond 150

Part 3 Solving a classical problem using a quantum algorithm 153

6 Evaluating classical functions on a quantum computer 155

6.1 Reversible computing: Mapping classical computation onto quantum 157

- 6.2 Evaluating single-bit functions 160
  - *Math 161 ▪ Qiskit 165 ▪ Q# 166*
- 6.3 Testing reversible computations 168
  - *Qiskit 170 ▪ Q# 171*
- 6.4 Evaluating Boolean operations 173
  - *Math 174 ▪ Qiskit 178 ▪ Q# 179*
- 6.5 Evaluating Boolean expressions 180
  - *Math 181 ▪ Qiskit 185 ▪ Q# 186*
- 6.6 Going beyond 188

7 Grover's search algorithm 190

- 7.1 Quantum oracles 193
  - *Math 194 ▪ Qiskit 199 ▪ Q# 201*
- 7.2 Grover's search algorithm 202
  - *Definitions 203 ▪ Math 208 ▪ Qiskit 211 ▪ Q# 212*
- 7.3 Going beyond 213

8 Solving N queens puzzle using Grover's algorithm 215

- 8.1 Naive solution 218
- 8.2 Encoding constraints in the search space 221
  - *Math 221 ▪ Qiskit 224 ▪ Q# 228*
- 8.3 Changing problem encoding 232
  - *Math 233 ▪ Qiskit 235 ▪ Q# 237*
- 8.4 Going beyond 239

9 Evaluating the performance of quantum algorithms 241

- 9.1 Choosing the classical solution for comparison 244
- 9.2 Performance comparisons: Asymptotic vs. practical 246
- 9.3 Estimating performance of a quantum solution 247
- 9.4 Azure Quantum Resource Estimator: An overview 251
- 9.5 Solutions' performance for the N queens puzzle 255
- 9.6 Further reading 256
- 9.7 Going beyond 256

appendix A Setting up your environment 259

index 263

preface

I joined Microsoft Quantum and, by extension, the world of quantum computing in early 2017, just as the team started developing the quantum programming language that later became Q#. I spent a big part of the next eight years learning quantum computing myself and helping others do the same, both as part of my job at Microsoft and in the course I teach at Northeastern University. And, while doing this, I noticed several gaps in the way quantum computing was taught.

First, a lot of material on quantum computing focused on its mathematical aspects only. I am an applied mathematician by training, so I'm comfortable with math. But I'm a software engineer by trade, and I'm a lot more comfortable with algorithms when I can implement them and experiment with running them! My first project in quantum computing education, the Quantum Katas, focused on introducing the basics—quantum states and gates, measurements, and simple algorithms—through a series of programming problems that the learner would solve to internalize the theory.

The second gap shows up later in the learning journey. There are plenty of "quantum computing 101" resources that focus on introductory concepts. But, once you've mastered the basics, what's next? What does "quantum computing 201" look like? If you've only ever run simple circuits, how do you start implementing real quantum algorithms? How do you test the quantum code you write? What do you need to know about quantum programming for future fault-tolerant quantum computers? And, ultimately, how do you figure out whether your quantum solution to the problem you're looking at is going to do better than a classical algorithm? This book aims to answer these questions.

The book offers you a selection of problems, from building quantum programming libraries to solving classical problems using quantum algorithms, and walks you through the solutions. As part of the discussion, I introduce the quantum software development workflow, from figuring out the algorithm suitable to solve the problem at hand to implementing the solution, testing it, and evaluating its performance. Each problem ends up being implemented as an end-to-end software project. Throughout the book I use Qiskit and Q#—two of the quantum programming languages used for quantum computing research today—to make sure the tools and methods I talk about are relevant to the current quantum programming landscape.

There are, of course, plenty of topics I could not include in the book: domain-specific applications, the architecture of fault-tolerant quantum computers and the software stack we're building for them, and debugging large-scale quantum algorithms, among others. I hope that this book will show you how to think about quantum computing as a software engineer and problem solver and thus equip you with the mindset you'll need to continue your pursuit of knowledge!

acknowledgments

First and foremost, I want to thank all the students I've had the privilege of teaching and all the learners and software developers I've had the pleasure of working with outside the formal classroom setting. It was their experiences, questions, and doubts that inspired me to write this book and helped me shape the answers and explanations it needed to provide.

Next, my gratitude goes to mentors and peers who taught me everything I know about quantum computing and quantum programming. Here is an incomplete list:

- Everybody in the Quantum Architectures and Computation group, for welcoming me to the world of quantum computing back in 2017 and guiding me through my first steps in it.
- Wim van Dam, for the discussions of quantum algorithms in general and phase estimation in particular.
- Mathias Soeken, Michal Stechly, and everybody at the Quantum Resource Estimation Workshop at IEEE Quantum Week, for the conversations about evaluating the performance of quantum algorithms that ultimately convinced me to dedicate a whole chapter to this topic.

Thanks to everyone who works on creating quantum software development toolkits, especially Azure Quantum Development Kit and Qiskit. It would be a lot harder to write a book about quantum programming if quantum programming tools didn't exist!

I want to thank the members of Manning's acquisitions, development, and production teams who made this book possible and helped it become the best version of itself. Many thanks go to the reviewers and the Manning Early Access Program

(MEAP) subscribers: Alain Couniot, Alberto Maldonado-Romo, Alexey Vyskubov, Amit Rambhai Modhwadia, Anup K Parikh, Bhagvan Kommadi, Brandon Darlington-Goddard, Christophe Pere, Daniel Guijo, Domingo Salazar, Fulvio Bruno, Gary Pass, James Weaver, Kaelyn Ferris, Kelvin D. Meeks, Krzysztof Kamyczek, Laud Bentil, Marco Venere, Maxime Boillot, Michael Wright, Michal Stechly, Nupur Baghel, Patrick Regan, Piero Giacomelli, Pierre Wan-Fat, Potito Coluccelli, Prasad Kukkamalla, Premkumar Reddy Jakkidi, Ricardo Verschueren, Saidaiah Yechuri, Mohammad Shahnawaz Akhter, Shivani Mayekar, Sonja Krause-Harder, Srikar Vedantam, Srinivas Vamsi Parasa, Tony Holdroyd, and William E. Wheeler. I am also grateful to my technical editor, Guen Prawiroatmodjo, experimental physicist and software engineer, as well as my technical proofer, Edoardo Altamura. Your feedback and suggestions helped make this a better book.

On a more personal note, I'd like to start by thanking my awesome husband, Sergii Dymchenko. From giving me Python advice to reminding me to exercise, he was there every step, helping me get this book done and keeping me sane. To my friends, thank you for your unwavering support and patience during the writing of this book; you will be seeing more of me now that I'm done! And finally, thanks to the creators of *Good Omens* TV show, the fandom, and the King County Library System: you were the perfect escape when I needed to take a break from all things quantum!

about this book

Quantum Programming in Depth isn't designed to teach you quantum computing from scratch, although I hope that you will learn a lot from it regardless of how much you already know when you start. It is meant to help you deepen your understanding of the fundamental concepts and apply them to solve problems, as well as expand your experience in quantum software development.

This is a book you should not just browse or flick through. Each chapter offers you a project to do or a series of problems to solve, and, while it walks you through the mathematical solutions and then the coding implementations, you will learn the most if you try to solve the tasks and write the code yourself, and then take the time to attempt the additional projects from Going Beyond idea lists. The more effort you invest into working through this book, the easier you'll find quantum computing problems you'll encounter afterward.

Who should read this book

This book was written for people who are interested in learning quantum computing and quantum programming beyond the basics. It is aimed at learners who have taken an introductory course and want to deepen their knowledge, or perhaps have studied the theory and want to get hands-on experience putting it into practice. You should already have an understanding of basic concepts and terminology, such as quantum gates, measurements, and Dirac notation.

This book will help you go from passing familiarity with the concepts of quantum computing to using them to solve realistic problems. You will become more confident as you write quantum programs, test them, and learn to think about their performance to better understand the potential use cases of quantum computing.

How this book is organized: A roadmap

This book has nine chapters. The first chapter gives you a quick overview of quantum computing, the kinds of problems it might solve more efficiently than classical computing, and quantum hardware and software development.

The remaining chapters are grouped into three parts. Part 1 includes two projects that can be used as building blocks for other, more complicated algorithms. This part also shows you how to write quantum code in Q# and Qiskit, run it on simulators, and test it:

- In chapter 2, you'll create a library that prepares arbitrary quantum states.
- In chapter 3, you'll learn to implement unitary transformations that are not part of the built-in gate set.

Part 2 offers a collection of smaller projects that focus on learning information about quantum systems:

- Chapter 4 focuses on using measurements to get the necessary information about quantum states.
- Chapter 5 uses the tools from the previous chapter to get information about unitary transformations. A big part of chapter 5 is dedicated to the phase estimation problem, one of important tools in the quantum computing toolbox.

Part 3 covers the end-to-end process of solving a classical problem using a quantum algorithm:

- Chapter 6 shows how classical functions can be represented and evaluated as part of quantum computations—this is the first step of quantum solutions to a lot of classical problems.
- Chapter 7 introduces Grover's algorithm, one of the most famous quantum algorithms for solving search problems.
- In chapter 8, you'll learn to use Grover's search algorithm to solve realistic problems and see the steps that are involved in that.
- Finally, chapter 9 discusses the performance of quantum programs and the way we think about comparing quantum solutions with classical ones to figure out whether a quantum algorithm can show a practical quantum advantage for a particular problem.

Each chapter is broken down into sections that focus on solving a specific task, learning to use a specific tool from the development toolkit, or implementing one part of the larger project. The goal of each section is to end up with working code in both Qiskit and Q#.

At the end of each chapter, you'll find a short section, Going Beyond, which provides a list of ideas of the ways to further develop the project from this chapter and similar projects you can do on your own. I encourage you to give them a try!

About the code

All the code written in this book can be found at https://github.com/tcNickolas/quantum-programming-in-depth. The project folder for each section includes the complete tests for the code developed in this section, even if they are omitted from the book itself. Sections 2.1–2.3, 3.1–3.2, and 6.2 are the exception to this rule, since I don't introduce the way to test the code written in these sections until later.

The code for each problem solved is available in both Qiskit and Q#. Installation instructions for both Qiskit and Azure Quantum Development Kit, as well as the pytest package, are available in the appendix and in the GitHub repository.

This book contains many examples of source code both in numbered listings and in line with normal text. In both cases, source code is formatted in a `fixed-width font like this` to separate it from ordinary text.

In many cases, the original source code has been reformatted; we've added line breaks and reworked indentation to accommodate the available page space in the book. Additionally, comments in the source code have often been removed from the listings when the code is described in the text. Code annotations accompany many of the listings, highlighting important concepts.

You can get executable snippets of code from the liveBook (online) version of this book at https://livebook.manning.com/book/quantum-programming-in-depth. The complete code for the examples in the book is available for download from the Manning website at https://www.manning.com/books/quantum-programming-in-depth and from GitHub at https://github.com/tcNickolas/quantum-programming-in-depth.

liveBook discussion forum

Purchase of *Quantum Programming in Depth* includes free access to liveBook, Manning's online reading platform. Using liveBook's exclusive discussion features, you can attach comments to the book globally or to specific sections or paragraphs. It's a snap to make notes for yourself, ask and answer technical questions, and receive help from the author and other users. To access the forum, go to https://livebook.manning.com/book/quantum-programming-in-depth/discussion. You can also learn more about Manning's forums and the rules of conduct at https://livebook.manning.com/discussion.

Manning's commitment to our readers is to provide a venue where a meaningful dialogue between individual readers and between readers and the author can take place. It is not a commitment to any specific amount of participation on the part of the author, whose contribution to the forum remains voluntary (and unpaid). We suggest you try asking the author some challenging questions lest her interest stray! The forum and the archives of previous discussions will be accessible from the publisher's website as long as the book is in print.

Other online resources

Are you looking to start with the very basics of quantum computing or even the linear algebra necessary for getting started? The Quantum Katas (https://quantum.microsoft.com/experience/quantum-katas) are online tutorials that follow the same practical hands-on approach to learning as this book. They offer plenty of programming problems and exercises in Q#, so completing them gives you a head start on the projects in this book!

As you work your way through the book and the code in each chapter, here are some additional resources to help you:

- Qiskit:
  - Qiskit documentation (https://docs.quantum.ibm.com/)—Complete documentation for using Qiskit and IBM Quantum in a quantum software development workflow
  - Qiskit on GitHub (https://github.com/Qiskit/)—Repositories that host Qiskit source code, as well as a collection of tools for working with Qiskit.
- Q#:
  - Q# documentation (https://learn.microsoft.com/azure/quantum/)—Complete documentation for using Q# and Azure Quantum in a quantum software development workflow.
  - Q# on GitHub (https://github.com/microsoft/qsharp/)—Source code for Q# compiler, simulators, and libraries, as well as a collection of Q# sample programs.

about the author

MARIIA MYKHAILOVA is a principal quantum software developer at PsiQuantum, working on software for fault-tolerant quantum computation. Prior to that, she was a quantum software engineer at Microsoft Quantum, joining the team in early 2017, just in time to participate in the development of the first version of the quantum programming language that became Q#. Mariia created the Quantum Katas project, an open source collection of hands-on tutorials and programming problems for learning quantum computing. She is also a part-time lecturer at Northeastern University, teaching Introduction to Quantum Computing since 2020, and the author of the O'Reilly book *Q# Pocket Guide*.

about the cover illustration

The figure on the cover of *Quantum Programming in Depth* is "Habitant de Juppa," taken from Balthasar Hacquet's *Images and Descriptions of Southwestern and Eastern Wenda, Illyrians, and Slavs*, published in 1815.

In those days, it was easy to identify where people lived and what their trade or station in life was just by their dress. Manning celebrates the inventiveness and initiative of the computer business with book covers based on the rich diversity of regional culture centuries ago, brought back to life by pictures from collections such as this one.

Quantum computing: The hype and the promise

This chapter covers
- The kinds of problems quantum computing might solve better than classical computing
- Three main components of quantum computing systems: algorithms, hardware, and software
- Major milestones of quantum hardware development, past and future
- Quantum software development workflow

Quantum computing uses quantum-mechanical phenomena to perform computations. It is a new computing paradigm that is fundamentally different from "classical computing"—the traditional technology that powers our world, from the home computers and smartphones we use on a daily basis to supercomputers that solve scientific problems.

Classical computing relies on the concepts that are familiar to us from our daily lives, and thus it feels intuitive to us, even if we often don't know the exact algorithms our computers employ to solve the problems we ask of them. For example, we can plan a trip using a paper map of the area, so a map application doing the same thing doesn't feel odd.

In contrast, we don't have a frame of reference for quantum-mechanical phenomena in our lives, so we don't have an opportunity to develop intuition for a model of computation that relies on them. Instead, we have to reason about quantum computing using mathematics and an occasional analogy that may or may not be helpful. Add to that the often-emphasized belief in the importance of mastering quantum physics for understanding quantum computing, and it's no wonder that this topic can feel mysterious and intimidating!

This chapter offers you the essential context around quantum computing and introduces a physics-free way to approach learning it—by solving problems and implementing the solutions to them as quantum programs.

1.1 Your second book on quantum computing: The prerequisites

This book is intended for readers who are already familiar with the basic concepts of quantum computing and seek to deepen their understanding of those basics and start using them to come up with solutions to nontrivial problems.

Here are the main quantum computing concepts you should be familiar with to get the most value out of this book:

- Quantum states and their representation as state vectors
- Quantum gates, their representation as matrices, and the ways to calculate their effect on quantum states by multiplying the state vector by the gate matrix
- Dirac notation for quantum states and performing computations in Dirac notation directly, without reverting to matrix computations
- The main quantum gates: Pauli gates X, Y, and Z, Hadamard gate H, rotation gate Ry, phase shift gates S and T, and CNOT and CCNOT gates
- Controlled and adjoint variants of gates
- Measurements for single- and multiqubit systems, their outcomes, and the relationship between the amplitudes of a state vector and the probabilities of measurement outcomes for it

I will include small refreshers in the text on these topics whenever they are required for the first time, but they aim to serve as reminders, not as detailed tutorials. Phrases such as "Given two qubits in the $|0\rangle$ state and an array of four floating-point numbers a, change the state of these qubits to $|\psi\rangle = \sum_{k=0}^{3} a_k |k\rangle$" (chapter 2) or "Apply a controlled variant of the rotation gate with the first $n-1$ bits as controls and the last bit as the target" (chapter 3) should make sense to you, even if you don't know how exactly to do that right away! If you are looking to get started with quantum computing from scratch, I recommend you combine this book with an additional resource that introduces the basic concepts slowly and thoroughly, be it another book, a set of online tutorials, or a series of video lectures.

The math of quantum computations is expressed in terms of complex numbers, vectors, and matrices. As you work with quantum computing, you should be comfortable doing basic linear algebra operations, such as multiplying matrices, finding inner and outer products of vectors, and computing tensor products of matrices. For example, you should understand the math-heavy sentences such as "The probability of the state $|\psi_0\rangle$ being measured as $|m_0\rangle$ is $|\langle\psi_0|m_0\rangle|^2$" (chapter 4) or "The state of the system becomes $\frac{1}{\sqrt{2}}(|0\rangle - |1\rangle) \otimes |1\rangle$" (chapter 5).

This book assumes familiarity with basic trigonometric functions such as sine, cosine, and tangent and includes reminders of the trigonometric identities used in the computations. Some projects additionally require some trigonometry or slightly more advanced linear algebra concepts such as eigenvectors and eigenvalues (chapter 5). I will introduce these more advanced concepts in the chapters that rely on them.

Finally, understanding the basics of computational complexity theory will be useful for the discussions of quantum algorithms' performance. I do not go into detailed analysis of asymptotic behavior of quantum algorithms considered in this book, but you should be familiar with the concept of asymptotic behavior itself and the basics of the big-O notation (for example, the term "quadratic speedup").

A great getting started resource is the Quantum Katas (https://mng.bz/GeoO)—an open source collection of hands-on tutorials and programming exercises that I created to help beginners learn the very basics of quantum computing. The tutorials include an introduction to working with complex numbers and linear algebra tools that are required to express quantum computations, as well as all basic concepts of quantum computing and some educational algorithms. Best of all, the programming exercises in the Quantum Katas provide immediate feedback on your work, helping you learn more effectively. If you prefer to start learning quantum computing by reading a book rather than by diving into programming right away, check out the book *Learn Quantum Computing with Python and Q#* by Sarah Kaiser and Cassandra Granade (Manning, 2021).

1.2 The hype and the promise: What kinds of problems can quantum computing solve?

You have most likely heard a lot about quantum computing and its promise to solve all kinds of problems. There is a lot of hype around quantum computing these days—one might even get an impression that it will replace classical computing altogether! This is, in fact, not true.

Even though quantum computing is still in its early days, scientists are quite certain that it is not going to be useful for every computing task that occurs in our lives. In principle, a large enough quantum computer can run any classical computation. However, it will take the quantum computer a lot longer to run an equivalent of a classical computation than it will take a classical computer to run the original classical program. So, if a classical computer is doing a good enough job of a mundane task like checking your email or searching through a database, there is no need to try to harness a quantum computer to do the same thing.

Instead, scientists are looking for problems that cannot be solved by classical computers efficiently and for algorithms that quantum computers can use to solve them better. Figure 1.1 illustrates the behavior of classical and quantum solutions for a problem that can benefit from quantum computing.

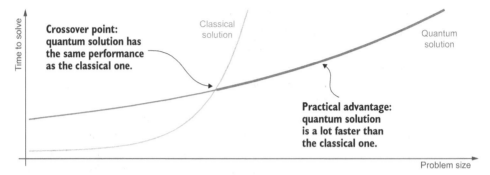

Figure 1.1 Quantum advantage might be achievable if the time a quantum computer takes to solve a certain problem grows at a slower rate as the problem size increases than the time a classical computer takes to do the same. In this case, problem instances that are much larger than the crossover size might be good candidates for quantum solutions. If the crossover time is months or more, quantum computing offers no practical advantage, since larger problem instances take much longer to solve, and running a quantum computer for months or years to solve a single problem is not practical.

A problem has to satisfy multiple requirements to show *practical quantum advantage*:

- A classical computer or even a supercomputer running the best known algorithm takes too long to solve the problem to be useful (years, decades, or even longer).
- A quantum computer can solve the same problem fast enough for the solution to be useful (at most, days and preferably hours).
- The problem is a meaningful, real-world application rather than an artificially constructed task with no practical value, and the answer is valuable regardless of how it has been obtained.

It is already clear that the problems that will show quantum advantage will be very specialized, similar to the ones that today's supercomputers tackle. Materials science and simulating quantum systems that occur in chemistry and physics problems are a few examples of such tasks. (Why? These kinds of problems involve accurately simulating behavior of quantum systems, such as electrons in molecules, and a simulation that uses a computer based on the same principles as the system being simulated turns out to be a lot more efficient compared to a classical simulation.)

Quantum algorithms research to date suggests several properties of the problems that might exhibit practical quantum advantage. First, the problems best suited for quantum computation are "small-data big-compute" problems—problems that have small inputs and require a massive computation to process them. For example, for integer factorization, a problem for which Shor's quantum algorithm promises to outperform the best classical algorithms, the input is a single number, but finding its divisors is computationally hard. Similarly, for quantum systems simulations, the input descriptions of the systems being simulated are much smaller than the computation required to find the required properties of the system.

Next, the problem has to have some sort of structure that can be exploited by the quantum algorithm. For example, Shor's algorithm for integer factorization relies on periodicity of a specific function defined based on the number that we aim to factor.

Finally, the asymptotic behavior of the quantum algorithm has to be significantly better than that of the classical algorithm. There are many factors that affect the practical performance of a quantum algorithm (we'll talk about them in chapter 9). Once we take them into account, we realize that a quantum algorithm that offers only a quadratic speedup over its classical counterpart (for example, Grover's search algorithm, which we'll discuss in chapter 7) is extremely unlikely to offer practical advantage. It is possible that only algorithms with exponential or better speedups will end up being practical.

The research of applications that will benefit from quantum computing is still ongoing, but even if the pool of these applications ends up being limited to highly specialized applications such as materials science and quantum systems simulations, they have the potential for having a huge effect on our lives. This kind of application can lead to discoveries of new materials with highly desirable properties that have the potential to revolutionize entire industries such as energy and manufacturing.

1.3 A peek inside the fridge: How does quantum computing work?

Quantum computing systems consist of three main components: algorithms, hardware, and software. These components tend to evolve in parallel, each of them informing the requirements for development of the others and boosting their progress in turn. Let's take a closer look at each of them.

> **NOTE** This book focuses on the gate-based model of quantum computation, in which the computation is represented as a sequence of single- and multiqubit quantum gates, similar to how digital computers represent the computation as a sequence of logic gates. Other models of quantum computation exist that are equivalent to the gate-based model and rely on the same principles, although implemented differently. Examples of such models are the measurement-based model, which represents the computation as a sequence of measurements and single-qubit gates, and the adiabatic model, which is similar to analog classical computers.

1.3.1 Algorithms

Even though quantum mechanics developed in the first decades of the 20th century, quantum computing did not emerge until the early 1980s, when Paul Benioff, Yuri Manin, and Richard Feynman independently suggested that quantum-mechanical systems can be used to perform computations that cannot be efficiently done on classical computers, such as simulation of quantum system evolution. It took another decade for scientists to come up with the first quantum algorithms that promised speedups for solving purely classical problems not related to physics simulations: Shor's integer factorization algorithm and Grover's search algorithm.

Quantum algorithms were the driving force behind the emergence of quantum computing as a separate field. After all, we're not building quantum computers just because we can: we do it because of their promise to solve problems that are of practical interest to the world. Continued progress in quantum algorithms development and discovery of new problems that quantum computers will be great at solving are essential to the long-term success of quantum computing.

It is also important to consider quantum algorithms not only in terms of their abstract computational complexity but also with an eye toward the practicality of their implementation. Sometimes quantum algorithms that theoretically have a better computational complexity than their classical counterparts turn out to be not so attractive under a more rigorous analysis that takes into account all the implementation details.

Grover's algorithm for unstructured search, or function inversion, is a great example of such an algorithm. It solves the following problem: given a black box function (a function that you can evaluate for a specific input but don't have any information about otherwise) with N possible inputs, find the input that produces a specific output. Grover's search can find the solution in $O(\sqrt{N})$ calls of this function, while the classical algorithm acting under the same limitations takes $O(N)$ calls. We say that the quantum algorithm offers a *quadratic speedup* in this case.

However, in practice, classical computing tends to take advantage of the structure of the problem to devise a much more efficient algorithm than the brute-force one relying on accessing the function as a black box. Database search is often mentioned as one of the applications of quantum computing, but you don't see a classical database searched by randomly picking an entry and checking whether it fits the search condition; instead, the databases have indices and partitions in place to improve the data retrieval speed. Grover's search cannot use the problem structure as efficiently as the classical algorithms, so for a lot of problems, it ends up being slower than the best classical algorithms even theoretically.

The search problems that do not have an efficient classical algorithm exploiting their structure, such as the hash inversion problem, encounter a different problem. We expect the elementary operations on quantum computers to be quite a bit slower than on classical ones, and implementing simple classical computations such as integer or floating-point arithmetic to be a lot more complicated. Consequently, one function evaluation on a quantum computer can be many orders of magnitude slower than on a classical one, dwarfing the theoretical complexity improvement. We discuss these and other factors that have to be taken into account when evaluating performance of quantum algorithms in more detail in chapter 9.

Increasingly thorough analysis of the quantum algorithms and the speedups offered by them is an important part of the quantum algorithm discovery. It is aided by the quantum software progress, and the results of this analysis, in turn, inform the decisions made about both software and hardware design.

1.3.2 Hardware

The suggestion to use the principles of quantum mechanics to perform computations launched the efforts to build a physical implementation of this idea—a working quantum computer. The first experimental implementations of quantum algorithms were demonstrated in 1998 using small nuclear magnetic resonance quantum computers.

The state of quantum hardware development now, two and a half decades after those early experiments, is aptly described as "noisy intermediate-scale quantum era" (NISQ), the term introduced by John Preskill in his keynote at Quantum Computing for Business in December 2017. The best available quantum devices are large enough that their behavior cannot be simulated classically, but still too small and too noisy to solve practical problems.

Multiple companies worldwide are building quantum computers based on different underlying technologies. The landscape of the approaches considered to be the most viable shifts over time; for example, nuclear magnetic resonance devices that played a prominent role in early demonstrations of experimental quantum computing are not suitable for building large quantum computers. The main technologies pursued today are (in no particular order) superconducting circuits, trapped ions, neutral atoms, and photons.

To reach maturity, quantum hardware has to hit four milestones shown in figure 1.2.

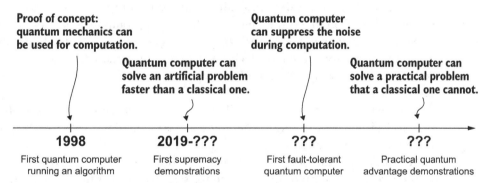

Figure 1.2 The major milestones of quantum hardware development. The first two, showing the use of quantum mechanics to perform a computation and having a quantum computer solve an artificial problem that a classical computer cannot, have already been achieved. The next milestone, building a fault-tolerant quantum computer that can run long computations, is the current focus. The final goal is to build a quantum computer that can solve practical problems that a classical computer cannot.

The first milestone is implementing a proof of concept device that shows the fundamental possibility of harnessing quantum-mechanical principles for performing a certain computation. This milestone has been achieved over two decades ago with the first nuclear magnetic resonance quantum computers that implemented small algorithms such as Deutsch, Deutsch-Jozsa and Grover's search algorithm. However, this milestone remains an important one, since it shifted quantum computation from being a theoretical conjecture to becoming an area of practical experimentation.

The second milestone is demonstrating a device solving a problem that cannot be solved on a classical computer in a reasonable amount of time, without the requirement that this problem is useful outside this demonstration, focusing on the scientific merit of the demonstration rather than on the practical one. There is no clear-cut way to recognize whether this milestone has been accomplished, since classical algorithms improve over time and such demonstrations can be challenged later. The first supremacy claims by Google and by the University of Science and Technology of China, published between 2019 and 2022, were refuted in the next few years by other researchers who demonstrated efficient classical algorithms for solving the same problems.

Next, the quantum computers need to become *fault-tolerant*—able to reduce the noise to arbitrarily low levels that would allow them to carry out long computations. This means that they have to run error correction continuously, as a layer that protects logical programs from the noise that occurs during their execution on hardware. The current systems cannot do that; instead, they rely on techniques like error mitigation to improve the accuracy of the results produced by the quantum devices. However, error correction is one of the requirements for fault-tolerant quantum computers, together with scaling up the number of qubits significantly. A lot of current research and experimentation focuses on demonstrating error correction on existing hardware on a small scale.

The final milestone is demonstrating a quantum computer solving a practically significant problem that cannot be solved by classical computers in reasonable time.

Notably, the raw parameters such as the number of qubits in a quantum computer are not the primary criteria for declaring a milestone achieved. What matters more is the kind of problems you can solve using that quantum computer and the quality of the results.

Despite the quantum hardware still having a long way to go before it can offer us a practical advantage over classical computers, it is fascinating to observe the progress happening in the industry.

When I joined the field of quantum computing in early 2017, IBM had just released a 5-qubit computer in the cloud for scientists and enthusiasts worldwide to experiment with, and unveiled a 17-qubit processor shortly after. In mid-2023, when I started writing this book, a lot of attention was still focused on building devices with more qubits (the highest number was 433 qubits in an IBM device) and looking for applications for them. In December 2024, during the final edits for this book, the world record for the most qubits in a quantum computer was held by a 1,180-qubit device announced by Atom Computing in October 2023.

By the end of 2023, though, the focus of the quantum computing community largely switched to the pursuit of the fault-tolerance milestone. The year 2024 saw a number of exciting error correction demonstrations by multiple companies, including Microsoft, Quantinuum, and Google. And the next decade is promising to bring even faster progress!

1.3.3 Software

The software stack plays a crucial role for quantum computers, same as it does for classical computers, serving as an interface between the theoretical algorithms and hardware that can run them. It includes multiple types of software that enable quantum application development, testing, evaluation, and execution on quantum hardware.

Based on its purpose, quantum software can be divided in two large classes: application software that utilizes the quantum computer to solve problems and system software that provides the platform for running application software. Figure 1.3 shows some of the most prominent layers of the quantum software stack.

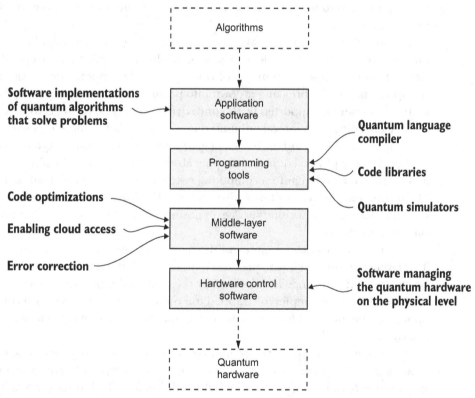

Figure 1.3 A quantum software stack serves as an interface between the quantum algorithms and the hardware running them. Its components mirror those of the classical software stack.

Let's take a closer look at examples of software within each layer shown in the figure. Application software uses the rest of the software stack and the quantum hardware to solve specific practical problems. This software directly implements the quantum algorithms developed for solving these problems. A program that evaluates properties of molecules using a quantum chemistry algorithm is an example of application software.

The next layer is the programming tools that support the programming language used to develop application software. This language will typically be hardware-agnostic, expressing the algorithm in terms of abstract concepts such as qubit allocation and gate application rather than commands specific to a certain hardware platform. This agnosticism enables running the same code on multiple hardware devices, possibly built based on completely different physical platforms, without rewriting it for each device. Depending on the language, its programming toolkit can include a standalone domain-specific language, like Q#, or libraries that allow you to embed the quantum program elements into a classical programming language, like Qiskit which is implemented as a Python library. It will also typically include a variety of quantum libraries—collections of prewritten programs and utilities that make developing quantum applications easier, similar to the ones available for classical programming languages.

The middle-layer software takes care of converting high-level application code into its representation suitable for running on the target hardware. Depending on the platform, various components of this layer can be responsible for optimizing the application code, breaking it down into primitive gates and measurements (elementary operations supported by the underlying system), applying error correction (that is, encoding each logical qubit used in a program into multiple physical qubits on a quantum device and each logical gate into a fault-tolerant sequence of gates applied to those physical qubits), mapping abstract qubits to specific physical objects, and so on. For cloud quantum computing systems, such as Azure Quantum and IBM Quantum, middle-layer software also includes the software that enables access to quantum hardware as a cloud service, exposing the APIs necessary to run programs on quantum devices.

Finally, control software manages the quantum hardware on the physical level. This layer communicates with quantum hardware directly and thus is specific to each hardware platform, since it is defined by the underlying physical implementation of the qubits. For example, for trapped ion qubits, this software controls the lasers applied to the ions, and for superconducting qubits, the microwave pulses applied to the circuits.

In addition to the typical programming tools that enable quantum code development, such as compilers, integrated development environments, and code libraries, quantum programming toolkits include additional tools that have no equivalent in classical software development. The primary example of such tools are *quantum simulators*—classical programs that can run simulations of small quantum systems. Quantum simulators can plug into the software stack at any layer, depending on the aspects of the system that need to be simulated. For example, on the highest level, they allow the developer to run the entire quantum program for small instances of the problem it solves on a classical computer, without accessing quantum hardware; on a lower level a quantum simulator can focus on imitating the noisy behavior of the quantum device, allowing to validate the error correction software. These kinds of tools are critically important for testing quantum programs, and you will use them extensively later in this book.

1.3.4 Quantum application software development workflow

The quantum application developer interacts primarily with the topmost system software layer, the programming tools (although understanding of the underlying layers certainly helps, same as in classical software development). These tools have to support the steps of the quantum application software development workflow, shown in figure 1.4.

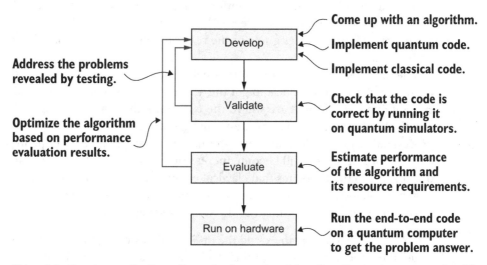

Figure 1.4 Quantum application software development workflow. From the developer perspective, it is similar to the classical software development workflow, with some differences to account for the nature of quantum computing. For example, using quantum simulators instead of the hardware makes testing quantum code on small problems faster and easier because it eliminates the need to account for noise.

The first step of creating a quantum software application is coming up with the algorithm to use and implementing it. This does not necessarily mean only the quantum code! A lot of practical quantum applications are expected to use *hybrid algorithms*, combining quantum subroutines that perform heavy computations with classical ones that take care of the tasks better suited for classical computers. Developing hybrid applications will include writing both quantum and classical code, tightly coupled together.

Once the code is written, the next step is validating its correctness. Testing and debugging quantum programs borrows some concepts from classical software testing, but the fundamental differences between quantum and classical computing mean that some techniques have to be reinvented from scratch. For example, the technique of checking the state of the variables used in a classical program at certain points of its execution cannot be replicated on quantum hardware, since it is impossible to get complete information about the state of a quantum system by observing it.

Instead, the developer can use quantum simulators that, being classical programs, allow peeking at their internal state, to validate the quantum program behavior on small problem instances.

After the code is written and tested, it is time to evaluate its performance and resource requirements. The currently available quantum devices are small and noisy enough that they can only run programs that require relatively few qubits and gates. This step helps evaluate whether the program can fit on a device with a certain number of qubits and be executed before the noise obscures the results. Another use of resource estimation for quantum programs is evaluating the efficiency of different implementations of the same subroutine or algorithm, thus enabling optimizing the program in advance of quantum devices being ready to successfully execute it, as well as informing hardware designers of the requirements of running large algorithms on hardware.

The final step of the quantum software development process is running the application on quantum hardware to get the answer to the problem it solves. Since the current quantum devices are still in the NISQ era, they cannot solve problems of practical importance yet, so this step is used as a part of the application validation process rather than as the end goal of the application development. As quantum hardware matures, this step will become increasingly more important, as it will provide the answers to the problems that classical computers cannot provide.

This book focuses on the first three steps of this workflow, developing and testing quantum programs and evaluating the resources they require.

> **TIP** You are welcome to extend the projects discussed in this book by trying to use the cloud quantum computing systems available today to run your programs on real quantum devices!

Quantum software is the critically important connective tissue between quantum algorithms and quantum hardware. The progress made in all layers of the software stack enables us to run new kinds of algorithms on hardware and allows us to shift from reasoning about quantum algorithms in terms of circuits to reasoning in terms of high-level programs and from estimating abstract runtime complexity of an algorithm to implementing it and getting accurate performance information. All these capabilities enable progress in both algorithms development and hardware design.

1.4 Why learn quantum computing?

The recent advances in all areas of quantum technologies bring attention and funding from governments and industry leaders around the globe. These areas include quantum computing, quantum communications (using quantum principles to enable safe communications), and quantum sensing (building sensors based on quantum systems) with quantum computing being the most promising of the three and attracting the most notice.

Governments of multiple countries recognize the potential effect of quantum science and invest billions of dollars in programs aiming to accelerate its progress. The National Quantum Initiative Act passed in 2018 defined the United States' plan of advancing quantum technology for the next 10 years. In the same year, the European Union launched a decade-long research initiative called Quantum Flagship with the goal of consolidating and expanding European scientific work in this area.

For several decades, quantum computing has been an area of primarily theoretical research. These days, though, industry involvement in the area is growing rapidly. As of late 2024, over 600 companies—both large companies with quantum-dedicated divisions and startups focused solely on one or several aspects of quantum technologies—and almost 200 universities worldwide are involved in quantum technologies research and development.

Increasing numbers of industry and academia jobs related to quantum technologies is driving the growing demand in workforce development in this area and broadening accessibility of quantum computing education. Ten or fifteen years ago, the main career path into quantum computing involved getting a PhD in quantum physics or theoretical quantum science and then staying in academia. As far as career choices went, it was an uncommon one. During my time earning a computer science degree at the Kyiv Polytechnical Institute, I learned about quantum physics but not about the idea of using its principles for computation, so it never occurred to me to consider it as an option for further studies. I've discovered the fascinating world of quantum computing only a decade later and had to learn everything from scratch after joining Microsoft Quantum.

These days, quantum computing is much more prominent in the public eye, and the education necessary to get involved in it is much more accessible. As of late 2024, 55 universities worldwide offer master's degree programs in quantum technologies. There are also countless software tools and online learning resources that make it possible to approach learning quantum computing from a computer science angle, without dedicating years to learning the underlying physics.

The abundance of opportunities to get involved in quantum computing and start contributing to the area makes the present moment a great time to learn quantum computing. Even if you end up not working in quantum computing domain full time, you'll reap the benefits of learning a new computing paradigm and that, same as learning new natural languages, is the best kind of brain teaser, making you a better thinker in the long run!

1.5 Learning quantum computing through quantum programming

This book takes a hands-on approach to quantum computing, focusing on problem-solving and quantum programming practice. It offers you a selection of introductory problems in quantum computing and walks you through the solutions, treating them as end-to-end software projects. Each project covers all the steps from the mathematical reasoning to working code, complete with unit tests. The offered projects, however, are not the ones that will yield practical advantage once quantum computers reach their maturity—materials science and quantum systems simulation are far from introductory topics! Rather, the problems I selected for the book emphasize the practice of manipulating the basic elements from which quantum algorithms are constructed and getting comfortable inventing and implementing algorithms, even if they're relatively simple.

What kind of projects will we build in this book? Some of them are implementations of useful library routines, such as preparing a given quantum state or implementing a given unitary transformation. Others explore well-known quantum algorithms and using them to solve problems, such as estimating eigenvalues of the given unitary or finding a solution to a simple classical puzzle using Grover's search.

At this point in the evolution of quantum computing, plenty of software tools are available for working with it, from frameworks designed to support the entire quantum software development workflow to specialized tools focused on specific areas. So, you have a lot of tools to choose from when solving the kind of problems discussed in this book.

I use two quantum programming languages, Qiskit and Q#, throughout the book. Qiskit is a Python library developed by IBM and currently the most popular circuit-level quantum programming language. Q# is a domain-specific language developed by Microsoft that focuses on high-level quantum algorithm design and can be integrated with Python code for pre- and postprocessing (for example, verifying the results of quantum code execution in tests). Both languages come with open source toolkits that support all steps of quantum software development workflow discussed earlier in this chapter. The appendix includes setup instructions for both Q# and Qiskit development environments. (You can find a pointer to the list of other open source quantum software tools in section 1.6.)

To get the most out of this book, you should be comfortable working with Python, creating test projects with it, and using basic language constructs such as variables, loops, methods, etc. I introduce the basic language elements of both Qiskit and Q# as we go.

Keep reading to start solving problems and writing your own quantum programs. And who knows, one day it might be you at the forefront of quantum computing progress!

1.6 Further reading

Here is a short list of references that are good starting points if you want to learn more about some topics I briefly mentioned in this chapter:

Section 1.2

- Hoefler, T., Haener, T., & Troyer, M. (2023). Disentangling hype from practicality: On realistically achieving quantum advantage. https://arxiv.org/abs/2307.00523
- Aaronson, S. (2022). How much structure is needed for huge quantum speed-ups? https://arxiv.org/abs/2209.06930

- Preskill, J. (2018). Quantum computing in the NISQ era and beyond. https://arxiv.org/abs/1801.00862

Section 1.3

Multiple groups demonstrated implementations of quantum algorithms nearly simultaneously. Examples include

- Jones, J. A., & Mosca, M. (1998). Implementation of a quantum algorithm to solve Deutsch's problem on a nuclear magnetic resonance quantum computer. https://arxiv.org/abs/quant-ph/9801027
- Chuang, I., Gershenfeld, N., & Kubinec, M. (1998). Experimental implementation of fast quantum searching. *Physical Review Letters, 80,* 3408-3411. http://cba.mit.edu/docs/papers/98.03.grover.pdf

The shift from the pursuit of useful algorithms that can run on NISQ machines to focus on overcoming noise in quantum devices is illustrated in

- Preskill, J. (2023). Crossing the quantum chasm: From NISQ to fault tolerance. https://quantumfrontiers.com/2023/12/09/crossing-the-quantum-chasm-from-nisq-to-fault-tolerance/

Section 1.5

Quantum Open Source Foundation maintains a list of open quantum software projects at https://qosf.org/project_list, which includes both general-purpose quantum software development kits and specialized tools.

Summary

- Quantum computing will not speed up arbitrary classical computing tasks. Instead, it will let us solve some highly specialized problems such as quantum systems simulations that are too complicated for classical (super)computers.
- To yield practical advantage over the best classical algorithms for the same problem, quantum algorithms have to offer significant speedups, featuring at least exponentially better asymptotic complexity compared to that of the classical algorithms.
- Quantum hardware is in its "noisy intermediate-scale" era, with devices too large to be simulated classically but too small and too noisy to solve practical problems.
- The software stack plays a critical role for quantum computers, enabling the execution of algorithms on hardware and accessing the quantum systems via the cloud, accelerating algorithms research and driving the requirements for hardware design.
- Governments and companies worldwide are paying increasing attention to quantum computing and investing in its continued development.
- Learning quantum computing can provide you with a lot of opportunities to contribute to this domain and, like learning any new computing paradigm, make you a better thinker!

Part 1

Building your own library

The first part of the book covers two projects that focus on manipulating quantum states using quantum gates. Conveniently, you can do these projects early on in your learning process, even before you learn how quantum measurements work!

Both projects in this chapter implement operations that act as building blocks for other, more complicated quantum algorithms, and can be reused later in the book. In chapter 2, we develop a library that prepares arbitrary quantum states. In chapter 3, we learn to implement arbitrary unitary transformations on multiple qubits.

This part covers the basics of writing quantum programs in Qiskit and Q#. It also introduces the principles of testing quantum code by running it on quantum simulators, as well as the tools that allow you to validate the behavior of quantum programs.

Preparing quantum states

This chapter covers
- Using quantum gates to change quantum states
- Using Q# and Qiskit to write quantum programs
- Running and testing quantum programs using simulators
- Watching the state of a quantum program during its execution

Quantum algorithms revolve around manipulating the states of quantum systems. Figure 2.1 shows the flow typical for many quantum algorithms. The algorithm starts with preparing the quantum system in a certain superposition state and then applies a sequence of transformations to it before performing a measurement to extract the results. The goal of the algorithm is to lead the system to a superposition state in which the basis states that are answers to the problem being solved have large amplitudes, and all the other basis states have much smaller amplitudes. This allows the final measurement to yield the answer to the problem with high probability.

> **NOTE** Not all quantum algorithms follow this approach. Some algorithms focus on estimating the probabilities of measurement outcomes instead; you'll see an example in chapter 5 when we discuss different phase estimation algorithms. However, preparing the quantum system in a certain initial state is an important step for these algorithms as well.

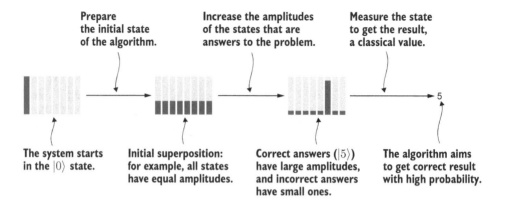

Figure 2.1 Any quantum algorithm can be broken down into several steps: prepare the initial state, evolve it following the algorithm, and measure the end state to get the result. The goal of many algorithms is to end up in a state in which the result of the final measurement is a correct answer with high probability. (Each block of eight bars represents the eight amplitudes of the basis states in a three-qubit quantum state.)

In this chapter, we'll focus on the first step of a quantum algorithm: state preparation. The goal of this step is as follows: given a freshly initialized system, typically in the $|0\rangle$ state, change its state to the given superposition state. This state is often simple—for example, a superposition in which all basis states are present and have equal amplitudes. (You've probably seen plenty of educational algorithms that start with "Prepare an equal superposition of all the basis states on the input qubits." Deutsch–Jozsa, Bernstein–Vazirani, and the basic Grover's search algorithm are just a few examples that come to mind.)

But the more elaborate the required state is, the more interesting the task of preparing it becomes. For example, a modification of Grover's search algorithm that we'll discuss in chapter 8 relies on preparing a state that is an equal superposition of only the basis states that are included in the search space, rather than of all the basis states. The first step of the Harrow–Hassidim–Lloyd (HHL) algorithm—the algorithm for solving a system of linear equations $Ax = b$—is preparing the arbitrary superposition state $|b\rangle = \sum b_k |k\rangle$. Variational quantum eigensolver—the algorithm for estimating the ground energy of the given physical system—relies on preparing the quantum state that describes the ground state of the system (called *ansatz* in this context).

More broadly, a lot of quantum algorithms, including quantum machine learning algorithms, rely on *quantum random access memory* (qRAM), an abstraction that represents the ability to load a large amount of classical data into a quantum computer fast. Finding an efficient way to implement qRAM is still an open problem. One variant of implementing qRAM stores the classical values and allows the algorithm to "read" all of them at once as a superposition state, which is just another way to describe the state preparation problem.

Occasionally, state preparation shows up as a part of the second step of the algorithm, state evolution. For example, the "reflection about the mean" step of Grover's search algorithm is commonly implemented using the same state preparation routine as the one used to prepare the initial state of the algorithm (we'll see examples in chapters 7 and 8).

Now that you have some idea about the applications of the state preparation, let's take a look at the problem itself, starting with its single-qubit variant and building up to preparing arbitrary multiqubit states with real amplitudes. Along the way, I will introduce writing quantum programs in Q# and Qiskit, using simulators to run these programs and observe their results, and writing tests for quantum software projects.

> **Why state preparation?**
>
> You are not likely to have to write the state preparation code in real quantum software projects yourself. Both Qiskit and Q# have libraries that do this for you: Qiskit's class `QuantumCircuit` offers a method `initialize` that initializes the given qubit array in the state described using the given array of complex amplitudes, and Q#'s `PreparePureStateD` and `ApproximatelyPreparePureStateCP` operations from the namespace `Microsoft.Quantum.Unstable.StatePreparation` do the same for real or complex amplitudes, respectively. I selected this problem as the first project for several reasons:
>
> - It is easy to define, and the solution relies only on the most basic concepts such as qubits and gates, not even using measurements. State preparation problems are some of the first exercises you can try solving when you're learning quantum computing.
> - It allows us to start simple and build up to fairly sophisticated concepts such as applying controlled gates and using recursion in quantum algorithms.
> - This problem is the kind that a beginner can approach and solve themselves rather than just implement somebody's algorithm, and helping you learn to come up with algorithms yourself is the whole point of this book!

2.1 Preparing a single-qubit state

Let's start with *almost* the simplest possible state preparation problem. Given a single qubit in the $|0\rangle$ state and two floating-point numbers α and β that, when squared, add up to 1 ($\alpha^2 + \beta^2 = 1$), change the state of this qubit to the state $\alpha |0\rangle + \beta |1\rangle$. In matrix notation, we're looking to perform the transformation

$$\begin{pmatrix} 1 \\ 0 \end{pmatrix} \rightarrow \begin{pmatrix} \alpha \\ \beta \end{pmatrix}$$

> **NOTE** The simplest possible state preparation tasks are preparing the qubit in the $|1\rangle$ state or in the "plus" state—the state $\frac{1}{\sqrt{2}}(|0\rangle + |1\rangle)$. Why not start with one of these? Neither of these states is a good building block for the state preparation problem because it's trickier to transform them into the uneven superposition state we're looking for than to start with the $|0\rangle$ state directly.

2.1.1 Math

For a problem that small, we're not so much inventing an algorithm to solve it as looking for a single-qubit quantum gate that can do it. Each quantum programming language comes with a set of built-in gates that implements the most common quantum logic gates, so a good first step is checking whether any of them performs the right transformation.

Table 2.1 gives a brief list of commonly used single-qubit quantum gates. You can find the more detailed explanations of these and other gates and the rules for applying gates to quantum states in the Single-Qubit Gates kata at https://mng.bz/AQrK.

Table 2.1 Commonly used single-qubit gates with real coefficients and their effects on an arbitrary state

Gate	Matrix representation	The result of applying the gate to $\|\psi\rangle = \gamma \|0\rangle + \delta \|1\rangle$
I	$\begin{pmatrix} 1 & 0 \\ 0 & 1 \end{pmatrix}$	$I\|\psi\rangle = \gamma\|0\rangle + \delta\|1\rangle$
X	$\begin{pmatrix} 0 & 1 \\ 1 & 0 \end{pmatrix}$	$X\|\psi\rangle = \delta\|0\rangle + \gamma\|1\rangle$
Z	$\begin{pmatrix} 1 & 0 \\ 0 & -1 \end{pmatrix}$	$Z\|\psi\rangle = \gamma\|0\rangle - \delta\|1\rangle$
H	$\frac{1}{\sqrt{2}}\begin{pmatrix} 1 & 1 \\ 1 & -1 \end{pmatrix}$	$H\|\psi\rangle = \frac{1}{\sqrt{2}}(\gamma+\delta)\|0\rangle + \frac{1}{\sqrt{2}}(\gamma-\delta)\|1\rangle$
$Ry(\theta)$	$\begin{pmatrix} \cos\frac{\theta}{2} & -\sin\frac{\theta}{2} \\ \sin\frac{\theta}{2} & \cos\frac{\theta}{2} \end{pmatrix}$	$Ry(\theta)\|\psi\rangle = (\gamma\cos\frac{\theta}{2} - \delta\sin\frac{\theta}{2})\|0\rangle + (\gamma\sin\frac{\theta}{2} + \delta\cos\frac{\theta}{2})\|1\rangle$

> **Applying quantum gates to quantum states**
>
> As a reminder, you can calculate the result of applying a gate to a quantum state by multiplying the column vector that describes that state by the matrix of that gate. Dirac notation represents arbitrary quantum states as linear combinations of basis states, denoting all column vectors as *ket symbols*. For example,
>
> $$X\|\psi\rangle = X(\gamma\|0\rangle + \delta\|1\rangle) = \begin{pmatrix} 0 & 1 \\ 1 & 0 \end{pmatrix}\begin{pmatrix} \gamma \\ \delta \end{pmatrix} = \begin{pmatrix} \delta \\ \gamma \end{pmatrix} = \delta\begin{pmatrix} 1 \\ 0 \end{pmatrix} + \gamma\begin{pmatrix} 0 \\ 1 \end{pmatrix} = \delta\|0\rangle + \gamma\|1\rangle$$

In our case, both amplitudes α and β are real rather than complex, so we're looking for a gate that doesn't have complex numbers in its matrix representation. (We will need gates with complex coefficients later, in chapter 5; I'll introduce them there.)

2.1 Preparing a single-qubit state

We're also looking for a parameterized gate that acts differently depending on the value of a parameter or several. Indeed, since we need to prepare a variety of states described by different parameters α and β, our solution should depend on the values of these parameters; nonparameterized gates such as X, Z, and H don't give us this flexibility.

The gate that looks like a good fit is the last gate in the table, the rotation gate $Ry(\theta)$. We can use the Ry gate information from table 2.1 to calculate the result of applying it to the $|0\rangle$ state:

$$Ry(\theta)|0\rangle = \cos\tfrac{\theta}{2}|0\rangle + \sin\tfrac{\theta}{2}|1\rangle$$

This looks just like the state we want to prepare! All we need to do is find θ for which

$$\cos\tfrac{\theta}{2}|0\rangle + \sin\tfrac{\theta}{2}|1\rangle = \alpha|0\rangle + \beta|1\rangle$$

In other words, $\cos\tfrac{\theta}{2} = \alpha$ and $\sin\tfrac{\theta}{2} = \beta$.

To consider a few examples, the states $|0\rangle, |1\rangle, |+\rangle = \tfrac{1}{\sqrt{2}}(|0\rangle + |1\rangle)$ and $|-\rangle = \tfrac{1}{\sqrt{2}}(|0\rangle - |1\rangle)$ can be prepared using parameter values 0, π, $\tfrac{\pi}{2}$, and $-\tfrac{\pi}{2}$, respectively. How can we find the value of the θ in the general case?

Here and later in the book we'll often need to find a rotation angle γ for which $\alpha = \cos\gamma$ and $\beta = \sin\gamma$. Multiple inverse trigonometric functions can be used. We'll choose the two-argument arctangent function $\mathrm{atan2}(\beta, \alpha)$ that returns a value in the interval $(-\pi, \pi]$ and calculate our parameter $\theta = 2 \cdot \mathrm{atan2}(\beta, \alpha)$.

Why is this function the best fit for our problem? Figure 2.2 shows several functions we could've used instead and the scenarios in which they return an incorrect angle.

Using the single-argument function $\mathrm{atan}(\tfrac{\beta}{\alpha})$, for example, considers only the ratio $\tfrac{\beta}{\alpha}$ and always returns an angle in the interval $(-\tfrac{\pi}{2}, \tfrac{\pi}{2}]$, thus producing an incorrect result for negative cosine inputs. (It also requires separate handling for the case $\alpha = 0$, making the code more bulky and error-prone.)

Similarly, functions $\arccos\alpha$ and $\arcsin\beta$ return angles in intervals $[0, \pi]$ and $[-\tfrac{\pi}{2}, \tfrac{\pi}{2}]$, respectively. These functions ignore the sign of the argument they don't use (β and α, respectively) completely, so they produce incorrect results for negative sine and cosine inputs, respectively. For example, if you try to prepare the state $|-\rangle$ and use the function $\arccos\alpha$ to figure out the parameter, you'll end up choosing parameter $\theta = \tfrac{\pi}{2}$ instead of $-\tfrac{\pi}{2}$, preparing the state $|+\rangle$ that is orthogonal to the state you needed!

Using the function $\mathrm{atan2}(\beta, \alpha)$ allows us to preserve the information about the signs of both amplitudes α and β and thus to implement the required state precisely without introducing an additional relative phase or a global phase.

> **TIP** Introducing a global phase does not matter as long as we only use this state preparation routine as a standalone program. However, later in this chapter, we'll use the controlled variant of this routine as a part of a larger program, and the effect of an incorrect global phase would become very noticeable!

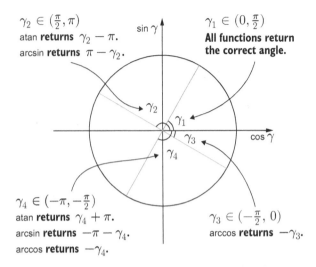

Figure 2.2 Different inverse trigonometric functions handle the signs of sine and cosine differently. The angle returned by the function atan2 has correct signs of both sine and cosine. The function atan preserves only their relative sign, always returning an angle with a nonnegative cosine. Functions arccos and arcsin ignore the sign of sine and cosine, respectively, assuming it is always nonnegative.

Note that the function atan2 does not require its arguments to be normalized to equal sine and cosine of some angle—that is, for their squares to add up to 1. We'll use that later in the chapter to simplify our code.

2.1.2 Qiskit

Let's see how to implement this solution in Qiskit. Qiskit is implemented as a Python library, so Qiskit projects are organized in the same way as the classical Python projects. The simplest way to set up a Qiskit project is as a standalone Python script in a .py file, so this is what I'll do for the first several code examples.

Quantum programs in Qiskit focus on constructing *circuits*—sequences of gates and measurements applied to a predefined set of qubits. The circuits are represented as instances of class QuantumCircuit, initialized with the number of qubits and the number of classical bits in the circuit. The gates are then appended to the circuit instances using either the append method or the shortcuts defined for the built-in gates such as Ry.

The ry gate in Qiskit takes two parameters: the rotation angle, in radians, and the qubit to which the gate should be applied. (The gates that don't have numeric parameters take only one argument, the qubit(s) to which they are applied.) The qubit can be identified in multiple ways, for example, using its index in the array of qubits on which the circuit is defined. In our case, the circuit contains a single qubit, so its index is 0.

Listing 2.1 shows the Qiskit code that implements our mathematical solution to prepare a single-qubit state with the given coefficients. This code creates a circuit consisting of one qubit that ends up in the required state.

Listing 2.1 Qiskit code to prepare a single-qubit state

```
from math import atan2
from qiskit import QuantumCircuit

alpha, beta = 0.6, 0.8            ◁── Defines an empty
                                      circuit with one qubit
circ = QuantumCircuit(1)          ◁──
theta = 2 * atan2(beta, alpha)    ◁── Calculates the parameter of the Ry gate
circ.ry(theta, 0)                 ◁──
                                      Appends the Ry gate acting
                                      on qubit 0 to the circuit
```

You can run this code just like a regular Python file, by navigating to the folder containing the file and running

```
python prep_one_qubit.py
```

You'll see, however, that it doesn't output anything yet. Indeed, so far we only construct a quantum circuit but do not attempt to execute it. We'll modify the code to actually run this circuit on a simulator and peek at the state it prepares in section 2.2.

2.1.3 Q#

Now let's take a look at the same solution in Q#. Q# is a domain-specific language that uses a separate file type with extension .qs. To start, we'll look at the simplest Q# project—a single .qs file that can be executed using Visual Studio Code extension called the Azure Quantum Development Kit.

Q# programs represent the computation slightly differently compared to Qiskit: they allocate qubits as needed using a `use` statement and then treat them as just a different kind of variable of type `Qubit`. Any operations can take parameters of type `Qubit` along with the other types. Quantum gates are defined in the namespace `Std.Intrinsic`, which is open in Q# programs by default. The Ry gate in Q# takes two parameters: the rotation angle, in radians, and the `Qubit` variable that defines the qubit to which the gate should be applied.

Listing 2.2 shows the Q# code that implements our mathematical solution to prepare a single-qubit state with the given coefficients. This code allocates a qubit and prepares it in the required state. At the end of the program the qubit is returned to the $|0\rangle$ state.

Listing 2.2 Q# code to prepare a single-qubit state

```
import Std.Math.ArcTan2;     ◁── Imports function from the Math namespace

@EntryPoint()                               ◁── Marks the entry point of the code
operation SingleQubitDemo() : Unit {        ◁── The quantum code is defined as operations.
    use q = Qubit();                        ◁── Allocates a qubit
    let (alpha, beta) = (0.6, 0.8);
    let theta = 2.0 * ArcTan2(beta, alpha); ◁── Calculates the parameter of the Ry gate
    Ry(theta, q);                           ◁── Applies the Ry gate to the qubit
    Reset(q);                               ◁── Resets the qubit to the 0 state
}
```

Releasing qubits in Q#

You might have noticed that the last command in Q# code does not have a match in the Qiskit listing 2.1 for the same problem. Q# requires that all qubits are returned to the $|0\rangle$ state before they are released. `Reset` operation does just that by measuring the qubit and applying the X gate if the measurement result was 1.

Where does this requirement come from, and how is it enforced? Q# allows you to allocate and release qubits at any point during the program execution. So far, you've only seen a very small Q# program that uses just one qubit, and it is released at the end of the program execution, so ending the program with it in a nonzero state would not have any weird side effects. Generally, when you work with larger programs that use multiple qubits, you need to be more careful about how you manage them. Releasing qubits that are entangled with the qubits still in use can change the computation in unexpected ways, for example, by preventing interference. (You will see a detailed example of this happening in section 6.5 when we discuss more complicated quantum programs.) Measuring the qubits automatically before releasing them is not safe in this scenario either, since doing so would affect the state of the qubits they are entangled with. Returning the qubits to the $|0\rangle$ state makes sure they are not entangled with any other qubits and can be released safely.

This restriction cannot be enforced at compile time because it would require the compiler to keep track of the state of the qubits, effectively simulating the whole program, and that is impossible for large programs. Instead, the Q# simulator checks the state of the qubits before releasing them during program execution and throws a `Released qubits are not in zero state` exception if the qubits are in any state other than $|0\rangle$. This way, the Q# developer can notice the potential problem with quantum memory management when they test their code and handle it appropriately.

The entry point of the Q# project is the operation from which code execution starts. Once you've annotated an operation as an entry point, the Azure Quantum Development Kit extension will show you several actions you can take for it (see figure 2.3).

```
@EntryPoint()
Run | Histogram | Estimate | Debug | Circuit
operation SingleQubitDemo() : Unit {
```

Figure 2.3 An example of code actions provided by the Azure Quantum Development Kit extension

The code actions are

- *Run*—Run this code on the simulator once and print any outputs and the return value. It is the same as using the `Run Q# File` command under the Play icon dropdown in the top-right of the editor window, provided by the same extension. Alternatively, you can press Ctrl + F5 to run your code.

- *Histogram*—Run this code multiple times and show a histogram of the return values.
- *Estimate*—Run resource estimation for this code (we'll discuss this action in detail in chapter 9).
- *Debug*—Run this code on the simulator with the debugger that allows you to watch the evolution of classical values and the quantum state during the program execution.
- *Circuit*—Show the quantum circuit implemented by this code.

In our case, you can use the `Run` command to run the code. However, its output in the debug console is rather underwhelming:

```
Result: "()"
Finished shot 1 of 1

Q# simulation completed.
```

This output means that the code ran successfully and returned `()`—the only value that the Q# data type `Unit` can take. It does not, however, offer us any insight into the quantum state during the program execution. We will learn to peek at the quantum states in the next section.

> **TIP** Using `Unit` as the return type indicates that the operation doesn't have a return value. Instead, it acts through side effects such as printing an output (we will modify the code to print the state it prepared in the next section) or changing the state of the qubits passed as its argument, as we'll see in section 2.3.

2.2 What does your solution do?

Now, we've written the code that prepares a quantum state, but it doesn't output anything. How can we see what it does to check that it's correct? Let's learn to do that.

In a physical quantum system, the only way to learn anything about its state is measurement, and the information it provides is limited: one bit of information per measurement performed. In a single-qubit system, this means exactly one bit of information—definitely not enough to check that the qubit has been prepared in the right superposition state.

Running the experiment that prepares the state and measures it multiple times would give us more information. We can collect the statistics of different measurement outcomes and estimate their probabilities and then estimate the amplitudes of the basis states as square roots of the corresponding outcome probabilities. However, this approach has its limitations: it doesn't preserve the information about the relative phase between the amplitudes, and it requires a lot of repetitions to get a reasonably accurate estimate of the amplitudes. Besides, running the program on quantum hardware yields noisy results, which, depending on the noise type, can introduce a bias in the amplitude estimates, making it unreliable. The techniques of running experiments to get an accurate analysis of the quantum system state exist, but are fairly advanced.

Fortunately, quantum programming tools offer a much simpler solution to this problem, at least for its small instances. *Quantum simulators* are classical programs that can run simulations of small quantum systems, allowing the developer to run the quantum program on a classical computer, without accessing quantum hardware. Since simulators are classical programs running on classical hardware, they are not subject to the same limitations as the physical processes in quantum systems. They represent the internal state of the quantum system as a classical data structure, allowing the developer to take a look at this state at any point of the program. The benefit of this approach is that the simulations are usually noiseless, so the results you get will be a perfect representation of the ideal state of your program. Unfortunately, the memory required to store the state of a quantum program grows exponentially with the number of qubits allocated, so this approach only works for small programs.

We are going to take advantage of quantum simulators and use toolkit-specific capabilities of accessing the program state directly to see what our code does.

2.2.1 Qiskit

The most common simulator used to run Qiskit programs is `AerSimulator`. Once you've obtained an `AerSimulator` instance to use as the simulator in your code, the `QuantumCircuit` class gains additional methods used to save its quantum state. The `save_statevector` method saves the current quantum state of the circuit as a vector of complex numbers, which can then be retrieved from the simulation results using the `get_statevector` method.

Listing 2.3 shows you how to modify listing 2.1 to run the circuit and to get the results of its execution. To do this, the code saves the state vector during the program simulation and extracts the saved state to print it after the simulation is complete.

Listing 2.3 Qiskit code to show the state prepared by the circuit

```
from math import atan2
from qiskit import QuantumCircuit
from qiskit_aer import AerSimulator

simulator = AerSimulator(method='statevector')     ← Gets a simulator instance to use

alpha, beta = 0.6, 0.8

circ = QuantumCircuit(1)
theta = 2 * atan2(beta, alpha)
circ.ry(theta, 0)
circ.save_statevector()                ← Saves the circuit state at this point

res = simulator.run(circ).result()             ← Runs the circuit on the simulator
state_vector = res.get_statevector()           ← Extracts the saved state
print(state_vector)
```

The output of this program is

```
Statevector([0.6+0.j, 0.8+0.j],
            dims=(2,))
```

The Statevector class is a wrapper around a list of complex numbers—the amplitudes of the basis states of the system, starting with $|0\rangle$. You can see that the state prepared by this code corresponds to the state $0.6\,|0\rangle + 0.8\,|1\rangle$, and that's exactly the state we aimed for when we defined $\alpha = 0.6$ and $\beta = 0.8$ in the code.

2.2.2 Q#

Q# simulators don't offer a direct way to access their internal state, either from Q# code itself or from the classical code that calls Q# code. Instead, Q# offers a library function DumpMachine (Std.Diagnostics namespace) that prints the state of the program at the point at which this function is called.

The Q# simulator represents the state of the program in the most generic way, as a vector of complex numbers storing the amplitudes of each basis state. The output of DumpMachine is the list of all basis states with their amplitudes, measurement probabilities, and phases.

Listing 2.4 shows you how to modify listing 2.2 to use DumpMachine to print the state of the program during its execution on a simulator. Unlike Qiskit, Q# code doesn't include explicit instructions for executing it on a simulator. The choice of the execution target—a simulator or a hardware endpoint available via Azure Quantum—is handled either by the Python host program (we'll see an example in section 2.4) or by the Visual Studio Code extension used to run standalone Q# programs.

> **Listing 2.4 Q# code to observe the state prepared by the circuit**

```
import Std.Diagnostics.DumpMachine;      ◁——┐ Imports the DumpMachine function from
import Std.Math.ArcTan2;                     │ the diagnostics tools namespace

@EntryPoint()
operation SingleQubitDemo() : Unit {
  use q = Qubit();
  let (alpha, beta) = (0.6, 0.8);
  let theta = 2.0 * ArcTan2(beta, alpha);
  Ry(theta, q);
  DumpMachine();     ◁—— Prints the state of the program
  Reset(q);
}
```

The output of this program will look as follows:

```
DumpMachine:

 Basis | Amplitude        | Probability | Phase
------------------------------------------------
  |0>  |  0.6000+0.0000i  |   36.0000%  |  0.0000
  |1>  |  0.8000+0.0000i  |   64.0000%  |  0.0000

Result: "()"
```

The columns of the `DumpMachine` output include the following information:
- The ket representation of the basis state
- The amplitude of this basis state as a complex number (only the basis states with non-zero amplitudes are listed)
- The probability to get this basis state when performing a measurement
- The phase of the amplitude, in radians

Now that we know how to see what our program does and check that it matches our intent, we can move on to solving the more challenging problems!

2.3 Preparing a two-qubit state

The next larger variant of the state preparation problem is preparing a two-qubit state. More accurately, the problem can be formulated as follows. Given two qubits in the $|0\rangle$ state and an array of four floating-point numbers a, change the state of these qubits to $|\psi_2\rangle = a_0 |0\rangle + a_1 |1\rangle + a_2 |2\rangle + a_3 |3\rangle$.

Same as in the single-qubit case, we can assume that the amplitudes we are given as inputs are normalized—that is, $a_0^2 + a_1^2 + a_2^2 + a_3^2 = 1$. We will see, however, that we don't need to rely on this assumption: our solution will be able to normalize the given amplitudes for us when preparing the state.

Note that here we've changed the input type from separate numbers to an array of amplitudes. This change helps us prepare to scale up this solution to handle an arbitrary number of qubits, since we'll handle the correspondence between basis states (represented as bit strings) and the indexes of the amplitudes in the array (represented as integers).

> **Converting bit strings into integers: Big-endian vs. little-endian**
>
> You'll notice that in the problem statement we're labeling the basis states using integers instead of bit strings. This method sets us up for working with arbitrary numbers of qubits, but we need to handle this transition with care.
>
> Bit strings can be converted into integers in two ways: big-endian encoding, in which the least significant bit is stored in the *last* bit of the bit string, and little-endian encoding, in which it is stored in the *first* bit of the string. For example, the two-qubit basis state $|01\rangle$ corresponds to the integer 1 if interpreted as a big-endian notation (the least significant bit is 1, and the most significant bit is 0) and to the integer 2 if interpreted as a little-endian binary notation (the least significant bit is 0, and the most significant bit is 1).
>
> Unfortunately, there is no universal agreement on which notation to use in quantum computing when converting basis states and measurement results to integers (for example, indices in an array of amplitudes). Books typically choose big-endian, and software tools can lean either way. Qiskit and Q# use different conventions: Qiskit uses little-endian notation, and Q# uses big-endian.

> In this book, I'll use little-endian notation to work through the math of solving the problem, and the convention used by the language when implementing the solution in that language. I'll try to stick to "least significant bit" and "most significant bit" terminology instead of "first bit" and "second bit" whenever possible. The advantage of this approach is that it matches the behavior of the libraries native to each language and simplifies interpreting the quantum states printed by our programs. The disadvantage is, of course, that Q# and Qiskit solutions will interpret the same array of amplitudes as different quantum states.

2.3.1 Refresher: Controlled gates in Dirac notation

Unlike the single-qubit case, we won't find a built-in two-qubit gate to execute the necessary transformation of the state all at once. Instead, we'll have to come up with a sequence of steps using single-qubit gates and their controlled variants. Before we dive into that, let's remind ourselves what controlled gates are and how to apply them to quantum states using Dirac notation.

> **NOTE** In this chapter, we focus on modifying individual states, and it's more convenient to express the effects of the gates on them using Dirac notation. We'll revisit the controlled gates in their matrix form in the next chapter, where we'll focus on matrices and their manipulation. Getting comfortable with different ways to represent the same computation is very useful, both for choosing the most convenient way to think about each specific problem and for following the calculations done, say, in research papers that use different representations.

A *controlled variant* of a gate is a gate that acts on two groups of qubits, called *control qubits* and *target qubits*, as follows:

- If the controlled variant of a gate U is applied to a basis state in which all control qubits are in the $|1\rangle$ state, the gate U is applied to the target qubits.
- If the controlled variant of a gate U is applied to a basis state in which at least one of the control qubits is in the $|0\rangle$ state, the state doesn't change.
- For the superposition states, the effect of the controlled gate is defined based on its effect on the basis states. Since all quantum gates are linear, the result of applying a gate to a linear combination of basis states can be calculated as a linear combination of the results of applying that gate to each basis state.

The simplest example of a controlled gate is the CNOT gate—a controlled X gate with one control qubit. The effects of this gate on a two-qubit state can be described in Dirac notation as follows (assuming the left qubit is the control and the right qubit is the target):

- If the control qubit is in the $|1\rangle$ state, apply the X gate to the target ("flip" its state):

$$CNOT\,|10\rangle = |11\rangle,\ CNOT\,|11\rangle = |10\rangle$$

- If the control qubit is in the $|0\rangle$ state, the target state is unchanged:

$$CNOT\,|00\rangle = |00\rangle,\ CNOT\,|01\rangle = |01\rangle$$

- For a superposition state—for example, $\alpha\,|10\rangle + \beta\,|01\rangle$—the CNOT gate is applied to each term separately:

$$CNOT(\alpha\,|10\rangle + \beta\,|01\rangle) = \alpha\,CNOT\,|10\rangle + \beta\,CNOT\,|01\rangle = \alpha\,|11\rangle + \beta\,|01\rangle$$

A slightly more complicated example of a controlled gate that we'll be using extensively in this section is $CRy(\theta)$, a controlled $Ry(\theta)$ gate with one control qubit. Its effects on a two-qubit state, if the left qubit is used as the control and the right one as the target, can be computed directly in Dirac notation as follows:

- If the control qubit is in the $|1\rangle$ state, apply the $Ry(\theta)$ gate to the target qubit:

$$CRy(\theta)\,|10\rangle = |1\rangle \otimes Ry(\theta)\,|0\rangle = \cos\tfrac{\theta}{2}\,|10\rangle + \sin\tfrac{\theta}{2}\,|11\rangle$$
$$CRy(\theta)\,|11\rangle = |1\rangle \otimes Ry(\theta)\,|1\rangle = -\sin\tfrac{\theta}{2}\,|10\rangle + \cos\tfrac{\theta}{2}\,|11\rangle$$

- If the control qubit is in the $|0\rangle$ state, the state doesn't change:

$$CRy(\theta)\,|00\rangle = |00\rangle$$
$$CRy(\theta)\,|01\rangle = |01\rangle$$

- For a superposition state, for example, $\alpha\,|10\rangle + \beta\,|01\rangle$, apply the $CRy(\theta)$ gate to each term separately and add the results:

$$CRy(\theta)(\alpha\,|10\rangle + \beta\,|01\rangle) = \alpha\,CRy(\theta)\,|10\rangle + \beta\,CRy(\theta)\,|01\rangle$$
$$= \alpha(\cos\tfrac{\theta}{2}\,|10\rangle + \sin\tfrac{\theta}{2}\,|11\rangle) + \beta\,|01\rangle$$

Similarly, *controlled-on-zero variant* of a gate applies the original gate to the target qubits if and only if all control qubits are in the $|0\rangle$ state. This variant is sometimes called an *open-controlled* gate to reflect the way it's drawn in circuit representations of quantum programs. You can implement a controlled-on-zero variant of a gate by applying the X gate to the control qubits, then using a regular controlled variant of a gate, and finally applying the X gate to the control qubits again to return them to their original state.

> **NOTE** Simplifying the calculation of the effects of gates on quantum states is one of the advantages of Dirac notation over matrix notation. It is especially useful when the control and the target qubits of the gate are not adjacent in the bit string that represents the basis state. For example, to apply a controlled Ry gate to a three-qubit state with the rightmost qubit as the control and the leftmost qubit as the target, you use the same conditional logic for each three-qubit basis state, applying the gate to the leftmost bit if the rightmost bit is 1 and leaving the state unchanged otherwise. (The state of the middle qubit that is not involved in the gate is always unchanged.) The same gate is a lot trickier to apply in the matrix form!

2.3.2 Math

With controlled gates in mind, we'll take a step-by-step approach: we'll start by preparing the least significant qubit in some state and then adjust the state of the most significant qubit conditionally depending on the state of the least significant one. Figure 2.4 shows the outline of this approach.

Let's figure out what each of the steps will look like, knowing their sequence and reverse-engineering the details based on the state that we want to prepare. As a reminder, we're using little-endian notation here, matching amplitude a_1 with basis state $|10\rangle$ and amplitude a_2 with basis state $|01\rangle$.

First, let's group the terms of the state expression based on the value of the first qubit:

$$a_0 |00\rangle + a_1 |10\rangle + a_2 |01\rangle + a_3 |11\rangle = |0\rangle (a_0 |0\rangle + a_2 |1\rangle) + |1\rangle (a_1 |0\rangle + a_3 |1\rangle)$$

Now, let's rewrite the expressions in brackets so that the norm of each of them equals 1, moving the normalization coefficients outside the brackets:

$$\sqrt{a_0^2 + a_2^2} |0\rangle \left(\frac{a_0}{\sqrt{a_0^2+a_2^2}} |0\rangle + \frac{a_2}{\sqrt{a_0^2+a_2^2}} |1\rangle \right) + \sqrt{a_1^2 + a_3^2} |1\rangle \left(\frac{a_1}{\sqrt{a_1^2+a_3^2}} |0\rangle + \frac{a_3}{\sqrt{a_1^2+a_3^2}} |1\rangle \right)$$

Each of the single-qubit states in brackets is normalized, so we can prepare them using our solution from section 2.1. For the first state, for example, the parameters we need to use are $\alpha = \frac{a_0}{\sqrt{a_0^2+a_2^2}}$ and $\beta = \frac{a_2}{\sqrt{a_0^2+a_2^2}}$. We can simplify this using the fact that our single-qubit state preparation routine doesn't require its inputs to be normalized. Thus, we can use it with simpler parameters $\alpha = a_0$ and $\beta = a_2$.

We can prepare the single-qubit state $\sqrt{a_0^2 + a_2^2} |0\rangle + \sqrt{a_1^2 + a_3^2} |1\rangle$ using the same solution from section 2.1, with parameters $\alpha = \sqrt{a_0^2 + a_2^2}$ and $\beta = \sqrt{a_1^2 + a_3^2}$.

The sequence of steps for preparing the two-qubit state ends up looking like this:

1. Prepare the first (least significant) qubit in the state $\sqrt{a_0^2 + a_2^2} |0\rangle + \sqrt{a_1^2 + a_3^2} |1\rangle$. We can do that using the single-qubit preparation routine with parameters $\alpha = \sqrt{a_0^2 + a_2^2}$ and $\beta = \sqrt{a_1^2 + a_3^2}$. The second (most significant) qubit remains in the $|0\rangle$ state for now, so the overall state of the system becomes

$$\left(\sqrt{a_0^2 + a_2^2} |0\rangle + \sqrt{a_1^2 + a_3^2} |1\rangle \right) \otimes |0\rangle = \sqrt{a_0^2 + a_2^2} |0\rangle \otimes |0\rangle + \sqrt{a_1^2 + a_3^2} |1\rangle \otimes |0\rangle$$

2. Adjust the first term of the superposition $\sqrt{a_0^2 + a_2^2} |0\rangle \otimes |0\rangle$ to $a_0 |00\rangle + a_2 |01\rangle$, leaving the second term unchanged. We can do that using the controlled-on-zero variant of the single-qubit preparation routine, with the first qubit as control, the second qubit as target, and parameters $\alpha = a_0$ and $\beta = a_2$. After this, the system state becomes

$$a_0 |00\rangle + a_2 |01\rangle + \sqrt{a_1^2 + a_3^2} |1\rangle \otimes |0\rangle$$

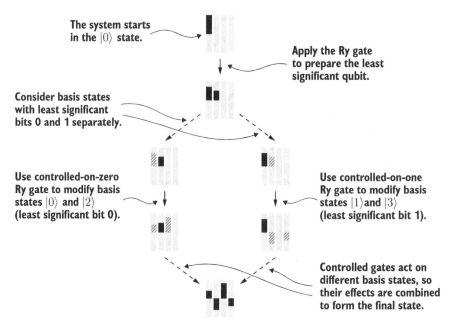

Figure 2.4 Preparing a two-qubit state. Each set of four bars represents the amplitudes of the basis states: from left to right, $|0\rangle$, $|1\rangle$, $|2\rangle$, and $|3\rangle$. Light bars indicate zero amplitudes (basis states not present in the superposition state), dark bars indicate nonzero amplitudes (positive or negative). We prepare the least significant qubit in a superposition state and then adjust the state of the most significant qubit depending on the state of the least significant qubit using controlled gates. The left path handles the case of the least significant qubit being in the $|0\rangle$ state, and the right path handles the $|1\rangle$ state. Striped bars represent the amplitudes of the basis states that are involved in each path.

3 Adjust the last term of the superposition $\sqrt{a_1^2 + a_3^2}\,|1\rangle \otimes |0\rangle$ to $a_1\,|10\rangle + a_3\,|11\rangle$, leaving the first two terms unchanged. We can do that using the controlled variant of the single-qubit preparation routine, with the first qubit as control, the second qubit as target, and parameters $\alpha = a_1$ and $\beta = a_3$. This process brings the system to our target state:

$$a_0\,|00\rangle + a_2\,|01\rangle + a_1\,|10\rangle + a_3\,|11\rangle$$

To implement this algorithm in code, we'll need to learn several new syntax elements that allow us to define a custom gate and to apply controlled and controlled-on-zero variants of a gate.

2.3.3 Qiskit

In Qiskit, you can define a custom gate as a Python function that constructs a circuit, appends the necessary gates to it, and then converts it into a gate using the `to_gate` method of the `QuantumCircuit` class. Then you can append that gate to other circuits using the `append` method of the `QuantumCircuit` class, passing it that gate and the array of indexes of the qubits it should be applied to.

2.3 Preparing a two-qubit state

To use a controlled variant of a gate, you can use the `control` method of a gate. This method takes an integer parameter that specifies the number of control qubits and returns a gate that acts on a combined list of target and control qubits, with the control qubits being first in the list, followed by the target qubits. Then, same as with any custom gates, you can append this gate to a circuit.

To implement a controlled-on-zero variant of a gate, you can use the additional parameter `ctrl_state` of the `control` method to specify the state on which the gate application is controlled. The value passed as this parameter should be a string or an integer representation of the control state. Since in this case there is a single control qubit and the gate should be applied when its state is $|0\rangle$, the control state should be `'0'` or `0`.

Listing 2.5 shows the Qiskit code that implements our mathematical solution to prepare a two-qubit state with the given coefficients. Note that as the code grows larger and more complex, we refactor it to break down the logic into smaller functions to make it easier to read and test. Like listing 2.3, the code executes the circuit that prepares the required state and prints the resulting state vector.

Listing 2.5 Qiskit code to prepare a two-qubit state

```
from math import atan2, sqrt
from qiskit import QuantumCircuit, transpile
from qiskit_aer import AerSimulator

simulator = AerSimulator(method='statevector')     ◁── Defines the one-qubit
                                                        state preparation
def prep_one_qubit(alpha, beta):                        as a gate
  circ = QuantumCircuit(1, name=f'Prep({alpha}, {beta})')
  theta = 2 * atan2(beta, alpha)
  circ.ry(theta, 0)
  return circ.to_gate()

def prep_two_qubit(a):
  b0 = sqrt(a[0]**2 + a[2]**2)
  b1 = sqrt(a[1]**2 + a[3]**2)

  circ = QuantumCircuit(2)
  circ.append(prep_one_qubit(b0, b1), [0])      ◁── Applies the state prep gate
                                                     to qubit 0 (least significant)

  circ.append(     ◁── Applies the controlled state prep gate to qubits 0 (control) and 1 (target)
    prep_one_qubit(a[1], a[3]).control(1),
    [0, 1])
                                                 ┌── Applies controlled-on-zero state prep
  circ.append(                                   │    gate to qubits 0 (control) and 1 (target)
    prep_one_qubit(a[0], a[2]).control(1, ctrl_state=0),
    [0, 1])

  return circ

def prep_two_qubit_demo(a):
  circ = prep_two_qubit(a)
  circ.save_statevector()

  circ = transpile(circ, backend=simulator)
  res = simulator.run(circ).result()
```

```
state_vector = res.get_statevector()
print([d.round(5) for d in state_vector.data])

prep_two_qubit_demo([0.36, 0.48, 0.64, -0.48])
```

This code produces the following output:

```
[(0.36+0j), (0.48+0j), (0.64+0j), (-0.48+0j)]
```

Note that once you start using custom and controlled gates in your Qiskit circuits, you'll need to *transpile* your circuit—that is, rewrite it to match the capabilities of a specific simulator or quantum device. In this case, the transpile method breaks the multiqubit gates down into simpler gates recognized by the simulator.

We observe the prepared state on multiple qubits using the same technique we used for the single-qubit case: save the state of the program after the state is prepared using save_statevector and extract the results from running it on the simulator using get_statevector. (Notice how the list of amplitudes returned by get_statevector is ordered by basis states as if they were integers in little-endian notation: the first element corresponds to the basis state $|00\rangle$, the second one corresponds to $|10\rangle$, and so on.) In this code listing, I changed the output format: instead of printing the saved state vector as is, the code now extracts just the list of amplitudes and limits the number of decimal places used to print the floating-point numbers. This change will come in handy later to keep the output size manageable when we work with larger states with more amplitudes.

2.3.4 Q#

Now let's see how to implement the same algorithm in Q#. In Q#, all gates are implemented as operations that take one or more qubits as one of their arguments and have return type Unit, indicating that they act by changing the state of these qubits.

The built-in Q# gates are defined in the Std.Intrinsic namespace. You can also define custom gates in the code just like any other Q# operation and then call them the same way as the built-in gates. For example, here is how you can modify the code from listing 2.4 to define a custom gate that prepares a qubit in the state $\alpha |0\rangle + \beta |1\rangle$ and then use it in the code:

```
import Std.Math.ArcTan2;

operation PrepOneQubit(q : Qubit, alpha : Double, beta : Double) : Unit {
    let theta = 2.0 * ArcTan2(beta, alpha);
    Ry(theta, q);
}

@EntryPoint()
operation SingleQubitDemo() : Unit {
    use q = Qubit();
    let (alpha, beta) = (0.6, 0.8);
    PrepOneQubit(q, alpha, beta);
    Reset(q);
}
```

Any Q# operation that implements a quantum gate can have adjoint and controlled *specializations*—that is, operations that implement the adjoint and controlled variants of the corresponding quantum gate. These specializations can be defined only for operations that act on qubits and have return type `Unit`, since otherwise an operation cannot implement a quantum gate. The adjoint specialization of an operation has exactly the same parameters as the original operation. The controlled specialization of an operation has two parameters: the first parameter is a qubit array that is used as the control qubits, and the second parameter is a tuple of parameters that match those of the original operation.

All built-in Q# gates have adjoint and controlled specializations defined for them. When defining a custom gate, you have to define its specializations yourself. The easiest way to do that is to specify the corresponding *characteristics* of the operation in its signature and let the Q# compiler generate the specializations automatically. For example, to specify that the operation `PrepOneQubit` has both adjoint and controlled specializations (as well as their combination, controlled adjoint), you need to add `is Adj + Ctl` to the end of its signature:

```
operation PrepOneQubit(q : Qubit, alpha : Double, beta : Double) : Unit
  is Adj + Ctl {
  // Operation body ...
}
```

To use an adjoint or a controlled variant of a gate, you can use `Adjoint` and `Controlled` keywords. These modifiers take an operation as an argument and produce the matching specialization of this operation. For example, `Controlled PrepOneQubit` returns the operation that implements the controlled specialization of the operation `PrepOneQubit`.

Finally, how can we invoke a controlled-on-zero variant of a Q# gate? Q# standard library offers two operations that allow you to call controlled variants of gates with various control patterns as long as the operation implementing the original gate has a controlled specialization defined:

- `ApplyControlledOnBitString` operation applies the original gate to the target qubits if the control qubits are in the basis state described by the given bit string—the control pattern. For example, using `ApplyControlledOnBitString` with control pattern `[false]` and the gate `PrepOneQubit` applies the controlled-on-zero variant of our custom state preparation gate.
- `ApplyControlledOnInt` operation applies the original gate to the target qubits if the control qubits are in the basis state described by the given integer (converted into a bit string using little-endian encoding). We can apply the controlled-on-zero variant of `PrepOneQubit` by using `ApplyControlledOnInt` with 0 as the control integer.

Listing 2.6 shows the Q# code that implements our mathematical solution to prepare a two-qubit state with the given coefficients. Like listing 2.4, the code prepares the required quantum state and prints its amplitudes.

Listing 2.6 Q# code to prepare a two-qubit state

```
import Std.Diagnostics.DumpMachine;
import Std.Math.ArcTan2, Std.Math.Sqrt;

operation PrepOneQubit(q : Qubit, alpha : Double, beta : Double) : Unit
  is Adj + Ctl {
  let theta = 2.0 * ArcTan2(beta, alpha);
  Ry(theta, q);
}

operation PrepTwoQubits(qs : Qubit[], a : Double[]) : Unit is Adj + Ctl {
  let b0 = Sqrt(a[0] * a[0] + a[2] * a[2]);         ◄── Applies the state prep gate
  let b1 = Sqrt(a[1] * a[1] + a[3] * a[3]);              to qubit 1 (least significant)
  PrepOneQubit(qs[1], b0, b1);

  Controlled PrepOneQubit(                          ◄── Applies the controlled state prep gate
    [qs[1]], (qs[0], a[1], a[3]));                       to qubits 1 (control) and 0 (target)

  ApplyControlledOnInt(0, PrepOneQubit,             ◄── Applies the controlled-on-zero
    [qs[1]], (qs[0], a[0], a[2]));                       state prep gate to qubits 1 (control)
}                                                        and 0 (target)

operation PrepTwoQubitsDemo(a : Double[]) : Unit {
  use qs = Qubit[2];
  PrepTwoQubits(qs, a);
  DumpMachine();
  ResetAll(qs);
}

@EntryPoint()
operation RunPrepTwoQubitsDemo() : Unit {
  PrepTwoQubitsDemo([0.36, 0.48, 0.64, -0.48]);
}
```

As in the single-qubit case, we use the `DumpMachine` operation to print the current state of the program. The output of this program looks as follows:

```
DumpMachine:

Basis | Amplitude       | Probability | Phase
-----------------------------------------------
 |00> |  0.3600+0.0000i |   12.9600%  |  0.0000
 |01> |  0.4800+0.0000i |   23.0400%  |  0.0000
 |10> |  0.6400+0.0000i |   40.9600%  |  0.0000
 |11> | -0.4800+0.0000i |   23.0400%  |  3.1416
```

Note that `DumpMachine` uses bit strings instead of integers to represent the basis states described by each line of its output, but orders the basis states as if they were integers in big-endian notation: the first line corresponds to the basis state $|00\rangle$, the second line corresponds to $|01\rangle$, the third line corresponds to $|10\rangle$, and so on.

2.4 Testing your solution

If you attempted to come up with a way to prepare the two-qubit state and implement it yourself rather than just read through the section 2.3, you might've noticed that it is very easy to make a mistake in the code. Making mistakes is perfectly normal; in fact, I made a couple myself when writing the code for this section! And that is exactly why it is very important to check that your solution is correct.

We've seen one way of validating the correctness of your code in section 2.2: run your code on one input, print the program state after your code finished, and check that the output matches the state you wanted to prepare. And for a single qubit, this method worked just fine: there were only a few distinct scenarios that were worth trying, and you could easily check that your code prepared the basis states and several superposition states with different amplitudes and relative phases correctly.

However, this semi-manual approach is not sustainable in the long run. When you work on a larger software project, you cannot run all the checks by hand and look at the outputs to verify that they are correct every time you change the code. The number of scenarios to test is just too great, and doing the validations this way would take a prohibitive amount of time and attention.

Classical software engineering solved this problem a long time ago by introducing *software testing*, a stage of software development that examines the software being developed to evaluate its behavior and analyze its correctness. There are many approaches to software testing depending on the goals and the resources available. For example, code reviews done by other engineers are a kind of *static testing* (software verification done without running the software), and running the program manually to check its output against the expected result is a kind of *dynamic testing* (software validation done by running the software).

Quantum software engineering can (and should!) borrow a lot of techniques from its classical counterpart. In this case, we'll automate the dynamic testing of our code by developing *unit tests*, which are automated tests written to ensure that a library operation behaves as intended by its design. These unit tests will rely on the same principle we discussed in section 2.2: run the code on a simulator and use the access to the internal state of the simulator to test that this state matches our expectations.

In this section, we'll take the next step of developing our state preparation library by writing unit tests for both Q# and Qiskit solutions that will automate the validation of the code. This step will let us feel more confident in our existing code as we approach the final step of our project—preparing a state on an arbitrary number of qubits.

> ### Testing state preparation code
> How do we select the test cases for the state preparation task to use, either in automated or manual testing? Very often a beginner will run their code on an equal superposition of all basis states (in the two-qubit scenario, the $\frac{1}{2}(|00\rangle + |10\rangle + |01\rangle + |11\rangle)$ state) and stop testing after getting the correct answer on that case.

(continued)

However, many incorrect programs will still get this state right:
- The code that misses the square root when calculating the amplitudes of the state to be prepared on the first qubit
- The code that does not consider negative amplitudes or handles them incorrectly, for example, by calculating the rotation angles in the single-qubit state preparation routine using the wrong inverse trigonometric function
- The code that gets the order of amplitudes wrong, using big-endian instead of little-endian

A better approach here, as when testing classical programs, is to consider the different properties of quantum states and pick test cases that exhibit these properties, as well as some corner cases that can expose various kinds of bugs in the code. For example, some good test cases for this library include
- States with all amplitudes distinct, to expose any bugs in the matching of the amplitudes to the basis states or in the rotation angles computation
- The basis states and other states with one or more zero amplitudes, to check that zero amplitudes are handled correctly and don't cause a division-by-zero exception
- States with amplitudes of different signs, to check that the code handles them correctly in addition to the absolute values of the amplitudes

Generally, there are two ways to write tests for quantum programs. *Unit tests* verify the behavior of a single small component, such as our state preparation routine. These tests typically need access to the detailed program state to implement the test logic. To implement these tests, you'll likely use the toolkit-specific capabilities for accessing the program state at run time on a simulator similar to those you used for observing it in section 2.2. *Integration tests* validate end-to-end scenarios to check that the quantum program gives the correct answer to the problem it solves. Integration tests are typically implemented as classical code that calls the quantum program to test it as a whole.

In this chapter, we'll look at the first approach, since we are testing a single component and need detailed access to the quantum state of the program to verify that it matches our expectations. We'll see examples of the second approach later in the book, in chapter 8, when we look at using quantum algorithms to solve classical problems and analyze success rates of a quantum solution.

2.4.1 Qiskit

As we've seen earlier, with Qiskit implemented as a Python library, any quantum code written in Qiskit can be treated as regular Python code. Consequently, we can set up the tests for our Qiskit code in the same way we'd set them up for any Python code. In this book, I use pytest, one of the most popular Python testing frameworks.

pytest will discover and run all functions with names starting with `test_` in all files named `test_*.py` or `*_test.py` in the current directory. This makes it easy to keep unit tests separate from the library logic being tested.

2.4 Testing your solution

We've seen in listings 2.3 and 2.5 that Qiskit allows you to save the state vector of the program using the method `save_statevector` and then get it after the program is executed on a simulator using `get_statevector`. Once this information has been extracted, we can treat it as a regular Python list and write arbitrary test logic for it.

In our case, we need to check that the amplitudes of the state that the simulation yielded match those passed as an argument to the `prep_two_qubit` function. We can implement this check using the standard Python tools for comparing lists of floating-point numbers.

Listing 2.7 shows the test code for the two-qubit state preparation operation in Qiskit. The code running the test for one set of amplitudes, `run_test_prep_two_qubit`, is very similar to the function `prep_two_qubit_demo` used in listing 2.5 to print the amplitudes of the prepared state, except this time instead of printing the state, we compare its amplitudes with the input list of amplitudes element by element.

Listing 2.7 Qiskit code to test preparation of an arbitrary state

```
from math import sqrt
from qiskit import transpile
from qiskit_aer import AerSimulator
import pytest
from .prep_two_qubit import prep_two_qubit

simulator = AerSimulator(method='statevector')

@pytest.mark.parametrize("a",
    [ [1., 0., 0., 0.],                    ◀—— Several test cases are omitted for brevity.
      [0., 1., 0., 0.],
      [0.36, 0.48, 0.64, -0.48],
      [1. / sqrt(3.), -1. / sqrt(3.), 1. / sqrt(3.), 0.]
    ])
def test_prep_two_qubit(a):
  circ = prep_two_qubit(a)
  circ.save_statevector()

  circ = transpile(circ, backend=simulator)
  res = simulator.run(circ).result()                    Compares amplitudes approximately
  state_vector = res.get_statevector().data             using default tolerance
                                                        for real numbers
  assert state_vector == pytest.approx(a)    ◀—┘
```

The statement that imports `prep_two_qubit` might differ depending on how you set up your Python test project. In my case, I placed the test file next to the file containing the state preparation library.

You can see that we can use any Python testing tools, such as the convenient decorator `pytest.mark.parametrize`, which allows us to run the test function `test_prep_two_qubit` on multiple state vectors we want to use to test our state preparation code.

Note that this code relies on the number of qubits in the state only implicitly: the number of qubits in the circuit is defined in the function `prep_two_qubit`. This allows us to reuse this test code for the multiqubit case without any changes.

2.4.2 Q#

Developing tests for Q# code requires splitting the test logic between Q# and Python. We can set up the tests using the standard Python tools for testing—in this case, pytest, one of the most popular Python testing frameworks—and then use specialized libraries to access the state of the Q# program from Python test code and validate it using Python.

The simplest Q# test project thus consists of several files:

- A Python file that defines the tests in the root of the project folder. The name of the file has to start with `test_` or end with `_test` for pytest to discover and run the tests defined in it.
- Q# file(s) with the code we want to test in the `\src` folder within the project folder.
- The manifest file `qsharp.json` that specifies the properties of the Q# project such as the author and the license of the project. The shortest possible manifest file is the empty JSON `{}`.

As we discussed earlier in section 2.2, Q# doesn't give you direct access to the state vector of the simulator in Q# code itself. Instead, when you create a Python host program for your quantum code, you can use Python functions from the `qsharp` module to load the Q# code in the project, simulate a Q# code snippet that prepares the state you want to examine, and then fetch the state vector of the simulation. Listing 2.8 shows the Python test code for the two-qubit state preparation operation implemented in Q#.

Listing 2.8 Python code to test Q# preparation of a two-qubit state

```
from math import sqrt
import qsharp
import pytest

@pytest.mark.parametrize("a",
    [ [1., 0., 0., 0.],
      [0., 1., 0., 0.],          ◁── Several test cases are omitted for brevity.
      [0.36, 0.48, 0.64, -0.48],
      [1. / sqrt(3.), -1. / sqrt(3.), 1. / sqrt(3.), 0.]
    ])
def test_prep_two_qubit(a):
  qsharp.init(project_root='.')
  qsharp.eval(f"use qs = Qubit[2]; StatePreparation.PrepTwoQubits(qs, a);")
  state_vector = qsharp.dump_machine().as_dense_state()

  assert state_vector == pytest.approx(a)    ◁── Compares amplitudes approximately using default tolerance for real numbers
```

Let's take a closer look at the Python functions that enable running Q# code and get the simulated state of the program for validation:

- `qsharp.init` loads the Q# project that will be used in the Python code. In our case, we'll need to specify the parameter `project_root='.'` to load the Q# files from the current Python folder.
- `qsharp.eval` simulates the Q# code snippet provided as the argument. In our case, the Q# library code we need to test (listing 2.6) is in the Q# file, so the small code fragment we'll define here will do only two things: allocate the qubits and call the Q# library method `StatePreparation.PrepTwoQubits` with the given list of amplitudes as the argument.

  > **NOTE** Notice that we don't want to release the qubits after the `PrepTwo-Qubits` call, so we're not enclosing the Q# code in the `eval` statement in curly brackets. As a result, `qsharp.eval` ends execution with the qubits still allocated, and we can access their state or modify it later by calling `qsharp.eval` again. Enclosing the two statements in curly brackets makes them a block, and the qubits allocated within the block are released at its end.

- `qsharp.dump_machine` returns the current state of the Q# simulator as a `StateDump` object, which includes the number of qubits allocated and the complex amplitudes of the basis states. This function is the Python API equivalent of the Q# operation `DumpMachine` you saw in section 2.2.2.
- The `as_dense_state()` method of the `StateDump` class converts the default sparse representation of the quantum state as a Python dictionary into a dense list of amplitudes that includes the zero amplitudes. This process allows us to compare the amplitudes of the prepared state with the input list of amplitudes element by element, just as we did in Qiskit.

2.5 Preparing a multiqubit state

Now that we've learned to test our quantum program automatically, we're finally ready to approach our main project for this chapter and generalize our code to handle the preparation of states with arbitrary numbers of qubits. More precisely, we want to write a library that, given n qubits in the $|0...0\rangle$ state and an array of 2^n floating-point numbers a describing the amplitudes of an n-qubit state, changes the state of these qubits to

$$|\psi_n\rangle_n = a_0 |0\rangle_n + a_1 |1\rangle_n + ... + a_{2^n-2} |2^n - 2\rangle_n + a_{2^n-1} |2^n - 1\rangle_n = \sum_{j=0}^{2^n-1} a_j |j\rangle_n$$

When working with multiqubit basis states, especially those with more than just a few qubits, representing them using bit strings becomes unwieldy. Basis states comprised of repetitions of the same bit, $|0...0\rangle$ and $|1...1\rangle$, can be written relatively conveniently, but any states with a varying bit pattern are not that easy to write out. That's why in this chapter I'm using the variant of Dirac notation that represents basis states as integers in little-endian notation. It allows us to write the state more concisely.

> **Using Dirac notation for multiqubit states**
>
> Dirac notation that uses integers to denote basis states, while convenient in a lot of scenarios, comes with its own set of challenges. For example, you need to be careful to keep track of the number of qubits in the basis states written like this; without this information, you cannot say whether the state $|0\rangle$ describes 1 or 100 qubits!
>
> Usually, the context in which the state is mentioned clarifies the number of qubits in it. In our case, the upper limit of the sum is $2^n - 1$, which, combined with the mention that this expression describes an arbitrary state, implies that the basis states in the sum $|j\rangle$ have n qubits.
>
> Since we'll be dealing with n-qubit, $(n-1)$-qubit, and one-qubit states in the same formulas, I'm using a subscript after the ket symbol to denote the number of bits explicitly: $|0\rangle_1$ is the zero state on a single qubit, and $|0\rangle_n$ is the n-qubit state in which every qubit is in the zero state. This method makes the notation bulkier, so most books or papers don't use it, but it can be convenient when manipulating states with different numbers of qubits simultaneously.

2.5.1 Math

In the two-qubit case, we used several steps to prepare the state: we started by getting the least significant qubit into the right state and then modified the state of the most significant qubit conditionally, depending on the state of the least significant qubit. To do that, we used a controlled variant of the same operation we used to prepare a single-qubit state earlier in the chapter.

This pattern of breaking the problem down into subproblems and solving each of them separately, with some subproblems being simpler versions of the original problem, looks very much like recursion. Can we come up with a recursive solution to the state preparation problem? Yes, we can, and figure 2.5 shows the outline of the general recursive approach.

The general approach is very similar to the one we took to prepare a two-qubit state: prepare the least significant qubit in some state and then adjust the state of the remaining $n-1$ qubits conditionally using controlled variants of the same state preparation routine called for $n-1$ qubits. Let's figure out the exact parameters to use on each step.

First, let's group the terms of the sum that expresses the state $|\psi_n\rangle_n$ we're preparing in the same manner we did for the two-qubit state: based on the bit value of the first qubit. The first qubit corresponds to the least significant bit in the little-endian notation of an integer, so this grouping will separate the terms with even and odd basis states.

We'll use the fact that if the little-endian binary notation of the integer j is a bit string "s", then integers $2j$ and $2j+1$ can be written as "$0s$" and "$1s$", respectively. Translating this to Dirac notation gives us $|2j\rangle_n = |0\rangle_1 \otimes |j\rangle_{n-1}$ and $|2j+1\rangle_n = |1\rangle_1 \otimes |j\rangle_{n-1}$.

2.5 Preparing a multiqubit state

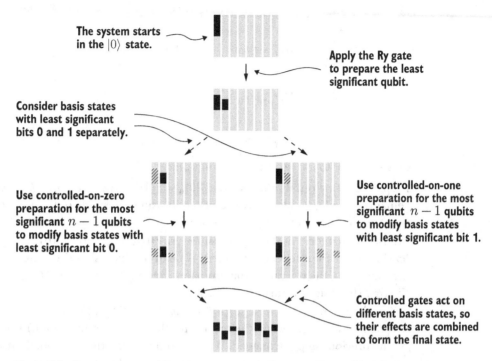

Figure 2.5 To prepare an n-qubit state, we prepare the least significant qubit in a superposition state and then adjust the state of the remaining $n-1$ qubits. Same as in the two-qubit case, controlled variants of the state preparation operation allow us to adjust the states of the most significant $n-1$ qubits conditionally, with separate handling of the least significant qubit being in $|0\rangle$ and $|1\rangle$ states.

With this in mind, we can rewrite the state we're preparing as follows:

$$|\psi_n\rangle_n = \sum_{k=0}^{2^n-1} a_k |k\rangle_n = \sum_{j=0}^{2^{n-1}-1} \left(a_{2j} |2j\rangle_n + a_{2j+1} |2j+1\rangle_n\right)$$

$$= \sum_{j=0}^{2^{n-1}-1} \left(a_{2j} |0\rangle_1 \otimes |j\rangle_{n-1} + a_{2j+1} |1\rangle_1 \otimes |j\rangle_{n-1}\right)$$

$$= |0\rangle_1 \otimes \sum_{j=0}^{2^{n-1}-1} a_{2j} |j\rangle_{n-1} + |1\rangle_1 \otimes \sum_{j=0}^{2^{n-1}-1} a_{2j+1} |j\rangle_{n-1}$$

Now, let's rewrite the sums so that the norm of each of them is 1 and the normalization coefficients are outside the sums. As in the two-qubit case, we can prepare the expressions in brackets as $(n-1)$-qubit states.

We'll define the helper real numbers $m_0 = \sqrt{\sum_{j=0}^{2^{n-1}-1} a_{2j}^2}$ and $m_1 = \sqrt{\sum_{j=0}^{2^{n-1}-1} a_{2j+1}^2}$. We know that $m_0^2 + m_1^2 = 1$, since this sum is the same as the sum of squares of all input amplitudes. Now we can write the sums as follows:

$$\sum_{j=0}^{2^{n-1}-1} a_{2j} |j\rangle_{n-1} = m_0 \sum_{j=0}^{2^{n-1}-1} \frac{a_{2j}}{m_0} |j\rangle_{n-1} = m_0 |\psi_{n-1}^{(0)}\rangle_{n-1}$$

$$\sum_{j=0}^{2^{n-1}-1} a_{2j+1} |j\rangle_{n-1} = m_1 \sum_{j=0}^{2^{n-1}-1} \frac{a_{2j+1}}{m_1} |j\rangle_{n-1} = m_1 |\psi_{n-1}^{(1)}\rangle_{n-1}$$

$$|\psi_n\rangle_n = m_0 |0\rangle_1 \otimes |\psi_{n-1}^{(0)}\rangle_{n-1} + m_1 |1\rangle_1 \otimes |\psi_{n-1}^{(1)}\rangle_{n-1}$$

And thus we arrive to a clear recursive solution:

1. Prepare the first qubit in the state $m_0 |0\rangle_0 + m_1 |1\rangle_1$ (the remaining $n-1$ qubits remain in the $|0\rangle_{n-1}$ state). We can do that using the single-qubit preparation routine with parameters $\alpha = m_0$ and $\beta = m_1$.
2. Adjust the first term of the superposition $m_0 |0\rangle_1 \otimes |0\rangle_{n-1}$ to $m_0 |0\rangle_1 \otimes |\psi_{n-1}^{(0)}\rangle_{n-1}$, leaving the second term unchanged. We can do that using the controlled-on-zero variant of the operation that prepares the $(n-1)$-qubit state $|\psi_{n-1}^{(0)}\rangle_{n-1}$ with the first (least significant) qubit as control.
3. Adjust the last term of the superposition $m_1 |1\rangle_1 \otimes |0\rangle_{n-1}$ to $m_1 |1\rangle_1 \otimes |\psi_{n-1}^{(1)}\rangle_{n-1}$, leaving all the other terms (the terms with the least significant bit 0) prepared on the previous step unchanged. We can do that using the controlled variant of the operation that prepares the $(n-1)$-qubit state $|\psi_{n-1}^{(1)}\rangle_{n-1}$ with the first qubit as control.

With all the work we've already done in this chapter, implementing this algorithm will not require us to learn any new quantum programming tools. We'll write some extra classical code to calculate the coefficients for the preparation of the least significant qubit and to separate the amplitudes into two groups for the recursive calls. Let's see how to do that.

2.5.2 Qiskit

Listing 2.9 shows the Qiskit code that implements our recursive solution to prepare a multiqubit state with the given coefficients.

Listing 2.9 Qiskit code to prepare a multiqubit state

```
from math import atan2, sqrt
from qiskit import QuantumCircuit

def prep_one_qubit(alpha, beta):
  circ = QuantumCircuit(1, name=f'Prep({alpha}, {beta})')
  theta = 2 * atan2(beta, alpha)
  circ.ry(theta, 0)
  return circ.to_gate()

def prep_multi_qubit(n, a):
  circ = QuantumCircuit(n)

  if n == 1:                                    ⬅ Base case of the recursion
    circ.append(prep_one_qubit(a[0], a[1]), [0])
```

```
    return circ

even_amps = a[0 : : 2]          ◄──── Groups amplitudes of even and odd basis states separately
odd_amps = a[1 : : 2]

m0 = sqrt(sum(a*a for a in even_amps))
m1 = sqrt(sum(a*a for a in odd_amps))        ┐ Prepares qubit 0
                                             │ (the least significant)
circ.append(prep_one_qubit(m0, m1), [0])  ◄──┘

circ.append(prep_multi_qubit(n - 1, even_amps)   ◄──┐ Prepares basis states with
    .to_gate().control(1, ctrl_state=0), range(n))  │ the least significant bit 0

circ.append(prep_multi_qubit(n - 1, odd_amps)    ◄──┐ Prepares basis states with
    .to_gate().control(1), range(n))                │ the least significant bit 1

return circ
```

Note that we didn't need to renormalize the amplitudes after splitting them in two groups before passing them as arguments to the recursive state preparation calls. We end up using the values of the amplitudes only to calculate the rotation angles for the various Ry gates, and we do that using the atan2 function, which ignores the magnitudes of its arguments and only uses their relative values. As a result, we don't need to normalize the amplitudes we use as the arguments for our state preparation function. We can always multiply all of them by the same constant value and get the same state prepared as a result, which certainly makes the code neater!

To test this code, we can reuse the code from listing 2.7, extending the set of test cases to include single-qubit and multiqubit states. For example, here are the tests that verify preparation of basis states on one, two, and three qubits and preparation of random states:

```
def test_basis_states():
  for n in range(1, 4):
    for basis in range(2 ** n):
      a = [0.] * 2 ** n
      a[basis] = 1.
      run_test_prep_multi_qubit(n, a)

def test_random_unequal_superpositions():
  for i in range(10):
    n = randint(2, 4)
    a = [uniform(-1.0, 1.0) for _ in range(2 ** n)]
    norm = sqrt(sum(a*a for a in a))
    a_norm = [j / norm for j in a]
    run_test_prep_multi_qubit(n, a_norm)
```

You can find the code for this project, complete with unit tests, in the GitHub repository.

2.5.3 Q#

Listing 2.10 shows the Q# code that implements our recursive solution to prepare a multiqubit state with the given coefficients.

Listing 2.10   Q# code to prepare a multiqubit state

```
import Std.Math.*;

operation PrepOneQubit(
  q : Qubit, alpha : Double, beta : Double
) : Unit is Adj + Ctl {
  let theta = 2.0 * ArcTan2(beta, alpha);
  Ry(theta, q);
}

operation PrepArbitrary(
  qs : Qubit[],
  a : Double[]
) : Unit is Adj + Ctl {
  if Length(qs) == 1 {                    ◄─── Base case of the recursion
    PrepOneQubit(qs[0], a[0], a[1]);
  } else {
    let N = Length(qs);
    let evenAmps = a[0 .. 2 ...];         ◄─┐ Groups amplitudes of even and
    let oddAmps = a[1 .. 2 ...];            │ odd basis states separately

    let m0 = PNorm(2.0, evenAmps);        ◄─┐ PNorm function calculates the root of the sum
    let m1 = PNorm(2.0, oddAmps);           │ of array elements raised to the given power.

    PrepOneQubit(qs[N - 1], m0, m1);      ◄─── Prepares qubit N-1 (the least significant)

    ApplyControlledOnInt(0, PrepArbitrary,  ◄─┐ Prepares basis states with the
      [qs[N - 1]], (qs[... N - 2], evenAmps));  │ least significant bit 0

    ApplyControlledOnInt(1, PrepArbitrary,  ◄─┐ Prepares basis states with the
      [qs[N - 1]], (qs[... N - 2], oddAmps));   │ least significant bit 1
  }
}
```

As in Qiskit code (listing 2.9), we don't need to renormalize the amplitudes before passing them as arguments to the recursive state preparation calls because the function we're using to compute the rotation angles for Ry gates relies only on the relative values of its arguments, not their individual magnitudes.

To test this code, we can reuse the code from listing 2.8, extending the set of test cases to include multiqubit states. The new tests—both the test cases covered, such as the basis states and random multiqubit states, and the logic of their implementation—will be similar to those included in section 2.5.2, so I'm not repeating them here. You can find the complete code for this project in the GitHub repository.

2.6   Further reading

The state preparation algorithm described in this chapter is easy to come up with and understand, but it is not the most efficient approach to this problem. The following includes an example of a more efficient state preparation algorithm:

- Shende, V. V., Bullock, S. S., & Markov, I. L. (2004). Synthesis of quantum logic circuits. https://arxiv.org/abs/quant-ph/0406176

2.7 Going beyond

Do you want to spend some more time building out this project before moving on to the next topic? Here are some additional ideas for ways to extend this project if you want to try your hand at something more challenging:

- Quantum algorithms often require preparing n-qubit states that are a superposition of only the first K basis states in the space (the basis states described by integers $0, 1, ..., K-1$) rather than all 2^n of them. Modify the project so that if the input array of amplitudes has fewer than 2^n amplitudes, it is padded with zeroes to the length 2^n.
- Consider n-qubit states that consist of only basis states of the given parity. For example, a two-qubit state of even parity would be some superposition of $|00\rangle$ and $|11\rangle$, and of odd parity, a superposition of $|01\rangle$ and $|10\rangle$. Modify the project to prepare such a state. (We will use this type of states later, in chapter 4.)
- The general state preparation problem considers states with arbitrary amplitudes, which does not leave a lot of space for "Aha" moments. However, if your state has some structure—for example, it has only a few nonzero amplitudes that follow some kind of pattern—you can often prepare it more efficiently than in the general case. Come up with some fun states and think of custom ways to prepare them. You can check out the Preparing Quantum States kata from the Quantum Katas project for some examples of such states https://mng.bz/gaQV.
- Implement the state preparation algorithm from Shende et al. (see section 2.6). Note that you can reuse the unit tests developed earlier in this chapter to test your new code without any modifications!
- We looked at preparation of quantum states with only real amplitudes to keep things simple. There are some algorithms that rely on this kind of states exclusively, such as Grover's search algorithm, but in general, quantum algorithms require states with complex amplitudes. How would you change the algorithm to deal with such states? (Of course, you'll need more gates than just Ry and its controlled variants; consider the other rotation gates Rx and Rz.)

Summary

- Any quantum algorithm can be represented as several steps: preparing the initial state, evolving it following the specific algorithm, and measuring the final state to get the result. The goal of the algorithm is either to get the correct answer as a result of the final measurement with high probability or to estimate the probabilities of the outcomes.
- The goal of state preparation task is as follows: given a freshly initialized system in the $|0\rangle$ state, change its state to the superposition state described by the given list of amplitudes.
- State preparation operation can be implemented recursively, by preparing one of the qubits in a certain superposition state and then using it to control state preparation operations applied to the remaining qubits.

- Quantum simulators are classical programs that allow you to run small quantum programs without access to quantum hardware.
- Using simulators during quantum software development allows you to inspect the state of the program mid-execution, which is not possible when running the program on a quantum device, and to test your code easily.

Implementing quantum operations

This chapter covers
- Implementing quantum operations based on their matrix notation
- Using Q# and Qiskit to write more complicated quantum programs
- Observing the matrix implemented by a quantum operation
- Writing tests for validating quantum operations

As we've seen in the previous chapter, a typical quantum algorithm can be represented as a standard sequence of steps (see figure 3.1). In chapter 2, we've learned to implement the first step, preparing the quantum system in the given state.

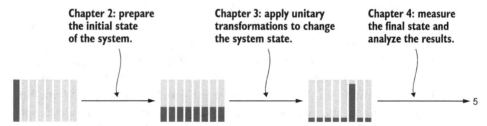

Figure 3.1 Any quantum algorithm can be broken down into several steps: prepare the initial state, evolve it by applying unitary transformations, and measure the final state. In this chapter, we'll learn to perform the second step: implementing unitary transformations as the algorithm dictates.

In this chapter, we'll focus on the second step: changing the state of the system using quantum operations. More specifically, we'll learn to implement quantum operations that change the state of the system the way the algorithm requires.

What do we mean by "implementing" a quantum operation? Figure 3.2 shows how quantum algorithms are decomposed into simpler building blocks on multiple levels.

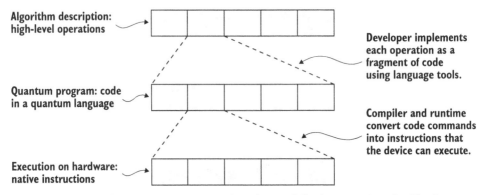

Figure 3.2 The transformation the quantum state undergoes following a quantum algorithm is typically broken down into simpler building blocks. First, the whole algorithm is expressed as a sequence of operations described in terms of the input parameters of the problem. These operations are further represented as sequences of primitives provided by the high-level programming language used to implement the algorithm. Finally, to execute the algorithm on a quantum device, programming language primitives have to be expressed as sequences of low-level instructions that are natively available on this device.

Most quantum algorithms don't prescribe the whole transformation that the quantum system needs to undergo as a single quantum operation. Instead, this transformation is typically broken down into simpler building blocks, and this process is repeated several times on different layers of abstraction that serve different purposes.

On the logical level, an algorithm is usually expressed as a sequence of high-level operations that are easy to understand in the context of the problem it solves. You'll find this level of algorithm description in papers and textbooks that propose new algorithms or explain well-known ones.

For example, Grover's search algorithm is an algorithm that searches for a value that satisfies a certain set of constraints. The algorithm is described as a sequence of Grover's iterations, where each iteration is composed of two logical operations. The first one is a quantum oracle that multiplies the amplitudes of certain basis states by −1 depending on the constraints of the problem. The second operation is the reflection about the mean—an operation that depends on the search space of the problem. Both these operations depend on the specific problem being solved, so the algorithm describes them in enough detail to allow the reader to reason about their effect in the general case, but not in so much detail as to narrow down the generic algorithm to a single problem instance.

> **NOTE** If you're not familiar with Grover's search algorithm, don't worry! We'll discuss it in chapters 7 and 8, where you'll learn about its structure and practice implementing the algorithm for solving specific problems.

Next, when the algorithm is implemented in a high-level quantum programming language, each of its logical building blocks has to be broken down into sequences of programming primitives provided by that language. Depending on the language and the libraries it provides, these primitives can be relatively high-level, such as quantum arithmetic operations, quantum Fourier transform, or other standard building blocks of quantum algorithms, or low-level, such as built-in gates that the language provides and automatically generated controlled variants of gates. Some of these building blocks can take input parameters that correspond to the parameters of the problem instance; these parameters then influence the exact sequence of primitives used to implement the block. This level of algorithm implementation allows the developer to run the program on quantum simulators to get the execution results for small problem instances or estimate the resources required to execute it on a quantum device.

To continue the Grover's search algorithm example, the simplest version of the reflection about the mean operation is implemented using low-level programming language primitives: H, X, and controlled Z gates. The more advanced versions take the search space description as an input and implement the operation using an additional higher-level state preparation primitive, such as the one we learned to implement in chapter 2, to prepare an equal superposition of all basis states that are part of the search space. The quantum oracle in Grover's search takes the description of the constraints for the problem instance and evaluates them for the input quantum state. Implementing this operation can be straightforward or quite challenging, depending on the problem that is being solved and the structure of its constraints (we'll see examples of this in chapter 8).

Finally, to run the algorithm on a quantum device, the program in a high-level language has to be converted into the lowest-level instructions that can be executed on that device. This compilation is usually performed by the middle-layer software, since the compilation algorithms require sophisticated math that is more convenient to implement in a classical programming language as part of the compiler stack, rather than in a quantum programming language as part of the quantum libraries code. In this case, quantum software developers don't have to do this decomposition by hand; they can use any gates and libraries provided by the language and trust that the compiler stack will take care of converting them into instructions for a specific device.

Hardware-specific compilation: Examples

The exact set of instructions available on a quantum device and the rules of their execution depend on several factors. Here are a few examples:

(continued)

Different hardware platforms use different physical objects acting as qubits, and thus support different gates that can be implemented natively using physical processes. The rest of the gates used by a programming language have to be decomposed into sequences of native instructions that approximate their effect and can be executed on a quantum device. This decomposition is called *unitary gate synthesis*. For example, a multicontrolled Z gate used by our reflection about the mean operation implementation will be decomposed into a sequence of one- and two-qubit gates, since most hardware platforms don't support gates acting on three or more qubits.

Different devices have different *qubit connectivity*—the map of pairs of qubits that are considered adjacent and can have multiqubit gates applied to them. Some platforms, such as trapped ion devices, might allow all-to-all connectivity. Others, such as devices based on superconducting qubits, are limited to planar connectivity, in which only pairs of physically adjacent qubits can share a gate. In this case, applying a two-qubit gate to two qubits that are not adjacent on a chip can be done by performing a sequence of other gates, each between two adjacent qubits.

In the long run, once quantum computers can run continuous error correction, this will affect the logical qubit connectivity and the set of gates natively available for them. Once a logical qubit is encoded as multiple physical qubits as part of an error-correction scheme, any gates applied to it have to be performed in a fault-tolerant manner to limit the spread of errors that occur during gate application. Quantum devices available today don't run error correction, but eventually this will affect the way operations are performed on a fault-tolerant quantum computer.

Now that you understand the levels at which quantum operations can be implemented, let's narrow down the problem we'll be solving and spell out the tools we're assuming are available to solve it. In this chapter, we'll focus on implementing the quantum operations as high-level programs, without diving into the intricacies of unitary gate synthesis and other details handled by the compiler stack. Consequently, we can use any built-in quantum gates offered by our programming languages, as well as convenient constructs such as controlled variants of gates with arbitrary number of control bits. We won't, however, use higher-level abstractions such as library operations that implement arbitrary unitary operations—that would take all the fun out of the project!

> **Why unitary implementation?**
>
> Just like with quantum state preparation, you're not likely to write the code to handle the general case of implementing unitaries yourself. This problem is common enough that quantum programming languages tend to have libraries that solve it for you. Qiskit's `unitary` method of the `QuantumCircuit` class and Q#'s `ApplyUnitary` operation from the namespace `Std.Intrinsic` both apply a unitary described with the given matrix of complex coefficients.

However, this problem makes for a great learning project.

- First, same as the state preparation task, it is easy to define, and the solution uses only the basic concepts of qubits and gates. However, while state preparation was easier to discuss in terms of Dirac notation, reasoning about unitary matrices is best done in matrix notation, so you'll get to practice a different, complimentary set of skills.
- Second, it has lots of special cases that are easier to handle than the most general case of the problem, so there are plenty of stepping stones that you can use for practice before approaching the general problem.
- Finally, it is a very practical problem, since most quantum algorithms rely on the use of nontrivial quantum transformations, and its special cases often show up in various algorithms on their own. Being able to come up with ways to handle these special cases can come in handy.

Quantum operations can be described in multiple ways; in this chapter we'll focus on implementing operations based on their descriptions as *unitary matrices*—square matrices for which their adjoint (also known as conjugate transpose) is equal to their inverse. In general, matrices that correspond to quantum operations can be complex-valued, but as in chapter 2, we'll simplify our project to only handle real-valued matrices.

Some unitary matrices of special shapes can be implemented more easily using specialized approaches. One example are *permutation matrices*—matrices that consist only of elements 0 and 1, and each row and each column has exactly one element 1. These matrices describe quantum operations that implement *reversible classical computations*—computations that map each classical input bit string to exactly one classical output bit string, and vice versa. Such operations can often be implemented more efficiently based on the analysis of the corresponding classical computation. We will revisit reversible computation in chapter 6, but in the current chapter, we will work with the general case of unitary matrices.

Now that we've established the problem we're solving and the tools we can use, let's get started! We'll begin with its single-qubit variant and build up to implementing arbitrary multiqubit unitary transformations with real coefficients. Along the way I will show you how to see the matrix of the unitary transformation implemented by the given code and how to write unit tests that verify that this matrix matches the one you want it to be.

3.1 Implementing a single-qubit gate

Let's again start with *almost* the simplest possible quantum operation implementation problem. Given a single qubit and a matrix of four floating-point numbers u_{00}, u_{01}, u_{10}, u_{11} that describe a single-qubit unitary transformation, implement an operation that applies this unitary transformation to the given qubit.

> **NOTE** Why start with this task? This implementation is the easiest possible task that does not boil down to just choosing the gate that matches the given matrix precisely. Instead, it requires some thought to figure out what the inputs can look like and which gate or gate combination allows us to implement the solution. In addition, this task is the essential building block for this problem that we'll use again and again later in the chapter.

3.1.1 Math

The matrix we need to implement as a quantum operation looks as follows:

$$U = \begin{pmatrix} u_{00} & u_{01} \\ u_{10} & u_{11} \end{pmatrix}$$

We know that the matrix we're given is a valid unitary transformation with real coefficients. What constraints does this impose on the input values?

By definition, for a unitary matrix its adjoint equals its inverse. In other words, the product of the matrix and its adjoint (in either order) is the identity matrix:

$$U \cdot U^\dagger = U^\dagger \cdot U = I$$

Since our matrix is real-valued, its adjoint equals its transpose ($U^\dagger = U^T$), so we can write this constraint as follows:

$$U^T \cdot U = \begin{pmatrix} u_{00} & u_{10} \\ u_{01} & u_{11} \end{pmatrix} \begin{pmatrix} u_{00} & u_{01} \\ u_{10} & u_{11} \end{pmatrix} = \begin{pmatrix} 1 & 0 \\ 0 & 1 \end{pmatrix} = I$$

Now we can unpack the matrix equality into a system of equations, one for each of the elements of the identity matrix. The pair of equations that correspond to the off-diagonal elements of the identity matrix end up being identical, so I'm listing only one of them:

$$\begin{cases} u_{00}^2 + u_{10}^2 = 1 \\ u_{00}u_{10} + u_{01}u_{11} = 0 \\ u_{01}^2 + u_{11}^2 = 1 \end{cases}$$

Based on the first equation, we can choose a variable α so that $u_{00} = \cos \alpha$ and $u_{10} = \sin \alpha$. (We always can do that for two numbers that, when squared, add up to 1.) Now, solving the system of equations completely gives us two options:

- The given matrix is *symmetric*: $u_{01} = \sin \alpha$ and $u_{11} = -\cos \alpha$. In other words, the two elements *off* the main diagonal are equal, and the two elements *on* the main diagonal have equal absolute values but opposite signs.
- The given matrix is *antisymmetric*: $u_{01} = -\sin \alpha$ and $u_{11} = \cos \alpha$. In other words, the two elements *on* the main diagonal are equal, and the two elements *off* the main diagonal have equal absolute values but opposite signs.

Depending on the input values, we might have one of the two scenarios to implement:

$$U = \underbrace{\begin{pmatrix} \cos\alpha & \sin\alpha \\ \sin\alpha & -\cos\alpha \end{pmatrix}}_{\text{symmetric matrix}} \text{ or } U = \underbrace{\begin{pmatrix} \cos\alpha & -\sin\alpha \\ \sin\alpha & \cos\alpha \end{pmatrix}}_{\text{antisymmetric matrix}}$$

> **Validating the solution for single-qubit gates**
>
> How can we validate this solution? The simplest "smoke test" is to think about the most commonly used gates and see whether all of them can be described using one of these two scenarios. And indeed, looking at the table 2.1, we can see that Z, X, and H are all examples of gates with symmetric matrices (with parameter α being 0, $\frac{\pi}{2}$, and $\frac{\pi}{4}$, respectively), while I and $Ry(\theta)$ have antisymmetric matrices (with parameters 0 and $\frac{\theta}{2}$, respectively).
>
> (The I gate is symmetric in the informal sense of the term, in that it is equal to its transpose. In the context of this chapter, however, we require the elements on the main diagonal of a symmetric matrix to have opposite signs. The elements on the main diagonal of the I matrix are equal, so by our definition, this gate is antisymmetric.)

A gate that is described with an antisymmetric matrix can be implemented using a single $Ry(2\alpha)$ gate, since the matrix describing it matches that of the Ry gate exactly:

$$Ry(\theta) = \begin{pmatrix} \cos\frac{\theta}{2} & -\sin\frac{\theta}{2} \\ \sin\frac{\theta}{2} & \cos\frac{\theta}{2} \end{pmatrix}$$

In the case of a symmetric matrix, though, we need to change the signs of the matrix elements in the right column, which we can do by applying the Z gate before applying the Ry gate. In matrix form, the solution can be expressed as $Ry(2\alpha) \cdot Z$, since the gates in the matrix product are applied to qubits in the order from right to left:

$$Ry(2\alpha) \cdot Z = \begin{pmatrix} \cos\alpha & -\sin\alpha \\ \sin\alpha & \cos\alpha \end{pmatrix} \cdot \begin{pmatrix} 1 & 0 \\ 0 & -1 \end{pmatrix} = \begin{pmatrix} \cos\alpha & \sin\alpha \\ \sin\alpha & -\cos\alpha \end{pmatrix}$$

The complete solution steps are as follows:

1. Check whether the input matrix is symmetric by checking that the elements off the main diagonal are equal and the elements on the main diagonal are the negation of each other. If the matrix is symmetric, apply the Z gate to the qubit.
2. Find the parameter α from the given matrix and apply the $Ry(2\alpha)$ gate to the qubit.

As a final note, we can use the same function atan2 to calculate the angle α that we used in section 2.1. We need, however, to take care when identifying the scenario described by the inputs to make sure diagonal and antidiagonal matrices are classified correctly. For example, if the solution only checks that the diagonal elements are equal to decide that the matrix is antisymmetric, the X gate will be classified as antisymmetric and thus be implemented incorrectly. We also need to keep in mind that the elements of the input matrix are floating-point numbers and thus have to be compared within certain tolerance rather than exactly, especially if the input matrix is not hardcoded in the tests but calculated on the fly, which we'll see later in the chapter.

3.1.2 Qiskit

The code for this task can be written using only the language constructs we've already seen in chapter 2. We'll implement the operation as a gate right away, since we'll use it extensively as a building block later in the chapter. The following listing shows the Qiskit code that implements a single-qubit unitary with the given real coefficients.

Listing 3.1 Qiskit code to implement a single-qubit unitary

```python
from math import atan2, isclose
from qiskit import QuantumCircuit

def apply_one_qubit(u):
  circ = QuantumCircuit(1)
  if isclose(u[0][0], -u[1][1]) and \
     isclose(u[1][0], u[0][1]):
    circ.z(0)
  theta = atan2(u[1][0], u[0][0])
  circ.ry(2 * theta, 0)
  return circ.to_gate()
```

Uses Python function math.isclose to compare real numbers approximately

This code doesn't output anything yet because it only defines a function that implements a gate. We'll learn to see its effect in the next section.

3.1.3 Q#

Now let's take a look at the same solution in Q#.

Listing 3.2 Q# code to implement a single-qubit unitary

```
import Std.Math.*;

operation ApplyOneQubit(
  qs : Qubit[], u : Double[][]
) : Unit is Adj + Ctl {
  if AbsD(u[0][0] - (-u[1][1])) < 1e-9 and
      AbsD(u[0][1] - u[1][0]) < 1e-9 {
    Z(qs[0]);
  }
  let angle = ArcTan2(u[1][0], u[0][0]);
  Ry(2.0 * angle, qs[0]);
}
```

Uses an array of one qubit as an argument to simplify the future code

Uses Q# function AbsD to compare real numbers approximately

As with Qiskit, this code doesn't produce an output yet (in fact, trying to run it will cause an error due to a missing entry point operation). We will modify it to see the result of implementing a unitary in the next section.

3.2 What does your solution do?

So far, the code we've written does not output anything or even apply the newly defined gate to any qubits. How can we see what it does to check that it's correct?

We could use the same technique we saw in the previous chapter to apply our gate to a quantum state or several (for example, all the basis states this unitary can act upon), get the amplitudes of the resulting state(s), and then assemble them into a matrix. But it is easier to use the built-in tools that run the operation on a quantum simulator to get the matrix representation of the unitary it implements.

3.2.1 Qiskit

One of the simulation methods available as part of `AerSimulator` is `unitary_simulator`. Under the hood, this simulator calculates the unitary matrix of the circuit itself rather than the result of the evolution of a specific initial quantum state. That's why it can only be used for simulating circuits that consist of gates that can be decomposed into gates with matrix definitions and will fail if the circuit contains measurements or conditional operations (`if` statements with classical conditions embedded into the circuit). In our code, we only use conditional statements to build the circuit; they are not part of the circuit itself, so we can use this simulator. Once the simulation is complete, the resulting matrix can be retrieved using the method `get_unitary`.

Listing 3.3 shows you how to modify listing 3.1 to get an instance of the simulator to use and get the matrix representation of the program after simulation is complete.

> **NOTE** For the rest of this chapter, I'll only include new and modified code in the listings, rather than the complete code necessary to solve the task. You can find the complete code for each problem in this chapter in the GitHub repository.

Listing 3.3 Qiskit code to get a circuit's matrix via unitary_simulator

```
from qiskit import transpile
from qiskit_aer import Aer

coef = [[0.6, -0.8], [0.8, 0.6]]

circ = QuantumCircuit(1)                          ⬅ Creates a circuit and appends our gate to it
circ.append(apply_one_qubit(coef), [0])

simulator = Aer.get_backend('unitary_simulator')
circ = transpile(circ, backend=simulator)
res = simulator.run(circ).result()
matrix = res.get_unitary().data    ⬅ Gets the unitary matrix of this circuit
print(matrix)
```

The `get_unitary` method returns the matrix of a unitary, represented as a two-dimensional array of complex numbers. The output of this program will look as follows:

```
[[ 0.6+0.j -0.8+0.j]
 [ 0.8+0.j  0.6+0.j]]
```

Alternatively, we can use the `Operator` class from the `qiskit.quantum_info` library. This class is used to represent unitary operations that act on a quantum system and can be initialized from a circuit or a gate—in this case, the gate `apply_one_qubit`. Like the `unitary_simulator`, this class computes the unitary matrix of the circuit instead of simulating its action on a specific starting state, and it can only be used for circuits composed of gates, without measurements or conditionals.

Listing 3.4 shows you how to modify listing 3.3 to convert a circuit or a gate into an `Operator` and extract the matrix from the properties of this class.

Listing 3.4 Qiskit code to get a gate's matrix via qiskit.quantum_info

```
from qiskit.quantum_info import Operator

coef = [[0.6, -0.8], [0.8, 0.6]]

op = Operator(apply_one_qubit(coef))     ← Initializes an Operator for our gate
print(op.data)                            ← Gets the matrix of this Operator
```

This code will produce the same output as the one printed by listing 3.3: the matrix of the quantum operation as a two-dimensional array of complex numbers.

3.2.2 Q#

In chapter 2, we saw how developing tests for Q# code that check the quantum state of the program required us to use Python. The Python module `qsharp` includes a function `dump_machine` you can use to peek at the current quantum state of a program. Similarly, a helper Python module `qsharp.utils` offers a function `dump_operation` you can use to get the matrix implemented by the given quantum operation.

Listing 3.5 shows you how to add Python code to listing 3.2. The new code uses `dump_operation` to print the matrix implemented by the operation `ApplyOneQubit` for a specific input set of coefficients. (At this point, you need to switch from working with Q# standalone files to using a Python + Q# project structure, as we discussed in section 2.4.2.)

Listing 3.5 Python code to get the matrix of a Q# operation

```
import qsharp
from qsharp.utils import dump_operation

coef = [[0.6, -0.8], [0.8, 0.6]]

qsharp.init(project_root='.')
print(dump_operation(f"UnitaryImplementation.ApplyOneQubit(_, {coef})", 1))
```

Partial application in Q#

This is the first time we're seeing partial application in Q# in this book, so let's inspect this code closer.

The Python function `dump_operation` takes two arguments, the Q# operation and the number of qubits on which it acts, and returns the matrix representation of this operation. The Q# operation passed as a parameter to `dump_operation` should take a single argument—an array of qubits—and have no return value (otherwise, it cannot be a unitary and have a matrix representation). That's why I used a qubit array as the first argument to the operation `ApplyOneQubit` instead of a single qubit.

However, the operation `ApplyOneQubit` takes two parameters: a qubit array and an additional parameter, the matrix of coefficients. We cannot pass it as an argument to `dump_operation` as is. We need to define another operation that takes a single parameter, the qubit array, and applies `ApplyOneQubit` to this array using the specific hardcoded matrix of coefficients as the second parameter.

We can do this using a *partial application*. Partial application is the process of fixing one or several arguments of an operation to produce a new operation with fewer arguments. In Q#, partial application looks similar to an operation call: the arguments that are provided indicate the arguments that will be fixed, and the underscores denote the arguments that are left unbound and will become arguments of the new operation.

Consider the following Q# code snippets:

```
use qs = Qubit[1];
ApplyOneQubit(qs, [[0.6, -0.8], [0.8, 0.6]]);

let op = ApplyOneQubit(_, [[0.6, -0.8], [0.8, 0.6]]);
use qs = Qubit[1];
op(qs);
```

The first snippet allocates a qubit array and applies `ApplyOneQubit` to it directly. The second snippet starts by defining an operation `op` that takes a single argument, a qubit array. When this operation is applied to a qubit array, it applies the operation `ApplyOneQubit` with the given matrix as a second argument to it. Then the snippet allocates a qubit array and applies the operation `op` to it. This way, the classical parameter can be defined before the qubits are allocated.

The code in listing 3.5 takes this approach one step further: it defines a single-argument operation using partial application and passes it to `dump_operation` immediately. `dump_operation` then allocates the qubits, prepares them in a certain state, and applies this operation to them to extract its matrix representation.

The output of this program will look as follows:

```
[[(0.6+0j), (-0.8+0j)], [(0.8+0j), (0.6+0j)]]
```

You can see that, as with the Qiskit code we saw in the previous section, the matrix is represented as a two-dimensional array of complex numbers. Note that since the values are floating-point numbers, they might differ slightly from the exact values we were aiming for (in this case, 0.6 and 0.8) due to floating-point imprecision. That's why in the next section, when we develop tests for this code, we'll compare the elements of the desired matrix with the elements of the one that was actually implemented within certain tolerance rather than exactly.

> **TIP** Q# namespace `Std.Diagnostics` offers a similar operation `DumpOperation` that prints the matrix of a unitary directly from Q#. You can use it when working with Q# standalone files; we will, however, need to write tests in Python, so I focused on the Python API of this tool.

3.3 Testing your solution

Hopefully your experience with the first project has convinced you that unit tests are best written as soon as possible! You might have noticed that in this chapter the project is trickier, and there are more scenarios and corner cases to test even in the very first task we tackled. Since we've already learned the general approach to writing unit tests for quantum code in chapter 2, let's learn how to validate the matrices implemented by quantum operations right now to make our life easier for the remainder of the chapter.

We will use the same approach we saw earlier: write unit tests to verify that our implementation of quantum operations indeed has the matrix representation we expect it to have and use quantum simulators and specialized tools to do this.

3.3.1 Qiskit

As we saw in section 3.2.1, Qiskit provides multiple ways to extract the matrix implemented by the circuit. We can use either of these ways to get the matrix of our implementation and then compare it to the matrix we needed to implement using standard Python tools. For the rest of this chapter, I'll use the approach that relies on the `Operator` class, since it makes the code more concise and has better performance for larger test cases we'll need in the end of the chapter.

The following listing shows the test code for the single-qubit unitary implementation in Qiskit.

Listing 3.6 Qiskit code to test a single-qubit unitary implementation

```
from math import cos, pi, sin
from random import randint, random
from qiskit.quantum_info import Operator
import pytest
from .one_qubit_unitary import apply_one_qubit

@pytest.mark.parametrize("u",
```
⟵ Defines several sets of diagonal and antidiagonal matrices as arguments for the test function

```
    [ [[1.0, 0.0], [0.0, 1.0]],
      [[0.0, -1.0], [-1.0, 0.0]] ])
def test_apply_one_qubit(u):
  op = Operator(apply_one_qubit(u))     ◀── Gets the matrix of the operation
  matrix = op.data                           implemented by our code

  for actual, expected in zip(matrix, u):    ◀── Compares the matrices row by row
    assert actual == pytest.approx(expected)
def random_one_qubit_unitary():   ◀── Helper function to generate a random unitary matrix
  theta = random() * 2 * pi
  sign = +1 if randint(0, 1) == 1 else -1
  return [[cos(theta), sign * sin(theta)],
          [-sin(theta), sign * cos(theta)]]

def test_dense():        ◀── Tests random matrices with no zero elements
  for _ in range(1, 20):
    test_apply_one_qubit(random_one_qubit_unitary())
```

The tests pay special attention to the diagonal and antidiagonal matrices, since they are a corner case for figuring out whether the input matrix is symmetric or antisymmetric. Since at this point the code is covered with tests, it will not print anything; the expected result of running the code is it passing all the tests.

3.3.2 Q#

Similarly to Qiskit, we'll use the approach from section 3.2.2, which allows us to get the matrix of a unitary in Python, and then use standard Python tools to compare it to the matrix we needed to implement. The following listing shows the Python test code for the single-qubit unitary implementation in Q#.

> **Listing 3.7 Python code to test a single-qubit unitary implementation in Q#**

```
from math import cos, pi, sin
from random import randint, random
import qsharp
from qsharp.utils import dump_operation
import pytest
                                    ┌── Defines several sets of diagonal and antidiagonal
@pytest.mark.parametrize("u",    ◀──┘ matrices as arguments for the test function
    [ [[1.0, 0.0], [0.0, 1.0]],
      [[0.0, -1.0], [-1.0, 0.0]] ])
def test_apply_one_qubit(u):
  qsharp.init(project_root='.')
  matrix = dump_operation(                       ◀── Gets the operation matrix
    f"UnitaryImplementation.ApplyOneQubit(_, {u})", 1)
  for actual, expected in zip(matrix, u):
    assert actual == pytest.approx(expected, abs=1e-6)   ◀──┐ Compares matrices
def test_dense():                                             row by row
  for _ in range(1, 20):
    test_apply_one_qubit(random_one_qubit_unitary())
                                              ◀──┐ Helper function is the
                                                  same as in Qiskit.
```

3.4 Matrix decomposition

Now that we've learned to implement single-qubit unitaries and to test our code, we can move on to the main problem: implementing multiqubit unitaries. This problem is challenging, so we'll break it down into several smaller building blocks, from which we'll then construct the solution to the more general case.

We will use a way to represent an arbitrary unitary matrix as a product of several matrices of simpler structure called *cosine-sine decomposition*. This decomposition can be obtained for matrices of even size ($2M \times 2M$) and looks as follows:

$$U = \begin{pmatrix} A_l & 0 \\ 0 & B_l \end{pmatrix} \begin{pmatrix} C & -S \\ S & C \end{pmatrix} \begin{pmatrix} A_r & 0 \\ 0 & B_r \end{pmatrix}$$

Here, A_l, A_r, B_l, B_r are unitary matrices of size $M \times M$, and C and S are diagonal matrices of size $M \times M$ that, when squared, add up to identity matrix: $C^2 + S^2 = I$. Consequently, all three matrices in the decomposition describe unitary transformations. Since we consider only matrices with real coefficients, all the matrices in the decomposition will also have real coefficients.

Figure 3.3 shows an example of a cosine-sine decomposition for a simple 4×4 matrix.

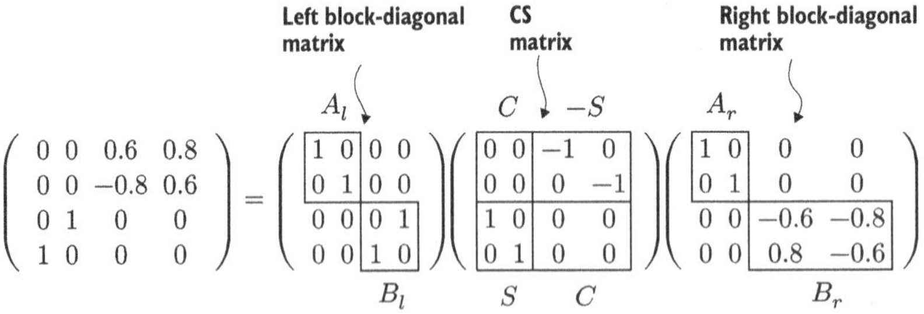

Figure 3.3 Cosine-sine decomposition for an example 4×4 matrix. This matrix is represented as a product of three matrices: a block-diagonal matrix defined by 2×2 matrices A_l and B_l, a block matrix of special shape called CS matrix defined by 2×2 diagonal matrices C and S, and another block-diagonal matrix defined by 2×2 matrices A_r and B_r.

The left and right matrices in the decomposition are *block-diagonal*—that is, they have square blocks of nonzero elements on the main diagonal of the matrix and zero elements everywhere else. The middle matrix in the decomposition is called the cosine-sine factor in the literature; for simplicity, I'll refer to it as the *CS matrix*, and the unitary transformation described by this matrix, the *CS unitary*.

This decomposition shows us the path to completing the project we're working on in this chapter. If we figure out how to implement each of the matrices used in the decomposition, taking advantage of their special shapes, we can use these to implement an arbitrary matrix.

3.4 Matrix decomposition

I don't derive the cosine-sine decomposition or the algorithm of obtaining it here. This is a well-studied classical algorithm, and I'll take advantage of it being available in a lot of matrix algebra software packages, including the SciPy library in Python. If you want to learn more about this decomposition, check out section 3.11 for additional resources.

Listing 3.8 shows you how to use the library function `cossin` from the SciPy library (https://mng.bz/6edA) to get the cosine-sine decomposition of the matrix from figure 3.3.

Listing 3.8 Python code for cosine-sine decomposition of a matrix

```
from numpy import allclose
from scipy.linalg import cossin

u = [[0, 0, 0.6, 0.8],
     [0, 0, -0.8, 0.6],
     [0, 1, 0, 0],
     [1, 0, 0, 0]]

left, cs, right = cossin(u,
    p=len(u) // 2, q=len(u) // 2)

print(allclose(u, left @ cs @ right))

print(left)
print(cs)
print(right)
```

p and q are the dimensions of the blocks in the decomposition.

Checks that the original matrix equals the product of matrices in decomposition

The output of this code looks like this:

```
True
[[1. 0. 0. 0.]
 [0. 1. 0. 0.]
 [0. 0. 0. 1.]
 [0. 0. 1. 0.]]
[[ 6.123234e-17  0.000000e+00 -1.000000e+00 -0.000000e+00]
 [ 0.000000e+00  6.123234e-17 -0.000000e+00 -1.000000e+00]
 [ 1.000000e+00  0.000000e+00  6.123234e-17  0.000000e+00]
 [ 0.000000e+00  1.000000e+00  0.000000e+00  6.123234e-17]]
[[ 1.   0.   0.   0. ]
 [ 0.   1.   0.   0. ]
 [ 0.   0.  -0.6 -0.8]
 [ 0.   0.   0.8 -0.6]]
```

We can see that, indeed, the matrices in the decomposition have the expected shapes, and we can double-check that their product equals the original matrix.

Now we know what building blocks we need to construct the general unitary matrix. Let's start with the small case—4×4 matrices describing two-qubit operations.

3.5 Implementing a two-qubit block-diagonal unitary with 2×2 blocks

The first of the building blocks we'll need is two-qubit unitaries that implement 4×4 block-diagonal matrices of the following shape:

$$U = \begin{pmatrix} A & 0 \\ 0 & B \end{pmatrix} = \begin{pmatrix} a_{00} & a_{01} & 0 & 0 \\ a_{10} & a_{11} & 0 & 0 \\ 0 & 0 & b_{00} & b_{01} \\ 0 & 0 & b_{10} & b_{11} \end{pmatrix}$$

Here, U is a 4×4 block-diagonal matrix, in which the 2×2 blocks on the main diagonal are two independent 2×2 matrices A and B, and the 2×2 blocks off the main diagonal consist of zeros.

In this task we'll implement an operation that takes two 2×2 matrices with real coefficients A and B and implements the block-diagonal unitary as previously described.

3.5.1 Refresher: Controlled gates in matrix notation

Before we start figuring out how to implement this kind of block-diagonal matrices in terms of simpler gates, let's remind ourselves how different types of controlled gates look in matrix form. We'll only consider controlled gates acting on two qubits for now and return to this topic for gates with more qubits later in the chapter.

To start, let's spell out the row and column indices of 4×4 matrices in their binary form. Figure 3.4 shows these indices written as pairs of least and most significant bits.

$$\begin{array}{c c} & \begin{array}{cccc} 0=00 & 1=10 & 2=01 & 3=11 \end{array} \\ \begin{array}{c} 0=00 \\ 1=10 \\ 2=01 \\ 3=11 \end{array} & \begin{pmatrix} a_{00} & a_{01} & 0 & 0 \\ a_{10} & a_{11} & 0 & 0 \\ 0 & 0 & b_{00} & b_{01} \\ 0 & 0 & b_{10} & b_{11} \end{pmatrix} \end{array}$$

Figure 3.4 The row and column indices of 4×4 matrices. The indices are written in binary using little-endian notation: the least significant bit is written first. You can see that the top-left and bottom-right blocks group the elements for which the most significant (the last) bit of the row index equals that of the column index: for the matrix A in the top-left block, the most significant bit is 0, and for the matrix B in the bottom-right block, the most significant bit is 1.

Keep this reference in mind when spelling out the shapes of controlled gates in their matrix form.

> **Converting bit strings into integers: Big-endian vs. little-endian (a refresher)**
>
> You'll notice that I'm describing the qubits as the "least significant bit" and the "most significant bit" rather than left and right or first and second. This is another example of the scenario in which we need to convert bit strings into integer indices

of basis states that correspond to the rows/columns in a matrix, (the first example was the ordering of state vector amplitudes we discussed in section 2.3). Qiskit and Q# use different conventions for mapping integers to bit strings: Qiskit uses little-endian notation, in which the least significant bit is stored in the first/leftmost bit, and Q# uses big-endian, in which the least significant bit is stored in the last/rightmost bit.

Since the shape of the matrix implemented by a quantum gate depends on how the indices of the rows/columns are converted to the basis states, it makes sense to re-emphasize the endianness of this conversion now and again. In this chapter, like in chapter 2, I'll use little-endian to work through the math of solving the problem, and the convention used by the language when implementing the solution in that language. This process will again match the behavior of the libraries native to that language.

You can apply four different variants of a controlled gate to two qubits if you start with a single-qubit gate U and use a single control qubit:

- A controlled gate with the most significant qubit as control and the least significant qubit as target
- A controlled gate with the least significant qubit as control and the most significant qubit as target
- A controlled-on-zero gate with the most significant qubit as control and the least significant qubit as target
- A controlled-on-zero gate with the least significant qubit as control and the most significant qubit as target

Let's spell out the process of figuring out the elements of the matrix for the first variant in detail and then look at the final matrices for the other three cases. We know how a controlled-U gate acts on the basis states, so we can write the following transformations in Dirac notation, using the first (the least significant) qubit as target and the second (the most significant) qubit as control:

$$|00\rangle \to |00\rangle$$
$$|10\rangle \to |10\rangle$$
$$|01\rangle \to U|0\rangle \otimes |1\rangle = (u_{00}|0\rangle + u_{10}|1\rangle) \otimes |1\rangle = u_{00}|01\rangle + u_{10}|11\rangle$$
$$|11\rangle \to U|1\rangle \otimes |1\rangle = (u_{01}|0\rangle + u_{11}|1\rangle) \otimes |1\rangle = u_{01}|01\rangle + u_{11}|11\rangle$$

Now we can convert the Dirac notation into the matrix notation: the results of applying the gate to each basis state are written as the corresponding column, and the element in each row of that column is the amplitude of the corresponding basis state in the result (or zero if that basis state is not present in the result). For this variant of the controlled gate, we get the familiar matrix you usually see in books and tutorials that introduce the matrix form of a controlled-U gate, in which the bottom-right block of the matrix is the matrix of the U gate itself:

$$\begin{pmatrix} 1 & 0 & 0 & 0 \\ 0 & 1 & 0 & 0 \\ 0 & 0 & u_{00} & u_{01} \\ 0 & 0 & u_{10} & u_{11} \end{pmatrix}$$

We can use the same approach to produce the matrices for the other three scenarios. Table 3.1 shows the summary of the results we'll get: the matrices for the four variants of controlled single-qubit gates.

Table 3.1 The variants of a controlled single-qubit gate with one control qubit

Control pattern	The most significant bit as control	The least significant bit as control
Controlled on one	$\begin{pmatrix} 1 & 0 & 0 & 0 \\ 0 & 1 & 0 & 0 \\ 0 & 0 & u_{00} & u_{01} \\ 0 & 0 & u_{10} & u_{11} \end{pmatrix}$	$\begin{pmatrix} 1 & 0 & 0 & 0 \\ 0 & u_{00} & 0 & u_{01} \\ 0 & 0 & 1 & 0 \\ 0 & u_{10} & 0 & u_{11} \end{pmatrix}$
Controlled on zero	$\begin{pmatrix} u_{00} & u_{01} & 0 & 0 \\ u_{10} & u_{11} & 0 & 0 \\ 0 & 0 & 1 & 0 \\ 0 & 0 & 0 & 1 \end{pmatrix}$	$\begin{pmatrix} u_{00} & 0 & u_{01} & 0 \\ 0 & 1 & 0 & 0 \\ u_{10} & 0 & u_{11} & 0 \\ 0 & 0 & 0 & 1 \end{pmatrix}$

You can see that if the most significant bit is used as control, the matrix U occupies a contiguous 2×2 block: the top-left one if the control is on zero or the bottom-right one is the control is on one. If the least significant bit is used as control, the elements of the matrix U are split so that they occupy corners of a square within the larger matrix.

Equipped with the knowledge on how to implement matrices of these shapes, let's see how this helps us solve our task.

3.5.2 Math

As a reminder, our goal is to implement an operation described by a block-diagonal matrix

$$U = \begin{pmatrix} A & 0 \\ 0 & B \end{pmatrix} = \begin{pmatrix} a_{00} & a_{01} & 0 & 0 \\ a_{10} & a_{11} & 0 & 0 \\ 0 & 0 & b_{00} & b_{01} \\ 0 & 0 & b_{10} & b_{11} \end{pmatrix}$$

3.5 Implementing a two-qubit block-diagonal unitary with 2×2 blocks

We can implement separately operations described by matrices $\begin{pmatrix} I & 0 \\ 0 & B \end{pmatrix}$ and $\begin{pmatrix} A & 0 \\ 0 & I \end{pmatrix}$ as controlled and controlled-on-zero variants of operations B and A, respectively, with the most significant bit as control. Conveniently, the product of these two matrices (in either order) is exactly the matrix we're looking for:

$$\begin{pmatrix} A & 0 \\ 0 & B \end{pmatrix} = \begin{pmatrix} A & 0 \\ 0 & I \end{pmatrix} \cdot \begin{pmatrix} I & 0 \\ 0 & B \end{pmatrix} = \begin{pmatrix} I & 0 \\ 0 & B \end{pmatrix} \cdot \begin{pmatrix} A & 0 \\ 0 & I \end{pmatrix}$$

So our solution for this problem consists of only two steps:

1. Apply the controlled variant of operation B with the most significant qubit as control.
2. Apply the controlled-on-zero variant of operation A with the most significant qubit as control.

The order of steps doesn't matter: because the gates have the same control qubit but different control patterns, they act independently of each other. (Mathematically, the matrices that describe these operations *commute*: their product is the same regardless of which matrix is on the left and which one is on the right.)

3.5.3 Qiskit

After all the work with the matrices we did so far, the code implementation is extremely straightforward and does not require learning any new language constructs or tools. Listing 3.9 shows the Qiskit code that implements a two-qubit block-diagonal unitary with the given real coefficients, using listing 3.1 as a building block.

Listing 3.9 Qiskit code for a two-qubit block-diagonal unitary

```
def apply_two_qubit_block_diagonal(a, b):
  circ = QuantumCircuit(2)
  circ.append(apply_one_qubit(b).control(1), [1, 0])
  circ.append(apply_one_qubit(a).control(1, ctrl_state=0), [1, 0])
  return circ
```

Here, the most significant qubit used as the control (given by the first element in the qubit indices array) is the last qubit in the circuit.

To test this code, we can modify listing 3.6 to handle two-qubit cases. The following listing shows the test code for the two-qubit block-diagonal unitary implementation in Qiskit.

Listing 3.10 Qiskit code to test a two-qubit block-diagonal unitary

```
from qiskit.quantum_info import Operator
from pytest import approx
from .two_qubit_block_diagonal import apply_two_qubit_block_diagonal
```

```
def run_test_apply_two_qubit_block_diagonal(a, b):
  op = Operator(apply_two_qubit_block_diagonal(a, b))
  matrix = op.data

  complete_coef = [
      a[0] + [0., 0.],          ◀── Reconstructs complete matrix
      a[1] + [0., 0.],              of the block-diagonal gate
      [0., 0.] + b[0],              from submatrices A and B
      [0., 0.] + b[1]]

  for actual, expected in zip(matrix, complete_coef):
    assert actual == approx(expected)

def test_two_qubit_block_diagonal():
  for _ in range(1, 20):
    a = random_one_qubit_unitary()    ◀── Reuses the helper function
    b = random_one_qubit_unitary()
    run_test_apply_two_qubit_block_diagonal(a, b)
```

Note that we had to construct the complete matrix U from the matrices A and B to compare it to the program simulation results. I'm also not including any tests for corner cases: this solution relies on operation `apply_one_qubit`, which has its own set of tests (including the corner cases for it), so the new tests only need to check that the new operation gets assembled from the building blocks correctly. The code is covered with unit tests, so the result of its execution is passing tests.

3.5.4 Q#

Like Qiskit, Q# code implementation is straightforward and relies on language constructs and tools we're already familiar with. The following listing shows the Q# code that implements a two-qubit block-diagonal unitary with the given real coefficients.

Listing 3.11 Q# code for a two-qubit block-diagonal unitary

```
operation ApplyTwoQubitBlockDiagonal(
  qs : Qubit[], a : Double[][], b : Double[][]
) : Unit is Adj + Ctl {
  Controlled ApplyOneQubit([qs[0]], ([qs[1]], b));
  ApplyControlledOnInt(0, ApplyOneQubit, [qs[0]], ([qs[1]], a));
}
```

Notice that in this code the most significant qubit, used as the control for the two gates we apply, is the first qubit of the register `qs`. This convention is the opposite of Qiskit, in which the most significant qubit is the last qubit of the register.

To test this code, we can modify listing 3.7 to handle two-qubit cases. This modification is very similar to the one we saw in listing 3.10, so I'm not including the code here. Again, the Q# solution code is covered with unit tests, so the results of its execution should be a set of passing tests.

3.6 Implementing a two-qubit CS unitary

The next building block we'll need to implement an arbitrary unitary is the CS unitary—an operation described by the CS matrix, the middle matrix in the cosine-sine decomposition. For the two-qubit case, the CS matrix looks like this:

$$CS = \begin{pmatrix} C & -S \\ S & C \end{pmatrix} = \begin{pmatrix} c_{00} & 0 & -s_{00} & 0 \\ 0 & c_{11} & 0 & -s_{11} \\ s_{00} & 0 & c_{00} & 0 \\ 0 & s_{11} & 0 & c_{11} \end{pmatrix}$$

Here, $C = \begin{pmatrix} c_{00} & 0 \\ 0 & c_{11} \end{pmatrix}$ and $S = \begin{pmatrix} s_{00} & 0 \\ 0 & s_{11} \end{pmatrix}$ are 2×2 diagonal matrices that have a property $C^2 + S^2 = I$ (in other words, $c_{00}^2 + s_{00}^2 = 1$ and $c_{11}^2 + s_{11}^2 = 1$).

3.6.1 Math

The matrices C and S themselves are not unitary. A diagonal unitary matrix with real coefficients can only have values 1 and -1 on the main diagonal, and matrices C and S can have other elements on the main diagonal. The decomposition from figure 3.3, for example, shows a matrix C consisting of zeroes. However, we can group the nonzero elements of the CS matrix into two 2×2 matrices that are unitary, as shown in figure 3.5.

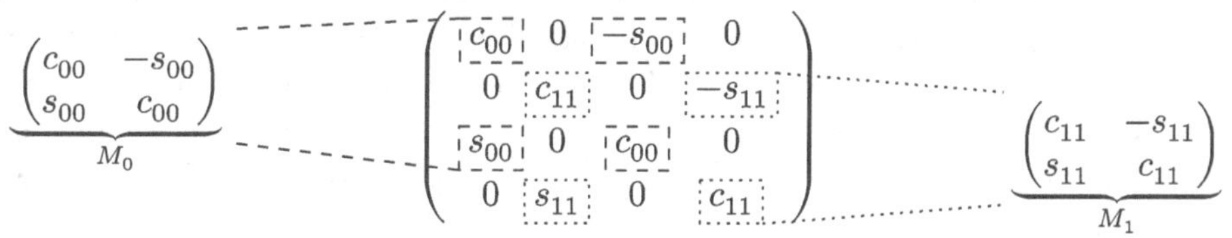

Figure 3.5 The nonzero elements of a two-qubit CS matrix can be separated and grouped together in two matrices M_0 and M_1. Each of these matrices is unitary.

The elements of these matrices are arranged in two patterns that look just like the matrices of controlled operations that we saw in the second column of the table 3.1—operations that use the least significant bit as control. Indeed, similarly to the block-diagonal matrices, we can represent the CS matrix as a product of two matrices that can each be implemented as a controlled single-qubit gate:

$$\begin{pmatrix} c_{00} & 0 & -s_{00} & 0 \\ 0 & c_{11} & 0 & -s_{11} \\ s_{00} & 0 & c_{00} & 0 \\ 0 & s_{11} & 0 & c_{11} \end{pmatrix} = \underbrace{\begin{pmatrix} c_{00} & 0 & -s_{00} & 0 \\ 0 & 1 & 0 & 0 \\ s_{00} & 0 & c_{00} & 0 \\ 0 & 0 & 0 & 1 \end{pmatrix}}_{\text{Controlled-on-zero } M_0} \cdot \underbrace{\begin{pmatrix} 1 & 0 & 0 & 0 \\ 0 & c_{11} & 0 & -s_{11} \\ 0 & 0 & 1 & 0 \\ 0 & s_{11} & 0 & c_{11} \end{pmatrix}}_{\text{Controlled } M_1}$$

So our solution to this problem consists of only two steps:

1. Apply the controlled variant of operation M_1 with the least significant qubit as control (the right matrix of the product).
2. Apply the controlled-on-zero variant of operation M_0 with the least significant qubit as control (the left matrix of the product).

As in the previous task, the order of steps doesn't matter: since the gates have the same control qubit but different control patterns, they act independently of each other.

3.6.2 Qiskit

The following listing shows the Qiskit code that implements a two-qubit CS unitary with the given real coefficients.

Listing 3.12 Qiskit code for a two-qubit CS unitary

```
def apply_two_qubit_cs_matrix(c0, s0, c1, s1):
  circ = QuantumCircuit(2)
  m0 = [[c0, -s0], [s0, c0]]
  m1 = [[c1, -s1], [s1, c1]]
  circ.append(apply_one_qubit(m1).control(1), [0, 1])
  circ.append(apply_one_qubit(m0).control(1, ctrl_state=0), [0, 1])
  return circ
```

The main difference compared to the way we handled two-qubit block-diagonal matrices is the parameters of the operation `apply_two_qubit_cs_matrix`: instead of passing the complete matrices C and S, we pass only their nonzero elements and then construct the unitary matrices M_0 and M_1 from them. This will be convenient later, when we work on implementing the CS matrix for an arbitrary number of qubits in section 3.9.

The test code for this task and the rest of this chapter is very similar to the code in listing 3.10, with only minor modifications to the logic of reconstructing the complete matrix of the operation we aim to implement, so I won't include the test code in the chapter. Rest assured, it's still included in the complete project code in the GitHub repository, and the code still should pass the tests!

3.6.3 Q#

The following listing shows the Q# code that implements a two-qubit CS unitary with the given real coefficients.

Listing 3.13 Q# code for a two-qubit CS unitary

```
operation ApplyTwoQubitCSMatrix(
  qs : Qubit[],
  (c0 : Double, s0 : Double),
  (c1 : Double, s1 : Double)
```

```
)  : Unit is Adj + Ctl {
    let m0 = [[c0, -s0], [s0, c0]];
    let m1 = [[c1, -s1], [s1, c1]];
    Controlled ApplyOneQubit([qs[1]], ([qs[0]], m1));
    ApplyControlledOnInt(0, ApplyOneQubit, [qs[1]], ([qs[0]], m0));
}
```

Notice that in this code the least significant qubit, used as the control for the two gates we apply, is the last qubit of the register qs.

The test code for this task and the rest of this chapter is very similar to the test code we used earlier in the chapter, in listings 3.7 and 3.10, with only minor modifications to the logic of reconstructing the complete matrix of the operation we aim to implement, so I won't include the test code in the chapter. It is included in the complete project code in the GitHub repository, and, as usual, the expected result of running the code is passing tests.

3.7 Implementing a two-qubit block-antidiagonal unitary with 2×2 blocks

Now that we have the building blocks for a cosine-sine decomposition of a two-qubit unitary, let's use them to implement an example of such unitary. Since this is still a stepping stone for our final project, we will not implement an arbitrary two-qubit unitary. Instead, we'll consider a unitary of a simpler shape for which the cosine-sine decomposition is simple enough to be derived by hand rather than using the Python library. The operation we'll implement in this section has the following matrix representation:

$$U = \begin{pmatrix} 0 & A \\ B & 0 \end{pmatrix} = \begin{pmatrix} 0 & 0 & a_{00} & a_{01} \\ 0 & 0 & a_{10} & a_{11} \\ b_{00} & b_{01} & 0 & 0 \\ b_{10} & b_{11} & 0 & 0 \end{pmatrix}$$

Here, U is a block-antidiagonal matrix, in which the 2×2 blocks off the main diagonal are two independent single-qubit unitaries (represented as 2×2 matrices, A and B), and the 2×2 blocks on the main diagonal consist of zeros.

3.7.1 Math

You can run the code for finding the cosine-sine decomposition from listing 3.8 for several block-antidiagonal matrices to find out that in this scenario, the CS matrix in the decomposition does not depend on the specific matrices A and B and has the following shape:

$$\begin{pmatrix} 0 & -I \\ I & 0 \end{pmatrix} = \begin{pmatrix} 0 & 0 & -1 & 0 \\ 0 & 0 & 0 & -1 \\ 1 & 0 & 0 & 0 \\ 0 & 1 & 0 & 0 \end{pmatrix}$$

Indeed, you can use matrix multiplication to verify the following equality:

$$\begin{pmatrix} 0 & A \\ B & 0 \end{pmatrix} = \begin{pmatrix} I & 0 \\ 0 & B \end{pmatrix} \begin{pmatrix} 0 & -I \\ I & 0 \end{pmatrix} \begin{pmatrix} I & 0 \\ 0 & -A \end{pmatrix}$$

This decomposition yields our solution for implementing an operation described with a block-antidiagonal matrix:

1. Apply the operation described with a block-diagonal matrix $\begin{pmatrix} I & 0 \\ 0 & -A \end{pmatrix}$.

2. Apply the CS unitary described with matrices $C = \begin{pmatrix} 0 & 0 \\ 0 & 0 \end{pmatrix}$ and $S = \begin{pmatrix} 1 & 0 \\ 0 & 1 \end{pmatrix}$.

3. Apply the operation described with a block-diagonal matrix $\begin{pmatrix} I & 0 \\ 0 & B \end{pmatrix}$.

3.7.2 Qiskit

The following listing shows the Qiskit code that implements a two-qubit block-antidiagonal unitary with the given real coefficients. Notice how the coefficients of the matrices C and S in the decomposition are hardcoded rather than computed on the fly.

Listing 3.14 Qiskit code for a two-qubit block-antidiagonal unitary

```
def apply_two_qubit_block_antidiagonal(a, b):
  circ = QuantumCircuit(2)
  id = [[1., 0.], [0., 1.]]
  minus_a = [[-a[0][0], -a[0][1]], [-a[1][0], -a[1][1]]]
  circ.append(apply_two_qubit_block_diagonal(id, minus_a), [0, 1])
  circ.append(apply_two_qubit_cs_matrix(0., 1., 0., 1.), [0, 1])
  circ.append(apply_two_qubit_block_diagonal(id, b), [0, 1])
  return circ
```

The results of this code are, again, passing tests, after they are modified appropriately.

3.7.3 Q#

The following listing shows the Q# code that implements a two-qubit block-antidiagonal unitary with the given real coefficients.

Listing 3.15 Q# code for a two-qubit block-antidiagonal unitary

```
operation ApplyTwoQubitBlockAntiDiagonal(
  qs : Qubit[], a : Double[][], b : Double[][]
) : Unit is Adj + Ctl {
  let id = [[1., 0.], [0., 1.]];
```

```
    let minusA = [[-a[0][0], -a[0][1]], [-a[1][0], -a[1][1]]];
    ApplyTwoQubitBlockDiagonal(qs, id, minusA);
    ApplyTwoQubitCSMatrix(qs, (0., 1.), (0., 1.));
    ApplyTwoQubitBlockDiagonal(qs, id, b);
}
```

The results of this code are, again, passing tests, after they are modified appropriately.

3.8 Implementing a two-block block-diagonal unitary of arbitrary size

We have successfully used a special case of a cosine-sine decomposition to implement a special case of a two-qubit unitary. Now we can finally approach the task we've been working toward: unitaries acting on an arbitrary number of qubits. The first building block required by the cosine-sine decomposition for matrices of arbitrary size is a block-diagonal unitary acting on n qubits consisting of two blocks of equal size:

$$U = \begin{pmatrix} A & 0 \\ 0 & B \end{pmatrix}$$

Here U is a block-diagonal matrix of size $2^n \times 2^n$, in which the $2^{n-1} \times 2^{n-1}$ blocks on the main diagonal are two independent unitary matrices A and B, and the remaining matrix elements are all zeros.

> **Multiplexers: Quantum if-then-else conditionals**
>
> This block-diagonal matrix is a special case of a *multiplexer*—a generalization of if-then-else conditionals for the quantum case. In general case, a multiplexer acting on n qubits is described with a block-diagonal matrix of size 2^n with 2^s blocks of size 2^{n-s} each. The s most significant qubits out of n qubits act as the condition of the multiplexer, and the blocks of the multiplexer describe the effects that should be applied to the $n-s$ least significant qubits for each value of the condition qubits.
>
> In our case we only need the variant with $s=1$, so we'll focus on implementing this variant alone. Another simple variant of a multiplexer is a diagonal matrix, for which the number of qubits that act as the condition is $s=n$. Indeed, consider a single-qubit diagonal matrix
>
> $$U = \begin{pmatrix} u_{00} & 0 \\ 0 & u_{11} \end{pmatrix}$$
>
> The result of applying a unitary described by this matrix to a quantum state $\alpha \ket{0} + \beta \ket{1}$ is $u_{00}\alpha \ket{0} + u_{11}\beta \ket{1}$, which can be described as "apply a phase u_{00} if the basis state is $\ket{0}$, and then apply a phase u_{11} if the basis state is $\ket{1}$." This behavior is exactly that of a multiplexer with the only qubit acting as the condition, and the effects that should be applied are 1×1 matrices—complex numbers applied as phases.
>
> Multiplexers defined for any value of s can come up in quantum algorithms, so they are a convenient tool to have in your toolbox.

In this task, we'll implement an operation that takes two $2^{n-1} \times 2^{n-1}$ matrices with real coefficients and implements the previously described $2^n \times 2^n$ block-diagonal unitary.

3.8.1 Math

Let's start with the same step we did when analyzing 4×4 block-diagonal matrices: spell out the binary representation of row and column indices of the matrix elements. Figure 3.4 shows the row and column indices for 4×4 matrices; figure 3.6 does the same for 8×8 matrices, showing the indices written as three-bit binary strings in little-endian (the string starts with the least significant bit and ends with the most significant one).

$$\begin{array}{c|cccccccc}
 & \begin{matrix}0=\\000\end{matrix} & \begin{matrix}1=\\100\end{matrix} & \begin{matrix}2=\\010\end{matrix} & \begin{matrix}3=\\110\end{matrix} & \begin{matrix}4=\\001\end{matrix} & \begin{matrix}5=\\101\end{matrix} & \begin{matrix}6=\\011\end{matrix} & \begin{matrix}7=\\111\end{matrix} \\
\hline
0=000 & a_{00} & a_{01} & a_{02} & a_{03} & 0 & 0 & 0 & 0 \\
1=100 & a_{10} & a_{11} & a_{12} & a_{13} & 0 & 0 & 0 & 0 \\
2=010 & a_{20} & a_{21} & a_{22} & a_{23} & 0 & 0 & 0 & 0 \\
3=110 & a_{30} & a_{31} & a_{32} & a_{33} & 0 & 0 & 0 & 0 \\
4=001 & 0 & 0 & 0 & 0 & b_{00} & b_{01} & b_{02} & b_{03} \\
5=101 & 0 & 0 & 0 & 0 & b_{10} & b_{11} & b_{12} & b_{13} \\
6=011 & 0 & 0 & 0 & 0 & b_{20} & b_{21} & b_{22} & b_{23} \\
7=111 & 0 & 0 & 0 & 0 & b_{30} & b_{31} & b_{32} & b_{33} \\
\end{array}$$

Figure 3.6 The row and column indices of an 8×8 block-diagonal matrix. The indices are written in binary using little-endian notation: the least significant bit is written first. The top-left and bottom-right blocks group the elements for which the most significant (the last) bit of the row index equals that of the column index, which is 0 for the top-left block and 1 for the bottom-right block.

You can see that in both figures the elements of the top-left and bottom-right blocks of the matrix that correspond to the smaller matrices A and B have the same most significant bit of their row and column indices. This bit equals 0 for the top-left block (matrix A) and 1 for the bottom-right block (matrix B). Larger matrices follow the same pattern.

Thinking back to section 3.5, the patterns of these blocks of elements look similar to the patterns we've seen in the first column of table 3.1 for controlled gates that use the most significant bit as control. Indeed, table 3.2 shows the matrices of controlled variants of $n-1$-qubit gates that use one additional qubit as control.

Using these two matrices as building blocks, we can construct the block-diagonal matrix we're looking for as their product:

$$\begin{pmatrix} A & 0 \\ 0 & B \end{pmatrix} = \begin{pmatrix} A & 0 \\ 0 & I \end{pmatrix} \cdot \begin{pmatrix} I & 0 \\ 0 & B \end{pmatrix}$$

Table 3.2 The variants of a controlled multiqubit gate with one most significant control qubit

Control pattern	Matrix representation	Effect of the n-qubit
Controlled on one	$\begin{pmatrix} I & 0 \\ 0 & B \end{pmatrix}$	If the most significant bit is 1, apply the unitary B to the $n-1$ least significant qubits; otherwise, do nothing.
Controlled on zero	$\begin{pmatrix} A & 0 \\ 0 & I \end{pmatrix}$	If the most significant bit is 0, apply the unitary A to the $n-1$ least significant qubits; otherwise, do nothing.

You'll notice that this formula is exactly the same one we saw in section 3.5 for the two-qubit block-diagonal unitaries. The only difference is the sizes of the matrices involved: in section 3.5, matrices A, B, and I are 2×2 matrices, and this time, they are matrices of size $2^{n-1} \times 2^{n-1}$.

Similarly to the solution in section 3.5, our implementation of the general block-diagonal matrix consists of only two steps:

1. Apply the controlled variant of operation B with the most significant qubit as control and the rest of qubits as targets.
2. Apply the controlled-on-zero variant of operation A with the most significant qubit as control and the rest of qubits as targets.

We have now completed the purely mathematical portion of the solution. However, before we get to coding it, we need to address one more question: How do we test this solution? So far in this chapter, we always expressed the solution to each task using the operations that solved the previous tasks and their controlled versions. But this time, to implement a general case of a block-diagonal unitary, we need to implement unitaries described by arbitrary matrices A and B, and we will not learn how to do that until section 3.10.2.

Ultimately, the algorithm for implementing arbitrary unitaries will be recursive, relying on applying itself for smaller problem instances to solve a larger instance. To implement an arbitrary n-qubit unitary, the algorithm will use the cosine-sine decomposition of the corresponding $2^n \times 2^n$ matrix to represent it as a sequence of matrices of the same size but of simpler structure, and those will be implemented using controlled variants of arbitrary matrices of size $2^{n-1} \times 2^{n-1}$. In the final version of this chapter's project, we'll use that recursive algorithm to implement arbitrary unitaries.

For now, though, we'll use a temporary placeholder for the building block "implement an arbitrary unitary of smaller size." We'll check whether the arbitrary unitary fits one of the special cases that we already know how to implement: single-qubit unitaries or two-qubit unitaries that have a block-diagonal or block-antidiagonal shape. If it does, we'll use the corresponding implementation, and if it doesn't, the building block will throw an exception. This placeholder, while not being particularly pretty, will let us test the logic of our implementation of block-diagonal matrices, as long as we stick to matrices with blocks of these special shapes in our tests.

3.8.2 Qiskit

The following listing shows the Qiskit code that implements an arbitrary two-block block-diagonal unitary.

Listing 3.16 Qiskit code for a two-block block-diagonal unitary

```
def apply_arbitrary_unitary(n, u):           ◄── Implements some special cases
  if n == 1:
    return apply_one_qubit(u)                ◄── We can implement single-qubit matrices, ...
  if n == 2:
    if all(isclose(v, 0) for v in
           u[0][2:4] + u[1][2:4] +
           u[2][0:2] + u[3][0:2]):
      tl = [u[0][0:2], u[1][0:2]]
      br = [u[2][2:4], u[3][2:4]]
      return apply_two_qubit_block_diagonal(tl, br).decompose().to_gate()

    if all(isclose(v, 0) for v in
           u[0][0:2] + u[1][0:2] +
           u[2][2:4] + u[3][2:4]):
      tr = [u[0][2:4], u[1][2:4]]
      bl = [u[2][0:2], u[3][0:2]]

      return apply_two_qubit_block_antidiagonal(tr, bl).decompose().to_gate()
    raise NotImplementedError("The case of " +
      "arbitrary 2-qubit unitaries is not implemented yet")
  raise NotImplementedError(
    "The case of 3+-qubit unitaries is not implemented yet")

def apply_two_block_diagonal(n, a, b):
  circ = QuantumCircuit(n)
  circ.append(apply_arbitrary_unitary(n - 1, b).control(1),    ◄── Uses the last, most significant bit as the control
              [n - 1] + list(range(n - 1)))
  circ.append(apply_arbitrary_unitary(n - 1, a).control(1, ctrl_state=0),
              [n - 1] + list(range(n - 1)))
  return circ
```

- ... two-qubit block-diagonal matrices (if elements in the top-right block and bottom-left block are all zeroes, separate the top-left and bottom-right blocks of the matrix), ...
- ...and block-antidiagonal matrices (if elements in the top-left block and bottom-right block are all zeroes, separate the top-right and bottom-left blocks of the matrix).

The largest block of code is the operation `apply_arbitrary_unitary`. However, at this point, instead of implementing the universal solution for an arbitrary unitary, it checks whether the input matrix fits one of the special cases:

- Single-qubit unitaries can be implemented using `apply_one_qubit`.
- We can implement two special cases of two-qubit unitaries, depending on the shape of the matrix. If all elements in the top-right and bottom-left blocks of the matrix are zeros, it is block-diagonal, implemented using `apply_two_qubit_block_diagonal`. If all elements in the top-left and bottom-right blocks of the matrix are zeros, it is block-antidiagonal, implemented using `apply_two_qubit_block_antidiagonal`.

Using this operation, `apply_two_block_diagonal` implements the general case of a block-diagonal unitary, assuming the ability to implement an arbitrary unitary (but using the placeholder implementation for now).

Note that the tests for apply_two_block_diagonal should be implemented based on the list of special cases handled by the code: if we try to run it for matrices of four qubits or for three-qubits matrices with arbitrary blocks, the implementation will fail. However, if the tests only include the cases handled by the code, they should pass as a result of executing this code.

3.8.3 Q#

The following listing shows the Q# code that implements an arbitrary two-block block-diagonal unitary.

Listing 3.17 Q# code for a two-block block-diagonal unitary

```
operation ApplyArbitraryUnitary(
  qs : Qubit[], u : Double[][]
) : Unit is Adj + Ctl {          ←— Implements some special cases
  let n = Length(qs);
  if n == 1 {
    ApplyOneQubit(qs, u);       ←— We can implement single-qubit matrices, ...
  } elif n == 2 {
    let isZeroD = x -> AbsD(x) < 1e-9;
    if All(isZeroD,
      u[0][2..3] + u[1][2..3] +
      u[2][0..1] + u[3][0..1]) {
      let tl = [u[0][0..1], u[1][0..1]];
      let br = [u[2][2..3], u[3][2..3]];
      ApplyTwoQubitBlockDiagonal(qs, tl, br);
    } elif All(isZeroD,
      u[0][0..1] + u[1][0..1] +
      u[2][2..3] + u[3][2..3]) {
      let tr = [u[0][2..3], u[1][2..3]];
      let bl = [u[2][0..1], u[3][0..1]];
      ApplyTwoQubitBlockAntiDiagonal(qs, tr, bl);
    } else {
      fail "The case of arbitrary 2-qubit unitaries" +
        " is not implemented yet";
    }
  } else {
    fail "The case of 3+-qubit unitaries is not implemented yet";
  }
}

operation ApplyTwoBlockDiagonal(
  qs : Qubit[], a : Double[][], b : Double[][]
) : Unit is Adj + Ctl {
  let n = Length(qs);
  Controlled ApplyArbitraryUnitary(   ←— Uses the first, most significant bit as the control
    [qs[0]], (qs[1...], b));
  ApplyControlledOnInt(0, ApplyArbitraryUnitary,
    [qs[0]], (qs[1...], a));
}
```

... two-qubit block-diagonal matrices (If elements in top-right block and bottom-left block are all zeroes, separate the top-left and bottom-right blocks of the matrix), ...

...and block-antidiagonal matrices (If elements in the top-left block and bottom-right block are all zeroes, separate the top-right and bottom-left blocks of the matrix).

As in Qiskit, this listing includes two operations. `ApplyArbitraryUnitary` is a placeholder for an arbitrary unitary preparation that for now implements several special cases we've seen before. `ApplyTwoBlockDiagonal` uses this placeholder to demonstrate the general logic of implementing a block-diagonal unitary. The tests should pass after they are modified to include the cases handled by the code.

3.9 Implementing a CS unitary of arbitrary size

The second building block required by the cosine-sine decomposition for matrices of arbitrary size is the CS matrix acting on n qubits—the middle matrix in the cosine-sine decomposition. It is a $2^n \times 2^n$ matrix of the following shape:

$$CS = \begin{pmatrix} C & -S \\ S & C \end{pmatrix}$$

Here C and S are $2^{n-1} \times 2^{n-1}$ diagonal matrices:

$$C = \begin{pmatrix} c_{00} & 0 & \cdots & 0 \\ 0 & c_{11} & \cdots & 0 \\ \vdots & \vdots & \ddots & \vdots \\ 0 & 0 & \cdots & c_{2^{n-1}-1, 2^{n-1}-1} \end{pmatrix} \quad S = \begin{pmatrix} s_{00} & 0 & \cdots & 0 \\ 0 & s_{11} & \cdots & 0 \\ \vdots & \vdots & \ddots & \vdots \\ 0 & 0 & \cdots & s_{2^{n-1}-1, 2^{n-1}-1} \end{pmatrix}$$

The matrices C and S, squared, add up to the identity matrix: $C^2 + S^2 = I$. In other words, these matrices are completely described by their diagonal elements $c_{00}, c_{11}, \ldots, c_{2^{n-1}-1, 2^{n-1}-1}$ and $s_{00}, s_{11}, \ldots, s_{2^{n-1}-1, 2^{n-1}-1}$, and for each index k from 0 to $2^{n-1}-1$, inclusive, the sum of squares of matching elements is 1: $c_{k,k}^2 + s_{k,k}^2 = 1$.

3.9.1 Math

Let's start our analysis with a slightly simpler scenario: an almost-diagonal matrix that matches the identity matrix I in all rows and columns except the intersection of rows and columns with indices k and $2^{n-1}+k$ (here, $k < 2^{n-1}$; that is, row k is in the top half of the matrix). The intersection of these rows and columns matches our CS matrix. Here, for example, is what this matrix looks like for $n = 3$ (an 8×8 matrix) and $k = 2$:

$$\begin{array}{c} \\ \\ \begin{array}{r} 0 = 000 \\ 1 = 100 \\ 2 = 010 \\ 3 = 110 \\ 4 = 001 \\ 5 = 101 \\ 6 = 011 \\ 7 = 111 \end{array} \end{array} \begin{array}{c} \begin{array}{cccccccc} 0= & 1= & 2= & 3= & 4= & 5= & 6= & 7= \\ 000 & 100 & 010 & 110 & 001 & 101 & 011 & 111 \end{array} \\ \begin{pmatrix} 1 & 0 & 0 & 0 & 0 & 0 & 0 & 0 \\ 0 & 1 & 0 & 0 & 0 & 0 & 0 & 0 \\ 0 & 0 & c_{22} & 0 & 0 & 0 & -s_{22} & 0 \\ 0 & 0 & 0 & 1 & 0 & 0 & 0 & 0 \\ 0 & 0 & 0 & 0 & 1 & 0 & 0 & 0 \\ 0 & 0 & 0 & 0 & 0 & 1 & 0 & 0 \\ 0 & 0 & s_{22} & 0 & 0 & 0 & c_{22} & 0 \\ 0 & 0 & 0 & 0 & 0 & 0 & 0 & 1 \end{pmatrix} \end{array}$$

3.9 Implementing a CS unitary of arbitrary size

Using the binary representations of row and column indices of a $2^n \times 2^n$ matrix from figure 3.6, we can see that the binary notation of index k as an n-bit string has 0 as its most significant bit, since k is less than 2^{n-1}, and the binary notation of index $2^{n-1} + k$ is the same but has 1 as the most significant bit. Thinking back to section 3.6, the pattern of this matrix resembles the patterns we've seen in the second column of the table 3.1 for controlled gates that use the least significant bit as control. Indeed, you can verify that this matrix corresponds to a controlled variant of a single-qubit gate with a matrix

$$M_k = \begin{pmatrix} c_{k,k} & -s_{k,k} \\ s_{k,k} & c_{k,k} \end{pmatrix}$$

which uses $n - 1$ additional bits as controls. The least significant bits of the n are used as controls, and the control pattern is exactly the binary representation of the index k in little-endian notation with $n - 1$ bits.

> **Verifying the matrix of controlled single-qubit gate**
>
> How can you verify that such controlled variant of a single-qubit gate is described with this matrix? To start, you can check that, for the two-qubit case (4×4 matrices), the controlled variants of the single-qubit rotation from the second column of the table 3.1 can be represented this way as well, using $k = 0$ and $k = 1$ for controlled-on-zero and controlled gates, respectively. In this case, the control pattern is one bit long.
>
> To simplify the math for the general case, you can apply this matrix to each of the basis states in turn. For all indices other than k and $2^{n-1} + k$ the columns of the matrix are the same as the corresponding columns of the identity matrix, so all these basis states remain unchanged. The basis states $|k\rangle$ and $|2^{n-1} + k\rangle$ are transformed into a superposition of two basis states each, and it's easy to see that the $n - 1$ least significant bits of these basis states all remain unchanged (and equal to the binary representation of k), and the most significant bit changes following the application of a rotation gate M to it. This is exactly the effect of the described controlled gate!

With this in mind, we can implement the full CS matrix as a product of 2^{n-1} matrices, each of them almost diagonal, differing from the identity in just two columns and two rows. (This is the same idea we used in section 3.6, but with 2^{n-1} matrices in the product instead of just two.) The complete solution consists of the following steps:

1. Iterate over indices k from 0 to $2^{n-1} - 1$, inclusive.
2. For each value of k, apply a controlled variant of the rotation gate M_k with $n - 1$ least significant bits as controls and the most significant bit as the target, using the binary notation of k in little-endian as the control pattern.

Since all control patterns are distinct, we're guaranteed that each controlled gate affects only two basis states, and no two controlled gates interfere with each other.

3.9.2 Qiskit

The following listing shows the Qiskit code that implements an arbitrary CS unitary with the given real coefficients.

Listing 3.18 Qiskit code to implement an arbitrary CS unitary

```
def apply_arbitrary_cs_matrix(n, cs):        ⟵ Uses an array of tuples
  circ = QuantumCircuit(n)                     to describe the CS matrix
  for (k, (c, s)) in enumerate(cs):
    m = [[c, -s], [s, c]]
    circ.append(apply_one_qubit(m).control(n - 1, ctrl_state=k), range(n))
  return circ
```

Conveniently, `control` method accepts both bit strings and integers as the `ctrl_state` argument, and interprets integers as their binary notations in little-endian, so we don't need to do the conversion manually in our code. With this code, the newly added tests that cover larger CS matrices should pass.

3.9.3 Q#

The following listing shows the Q# code that implements an arbitrary CS unitary with the given real coefficients.

Listing 3.19 Q# code to implement an arbitrary CS unitary

```
import Std.Arrays.*;

operation ApplyArbitraryCSMatrix(
  qs : Qubit[],
  cs : (Double, Double)[]    ⟵ Uses an array of tuples to describe the CS matrix
) : Unit is Adj + Ctl {
  for (k, (c, s)) in Enumerated(cs) {
    let m = [[c, -s], [s, c]];
    ApplyControlledOnInt(k, ApplyOneQubit,
      Reversed(qs[1...]), ([qs[0]], m));
  }
}
```

In this code, the least significant qubits, used as the controls for the gates we apply, are the last qubits of the register `qs`. Notice that we reverse their order before using them as controls with the control pattern k. `ApplyControlledOnInt` uses little-endian to convert its integer argument into a control pattern bit string, but our convention for Q# is to store the most significant bit first, which corresponds to big-endian notation. To reconcile these notations, we need to reverse either the bit pattern we use or the order of qubits in the array, and reversing the qubits turns out to be easier. (This reverse doesn't apply any gates; it just produces an array of qubit variables in a reverse order compared to the input array.) With this code, the newly added tests that cover larger CS matrices should pass.

3.10 Implementing an arbitrary unitary of arbitrary size

Now, we can use our code that implements block-diagonal unitaries and CS unitaries for an arbitrary number of qubits as building blocks for our final project: implementing an arbitrary unitary on an arbitrary number of qubits.

3.10.1 Math

As a reminder, the cosine-sine decomposition of a unitary matrix is its representation as a product of several matrices of special shapes:

$$U = \begin{pmatrix} A_l & 0 \\ 0 & B_l \end{pmatrix} \begin{pmatrix} C & -S \\ S & C \end{pmatrix} \begin{pmatrix} A_r & 0 \\ 0 & B_r \end{pmatrix}$$

This decomposition gives us the solution for implementing an operation described with an arbitrary unitary matrix:

1. Obtain the cosine-sine decomposition of the given matrix.
2. Apply the operation described with a block-diagonal matrix $\begin{pmatrix} A_r & 0 \\ 0 & B_r \end{pmatrix}$.
3. Apply the CS unitary described with matrices C and S.
4. Apply the operation described with a block-diagonal matrix $\begin{pmatrix} A_l & 0 \\ 0 & B_l \end{pmatrix}$.

This is a recursive solution, since implementing operations described as block-diagonal matrices relies on using controlled variants of unitaries of smaller sizes. As a result, we'll also need to update our implementation of the operations described with block-diagonal matrices to use our new implementation of arbitrary unitaries instead of the placeholder we used in section 3.8.

> **Calling Python libraries from quantum code**
>
> Getting the cosine-sine decomposition of the given matrix is a big part of the final solution for this project. This is a purely classical linear algebra exercise, so earlier in the chapter I opted for doing it using a SciPy library function. We can use the same function in the Qiskit code, since Qiskit is implemented in Python and allows easy access to other Python libraries.
>
> Q#, however, does not offer an interface for API calls to arbitrary libraries written in other programming languages and does not offer its own library implementation of the cosine-sine decomposition. As I mentioned in section 3.4, implementing this decomposition by hand is out of scope for this book, so in this chapter, we won't implement the final project in Q#.
>
> In practice, this kind of functionality—breaking the arbitrary unitaries down into sequences of simpler gates—is often implemented as part of the compiler stack or a specialized library in the quantum programming language rather than as application code, so that it can take advantage of the full power of classical software libraries.

3.10.2 Qiskit

The following listing shows the Qiskit code that implements an arbitrary unitary with the given real coefficients.

Listing 3.20 Qiskit code to implement an arbitrary unitary

```
from scipy.linalg import cossin

def apply_arbitrary_unitary(n, u):
  if n == 1:
    return apply_one_qubit(u)

  circ = QuantumCircuit(n)
  left, cs, right = cossin(u, p=len(u) / 2, q=len(u) / 2)

  ar, br = extract_blocks(right)
  circ.append(apply_two_block_diagonal(n, ar, br), range(n))

  cs_pairs = []
  for i in range(len(cs) // 2):
    cs_pairs += [(cs[i][i], cs[i + len(cs) // 2][i])]
  circ.append(apply_arbitrary_cs_matrix(n, cs_pairs), range(n))

  al, bl = extract_blocks(left)
  circ.append(apply_two_block_diagonal(n, al, bl), range(n))
  return circ.decompose().to_gate()

def extract_blocks(matrix):      ◁─── Helper function to extract two main
  block_len = len(matrix) // 2        blocks from a block-diagonal matrix
  a = [row[0 : block_len] for row in matrix[0 : block_len]]
  b = [row[block_len : ] for row in matrix[block_len : ]]
  return a, b
```

The updated variant of `apply_arbitrary_unitary` in this listing now implements an arbitrary unitary instead of just a few special cases. Note that `apply_two_block_diagonal` uses the code from listing 3.16, but now it can handle the general case of the block-diagonal unitary. The base case of recursion is the operation `apply_one_qubit` that implements the single-qubit case. In the multiqubit case, the first step is getting the cosine-sine decomposition, followed by applying the operations implementing each matrix of the decomposition: the right block-diagonal matrix, the CS matrix, and the left block-diagonal matrix.

At this point, we can update our tests to include arbitrary unitaries of any size, and they should pass. (I limited my tests to unitaries acting on at most four qubits in the interest of keeping the tests fast, but if you're willing to wait longer, you can include larger matrices.)

3.11 Further reading

Here is a short list of references that are good starting points if you want to learn more about unitary matrix decomposition:

- Sutton, B. D. (2007). Computing the complete CS decomposition. https://arxiv.org/abs/0707.1838
- Shende, V. V., Bullock, S. S., & Markov, I. L. (2004). Synthesis of quantum logic circuits. https://arxiv.org/abs/quant-ph/0406176
- Mottonen, M., & Vartiainen, J. J. (2005). Decompositions of general quantum gates. https://arxiv.org/abs/quant-ph/0504100

3.12 Going beyond

Do you want to spend some more time exploring variations of this project before moving on to the next topic? Here are some additional ideas for simpler examples, similar problems, and ways to extend this project:

- Implement a general case of a multiplexer for an arbitrary number of control qubits. How would you change the input data and the logic of its implementation compared to the multiplexer with one control qubit from section 3.8?
- In this chapter, we focused on implementing the general case of unitary matrices and a couple of matrices of special shapes that were the necessary building blocks for the general case. However, different algorithms rely on different unitaries, some of which might have different, more efficient implementations. Find some other matrices of special shapes and try to implement them.
- In this chapter, we considered only unitaries with real coefficients. Same as for the state preparation problem, some algorithms can be expressed using only this kind of operations, but in general, quantum algorithms rely on unitaries with complex coefficients. Extend this project to handle arbitrary unitaries with complex coefficients. You can start by exploring the standard algorithms for small cases: the Pauli decomposition for single-qubit unitaries and the Krauss-Cirac decomposition for the two-qubit case. Then, you can look into the cosine-sine decomposition for complex-valued matrices and implement the building blocks it uses, same as we did for real-valued matrices in this chapter.
- If you're curious about low-level algorithms of implementing unitaries using a smaller set of primitive gates than the one we used here, unitary gate synthesis is a great topic to dig into. In this scenario, the unitaries are implemented approximately, allowing a small discrepancy between the given matrix and the matrix implemented by the sequence of gates, and the implementations use a very limited set of gates (for example, CNOT, H, and T gates).

We will revisit a different aspect of unitary implementation problem later, when we cover unitary transformations that correspond to classical computations in chapter 6.

Summary

- Quantum operations that make up an algorithm can be expressed in different ways. On the conceptual level, the operations are described in terms of the problem solved by the algorithm and its input parameters.
- When writing the code, these operations are implemented in a quantum programming language as sequences of primitive gates, language constructs, and library operations available in that language.
- On the lowest level, the gates used in the high-level program are represented as sequences of low-level instructions native to the hardware device and/or the error correction scheme used with the hardware.
- The goal of the unitary implementation task is to convert the matrix description of a unitary operation into a sequence of quantum gates that implements the unitary described by this matrix.
- Unitary operations can be implemented recursively, by decomposing their matrices as products of matrices of special shapes and implementing each of these matrices using controlled variants of unitary operations acting on fewer qubits.
- Many quantum algorithms are hybrid, combining classical and quantum computation; getting the cosine-sine decomposition as a step of unitary implementation is one example. It is important for a quantum programming language to express hybrid computations efficiently.
- We can use quantum simulators and the way they allow us to access quantum states during the program execution to get the matrices implemented by quantum operations and test that a quantum operation implements the right matrix.

Part 2
Learning information about a quantum system

The second part of the book focuses on quantum measurements and the ways to use them to read out information from a quantum system, whether it is information about a quantum state or a quantum operation.

Chapter 4 focuses on using measurements to get the necessary information about quantum states in a variety of settings. Chapter 5 builds on top of the previous chapter, offering several exercises on getting information about unitary transformations. A big part of chapter 5 is dedicated to the phase estimation problem—finding an eigenvalue associated with the given eigenvector of the given unitary. A lot of quantum computing algorithms include phase estimation as a subtask, and the variety of the approaches they take to solving this problem is a great example of the different types of quantum algorithms.

Analyzing quantum states

This chapter covers

- Using quantum measurements to extract information about quantum states
- Implementing quantum measurements using Q# and Qiskit
- Analyzing quantum measurement outcomes
- Writing tests to validate information extracted using measurements

As we discussed in chapter 2, a typical quantum algorithm follows a standard sequence of steps (see figure 4.1): prepare the initial state of the quantum system, modify it as prescribed by the algorithm, and then extract the answer using measurements. In chapter 2, we learned to implement the first step, preparing the quantum system in the given state, and in chapter 3, we covered the second step, implementing the unitary transformations to modify the quantum state as required by the algorithm.

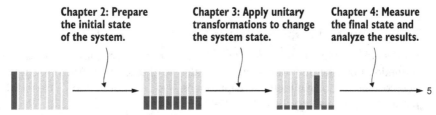

Figure 4.1 Any quantum algorithm can be broken down into several steps: prepare the initial state, evolve it following the algorithm, and measure the end state to get the result. In this chapter, we'll learn to work with the final step, measuring the state of the system to extract information about it.

In this chapter, we'll focus on the final step of a quantum algorithm: extracting the information about the state of the system. We will learn to use quantum measurements—the only way to get information out of a quantum system.

One of the most prominent ways in which quantum computing differs from classical is how you read out information about the system. In the classical world,

- Observing the system to get information about it is a deterministic process: it always gives the same readout for the same state of the system.
- You can get the complete information about the state of the system. If the system has n bits, it is described with n bits of information, and you can get all n bits out of it when observing it.
- Observing the system doesn't change the state of the system: after reading out the information, you can resume your computation as if the observation didn't happen.

In the quantum world, though, getting information about the system obeys different rules:

- System observation is a probabilistic process. Observing the system in a superposition state produces a random outcome, one of the set of possible outcomes with probabilities defined by the state of the system.
- You cannot get the complete information about the state of the quantum system by observing it. If the system has n qubits, it is described with 2^n complex numbers, but you still can get only n bits of information when observing it.
- Finally, observing the system generally changes the state of the system. You cannot take a peek at the system during your computation and then continue it as if nothing happened; you have to restart your computation from scratch.

The rules of quantum measurement limit the power of quantum algorithms quite a lot. Extracting information about the problem's solution in the end of the algorithm is like trying to drink an ocean through a straw: you have a huge amount of information in the system, but you can only read out a tiny fraction of it. You have to be mindful of this limitation when constructing a quantum algorithm: you need to end up in a state that contains the information necessary to solve your problem, and you need to make sure that this information can be extracted from the system using measurements.

> **Using quantum measurements to perform computations**
>
> On the bright side, quantum measurements can be used not only to read the information from the quantum system but also to change its state. This opens new possibilities for doing quantum computations—you cannot perform a classical computation by just reading the data in the right way!
>
> To give you one example, multiqubit measurements, similar to those we'll discuss in section 4.6, enable *error correction*—a method of protecting quantum information from errors caused by noise by encoding it with redundancy and then performing special kinds of measurements to extract the information about the errors that occurred without damaging the useful information.

> Unfortunately, error correction and using measurements to purposefully change the state of a quantum system are out of scope for this book, but if you're curious, I encourage you to dig deeper into these topics.

In this chapter, I'll take a different approach to selecting our practice problems than in the previous two chapters. Using measurements to extract information from a system is a pretty straightforward task on its own; it is more interesting to see what kinds of problems can be solved using measurements as a tool. So instead of choosing one large project and building up to it in smaller steps, I'll offer you several smaller projects that highlight different aspects of using measurements to extract information about quantum states. Some of these projects will obviously build up on the previous ones, but some will be a step sideways to consider a different kind of problem. I will also discuss specific examples of problems rather than their most generic form like I did in the previous chapters, to simplify the math and the code needed for the solutions while illustrating the core principles used to solve them.

Let's dive right into our first problem: how to use quantum measurements to get information from a quantum system and, ultimately, retrieve the result produced by our quantum algorithm.

4.1 Reading out information from a quantum system

We'll start with the simplest possible problem in extracting information about a quantum system. Given a quantum system, represented as an array of qubits, and knowing that it is in some basis state, how can you find that basis state?

> **NOTE** As usual, this task is an essential building block for all the later ones in this chapter. It also covers the more general version of the task of extracting information out of the system, in which the system is in a superposition of basis states and the measurement extracts information about one of these basis states. In this scenario, the steps you take to read out the information and the code you write to implement them are exactly the same as in the simpler version; the only difference is the outcomes you can get and how you interpret them.

4.1.1 Math

There are many ways to represent quantum measurements depending on what exactly you need to describe and how you will use it—from the simple verbal description of the outcomes and their probabilities to the formal Dirac notation of the measurement as a set of projection operators. (If you're not familiar with the projection operators formalism, don't worry; we won't use it in this book.) I'll use the simplest description that will do the job: listing the possible measurement outcomes and the probabilities associated with them.

The smallest case to consider is measuring a single-qubit system in the superposition state $\alpha |0\rangle + \beta |1\rangle$ with real amplitudes α and β. (States with complex amplitudes behave similarly, so I'll stick with real amplitudes for simplicity.) In this case, the measurement can yield one of the two results: 0, with probability α^2, and 1, with probability β^2.

> **NOTE** Unless otherwise specified, "measurement" means the measurement in the computational basis (the $\{|0\rangle, |1\rangle\}$ basis) that maps the basis state $|0\rangle$ to measurement outcome 0 and the basis state $|1\rangle$—to 1. This convention is commonly used in quantum computing, and this kind of measurement is most frequently used when describing high-level algorithms. We'll talk more about measurements in other bases in section 4.3.

Since in our problem the qubit we are given is guaranteed to be in a basis state, measuring it gives us the result that corresponds to that basis state with probability 1. The same logic can be applied to measuring a multiqubit system. Figure 4.2 shows the possible outcomes of measuring a two-qubit system and their relevance to our task.

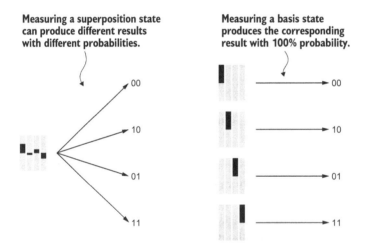

Figure 4.2 Measuring two qubits in a superposition of all basis states can give any of the results 00, 01, 10, and 11, with probabilities equal to squares of the amplitudes of the corresponding basis states in the superposition state. When we measure a system that is in a specific basis state, we can only get the result that corresponds to that state, with 100% probability.

Let's say our two qubits are in a state $a_0 |00\rangle + a_1 |10\rangle + a_2 |01\rangle + a_3 |11\rangle$. When we measure them, the result we get is probabilistic: we get output 00 with probability a_0^2, 10 with probability a_1^2, and so on. The probability of getting each result equals the square of the amplitude of the corresponding basis state. If the qubits are in a basis state, for example, $|01\rangle$, the amplitude of that state is 1, and the probability of getting the corresponding measurement result is also 1. The amplitudes of the other basis states are 0, so the probabilities of getting them as a measurement result are 0.

For the more general case of n qubits, if the system starts in a superposition state $\sum_{k=0}^{2^n-1} a_k |k\rangle$, measuring all n qubits yields a bit string of 0s and 1s that is the binary notation of the integer k with probability a_k^2. But, since we're dealing with a system in the specific basis state $|b\rangle$, measuring all qubits will yield the binary notation of this basis state, again with probability 1.

To summarize, to get information about the state of the system that is known to be in a basis state, all we need to do is measure all qubits. In this scenario, quantum measurements behave exactly like the information readout from a classical system. The measurement outcome is deterministic; we get complete information about the state of the system, and the state of the system doesn't change when it is measured. That's because our system is not in the superposition state at all, but in a much simpler state—a basis state.

> **NOTE** Ideally, we want to construct our quantum algorithms in such a way that at the end of the computation, the system ends up in a basis state describing the answer or a superposition state that is very close to such a basis state. In this case, reading out the answer from the quantum system is easy.

Before we go into the details of how measurements are implemented in the code, let's consider how to test our solution if it involves measurements. Unlike the previous chapters, now we're dealing with the code that produces classical values—the results of the measurements. Consequently, we can use classical tools to validate the results of the code execution. For this problem, each test should prepare a basis state as the input to our solution, run our code on it, get the results, and check that the results of the measurement match the basis state that was prepared.

4.1.2 Qiskit

In Qiskit, measurement results are represented as a part of the circuit, an array of classical bits to complement the qubit array. The simplest way to define a classical register in a circuit is by specifying two numbers instead of one when defining a `QuantumCircuit`: the first number specifies the number of qubits in the circuit and the second number specifies the number of classical bits. Then, the measurements are appended to the circuit using syntax similar to that of gates. A single-qubit measurement `measure` has to specify the index of the qubit on which it is performed and the index of the classical bit to which the result is written. Specifying lists of indices instead of individual indices means applying single-qubit measurements to pairs of corresponding qubits/classical bits: the measurement result on the first qubit in the first list will be stored in the first classical bit in the second list, and so on. The following listing shows the Qiskit code that measures each of the qubits in the given array and writes measurement results into an array of classical bits.

Listing 4.1 Qiskit code to measure all qubits

```
from qiskit import QuantumCircuit

def read_info(n):
    circ = QuantumCircuit(n, n)
    circ.measure(range(n), range(n))
    return circ
```

94 CHAPTER 4 *Analyzing quantum states*

This listing on its own doesn't output anything. How can we see what this code does, and how can we test it?

In Qiskit, you cannot write arbitrary post-processing code as part of the circuit itself. Instead, you have to first run the circuit on a backend (a simulator or, in a general case, a cloud backend representing a quantum device), fetch the results of its execution, and then print or analyze those results.

Here is a simple Qiskit code snippet that creates a two-qubit circuit that consists of one call to read_info, runs this circuit 100 times, and prints the results:

```
from qiskit import QuantumCircuit, transpile
from qiskit_aer import AerSimulator
from .read_info import read_info

n = 2
circ = QuantumCircuit(n, n)
circ.append(read_info(n), range(n), range(n))

simulator = AerSimulator(method='statevector')
circ = transpile(circ, backend=simulator)
res_map = simulator.run(circ, shots=100).result().get_counts()
print(res_map)
```

The method get_counts of the simulation results returns the results of individual runs ("shots"), aggregated into a map, where the keys are bit strings representing measurement results, and the values are the numbers of times that each of these bit strings occurred in the results. This code snippet prints {'00': 100}, meaning that all shots returned measurement results 00. Indeed, freshly allocated qubits in Qiskit start in the $|0\rangle$ state, and we didn't apply any gates to change their state before measuring them.

The following listing shows an example Qiskit code that defines a helper operation to run the code from listing 4.1 on one test case and validate the result, and another operation to run it on multiple test cases.

Listing 4.2 Qiskit code validating the information readout

```
from random import randint
from qiskit import QuantumCircuit, transpile
from qiskit_aer import AerSimulator
from .read_info import read_info

sim = AerSimulator(method='statevector')

def run_test_read_info(n, basis_state):
    circ = QuantumCircuit(n, n)
    for i in range(n):                      ◄── Prepares the input basis state
        if basis_state & (1 << i) > 0:      ◄──┐ Uses bitwise AND and bitwise
            circ.x(i)                          │ left shift to get the i-th bit
    circ.append(read_info(n), range(n), range(n))   ◄── Measures each qubit

    circ = transpile(circ, backend=simulator)   ◄──┐ Runs simulation and
                                                   │ fetches the results
```

```
res_map = simulator.run(circ, shots=100).result().get_counts()
assert len(res_map) == 1     ◀── Checks that the execution result of all shots is the same
res_bitstring = list(res_map.keys())[0]
res = int(res_bitstring, 2)                  ◀─┐ Checks that the execution
assert res == basis_state                      └ result equals the input
def test_read_info():
    for _ in range(1, 20):   ◀── Runs the test on multiple inputs
        n = randint(1, 5)
        num = randint(0, 2 ** n - 1)
        run_test_read_info(n, num)
```

The operation `run_test_read_info` takes two parameters: the number of qubits and the basis state to use in the test. The basis state is described as an integer, so we have to convert it to an array of bits within the operation. We have a choice between using little-endian or big-endian here, as long as we stay consistent within this operation. Here, I used little-endian to convert the basis state to an array of bits. Qiskit reverses the order of measurement results in the output, so the measured bit string uses big-endian, which is easy to convert to an integer using standard Python tools.

To prepare the given basis state on the allocated qubits, we iterate over all n bits of the integer denoting the basis state. If a bit is set to 1, we apply the X gate to the corresponding qubit.

To validate the results, we run the simulation for 100 shots. The result should be the same for all of them, since we're measuring a basis state, and in this case, measurement outcomes are deterministic. As a result, the map should consist of a single key-value pair, and the value should be 100 (the number of shots we ran), so we only need to extract and validate the key of this pair.

Finally, we convert the key bit string into an integer using the Python function `int` with base 2. We could also print these measurement results as a string or as an integer, break down the string into measurement results for individual qubits, and so on.

The method `test_read_info` uses the operation `run_test_read_info` to validate the code behavior on multiple test cases. This method will be recognized as a test by pytest, so the result of executing these two listings, taken together, is a passing test.

4.1.3 Q#

Q# has a separate data type, `Result`, for representing measurement results instead of reusing integer or Boolean type. This type has two values, `Zero` and `One`, which correspond to the measurement results 0 and 1, respectively.

> **TIP** Using a separate type to store measurement results emphasizes their domain-specific meaning and behavior. This type serves to capture results of measuring quantum systems and does not naturally support arithmetic or logical operations that are well-defined for integer and Boolean values, respectively.

Indeed, what does it mean to add or multiply two measurement results? If a quantum algorithm implicitly treats measurement results as a numeric or a Boolean type, Q# code will need to convert `Result` type into the required value explicitly.

Q# libraries offer several operations for different types of measurements. In our case, we can use operation `MResetZ` from the `Std.Measurement` namespace that is open by default in all Q# programs. This operation measures a qubit in the computational basis, resets it back to $|0\rangle$ state, and returns the measurement result. The following listing shows the Q# code that measures each of the qubits in the given array and returns the array of measurement results.

Listing 4.3 Q# code to measure all qubits and return the results

```
operation ReadInformation(qs : Qubit[]) : Result[] {    Defines a mutable
  mutable res = [];                                      array to store the
  for q in qs {                                          measurement results
    set res += [MResetZ(q)];    Measures each qubit
  }                             and appends measurement
  return res;                   results to the array
}
```

> **TIP** Q# uses two kinds of variables. *Immutable* variables, declared using the `let` keyword, are effectively constants: they keep the value assigned to them initially and don't allow it to be reassigned. *Mutable* variables, declared using the `mutable` keyword, are regular variables: they can be assigned different values during program execution.

This listing on its own doesn't output anything. How can we see what this code does? Measurement results, despite being a quantum-specific data type in Q#, are classical information. Thus, they can be printed and processed just like any other classical data type. You can use Q# built-in function `Message` to print an *interpolated string* containing any classical expressions, including arrays and individual variables of `Result` type. Here is a simple Q# code snippet that allocates an array of qubits, calls `ReadInformation` on them immediately and prints the value returned by this operation:

```
@EntryPoint()
operation DemoReadInformation() : Unit {
  use qs = Qubit[2];
  Message($"{ReadInformation(qs)}");
}
```

This code prints `[Zero, Zero]`, indicating that both measurement results were 0. Indeed, newly allocated qubits in Q# always start in the $|0\rangle$ state, and we didn't do anything to change their state before measuring them.

4.1 Reading out information from a quantum system

Now, how can we test our code? In Q#, processing the measurement results can be implemented as a part of the overall program, similarly to many other classical computations. When we write the tests for the code, we can implement all steps of the test as a single program and run all of it at once on a simulator.

The following listing shows Q# code that defines a helper operation to run the code from listing 4.3 on one test case and validates the result and another operation to run the tests on multiple test cases.

Listing 4.4 Q# code validating the information readout

```
import Std.Diagnostics.Fact;
import Std.Random.DrawRandomInt;
import AnalyzeStates.ReadInformation;

operation RunTestReadInformation(n : Int, basisState : Int) : Unit {
  use qs = Qubit[n];
  for i in 0 .. n - 1 {                    ◄── Prepares the input basis state
    if basisState &&& (1 <<< i) > 0 {      ◄── Uses bitwise AND and bitwise
      X(qs[i]);                                left shift to get i-th bit
    }
  }
  let res = ReadInformation(qs);           ◄── Measures each qubit
  mutable resInt = 0;
  for i in n - 1 .. -1 .. 0 {
    set resInt = resInt * 2 + (res[i] == One ? 1 | 0);
  }
  Fact(resInt == basisState,
    $"Expected {basisState}, got {resInt}");   ◄── Compares the obtained integer to
                                                   the input; fails if they are different
}

operation TestReadInformation() : Unit {
  for _ in 1 .. 20 {                       ◄── Runs the test on multiple inputs
    let n = DrawRandomInt(1, 5);
    let basisState = DrawRandomInt(0, 2 ^ n - 1);
    RunTestReadInformation(n, basisState);
  }
}
```

Converts the array of measurement results into an integer

The operation `RunTestReadInformation` takes two parameters—the number of qubits and the basis state to use in the test. The basis state is described as an integer instead of an array of bits, so we have to do the conversion within the operation. Q# libraries offer functions to convert integers to arrays of bits of different types and vice versa, but for the purpose of learning to deal with measurement results, I'm doing these conversions by hand.

First, we prepare the given basis state on the allocated qubits by iterating over all n bits of the integer denoting the basis state and, if a bit is set to 1, applying the X gate to the corresponding qubit. Then, we call the operation `ReadInformation` to measure all qubits and convert the measurement array back into an integer. To do this, we iterate over the elements of the array, from the most significant bit to the least significant one. On each iteration, we double the current integer, and if the measurement result is equal to the `Result` literal `One`, we add 1 to the current integer. The resulting integer should match the integer `basisState` used to initialize the qubit state.

> **TIP** In this test, we have the freedom to choose the way to map integers to bit strings, since our project doesn't impose any limitations on this; we only need to make sure we use the same encoding to convert `basisState` to a bit string and the measurement results back to an integer. I chose to use little-endian encoding, to match Q# library operations that do similar conversions.

The operation `TestReadInformation` uses the operation `RunTestReadInformation` to validate the code behavior on multiple test cases.

The final code fragment that we need to run the code from section 4.4 as a test is a Python wrapper. (The test project will follow the structure we saw earlier in section 2.4.2.) In this case, the Python code will be very simple: since all the testing logic is implemented in Q#, the Python code only needs to call the Q# operation `TestReadInformation`:

```
import qsharp

def test_read_info():
    qsharp.init(project_root='.')
    qsharp.run("Test.TestReadInformation()", shots=100)
```

Here, I use the method `qsharp.run` instead of `qsharp.eval` to execute the Q# test 100 times, each one with a new simulator instance and with different random test cases. To reproduce the Qiskit test behavior and run each of random test cases 100 times, you can modify the Q# code from listing 4.4 to call `RunTestReadInformation` in a `for` loop once each test case is generated. The result of executing these listings, taken together, is a passing test.

4.2 Distinguishing superposition states consisting of distinct basis states

Now that we've learned to use measurements to read out the information about the basis state the quantum system is in, let's see what kind of tasks can we try to accomplish using measurements as a tool. We'll spend most of this chapter on tasks of one type: given a quantum system in one of the known states, figure out which state it is in. These kinds of tasks are known as *quantum state discrimination.*

In the simplest scenario, you are given the complete list of states in which the system can be, and all of these states are orthogonal to each other. More formally, you are given a quantum register in a state $|\psi\rangle$ and a promise that this state is one of the given list of K orthogonal states $|\psi_0\rangle, \cdots, |\psi_{K-1}\rangle$. You have to figure out which one of this list of states you are given by doing the appropriate measurements on it.

4.2 Distinguishing superposition states consisting of distinct basis states

> **NOTE** Why is this scenario the simplest? The principles of quantum computing dictate that you can distinguish orthogonal states perfectly in one experiment, but you cannot do the same with nonorthogonal states. We'll explore dealing with nonorthogonal states in section 4.4.

This problem has two main variants with different solutions. Let's start with the simpler variant of the problem and say that each pair of the states in this list consists of different basis states. In other words, each basis state can be present in, at most, one of the states on the list or might not be present in either of these states. (We'll consider the more sophisticated variant in the next section.) For example, the following list of four states fits this description:

- $|\psi_0\rangle = \frac{1}{\sqrt{2}}(|000\rangle + |111\rangle)$
- $|\psi_1\rangle = \frac{1}{\sqrt{2}}(|100\rangle + |011\rangle)$
- $|\psi_2\rangle = \frac{1}{\sqrt{2}}(|010\rangle + |101\rangle)$
- $|\psi_3\rangle = \frac{1}{\sqrt{2}}(|001\rangle + |110\rangle)$

Indeed, each of the eight three-qubit basis states is present in exactly one of the states from this list. For two states to be nonorthogonal, they have to share at least one basis state. All pairs of the states from the list are orthogonal, so we don't need to check this condition separately.

4.2.1 Math

Figure 4.3 illustrates the solution to this problem: just measure the given state!

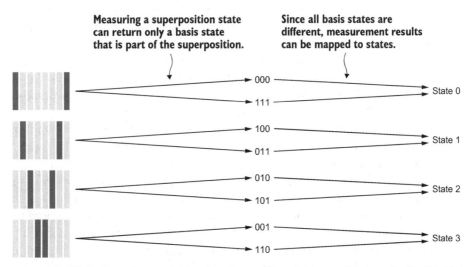

Figure 4.3 Measuring a quantum system in a superposition state can only return a basis state that was part of that superposition. Since all states consist of different basis states, the measurement result points back to the state that was measured uniquely.

Indeed, quantum measurement can only return one of the basis states that were a part of the superposition state being measured (the probability of getting any other basis state is 0). Since each basis state is part of, at most, one state from the list, we can use the measurement result to track the state that included the measured basis state.

Let's look again at our example list of four three-qubit states. If we measure all three qubits, we can map the results to the input states as follows:

- *Measurement results* 000 *or* 111—The input state is $\frac{1}{\sqrt{2}}(|000\rangle + |111\rangle)$.
- *Measurement results* 100 *or* 011—The input state is $\frac{1}{\sqrt{2}}(|100\rangle + |011\rangle)$.
- *Measurement results* 010 *or* 101—The input state is $\frac{1}{\sqrt{2}}(|010\rangle + |101\rangle)$.
- *Measurement results* 001 *or* 110—The input state is $\frac{1}{\sqrt{2}}(|001\rangle + |110\rangle)$.

To simplify comparing the measurement results to specific bit strings, we can convert the array of bits we get as a result of measurement into an integer, like we did when writing the tests in the previous section, and compare these integers.

> **TIP** In this particular case, there is a nice formula to convert the integer representation of the basis states that comprise the input states into the indices of these states. Indeed, basis states $|000\rangle$, $|100\rangle$, $|010\rangle$, and $|110\rangle$ correspond to little-endian notations of numbers 0, 1, 2, and 3—the indices of the states in which they are included. The basis states $|111\rangle$, $|011\rangle$, $|101\rangle$, and $|001\rangle$ correspond to notations of the numbers 7, 6, 5, and 4—the numbers that equal 7 minus the index of the input state. In general, such a neat formula might not exist, so you might have to map each combination of measurement results onto an output value separately.

Now, before we jump into writing the code, let's consider how we will test it. As in the previous section, the code we want to test returns a classical value—the index of the input state it recognized. We can use the same general approach to testing: prepare the input state, pass it to the solution, and check that its return identifies the input state correctly. However, this time, the exact measurement results for each possible input state will vary from run to run because each input state is a superposition and will yield different measurement results. So, we should run the code on each possible input state multiple times to make sure that the code identifies each input state correctly, regardless of the basis state the measurement yielded.

Depending on how likely the code is to be refactored and how helpful we want the test outputs to be in case of a failure, we could process incorrect returns of the code being tested in different ways. The most straightforward approach that I use here is to fail the test as soon as one of the input states is identified incorrectly and to include the index of the actual input state and the value returned by the code. If you want the test code to provide more detailed information about the failure (for example, if you're developing the tests and somebody else will write the code), you can keep running the test on this and other input states and gather the statistics: which input states were identified incorrectly, how often this happened, and which values the code returned instead of the correct ones. This information can help pinpoint the cause of code failure:

4.2 Distinguishing superposition states consisting of distinct basis states

- If a state is consistently misidentified as another state, the problem may be related to labeling the results of an otherwise correct measurement and classification process.
- If a state is misidentified as another one only sometimes, check whether mapping of basis states to input states matches the problem description.
- If multiple states are misidentified as others part of the time, the measurement procedure itself might be incorrect. In the next section, we'll see a task in which this problem is a lot more likely.

4.2.2 Qiskit

The following listing shows the Qiskit code that distinguishes the four three-qubit states we discussed earlier by measuring all qubits and analyzing the results, as well as the test code for it.

Listing 4.5 Qiskit code to distinguish four three-qubit states

```
from qiskit import QuantumCircuit, transpile
from qiskit_aer import AerSimulator

def prep_test_state(ind):
  circ = QuantumCircuit(3)          # Prepares the first state
  circ.h(0)                         # as the starting point
  circ.cx(0, 1)
  circ.cx(0, 2)                     # To prepare one of the other states,
  if ind > 0:                       # flips the state of the right qubit
    circ.x(ind - 1)
  return circ

def read_info(n):
  circ = QuantumCircuit(n, n)
  circ.measure(range(n), range(n))
  return circ
                                    # Interprets bit string of measurement
def interpret_measurements(str):    # results as the index of a state
  res = int(str, 2)
  return res if res < 4 else 7 - res

def test_distinguish_states():
  for state_ind in range(4):
    circ = QuantumCircuit(3, 3)
    circ.append(prep_test_state(state_ind), range(3))
    circ.append(read_info(3), range(3), range(3))

    simulator = AerSimulator(method='statevector')
    circ = transpile(circ, backend=simulator)
    res_map = simulator.run(circ, shots=100).result().get_counts()
    for key in list(res_map.keys()):           # Goes through all possible
      assert interpret_measurements(key) == state_ind  # measurement results and
                                                       # checks that each one is
                                                       # interpreted correctly
```

In this case, the measurement results for each of the input states can be different. The operation `interpret_measurements` contains the logic of converting the measurement results into the index of the state they correspond to. The test logic focuses on validating that each of the measurement results is converted to a state index correctly. This code includes the test code, which should pass as a result of its execution.

4.2.3 Q#

The following listing shows the Q# code that distinguishes the four three-qubit states we discussed earlier by measuring all qubits and analyzing the results.

Listing 4.6 Q# code to distinguish four three-qubit states

```
operation ReadInformationInt(qs : Qubit[]) : Int {
  mutable res = 0;
  for k in Length(qs) - 1 .. -1 .. 0 {
    set res = res * 2 + (MResetZ(qs[k]) == One ? 1 | 0);
  }
  return res;
}
operation DistinguishStates(qs : Qubit[]) : Int {
  let res = ReadInformationInt(qs);
  return res < 4 ? res | 7 - res;
}
```

Operation `ReadInformationInt` combines measuring all qubits and converting the results into an integer, the steps that were done separately in listings 4.3 and 4.4. We don't need to store measurement results between these steps because they are converted into an integer on the fly. This code should be invoked from a test similar to that in section 4.1.3 (see the GitHub repository for the complete code), so the result of its execution should be a passing test.

4.3 Distinguishing superposition states consisting of overlapping basis states

Now let's consider the more general variant of the problem of identifying one of a set of orthogonal states. This time, we remove the constraint on all states consisting of different basis states. Consequently, some states in the list can include the same basis state; in other words, a basis state can be present in at least two of the states on the list.

The smallest example of such problem is distinguishing $|+\rangle = \frac{1}{\sqrt{2}}(|0\rangle + |1\rangle)$ from $|-\rangle = \frac{1}{\sqrt{2}}(|0\rangle - |1\rangle)$. These states are orthogonal, and each includes both $|0\rangle$ and $|1\rangle$ basis states.

Another, slightly larger, example is the following list of four two-qubit states (known as Bell states) that also fits this description:

4.3 Distinguishing superposition states consisting of overlapping basis states

- $|\psi_0\rangle = \frac{1}{\sqrt{2}}(|00\rangle + |11\rangle)$
- $|\psi_1\rangle = \frac{1}{\sqrt{2}}(|00\rangle - |11\rangle)$
- $|\psi_2\rangle = \frac{1}{\sqrt{2}}(|01\rangle + |10\rangle)$
- $|\psi_3\rangle = \frac{1}{\sqrt{2}}(|01\rangle - |10\rangle)$

Indeed, each of the four two-qubit basis states is present in exactly two of the Bell states. In this scenario, the states can still be orthogonal (and you can check that Bell states are), but you might want to check this separately to convince yourself, especially if the states have complex amplitudes so that their orthogonality is not immediately obvious.

4.3.1 Math

This time, just measuring the states right away won't solve our problem: we can't always track the basis state that is the measurement result back to the unique input state that could've produced it. For example, if our measurement gives us result 00, we don't know if we measured state $|\psi_0\rangle$ or $|\psi_1\rangle$.

Instead, we need to find a way to set up the measurement in a way that gives a unique outcome for each of the possible input states. To do this, we need to perform a measurement *in a different basis*.

So far in this chapter, we've only considered measurements in the computational basis. They are convenient in many cases—for example, when the state we measure is a single basis state or when different superposition states consist of non-overlapping sets of basis states. However, now we need a different way to extract information about orthogonal states that would map outcomes 0 and 1 (or longer strings of measurement outcomes) to orthogonal states other than $|0\rangle$ and $|1\rangle$.

Let's start with an example of how we can do that for $|+\rangle$ and $|-\rangle$ states (this measurement is called *measurement in the Hadamard basis*) that is illustrated in figure 4.4.

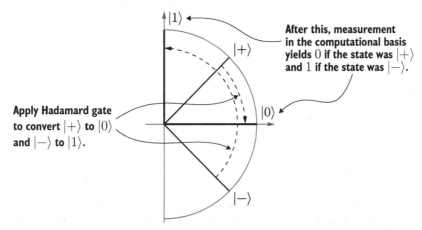

Figure 4.4 To do a measurement in Hadamard basis, we need to find a unitary transformation that maps the states of the Hadamard basis, $|+\rangle$ and $|-\rangle$, into the computational basis states $|0\rangle$ and $|1\rangle$. This is exactly the effect of the Hadamard gate! After this, a measurement in the computational basis will let us figure out which of the states we started with, $|+\rangle$ or $|-\rangle$.

If we can apply some unitary to these states to convert them into $|0\rangle$ and $|1\rangle$ states, we can then measure the qubit in the computational basis to figure out which input state we had originally. If the measurement yields 0, we know the input state was $|+\rangle$, and if it yields 1, we know it was $|-\rangle$. And this unitary is easy to find: it's a Hadamard gate!

This small example leads us to the general strategy of performing measurements in a basis other than the computational basis, shown in figure 4.5:

1 Find a transformation that maps each of the basis states of the other basis (in our case, the states we want to distinguish) to the computational basis states. This is always possible (although this transformation will not always look as neat as the one we just saw!), since the main property of unitary transformations is that they preserve orthogonality of the states they're applied to, and both sets of states are orthogonal.
2 Apply this transformation to the input state.
3 Perform the measurement in the computational basis.
4 Interpret the results, keeping in mind the mapping of the input states to the computational basis states.
5 If we need the quantum system to end up in the state that matches the measurement outcome in that basis (in the example of measurement in the Hadamard basis, the qubit should end up in the state $|+\rangle$ or $|-\rangle$ after the measurement yielded 0 or 1, respectively), we need to apply the adjoint of the unitary transformation we applied on the first step. However, for our problem, we don't care about the state of the qubits after the measurement because we're not planning to run further computation on them, so we can skip this step.

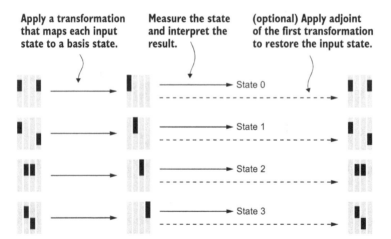

Figure 4.5 Performing a measurement in a noncomputational basis, using the Bell measurement as an example. First, we apply an operation that maps the basis states of the measurement basis (in this case, the Bell states) to the computational basis states. Then, we measure the qubits in the computational basis and interpret the measurement results. Finally, if the state of the system after the measurement has to match the measurement outcome, we apply the adjoint of the operation we applied in the first step.

4.3 Distinguishing superposition states consisting of overlapping basis states

Let's see how to apply this strategy to our second example, distinguishing the Bell states. The measurement we'll do in this case is called *Bell measurement*. We need to find a transformation that maps the four Bell states to the four basis states of the computational basis. Alternatively, we can start by finding a transformation that maps the states of the computational basis to the Bell states and then use its adjoint in the first step of the measurement process. (This method often turns out to be more convenient because it's easier to reason about converting basis states to some other states than vice versa.)

For the Bell states, this transformation is well known: you need to apply the Hadamard gate to the first qubit, followed by a CNOT gate with the first qubit as the control and the second qubit as the target. Table 4.1 shows the evolution of the two-qubit basis states when these two gates are applied to them.

Table 4.1 Preparing the Bell states from the basis states

Initial basis state	State after applying the Hadamard gate	State after applying the CNOT gate
$\|00\rangle$	$\frac{1}{\sqrt{2}}(\|00\rangle + \|10\rangle)$	$\frac{1}{\sqrt{2}}(\|00\rangle + \|11\rangle) = \|\psi_0\rangle$
$\|10\rangle$	$\frac{1}{\sqrt{2}}(\|00\rangle - \|10\rangle)$	$\frac{1}{\sqrt{2}}(\|00\rangle - \|11\rangle) = \|\psi_1\rangle$
$\|01\rangle$	$\frac{1}{\sqrt{2}}(\|01\rangle + \|11\rangle)$	$\frac{1}{\sqrt{2}}(\|01\rangle + \|10\rangle) = \|\psi_2\rangle$
$\|11\rangle$	$\frac{1}{\sqrt{2}}(\|01\rangle - \|11\rangle)$	$\frac{1}{\sqrt{2}}(\|01\rangle - \|10\rangle) = \|\psi_3\rangle$

We can see that, conveniently, the integer representation of the basis state (using little-endian notation) is exactly the index of the Bell state $|\psi_k\rangle$ into which it is transformed by these two gates. Therefore, we can apply the adjoint of these pair of gates—first the CNOT gate and then the Hadamard gate—to our input state, measure both qubits, and convert the measurement results into an integer to get our answer. Now let's see what this looks like in the code.

4.3.2 Qiskit

The following listing shows the Qiskit code that distinguishes the four Bell states.

Listing 4.7 Qiskit code to distinguish the Bell states

```
from qiskit import QuantumCircuit
def distinguish_bell_states():
  circ = QuantumCircuit(2, 2)
  circ.cx(0, 1)
  circ.h(0)
  circ.measure(range(2), range(2))
  return circ
```

The tests for this code look very similar to the ones used in the previous section. The only part that is different is the operation that prepares the input states for this code. The outcome of executing this code should be a passing test.

4.3.3 Q#

The following listing shows the Q# code that distinguishes the four Bell states, reusing the operation `ReadInformationInt` from listing 4.6 as a building block.

Listing 4.8 Q# code to distinguish the Bell states

```
operation DistinguishBellStates(qs : Qubit[]) : Int {
  CNOT(qs[0], qs[1]);
  H(qs[0]);
  let res = ReadInformationInt(qs);
  return res;
}
```

The tests for this code look very similar to the ones used in the previous section. The only part that is different is the operation that prepares the input states for this code. The outcome of executing this code should be a passing test.

4.4 Distinguishing nonorthogonal states with minimum error

So far in this chapter, we've dealt only with orthogonal states, which can be distinguished perfectly with the right choice of measurement. Now let's switch gears and talk about what happens if we try to distinguish nonorthogonal states.

Two quantum states that are not orthogonal cannot be distinguished perfectly (this rule can be derived from the main principles of quantum computing). As a result, we cannot aim to write a program that identifies which one of the nonorthogonal states it is given perfectly every time. Instead, we need to adjust the requirements to account for the inevitable error or uncertainty in the state identification.

One of the variants of this problem is called *state discrimination with minimum error*, and its simplest case is formulated in the following way. You participate in multiple independent trials; in each trial, you are given one of the two nonorthogonal states, selected randomly with equal probability. You have to devise a measurement that will let you identify which state you are given in each trial as often as possible (in other words, you have to minimize the probability of being incorrect, averaged across all trials).

To make the problem more specific, let's say that the two nonorthogonal states we aim to distinguish are the single-qubit states $|\psi_0\rangle = |0\rangle$ and $|\psi_1\rangle = \alpha|0\rangle + \beta|1\rangle$ (with known coefficients α and β). For simplicity, we will consider the case of real positive α and β.

4.4.1 Math

Let's dig into the problem statement in a way that will help us start looking for a solution. We know that the only way to get information about the state of a qubit is to measure it, but we can choose whatever measurement basis we want to use. This basis will consist of two orthogonal states, $|m_0\rangle$ and $|m_1\rangle$, that correspond to measurement outcomes 0 and 1. Figure 4.6 shows the geometric representation of all four states involved in the problem on a unit circle.

4.4 Distinguishing nonorthogonal states with minimum error

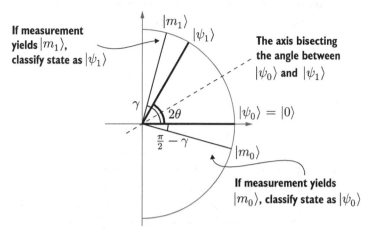

Figure 4.6 Choosing the measurement basis for distinguishing $|\psi_0\rangle = |0\rangle$ from $|\psi_1\rangle = \frac{1}{2}|0\rangle + \frac{\sqrt{3}}{2}|1\rangle$ with minimum error. We can describe the state $|\psi_1\rangle$ using only one parameter, the angle θ (for this example, $2\theta = \frac{\pi}{3}$), and the measurement basis using the second parameter, the angle γ. We want to choose the measurement basis states so that they are as close to the states being distinguished as possible while remaining orthogonal.

Let's spell out our states $|\psi_1\rangle$, $|m_0\rangle$, and $|m_1\rangle$ using sines and cosines of two angles to reduce the number of parameters we're working with:

$$|\psi_1\rangle = \alpha|0\rangle + \beta|1\rangle = \cos 2\theta |0\rangle + \sin 2\theta |1\rangle$$
$$|m_0\rangle = \cos(\tfrac{\pi}{2} - \gamma)|0\rangle + \sin(\tfrac{\pi}{2} - \gamma)|1\rangle = \sin\gamma |0\rangle - \cos\gamma |1\rangle$$
$$|m_1\rangle = \cos\gamma |0\rangle + \sin\gamma |1\rangle$$

Next, we know that the only information we can use to make the decision about which state we were given is the measurement outcome. So, the simplest way to make our decision is to say that if the measurement outcome is 0, we were given the state $|\psi_0\rangle$; otherwise, we were given the state $|\psi_1\rangle$.

With this strategy in mind, how can we calculate the probability of our guess being correct (which is the value that we need to maximize)? The probability of the state $|\psi_0\rangle$ being measured as $|m_0\rangle$ is

$$|\langle\psi_0|m_0\rangle|^2 = \sin^2\gamma$$

The probability of the state $|\psi_1\rangle$ being measured as $|m_1\rangle$ is

$$|\langle\psi_1|m_1\rangle|^2 = (\cos\gamma\cos 2\theta + \sin\gamma\sin 2\theta)^2 = \cos^2(\gamma - 2\theta)$$

The total probability of a state being identified correctly is the average of these two probabilities (remember that we're given one of the states $|\psi_0\rangle$ or $|\psi_1\rangle$ with equal probability):

$$P_{success} = \tfrac{1}{2}\left(\sin^2\gamma + \cos^2(\gamma - 2\theta)\right)$$

Our goal is to find the value of the angle γ that would maximize this expression. We can do this mathematically, by taking the derivative of this expression as a function of γ, equating it to 0, and solving the resulting equation. The solution will give us

$$\gamma = \theta + \tfrac{\pi}{4}$$

The maximum success probability that can be achieved using this γ is then

$$P_{max} = \tfrac{1}{2}\left(\sin^2(\theta + \tfrac{\pi}{4}) + \cos^2(\theta - \tfrac{\pi}{4})\right) = \tfrac{1}{2}(1 + \sin 2\theta)$$

NOTE Alternatively, we can look at figure 4.6 again to consider the geometric properties of the optimal measurement basis. The probability of the input state $|\psi_j\rangle$ identified correctly is proportional to the square of the cosine of the angle between it and the corresponding state of the measurement basis $|m_j\rangle$, which grows larger as the angle between these vectors grows smaller. The basis states $|m_0\rangle$ and $|m_1\rangle$ should be as close to the states $|\psi_0\rangle$ and $|\psi_1\rangle$, respectively, as they can be while remaining orthogonal. The input states are selected with equal probability, so our solution will be symmetric with respect to the axis that bisects the angle between the states $|\psi_0\rangle$ and $|\psi_1\rangle$ (the axis tilted at θ radians to the horizontal axis). The angles between $|\psi_j\rangle$ and $|m_j\rangle$ should be equal for both pairs of basis states. These angles then have to equal $\tfrac{1}{2}(\tfrac{\pi}{2} - 2\theta) = \tfrac{\pi}{4} - \theta$, giving us the final answer $\gamma = 2\theta + (\tfrac{\pi}{4} - \theta) = \tfrac{\pi}{4} + \theta$.

Before we implement this solution in code, let's run it through a couple of sanity checks. What happens if the states we aim to distinguish are orthogonal, that is, $|\psi_1\rangle = |1\rangle$? In this case, $\theta = \tfrac{\pi}{4}$, $\gamma = \tfrac{\pi}{2}$, and the basis we need to use for measurement is the basis that consists of the input states themselves. The probability of distinguishing the states correctly is $P_{max} = \tfrac{1}{2}\left(1 + \sin \tfrac{\pi}{2}\right) = 1$, as it should be when dealing with orthogonal states.

What happens if the states we aim to distinguish are the same—that is, $|\psi_1\rangle = |0\rangle$? In this case, $\theta = 0$, $\gamma = \tfrac{\pi}{4}$, and each of the states has a 0.5 probability of being identified correctly, giving us a 50% probability of the overall success. This matches our expectation: we cannot really guess which label was assigned to the $|0\rangle$ state when it was given to us as an input, $|\psi_0\rangle$ or $|\psi_1\rangle$, so we cannot do better than a random guess.

To summarize, two steps to our solution are as follows:

1 Perform the measurement in the basis $\{|m_0\rangle, |m_1\rangle\}$ using the procedure described in the previous section. The transformation that maps the states $|m_0\rangle$ and $|m_1\rangle$ to the computational basis states is the Ry gate with the parameter $2(\tfrac{\pi}{4} - \theta)$. (You can see this from figure 4.6: you need to rotate the states $|m_0\rangle$ and $|m_1\rangle$ counterclockwise by the angle $\tfrac{\pi}{2} - \gamma = \tfrac{\pi}{4} - \theta$ for them to become $|0\rangle$ and $|1\rangle$, respectively.)
2 If the measurement result is 0, identify the input state as $|\psi_0\rangle$; otherwise, as $|\psi_1\rangle$.

To test this solution, we need to account for a certain percentage of our attempts to identify the given state ending up incorrect, so we'll need to gather the statistics about the percentage of states identified correctly and then compare it with the theoretically computed maximum success probability. If our solution fails to identify the state too often, it is probably incorrect. However, if it identifies the state correctly too often, that's not great either. It might mean that our test setup is incorrect, and the states prepared as the input for the solution are wrong.

4.4.2 Qiskit

The following listing shows the Qiskit code that distinguishes the given nonorthogonal states with the minimum possible error.

Listing 4.9 Qiskit code to distinguish nonorthogonal states

```
from math import atan2, pi
from qiskit import QuantumCircuit

def distinguish_zero_and_sup(alpha, beta):
    circ = QuantumCircuit(1, 1)
    theta = atan2(beta, alpha) / 2
    circ.ry(- 2 * (theta - pi / 4), 0)
    circ.measure(0, 0)
    return circ
```

The test for this code, included in the GitHub repository, shows how to gather statistics across multiple trials and verify that the success probability is in the expected range. The outcome of executing the complete code should be this test passing.

4.4.3 Q#

The following listing shows the Q# code that distinguishes the given nonorthogonal states with the minimum possible error.

Listing 4.10 Q# code to distinguish nonorthogonal states

```
import Std.Math.*;

operation DistinguishZeroAndSup(
    q : Qubit, alpha : Double, beta : Double
) : Int {
    let theta = ArcTan2(beta, alpha) / 2.;
    Ry(- 2. * (theta - PI() / 4.), q);
    return MResetZ(q) == Zero ? 0 | 1;
}
```

The test for this code, included in the GitHub repository, shows how to gather statistics across multiple trials and verify that the success probability is in the expected range. The outcome of executing the complete code should be this test passing.

4.5 Reconstructing the state from multiple copies

The next problem we'll tackle is reconstructing a quantum state by using measurements on a set of identical quantum states. More specifically, you're given multiple systems, each in the same quantum state, and your goal is to reconstruct this state as accurately as possible.

For simplicity, we'll focus on a single-qubit state again, $\alpha |0\rangle + \beta |1\rangle$, and aim to estimate the unknown real coefficients α and β. Since there is no physical way to distinguish a state from the same state multiplied by a global phase of -1, we'll assume that α is nonnegative.

> **NOTE** This problem and the processes used to solve it are collectively known as *quantum state tomography*. It is based on the general idea that while performing a measurement on a single quantum system yields very little information about its state before measurement, performing different measurements on multiple copies of the same system and analyzing the results allows us to reconstruct the original state with high accuracy.

4.5.1 Math

In this section, I'm aiming to give you a general sense of the kinds of problems that can be solved using measurements, rather than the state-of-the-art algorithms for solving each problem. In this vein, the algorithm for reconstructing the state from measurements I show here will be very straightforward and built on top of the topics we've covered earlier in the chapter, but it will not provide statistically accurate analysis. Figure 4.7 shows the geometric representation of the two steps of the approach we'll take to reconstruct the state.

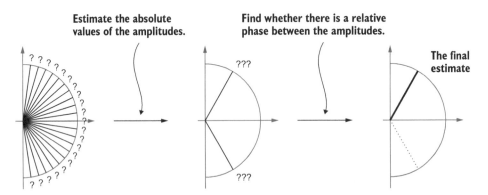

Figure 4.7 Reconstructing a single-qubit state $\alpha |0\rangle + \beta |1\rangle$ from multiple copies. We start by estimating the absolute values of the coefficients α and β and then figure out whether these coefficients have the same sign or different signs.

First, we estimate the absolute values of the coefficients α and β. We can do this by measuring multiple copies of the state and collecting frequency counts of the measurement outcomes 0 and 1. As we know from the properties of quantum measurements, these frequencies are proportional to squares of the coefficients α and β, respectively, so we can estimate the coefficients as square roots of the frequencies. Let's call our estimates α' and β' (both values are nonnegative).

Second, we need to figure out the sign of the coefficient β (remember we assumed α is nonnegative, since a global phase doesn't affect the behavior of a state during measurements and thus is undetectable). We can treat this task as a problem of deciding which of the states $\alpha'|0\rangle + \beta'|1\rangle$ or $\alpha'|0\rangle - \beta'|1\rangle$ we are given. This is exactly the problem we solved in section 4.4! We'll have to modify the solution slightly to account for the fact that this time the possible nonorthogonal states we're given are both different from $|0\rangle$.

Our solution in section 4.4 effectively boiled down to rotating the input state so that the axis that bisects the angle between the possible input states became tilted at the degree $\frac{\pi}{4}$ to the horizontal axis. We can generalize this for our current problem without doing all the math: the axis that bisects the angle between the possible input states now is just the horizontal axis, so we need to rotate our input states by $\frac{\pi}{4}$ before measuring them. (Remember the angle used as a parameter of the rotation gate Ry is double the angle of the geometric rotation.) If these measurements yield 0 more often than 1, our state estimate ends up being $\alpha'|0\rangle - \beta'|1\rangle$; otherwise, it is $\alpha'|0\rangle + \beta'|1\rangle$.

Notice that some quantum states are easier to reconstruct than the others. For example, if you run measurements on 100 copies of the state $\frac{1}{\sqrt{2}}(|0\rangle + |1\rangle)$, you'll get a reasonable estimate of two approximately equal amplitudes, and afterward, you'll need just a couple of experiments to find out the relative phase. However, for the state $\frac{1}{10}(\sqrt{99}|0\rangle + |1\rangle)$, the probability of measuring 1 is only 1%. After doing measurements on 100 copies of this state, you might not even realize that the state is not exactly $|0\rangle$. Similarly, the states $\frac{1}{10}(\sqrt{99}|0\rangle + |1\rangle)$ and $\frac{1}{10}(\sqrt{99}|0\rangle - |1\rangle)$ are almost the same, so it takes more experiments to decide which of these states we are given.

Generally, the smaller the absolute value of one of the amplitudes, the more experiments you need to run to get a good estimate of that value and to figure out the relative phase between the basis states. I will not go into further details of deciding how many trials are needed in each phase of the algorithm to make an estimate with a certain absolute or relative precision; you can experiment with that by tweaking the code and the input states.

4.5.2 Qiskit

The following listing shows the Qiskit code that reconstructs the coefficients of the given state.

Listing 4.11 Qiskit code to reconstruct the coefficients of a state

```
from math import pi, sqrt
from qiskit import QuantumCircuit, transpile
from qiskit_aer import AerSimulator

simulator = AerSimulator(method='statevector')

def reconstruct_state(state_prep):         # Step 1: Estimate the absolute values
    circ1 = QuantumCircuit(1, 1)           # of amplitudes alpha and beta.
    circ1.append(state_prep, [0])
    circ1.measure(0, 0)
```

```
circ1 = transpile(circ1, backend=simulator)        ◀─┐ Runs multiple trials
n_trials = 200                                       │ on the same circuit
res_map = simulator.run(circ1, shots=n_trials).result().get_counts()
if '0' in res_map:
   (n0, n1) = (res_map['0'], n_trials - res_map['0'])
else:                                              ◀─┐ Special case: The
   (n0, n1) = (n_trials - res_map['1'], res_map['1']) │ input state is |1>.
alpha = sqrt(n0 / n_trials)
beta = sqrt(n1 / n_trials)

circ2 = QuantumCircuit(1, 1)      ◀─┐ Step 2: Figure out whether
circ2.append(state_prep, [0])       │ there is a relative phase of -1.
circ2.ry(pi / 2, 0)
circ2.measure(0, 0)
circ2 = transpile(circ2, backend=simulator)

res_map = simulator.run(circ2, shots=n_trials).result().get_counts()
if '0' in res_map and 2 * res_map['0'] > n_trials:
   return (alpha, -beta)
else:
   return (alpha, beta)
```

Note that this code is different from the earlier Qiskit listings in this chapter: it handles all steps of working with a Qiskit circuit, from constructing the circuits required for each step of the algorithm to running them on a simulator and analyzing the results. This code needs to construct a complete circuit, including the preparation of the input state before measuring it, rather than just a fixed part of the circuit like the previous listings did. To enable this, the code takes the circuit that prepares the input state as an input parameter and uses it in the circuits it constructs.

The test for this code, included in the GitHub repository, is also different from the tests for the previous problems. Since all the quantum logic used in the algorithm is handled by the solution code, the test does only one completely classical check to see how close the estimate of the state coefficients is to the actual coefficients. The outcome of executing the complete code should be this test passing.

4.5.3 Q#

The following listing shows the Q# code that reconstructs the coefficients of the given state.

Listing 4.12 Q# code to reconstruct the coefficients of a state

```
import Std.Convert.IntAsDouble;
import Std.Math.*;

operation ReconstructState(statePrep : Qubit => Unit) : (Double, Double) {
   mutable nZeros = 0;          ◀─┐ Step 1: Estimate the absolute
   mutable nTrials = 200;         │ values of amplitudes alpha and beta.
   for _ in 1 .. nTrials {
      use q = Qubit();
      statePrep(q);
```

```
      if MResetZ(q) == Zero {
        set nZeros += 1;
      }
    }
    let alpha = Sqrt(IntAsDouble(nZeros) / IntAsDouble(nTrials));
    let beta = Sqrt(IntAsDouble(nTrials - nZeros) / IntAsDouble(nTrials));
    set nZeros = 0;              ←———— Step 2: Figure out whether
    for _ in 1 .. nTrials {              there is a relative phase of -1.
      use q = Qubit();
      statePrep(q);
      Ry(PI() / 2., q);
      if MResetZ(q) == Zero {
        set nZeros += 1;
      }
    }
    return 2 * nZeros > nTrials ? (alpha, -beta) | (alpha, beta);
}
```

This solution, unlike the Qiskit code for the same task, doesn't call a quantum simulator explicitly. Instead, the program expresses both the quantum parts of the computation and the classical analysis of their outputs in Q#, and then the whole program is executed on a simulator to get the result.

The test for this code, included in the GitHub repository, is also different from the Q# tests for the previous problems (and similar to the Qiskit test for this task). Since all the quantum logic used in the algorithm is handled by the solution code, the test does only the classical check to see how close the estimate of the state coefficients is to the actual coefficients. The outcome of executing the complete code should be this test passing.

4.6 Joint/parity measurements: Extracting partial information from a state

To wrap up this chapter, let's pivot to a completely different kind of problem: How can we extract some information about a quantum state while preserving the superposition (that is, without collapsing the state of the system all the way to a single basis state that corresponds to the measurement result)? Figure 4.8 shows a typical example of such problem.

The *parity* of a basis state is 0 if it has an even number of 1s in its bit string notation, and 1 otherwise. For example, in the two-qubit case, basis states $|00\rangle$ and $|11\rangle$ have parity 0, and $|01\rangle$ and $|10\rangle$ have parity 1.

You are given a state that is either a superposition of basis states with parity 0 or a superposition of basis states with parity 1. You want to figure out what kind of state you are given. However, you don't know the exact superposition you might be given, and you want to find the parity of the state while preserving the superposition.

If you measure both qubits as usual, like we did in section 4.2, you can count the number of 1s in the measurement results and thus learn the parity of the state you were given, but you will collapse the superposition in the process and have no way of restoring it. In fact, measuring even one of the qubits will ruin the superposition (but not actually answer your question). Is there a different way to extract information from a quantum state?

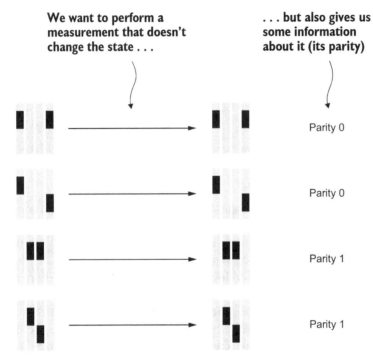

Figure 4.8 Measuring the parity of a quantum state. You are given a state that is a superposition of basis states with the same parity: $|00\rangle$ and $|11\rangle$ or $|01\rangle$ and $|10\rangle$. The goal is to perform a measurement to learn the parity of this state in a way that doesn't change the state.

4.6.1 Math

A special type of measurements called *joint measurements* allows us to solve this problem. Joint measurements are a multiqubit generalization of single-qubit measurements; they allow us to extract some information about the correlations between the qubits, where single-qubit measurements focus on information about the states of individual qubits.

Joint measurements can give information about different kinds of correlations, but for the purposes of this chapter, I'll talk only about one kind of measurements, *parity measurements*, which measure the parity of the state. Focusing on this special case will also let us avoid discussing the general-scenario math that is bulkier than we need at the moment.

To perform a parity measurement, we need to perform the following steps:

1 Allocate an auxiliary qubit in the $|0\rangle$ state.

4.6 Joint/parity measurements: Extracting partial information from a state

2. Calculate the parity of the state and store it in the auxiliary qubit. We can do this using a series of CNOT gates, one per qubit of the input state, with each of the input qubits as control and the auxiliary qubit as the target. This computation is based on the use of the CNOT gate to compute XOR of its arguments (we'll talk about this in more detail in chapter 6).
3. Measure the auxiliary qubit to read out the parity of the state. Importantly, in our case this measurement doesn't change the state of the input qubits! Since all the basis states that are included in that superposition state have the same parity, the value of the parity bit computed for all of them will be the same. The auxiliary qubit will end up not being entangled with the input qubits, and measuring it will not affect their state.

Let's see what the math for these steps looks like for the case of two input qubits. Table 4.2 shows the states of the system after each step of the process, using two examples of states of different parity as the input states.

Table 4.2 The steps of performing a parity measurement on a two-qubit state

The input state	$0.8\|00\rangle + 0.6\|11\rangle$	$0.8\|01\rangle + 0.6\|10\rangle$
Parity of the input state	0	1
Allocate auxiliary qubit (last bit)	$0.8\|00\rangle\|0\rangle + 0.6\|11\rangle\|0\rangle$	$0.8\|01\rangle\|0\rangle + 0.6\|10\rangle\|0\rangle$
Apply a CNOT gate with the first qubit as control (the state becomes entangled)	$0.8\|00\rangle\|0\rangle + 0.6\|11\rangle\|1\rangle$	$0.8\|01\rangle\|0\rangle + 0.6\|10\rangle\|1\rangle$
Apply a CNOT gate with the second qubit as control (the state becomes unentangled)	$0.8\|00\rangle\|0\rangle + 0.6\|11\rangle\|0\rangle$	$0.8\|01\rangle\|1\rangle + 0.6\|10\rangle\|1\rangle$
The state of the auxiliary qubit (the same for both basis states)	$\|0\rangle$	$\|1\rangle$

Notice that the basis states in each of the example states used in table 4.2 have different amplitudes (0.6 and 0.8). Using such uneven superposition states simplifies tracing the state changes during the computation; this way, you won't miss the basis states of the superposition changing into each other. (For example, if you start with an even superposition of $|00\rangle$ and $|11\rangle$, you won't notice if your transformation swaps these basis states accidentally.)

You can see that, indeed, the auxiliary qubit ends up in the same state for all the basis states in each of the input states (you can try out this computation yourself for the three-qubit case). This result makes sense because the state of this qubit is the parity of all bits of the basis state, and we are solving this problem under the assumption that each input state consists of basis states of the same parity.

NOTE If the input state had basis states of different parities, measuring the auxiliary qubit would have changed the input state, leaving only the basis states with parity matching the measurement outcome. This effect allows us to use measurements for computation, including error correction!

Before we start writing the code, let's take a moment to think about how we will test it. For this scenario, testing has to differ slightly from the previous cases in this chapter. Until now, we were willing to sacrifice the state of the quantum system to learn the necessary information about it, so we didn't care about the state of the qubits after the measurement. This time, though, we're trying to learn some information about the state without changing this state. Consequently, our tests need to check that the state of the qubits after the measurement is the same as their initial state, in addition to verifying that the information we learned about that state is accurate. There are two ways to do this:

- We can reuse the approach we saw in section 2.4: use the built-in language tools to access the quantum state after the measurement and check that it matches the input state. I'll use this approach for testing the Qiskit code for this problem.
- Alternatively, we can change our quantum code to do an extra step after the measurements are complete. We'll take the operation we used to prepare the input state from the $|0\rangle$ state (let's call it U and note that $U|0\rangle = |\psi\rangle$) and apply its adjoint $U^\dagger$ to the post-measurement state:
  - If the state after the measurement is the same as it was before the measurement, $|\psi\rangle$, applying $U^\dagger$ to it will convert it to $U^\dagger |\psi\rangle = U^\dagger U |0\rangle = |0\rangle$.
  - If the state after the measurement is different, applying $U^\dagger$ to it will result in some state other than $|0\rangle$ (remember U and $U^\dagger$ are unitary transformations and always map different states to different states).

Thus, we can distinguish these two scenarios by accessing the quantum state of the program and checking whether it is $|0\rangle$. I'll use this approach to test the Q# implementation of the solution to this problem.

Now, let's see how this solution looks implemented in code.

4.6.2 Qiskit

The following listing shows the Qiskit code that measures the parity of the given state.

Listing 4.13 Qiskit code to measure the parity of a state

```
from qiskit import QuantumCircuit

def state_parity(n):
  circ = QuantumCircuit(n + 1, 1)
  for i in range(n):
    circ.cx(i, n)
  circ.measure(n, 0)
  return circ
```

Note that this circuit requires one extra qubit in addition to the qubits that represent the given state and a classical bit used to store the measurement results. This auxiliary qubit is assumed to start in the $|0\rangle$ state and is used to compute the parity of the state. It is measured in the end, so its state is returned to $|0\rangle$. Since Qiskit requires that all the qubits used in a circuit are allocated up front and doesn't allow allocating and

4.6 Joint/parity measurements: Extracting partial information from a state

releasing auxiliary qubits during the program execution, you have to keep in mind the behavior of the auxiliary qubits when you use operations that rely on them. We'll practice writing programs that use auxiliary qubits a lot more in chapter 6.

The test for this program will repeatedly generate states of a certain parity (either random or predetermined), prepare input qubits in those states, run this measurement on them, check that the parity obtained this way matches the parity of the state that was prepared, and finally check that the state itself has not been modified by the measurement. You can use the code we wrote in chapter 2 to prepare the input state, but I used the built-in library method `QuantumCircuit.initialize`, which helps keep the code shorter. You can find the complete test code in the GitHub repository. The result of running the project should be a passing test.

4.6.3 Q#

The following listing shows the Q# code that measures the parity of the given state.

Listing 4.14 Q# code to measure the parity of a state

```
operation StateParity(qs : Qubit[]) : Int {
  use parityQ = Qubit();
  for q in qs {
    CNOT(q, parityQ);
  }
  return MResetZ(parityQ) == Zero ? 0 | 1;
}
```

This code takes the same approach as the Qiskit code in listing 4.13, allocating an auxiliary qubit and using it to compute the parity of the state. Q# allows you to allocate qubits temporarily to be used within the scope of one operation, so there is no need to preallocate extra qubits in the main program and pass them as arguments to the parity measurement operation like we did in Qiskit.

Alternatively, the same logic can be implemented using a built-in library operation `MeasureAllZ` (listing 4.15). This operation is a special case of a more general operation, `Measure`, which supports a variety of multiqubit measurements in different bases. The operation `MeasureAllZ` is a wrapper for one of its simplest variants that measures the parity of the given array of qubits.

Listing 4.15 Q# code to measure parity using MeasureAllZ

```
operation StateParityBuiltIn(qs : Qubit[]) : Int {
  return MeasureAllZ(qs) == Zero ? 0 | 1;
}
```

The test for this program would repeatedly generate states of a certain parity (either random or predetermined), prepare input qubits in those states, run this measurement on them, check that the parity obtained this way matches the parity of the state that was prepared, and finally check that the state itself has not been modified by the measurement. You can use the code we wrote in chapter 2 to prepare the input state, but I used the built-in library operation `PreparePureStateD`, which helps keep the code shorter. You can find the complete test code in the GitHub repository. The result of running the project should be a passing test.

4.7 Further reading

Here is a short list of references that are good starting points if you want to learn more about extracting information about quantum states:

- Chefles, A. (2000). Quantum state discrimination. https://arxiv.org/abs/quant-ph/0010114
- Bagan, E., Monras, A., & Munoz-Tapia, R. (2004). Estimation of pure qubit states with collective and individual measurements. https://arxiv.org/abs/quant-ph/0412027

4.8 Going beyond

Do you want to spend some more time exploring variations of the problems discussed in this chapter before moving on to the next topic? Here are some additional ideas for simpler examples, similar problems, and ways to extend these problems if you want to try your hand at something more challenging:

- In section 4.2, our code solved only one specific problem instance. Try to implement the solution to the general problem of identifying one state from an arbitrary list of states that don't share a basis state.

  Note that we don't care about the exact amplitudes of the basis states within the given states, only that they are all distinct. In the code for the general case, you can describe the states as arrays of basis states they're composed of instead of a more complicated structure that would also include their amplitudes.

- In section 4.3, we solved only the problem of distinguishing the Bell states. Try implementing the solution for a more general variant of the problem.

  The hardest part of the general solution is finding the transformation that maps the states we want to distinguish to basis states (or vice versa). To do this in general case, remember that the columns of a unitary matrix describe the results of applying the unitary to the computational basis states. If you need to distinguish 2^n orthogonal states on n qubits, you can write down the complete matrix of the transformation by just writing the amplitudes of these states in each of the matrix columns. If you have fewer than 2^n states to distinguish, you'll need to figure out how to fill the missing columns of the matrix with values that would make the matrix unitary first.

- In section 4.4, we considered the simplest case of state discrimination with minimum error: in each trial, each of the two nonorthogonal states was selected as the input state with equal probability. Consider the more complicated variant of the same problem, in which one of the states is selected as input more often

than the other—that is, the probabilities of the two states being selected are p and $1-p$, respectively, with $p \neq 0.5$. How does this affect the choice of the measurement basis and the probability of identifying the state correctly?
- An alternative approach to the problem of distinguishing nonorthogonal states is called *unambiguous state discrimination*. In this variant, you are given one of the two nonorthogonal states at random across multiple trials, but this time you're allowed to either identify the state as one of the input states or say "I don't know." The goal is to never give an incorrect answer while minimizing the frequency with which you use the third option. After all, it wouldn't be very useful to never be wrong by always saying "I don't know"! How would you approach this problem?
- Play with quantum state tomography; try to come up with a better algorithm than the one discussed in this chapter or a solution for the two-qubit (or multiqubit!) case.

We will keep using measurements for accomplishing different tasks in chapter 5, when we talk about analyzing operations. After all, measurements are a key component of quantum algorithms, so it's natural to learn to use them in as many contexts as possible!

Summary

- Measurements are an important part of quantum algorithms, since they're the only way to learn information about the state of a quantum system. They also limit the power of quantum computing, since they limit the amount of information you can get out of a system!
- Measurement allows us to identify the basis state in which the system is or, if the system is in a superposition state, to read out one of the basis states that have nonzero amplitudes in the superposition. The probability of getting each state as the result of a measurement equals the square of its amplitude in the superposition.
- The goal of many quantum algorithms is to get the quantum system into a state in which a measurement produces a problem solution with high probability. Some algorithms aim to estimate the probabilities of different measurement outcomes instead.
- Orthogonal states can be distinguished with perfect accuracy, as long as you use the right measurement procedure. This procedure can involve doing a measurement in a basis other than the default (computational) basis.
- Nonorthogonal states cannot be distinguished with perfect accuracy. A measurement procedure can be set up to maximize the probability of identifying the given state correctly over multiple independent trials.

- Quantum state tomography allows us to learn more detailed information about a quantum state compared to the information returned by a single measurement, as long as we're given multiple copies of the state.
- Joint measurements are a way to extract partial information about the quantum system—for example, the parity of the basis states included in the superposition—while preserving the state of this system. Joint measurements extract information about correlations between qubit states, while single-qubit measurements extract information about individual qubit states.

Analyzing quantum operations

This chapter covers
- Getting information about quantum operations
- Finding the matrix that describes the given quantum gate
- Estimating the eigenvalues of quantum gates
- Using Q# and Qiskit to analyze operations

In chapter 4, we learned to use measurements to analyze quantum states in different situations. In this chapter, we'll consider several new types of tasks that involve analyzing unitary transformations. Of course, these tasks will build on top of our learnings from the earlier chapters, since you can only learn things about operations by preparing certain states, applying these operations to those states, and then extracting information about the resulting states using measurements.

Quantum states are the most common kind of input data for quantum algorithms, but they are not the only ones. While typically unitary operations appear in algorithms as their building blocks, they can also be used as input data. In fact, algorithms that take a unitary as an input and aim to learn something about it can be just as important as the ones that learn something about a quantum state.

For example, the *phase estimation problem*, the task of estimating the eigenvalue of a unitary operation, is used as a subroutine in a lot of other quantum algorithms, including Shor's integer factorization algorithm, Harrow–Hassidim–Lloyd (HHL) algorithm for solving a system of linear equations, and the quantum counting algorithm that estimates the number of solutions for a search problem. The phase estimation problem uses both types of inputs: a unitary operation and a quantum state that is an eigenvector of this unitary. (We will spend a lot of time discussing different phase estimation algorithms in this chapter!)

Algorithms that are designed to learn a property of the given unitary operation follow a pattern, shown in figure 5.1, similar to that of the algorithms designed to learn a property of a quantum state:

1 We start by choosing the initial state and preparing it.
2 We apply one or several unitary transformations. Each of these transformations can be the unitary we're analyzing, its controlled or adjoint variant, or a different unitary that allows us to extract useful information from the system. Of course, at least one of these unitaries has to be related to the one we're analyzing; otherwise, we won't learn anything about it!
3 We measure the resulting state to get the information out of the system and use this information to learn something about the unitary.

In fact, this pattern follows the generic pattern of quantum algorithms we saw in figure 2.1, applied to our problem.

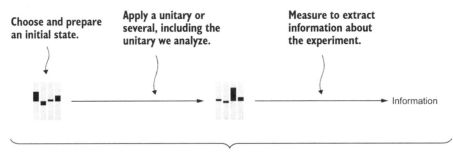

Figure 5.1 To learn a property of a given unitary operation, we choose an initial state, apply one or several quantum operations, including the operation we're analyzing or its variants, and measure the resulting state. Depending on the problem we're solving, we might have to repeat this sequence of steps multiple times to gather statistics about the measurement outcomes and/or vary the initial state and the unitaries applied.

Depending on the problem we're solving, running this sequence of steps just once might give us all the information we need, or we might need to run it multiple times to gather enough statistics about the measurement outcomes to arrive to the answer. We might even have to vary the initial state and the unitaries applied on each run to gather statistics on different aspects of the problem represented by different numerical properties of the unitary. We'll see examples of all these scenarios throughout this chapter.

In this chapter, I'll once again lean toward using specific examples of problems to illustrate the principles of extracting information about quantum operations. This approach will lead to simpler solutions compared to attempts to solve the general-case scenarios, which would now be even bulkier than they were in chapter 4. We'll start with the task of figuring out which of the two possible quantum gates you were given and solve several example problems for it. Then, we'll switch gears to an algorithm that learns the matrix representation of an unknown single-qubit gate. Finally, we'll explore several algorithms that solve the phase estimation problem—the task of finding the eigenvalue that corresponds to the given eigenvector of the given unitary gate.

5.1 Distinguishing unitaries

We'll start with a task similar to one of the problems we learned to solve in chapter 4: distinguishing two quantum operations. In this task, you are given an operation and a promise that it is one of the two specific unitaries. Your goal is to figure out which unitary you are given by running some experiments with it and analyzing the results.

When we talked about distinguishing quantum states in chapter 4, we had a clear condition they had to satisfy to make it possible to identify the given state in a single experiment: each pair of the states in the list had to be orthogonal. Now that we're talking about unitaries, there is no such obvious condition. Some pairs of unitaries are easy to distinguish by running a single experiment which includes applying the input unitary or its variant only once. Sometimes you can make do with one experiment but have to apply the unitary several times during it. And sometimes, if the unitaries you want to distinguish are similar enough, you have to run a lot of experiments to gather enough information.

In this section, we'll look at several tasks that can be solved using one experiment each. I'll try to use as few unitary applications as possible for each task we solve, but I won't dig into the mathematical proofs of the results being optimal.

> **TIP** I encourage you to experiment with similar tasks involving different pairs of unitaries that are not as easy to distinguish. Even a set of standard single-qubit gates such as the Pauli gates, the Hadamard gate, and the Ry gate offers plenty of possibilities for exploration!

Let's take a look at some examples of pairs of single-qubit unitaries that are easy to distinguish and see some common approaches to solving this problem.

5.1.1 Math

The general approach to attempting to solve the task of distinguishing two unitaries in a single experiment is shown in figure 5.2. The solution has two main components:

- Choose the initial state and the sequence of unitaries that will convert that initial state to orthogonal states when we use each of the two unitaries we aim to distinguish as a part of that sequence. Then, we can prepare that initial state and implement any additional unitaries using the techniques from chapters 2 and 3, respectively.

  The examples we'll explore in this chapter, though, will be small enough that we won't need the general multiqubit state preparation and unitary implementation routines. We can use simple single- and two-qubit gates instead.

- Figure out a way to distinguish the orthogonal states we obtain as a result of the first step for each of the two unitaries we aim to distinguish. This is exactly what we did in chapter 4, though again, we will need to do this only for very simple states.

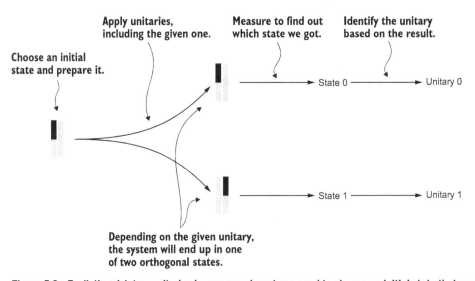

Figure 5.2 To distinguish two unitaries in one experiment, we need to choose an initial state that can be converted to different orthogonal states by applying each of these two unitaries, possibly as part of a longer sequence of unitaries. We then run the experiment by preparing that initial state, applying that sequence of unitaries, and identifying which of the orthogonal states we got using measurements.

Let's see how this approach works for several simple examples.

X OR Z?

In the first example, we are given a single-qubit gate, and we need to decide whether it is the X gate or the Z gate. We know that the X gate flips the basis states it acts on, transforming $|0\rangle$ to $|1\rangle$ and vice versa, and the Z gate leaves the basis states unchanged, affecting only the relative phase of the $|1\rangle$ state. This observation leads us to our solution right away:

- We can apply our input gate to the $|0\rangle$ state.
  - If the resulting state is $|0\rangle$, our input gate was the Z gate.
  - If the resulting state is $|1\rangle$, our input gate was the X gate.

- We can distinguish the resulting states by measuring them in the computational basis: measurement results 0 and 1 indicate the input gate being Z or X, respectively.

X OR H?

Can we always find an initial state that we can use to distinguish the given unitaries without using any additional unitaries? Let's think about this in the next example, in which we need to decide whether the given single-qubit gate is the X gate or the H gate.

Can we find an initial state $|\psi\rangle = \alpha |0\rangle + \beta |1\rangle$ that will be converted to orthogonal states by applying each of the given gates? For this to work, the states we get after applying our unitaries to this state $X|\psi\rangle$ and $H|\psi\rangle$ have to be orthogonal:

$$X|\psi\rangle = \beta |0\rangle + \alpha |1\rangle$$
$$H|\psi\rangle = \tfrac{1}{\sqrt{2}}(\alpha + \beta)|0\rangle + \tfrac{1}{\sqrt{2}}(\alpha - \beta)|1\rangle$$

We can check whether these states are orthogonal by writing their inner product. This product will look as follows (here, we rely on the fact that $|\psi\rangle$ is a quantum state and thus its norm $\alpha\alpha^* + \beta\beta^*$ is 1 to simplify the result):

$$\langle\psi|XH|\psi\rangle = \tfrac{1}{\sqrt{2}}\beta^*(\alpha+\beta) + \tfrac{1}{\sqrt{2}}\alpha^*(\alpha-\beta) = \tfrac{1}{\sqrt{2}}(\underbrace{\alpha\alpha^* + \beta\beta^*}_{=1} + \alpha\beta^* - \alpha^*\beta)$$

For the states $X|\psi\rangle$ and $H|\psi\rangle$ to be orthogonal, their inner product should equal 0. This leads us to the following equation:

$$\alpha\beta^* - (\alpha\beta^*)^* = -1$$

This equation, however, doesn't have a solution, since the difference between a complex number $\alpha\beta^*$ and its conjugate is either a complex number or 0 and cannot be equal to -1.

Does this mean that we cannot solve this task in a single experiment? Turns out that we can, as long as we apply the unitary we're given more than once during that experiment! We can use the Hadamard gate to switch between the computational basis and the Hadamard basis, and as part of that switch, it can convert the X gate into the Z gate and vice versa. With that in mind, let's consider the following sequence of gates: our input unitary—the X gate—our input unitary again:

- If our input unitary is X, this triplet of gates becomes $XXX = X$.
- If our input unitary is H, this triplet becomes $HXH = Z$.

We can solve our problem by distinguishing X and Z gates, which we learned to do earlier in the chapter. To do this, we start with a qubit in the $|0\rangle$ state; apply our input unitary, the X gate, and our input unitary again; and measure the qubit. Measurement results 0 and 1 point to the input gate being H and X, respectively.

X OR -X?

Can we always solve this kind of tasks by applying only the input unitary and some other gates, using only as many qubits as the input unitary itself acts upon? We'll think about this question in the next example, in which we need to decide whether the given single-qubit gate is the X gate or the $-X$ gate. The $-X$ gate is a gate that acts as the X gate but additionally multiplies the resulting state by the global phase of -1.

Remember that the global phase of a quantum state is not observable, since it doesn't affect the outcomes of any measurements that can be done on this state. Consequently, if we use only one qubit, we can't figure out whether the input gate is the X gate on its own or whether it introduces the additional global phase to the state.

We can, however, detect this additional global phase using the controlled variant of the input gate. Table 5.1 shows the effects of the controlled X and controlled $-X$ gates on all two-qubit basis states, with the first qubit as control and the second qubit as target.

Table 5.1 Effects of controlled X and controlled $-X$ gates on two-qubit basis states

The basis state	After applying controlled X	After applying controlled $-X$
$|00\rangle$	$|00\rangle$	$|00\rangle$
$|01\rangle$	$|01\rangle$	$|01\rangle$
$|10\rangle$	$|11\rangle$	$-|11\rangle$
$|11\rangle$	$|10\rangle$	$-|10\rangle$

You can see that if we apply the controlled variant of the input gate to any one of the basis states, we still can't detect the phase this basis state might have acquired. But some basis states acquire the phase, and some don't. This means that if we apply the controlled unitary to the right superposition state, the phase becomes relative rather than global, and it can be detected! We just need to decide which superposition state to use as the input to make detecting the relative phase easy.

The simplest input state we can use is an even superposition of all four basis states, $|++\rangle = \frac{1}{2}(|0\rangle + |1\rangle)(|0\rangle + |1\rangle)$. It can be prepared by applying an H gate to both qubits. Indeed, when we apply the controlled variant of the input unitary to this state with the first qubit as control and the second qubit as the target, we get the following results:

- If our input unitary is X, applying controlled X to this state doesn't change it.
- If our input unitary is $-X$, applying controlled X to this state changes it to $\frac{1}{2}(|0\rangle - |1\rangle)(|0\rangle + |1\rangle)$, since both basis states that have the first (control) qubit in the $|1\rangle$ state acquire the relative phase -1. This effect is called *phase kickback*—the fact that controlled operations can change the state of their control qubits, not only of their target qubits, by changing the relative phase of some basis states.

After applying the controlled variant of our input unitary we need to check the state of the first qubit: if it is $|+\rangle$, our gate is X, and if it is $|-\rangle$, our gate is $-X$.

How did we select this state to use as the input? The control qubit has to be in a superposition state to allow us to convert the global phase introduced by applying the gate to the second qubit into a relative phase. The states $|+\rangle$ and $|-\rangle$ are the most convenient ones to use on the control qubit to detect the -1 phase introduced on one of the basis vectors, since they are two orthogonal states that differ by a relative phase of -1. If we used a different superposition state for the control qubit, such as $0.6|0\rangle + 0.8|1\rangle$, the relative phase -1 would convert it into a state $0.6|0\rangle - 0.8|1\rangle$ that is not orthogonal to the original state. In this case, we would need multiple experiments to figure out whether a relative phase was introduced, as we discussed in section 4.4.

The target qubit has to be in a state that doesn't change when the gate is applied besides getting multiplied by a global phase. Such states are called *eigenstates* of the gate, and we'll talk a lot more about them later in this chapter. For the X and $-X$ gates, we see that $|+\rangle$ and $|-\rangle$ are such states.

> **TIP** The phase kickback trick can be applied in other scenarios as well: whenever we need to detect a global or relative phase introduced by a gate or to use it in computations. We will learn more about it in section 5.3.1 and then again in chapter 7, when we use it to implement the quantum oracle for Grover's search algorithm. In particular, we'll talk more about the choices of the states that are the best inputs to algorithms that detect the introduced phase.

We cannot always solve this kind of problems in a single shot, the way we could do for these three examples. Generally, we need to find states that are converted into states that are as different as possible by applying the input unitaries (or their variants) and then run the experiment loop multiple times and analyze the aggregated statistics, similar to what we did in section 4.4. The closer the resulting states are to being orthogonal, the easier it is to distinguish them. We will see an example of how to do this in the next section, where we'll need to distinguish between two unitaries as part of the unitary reconstruction problem.

Testing these solutions is very similar to how we tested the code that distinguished quantum states in chapter 4. The test for each pair of unitaries needs to select one of the two unitaries at random, pass it to the solution, and check that the solution identifies the input unitary correctly. The main difference is the type of the input to the solution: instead of qubits in the input state (for Q#) or circuits that prepare the necessary state (for Qiskit), we pass it quantum operations (Q#) or circuits that apply them (Qiskit). Let's see how to implement these solutions as code.

5.1.2 Qiskit

For Qiskit, the code written to solve the problem has an extra requirement. Qiskit circuits cannot do any classical decision-making steps based on the measurement outcomes: the result of a circuit execution is a measurement result or several, not an arbitrary return value like in Q#. Consequently, the measurement outcomes 0 and 1 have to correspond to the first and second unitaries in the pair of unitaries being distinguished, respectively. If we chose the input state and the sequence of gates applied to it so that the first unitary maps the state to $|1\rangle$ and the second unitary maps it to $|0\rangle$, we'll need to switch these states right before doing the final measurement by applying the X gate (you'll see this in the code for the first two tasks). Alternatively, we can keep the circuit as is and take this mapping into account when analyzing the circuit execution results later, in the classical code. Q# code can calculate the index of the unitary based on the measurement outcome, so you won't see those extra X gates applied in Q# solutions.

Listing 5.1 shows the Qiskit code that solves three examples of distinguishing the unitaries problem discussed in this section.

Listing 5.1 Qiskit code to distinguish three pairs of unitaries

```
from qiskit import QuantumCircuit

def distinguish_x_z(unitary_circ):
  circ = QuantumCircuit(1, 1)
  circ.append(unitary_circ, [0])
  circ.x(0)
  circ.measure(0, 0)
  return circ

def distinguish_x_h(unitary_circ):
  circ = QuantumCircuit(1, 1)
  circ.append(unitary_circ, [0])
  circ.x(0)
  circ.append(unitary_circ, [0])
  circ.x(0)
  circ.measure(0, 0)
  return circ

def distinguish_x_minusx(unitary_circ):
  circ = QuantumCircuit(2, 1)
  circ.h(0)
  circ.h(1)
  circ.append(unitary_circ.to_gate().control(1), [0, 1])
  circ.h(0)
  circ.h(1)
  circ.measure(0, 0)
  return circ
```

The complete test code for these solutions is included in the GitHub repository. The results of running the whole project should be three passing tests, one per pair of unitaries we want to distinguish.

5.1.3 Q#

Listing 5.2 shows the Q# code that solves three examples of distinguishing the unitaries problem discussed in this section. You can see that this code includes only the steps described in the mathematical solution, without the extra X gates needed in Qiskit.

> **Listing 5.2   Q# code to distinguish three pairs of unitaries**

```
operation DistinguishXZ(gate : Qubit => Unit is Adj+Ctl) : Int {
  use q = Qubit();
  gate(q);
  return MResetZ(q) == One ? 0 | 1;
}
operation DistinguishXH(gate : Qubit => Unit is Adj+Ctl) : Int {
  use q = Qubit();
  gate(q);
  X(q);
  gate(q);
  return MResetZ(q) == One ? 0 | 1;
}
operation DistinguishXMinusX(gate : Qubit => Unit is Adj+Ctl) : Int {
  use qs = Qubit[2];
  H(qs[0]);
  H(qs[1]);
  Controlled gate([qs[0]], qs[1]);
  H(qs[0]);
  H(qs[1]);
  return MResetZ(qs[0]) == Zero ? 0 | 1;
}
```

The complete test code for these solutions is included in the GitHub repository. The results of running the whole project should be three passing tests, one per pair of input unitaries.

5.2   Reconstructing the unitary

Let's now consider a more challenging task: given an unknown unitary operation, find out what unitary it is. More specifically, you are given an operation that applies a single-qubit gate to a qubit, and you need to reconstruct its matrix representation U. For simplicity, we'll limit the problem to unitary gates with real-valued matrices and assume that the top-left element of the matrix is nonnegative.

> **NOTE**   The more general case of this problem is called *quantum process tomography*. In this problem, you aim to reconstruct the description of a given process. In general, this process can be more complicated than just a unitary transformation. For example, it can involve choosing a random unitary from the list and applying it, or applying noise of unknown model to the qubits. Here we'll look at the simplest example just to get a feeling for what steps are involved in solving this type of problems.

5.2.1 Math

As we've seen in section 3.1, the matrix representation of a single-qubit unitary gate can have one of the two following shapes:

$$U_{diag} = \begin{pmatrix} a & b \\ b & -a \end{pmatrix} \quad \text{or} \quad U_{antidiag} = \begin{pmatrix} a & -b \\ b & a \end{pmatrix}$$

Here, we denoted $a = \cos \alpha$ and $b = \sin \alpha$. We're not interested in the parameter α like we were in chapter 3, since we're focusing on learning the coefficients of the matrix rather than on finding a way to implement it using rotation gates, and the notation change emphasizes this.

Figure 5.3 shows the two phases of the approach we'll take to reconstruct the unitary, adapting the general flow of the algorithm from figure 5.1 to our specific task.

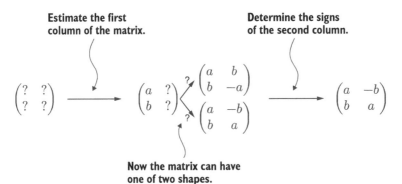

Figure 5.3 Reconstructing a single-qubit unitary from multiple experiments. We start by running a series of experiments to estimate the coefficients in the first column of the matrix and then a second series of different experiments to figure out the relative signs of the coefficients in the second column.

First, we estimate the coefficients a and b in the first column of the matrix we're looking for. The first column of the matrix U describes the amplitudes of the state $U|0\rangle = a|0\rangle + b|1\rangle$ that we can get by applying the given operation to the $|0\rangle$ state. We can estimate these amplitudes—both their absolute values and their relative sign—using the state tomography code we implemented in section 4.5.

Second, we need to figure out which of the scenarios we're looking at—a diagonal matrix (elements off the main diagonal have the same sign) or an antidiagonal matrix (elements off the main diagonal have opposite signs). To determine the scenario, let's consider the effects of the diagonal and antidiagonal matrices when they are applied to a qubit in the state $a|0\rangle + b|1\rangle$:

> **NOTE** Conveniently, we don't need to use our estimates of a and b from the first step to prepare this state! Instead, we can prepare it exactly by applying our given unitary U to the state $|0\rangle$.

$$U_{diag}(a\,|0\rangle + b\,|1\rangle) = a(a\,|0\rangle + b\,|1\rangle) + b(b\,|0\rangle - a\,|1\rangle)$$
$$= (a^2 + b^2)\,|0\rangle + (ab - ba)\,|1\rangle = |0\rangle$$
$$U_{antidiag}(a\,|0\rangle + b\,|1\rangle) = a(a\,|0\rangle + b\,|1\rangle) + b(-b\,|0\rangle + a\,|1\rangle)$$
$$= (a^2 - b^2)\,|0\rangle + 2ab\,|1\rangle$$

We can decide whether our given unitary is more likely to have a diagonal matrix or an antidiagonal matrix by applying it to the state $a\,|0\rangle + b\,|1\rangle$ and deciding whether the resulting state is more likely to be $|0\rangle$ (which corresponds to the diagonal matrix) or $(a^2 - b^2)\,|0\rangle + 2ab\,|1\rangle$ (the antidiagonal matrix). And this turns out to be exactly the problem of distinguishing nonorthogonal states that we've solved in section 4.4! The only difference with the problem we considered in section 4.4 is that the amplitude $2ab$ of the basis state $|1\rangle$ of the second state might be negative. We can account for this either by flipping the sign of the basis state $|1\rangle$ in the state we prepare before measuring it or by modifying the math we did to decide on the measurement to perform. The first approach turns out to be easier—just apply a Z gate to the state if b is negative.

These two steps, put together, let you reconstruct the matrix of the unitary you are given. The more experiments you run, the better your estimate will end up. Similarly to the state tomography problem from section 4.5, matrices that have some coefficients with very small absolute values take more experiments to reconstruct accurately compared to matrices in which all coefficients have roughly the same order of magnitude.

NOTE This solution is an excellent illustration of how the basic problems you learn to solve become tools that come in handy again and again. The more you practice solving these kinds of tasks, the larger and more versatile your toolbox becomes!

5.2.2 Qiskit

Listing 5.3 shows the Qiskit code that reconstructs the matrix representation of a given single-qubit unitary. It reuses the function reconstruct_state from listing 4.11.

Listing 5.3 Qiskit code to reconstruct the matrix of a unitary

```
from math import atan2, pi, sqrt
from qiskit import QuantumCircuit, transpile
from qiskit_aer import AerSimulator

simulator = AerSimulator(method='statevector')

def reconstruct_unitary(gate):
    (a, b) = reconstruct_state(gate)

    circ = QuantumCircuit(1, 1)
```

Step 1: Reconstruct the first column of the matrix.

Step 2: Figure out the relative sign of the second column.

```
circ.append(gate, [0])    ← Prepares the state a|0> + b|1> using the unitary itself
circ.append(gate, [0])    ← Applies the unitary again
if b < 0:                 ← Makes sure the amplitude of |1> is not negative
  circ.z(0)

theta = atan2(2 * a * abs(b), a * a - b * b) / 2
circ.ry(- 2 * (theta - pi / 4), [0])
circ.measure(0, 0)                                    ⎤ Decides which of the
circ = transpile(circ, backend=simulator)             ⎬ states this likely is to
                                                      ⎦ figure out the relative sign
n_trials = 200
res_map = simulator.run(circ, shots=n_trials).result().get_counts()
if '0' in res_map and 2 * res_map['0'] > n_trials:
  return [[a, b], [b, -a]]
else:
  return [[a, -b], [-b, a]]
```

You can find the complete project, including the test for this operation, in the GitHub repository. Running the project should result in passing tests.

5.2.3 Q#

Listing 5.4 shows the Q# code that reconstructs the matrix representation of a given single-qubit unitary. It reuses the operation `ReconstructState` from listing 4.12.

Listing 5.4 Q# code to reconstruct the matrix of a unitary

```
import Std.Convert.IntAsDouble;
import Std.Math.*;

operation ReconstructUnitary(gate : Qubit => Unit) : Double[][] {
  let (a, b) = ReconstructState(gate);    ⎤ Step 1: Reconstruct the first
                                          ⎦ column of the matrix.
  let nTrials = 200;        ⎤ Step 2: Figure out the relative
  mutable nZeros = 0;       ⎦ sign of the second column.
  for _ in 1 .. nTrials {
    use q = Qubit();
    gate(q);    ← Prepares the state a|0> + b|1> using the unitary itself
    gate(q);    ← Applies the unitary again
    if b < 0. {       ⎤ Makes sure the amplitude
      Z(q);           ⎦ of |1> is not negative
    }
    let theta = ArcTan2(2. * a * AbsD(b), a * a - b * b) / 2.;
    Ry(- 2. * (theta - PI() / 4.), q);
    if MResetZ(q) == Zero {                        ⎤ Decides which of the states
      set nZeros += 1;                             ⎬ this likely is to figure out
    }                                              ⎦ the relative sign
  }
  return 2 * nZeros > nTrials ? [[a, b], [b, -a]] | [[a, -b], [b, a]];
}
```

You can find the complete project, including the test for this operation, in the GitHub repository. Running the project should result in passing tests.

5.3 Finding eigenvalue of the given eigenvector: The phase estimation problem

The last problem we'll discuss in this chapter is a key building block of multiple quantum algorithms. Unlike the first two tasks we solved in this chapter, it does not aim to identify the given unitary itself but rather to estimate its numerical properties. Before I define the problem itself, let me introduce several new concepts, illustrated in figure 5.4, and show several examples.

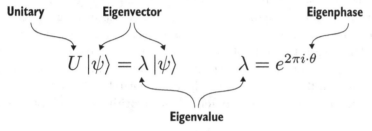

Figure 5.4 An eigenvector of a unitary is a vector that is multiplied by a scalar when this unitary is applied to it. This scalar is called the eigenvalue. An eigenvalue of a unitary can only be a complex number with absolute value 1, so it can be represented as an exponent using the real-valued eigenphase.

An *eigenvector* of a unitary transformation U, sometimes called an *eigenstate*, is a quantum state $|\psi\rangle$ that, when this unitary is applied to it, is only multiplied by a global phase and remains unchanged otherwise. For example, consider the Z gate: it has two eigenvectors, $|0\rangle$ and $|1\rangle$, since $Z|0\rangle = |0\rangle$ and $Z|1\rangle = -|1\rangle$.

> **NOTE** Of course, any quantum states that differ from one of these eigenvectors by a global phase, such as $-|0\rangle$ or $i|1\rangle$, are also eigenvectors of the Z gate. It is common to use the simplest possible quantum state to represent the class of eigenvectors that differ from each other by a global phase, usually states with real amplitudes.

The global phase by which an eigenvector is multiplied as a result of applying the unitary is called the *eigenvalue* that corresponds to that eigenvector. In the Z gate example, the eigenvalues that correspond to eigenvectors $|0\rangle$ and $|1\rangle$ are 1 and -1, respectively.

Since the transformations we're considering in quantum computing are unitary and thus preserve the norm of the vectors they act upon, we know that any eigenvalues we encounter have to be complex or real numbers with absolute value equal to 1. As a result, we can write any eigenvalue λ as $\lambda = e^{2\pi i \cdot \theta}$, where θ is a real number between 0 and 1. The number θ is the *eigenphase* that corresponds to the eigenvector. For the Z gate, the eigenphases that correspond to eigenvectors $|0\rangle$ and $|1\rangle$ are 0 and 0.5, respectively, since $e^{2\pi i \cdot 0} = 1$ and $e^{2\pi i \cdot 0.5} = e^{\pi i} = -1$.

Now that we're familiar with the concepts of eigenvectors, eigenvalues, and eigenphases, we can finally define the problem we aim to solve. You are given a unitary transformation U and one of its eigenvectors $|\psi\rangle$. These inputs are given as quantum operations that you can use to apply the unitary U and to prepare the state $|\psi\rangle$ instead of their matrix and vector representations that you could analyze mathematically. You need to find the eigenphase that corresponds to the eigenvector $|\psi\rangle$.

Formulating the phase estimation task in terms of eigenphases and not eigenvalues is customary. These two descriptions are equivalent, but the applications of this problem usually rely on the value of the real phase rather than the complex eigenvalue.

NOTE Phase estimation problem is an important part of several quantum algorithms, including Shor's algorithm for integer factorization, quantum counting algorithm that estimates the number of solutions to the given search problem, and the HHL algorithm for solving a system of linear equations. In each of them, the input problem is converted into a unitary transformation and its eigenvector, and the corresponding eigenphase can be used to calculate the answer to the problem. Unfortunately, these algorithms are out of scope for this book.

Before we start thinking about solving this task, let's list several examples of unitaries and eigenvector–eigenphase pairs (table 5.2) that we'll use to walk through the math of our solutions and then to test our code.

Table 5.2 Unitaries, their eigenvectors, and corresponding eigenphases with different values of phase

Unitary U	Eigenvector $|\phi\rangle$	Eigenvalue	Eigenphase (decimal)	Eigenphase (binary)
$Z = \begin{pmatrix} 1 & 0 \\ 0 & -1 \end{pmatrix}$	$|0\rangle$	1	0.0	0.0
	$|1\rangle$	-1	0.5	0.1
$INC = \begin{pmatrix} 0 & 0 & 0 & 1 \\ 1 & 0 & 0 & 0 \\ 0 & 1 & 0 & 0 \\ 0 & 0 & 1 & 0 \end{pmatrix}$	$\frac{1}{2}(|0\rangle + |1\rangle + |2\rangle + |3\rangle)$	1	0.0	0.00
	$\frac{1}{2}(|0\rangle - |1\rangle + |2\rangle - |3\rangle)$	-1	0.5	0.10
	$\frac{1}{2}(|0\rangle - i|1\rangle - |2\rangle + i|3\rangle)$	i	0.25	0.01
	$\frac{1}{2}(|0\rangle + i|1\rangle - |2\rangle - i|3\rangle)$	$-i$	0.75	0.11
$T = \begin{pmatrix} 1 & 0 \\ 0 & e^{i\pi/4} \end{pmatrix}$	$|0\rangle$	1	0.0	0.000
	$|1\rangle$	$e^{i\pi/4}$	0.125	0.001

The unitaries Z, INC, and T have eigenphases that require one, two, and three bits of precision, respectively, to represent their eigenphases in binary. Z and T gates are called *phase shift gates*—gates that don't change the $|0\rangle$ state but multiply the $|1\rangle$ state by a relative phase—in this case, -1 and $e^{i\pi/4}$, respectively. Another phase shift gate, the S gate, is commonly used to illustrate phase estimation for phases with two bits of precision, but it only has two different eigenvalues, 1 and $e^{i\pi/2}$. I wanted to use a unitary with all four possible two-bit eigenphases corresponding to four different eigenvectors, which requires a gate to act on two or more qubits. For this reason, I chose INC—a unitary that increments a two-bit integer modulo 4. It has the following effect on the basis states:

$$|0\rangle \to |1\rangle, |1\rangle \to |2\rangle, |2\rangle \to |3\rangle, |3\rangle \to |0\rangle$$

> **Verifying that a state is an eigenvector of the unitary**
>
> How can we check that these states are indeed eigenvectors of these unitaries?
>
> Mathematically, we can calculate the result of applying each unitary to each eigenvector and verify that it matches the result of multiplying this eigenvector by the corresponding eigenvalue. For example, to verify that the second eigenvector of the unitary INC has eigenvalue -1, we apply the unitary INC to it:
>
> $$INC \tfrac{1}{2}(|0\rangle - |1\rangle + |2\rangle - |3\rangle) = \tfrac{1}{2}(|1\rangle - |2\rangle + |3\rangle - |0\rangle)$$
>
> Then we verify that the result is, indeed, $(-1) \cdot \tfrac{1}{2}(|0\rangle - |1\rangle + |2\rangle - |3\rangle)$.
>
> In our code, we can use a technique similar to that we saw in the test code for chapter 2: prepare a qubit register in the state that is the eigenvector of the unitary, apply the unitary to this register, and check that the resulting state vector matches the result of multiplying the eigenvector by the eigenvalue.
>
> Alternatively, we can prepare the eigenvector and apply a unitary and then apply the adjoint of the procedure we used to prepare the eigenvector. The resulting state should be the $|0\rangle$ state (up to a global phase). This approach, however, doesn't allow us to verify the eigenvalue associated with this eigenvector, just that this state is an eigenvector. You can see the implementation of this approach in the tests I wrote for this section in the GitHub repository.

The phase estimation problem has a plethora of ways to approach solving it. I'll introduce three algorithms that represent different classes of quantum algorithms, not just slight variations of the same algorithm, and are each interesting in their own way:

- The iterative phase estimation algorithm (section 5.3.2) runs the same circuit multiple times and estimates the answer based on the evaluated probability distribution of the outcomes.
- The quantum phase estimation algorithm (section 5.3.5) obtains the answer from the most likely outcome of running a circuit.
- Adaptive phase estimation algorithms (section 5.3.3) learn the answer piece by piece, adjusting the program they execute on the go based on the parts of the answer they already learned.

NOTE Sometimes you'll see the last class of algorithms referred to as "iterative phase estimation." I prefer the terms "iterative" and "adaptive" to emphasize the difference between *iterating* over the same circuit multiple times and *adapting* the circuit on the later steps based on the information learned earlier.

Before we proceed to learning these algorithms, let's take a closer look at the common principle on which they're all built, known as the *phase kickback trick*.

5.3.1 Phase kickback

All phase estimation algorithms rely on the same technique—the phase kickback trick we've seen in section 5.1. It makes use of the fact that applying the controlled version of a unitary can "kick" a relative phase back to the control qubit instead of changing the state of the target qubit. Figure 5.5 shows the structure of the phase kickback trick as used in phase estimation algorithms.

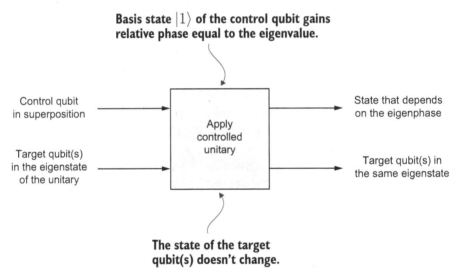

Figure 5.5 To use the phase kickback trick for phase estimation, we need a control qubit in a superposition state (the $|+\rangle$ state is commonly used) and a target register of qubits in the state that is an eigenvector of the unitary we're exploring. When we apply the controlled variant of this unitary, the target register remains unchanged, but the control qubit acquires a relative phase on the basis state $|1\rangle$. This relative phase can be analyzed to extract information about the eigenphase that corresponds to the eigenvector.

Let's see how the phase kickback trick allows us to get information about the eigenphase that corresponds to the given eigenvector. We'll use the Z gate and its two eigenvectors as the simplest example of a phase estimation problem that we can solve with a single measurement:

- We start with two qubits: the control qubit in the state $|+\rangle = \frac{1}{\sqrt{2}}(|0\rangle + |1\rangle)$ and the target qubit in the eigenstate—either the $|0\rangle$ or $|1\rangle$ state.
- When we apply the controlled Z gate, one of the following scenarios happens:
  - If the eigenvector we used was $|0\rangle$, the state of the system remains $\frac{1}{\sqrt{2}}(|0\rangle + |1\rangle) \otimes |0\rangle$, since the Z gate has no effect on the $|0\rangle$ state.
  - However, if the eigenvector we used was $|1\rangle$, the state of the system becomes $\frac{1}{\sqrt{2}}(|0\rangle - |1\rangle) \otimes |1\rangle$, since the Z gate flips the sign of the $|1\rangle$ state, and this only happens to the basis state in which the control qubit is $|1\rangle$.

5.3 Finding eigenvalue of the given eigenvector: The phase estimation problem

- We see that depending on the value of the eigenvalue that corresponds to the eigenvector we used (+1 for $|0\rangle$ or −1 for $|1\rangle$) the state of the control qubit either remains $|+\rangle$ or becomes $|-\rangle$. At the same time, the state of the target qubit doesn't change, and the target qubit remains unentangled with the control qubit.
- We can figure out whether the eigenvalue that corresponds to the given eigenvector is +1 or −1 by measuring the control qubit to find out whether it ended up in the $|+\rangle$ or $|-\rangle$ state after the application of the controlled Z gate.

This example shows how to learn the eigenvalue of the unitary, although only in the simplest scenario, in which it is exactly +1 or −1. Nonetheless, it is a great introduction to the phase kickback trick. And now that we're familiar with this trick, we can build more sophisticated phase estimation algorithms on top of it.

5.3.2 Iterative phase estimation

The first algorithm we'll see is *iterative phase estimation*. It follows the pattern shown in figure 5.6.

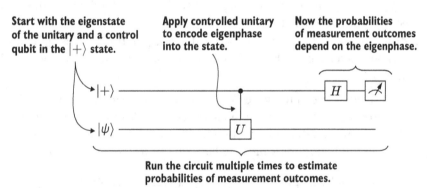

Figure 5.6 In iterative phase estimation, we come up with a fixed quantum circuit that produces measurement outcomes with probabilities that are a function of the eigenphase. The circuit starts with the qubits in a specific state, applies a controlled variant of the unitary to get the information about the eigenphase into the phase of the control qubit and then performs a specific measurement. We run this circuit multiple times, gather enough statistics about the measurement outcomes to estimate the probabilities of measurement outcomes, and calculate the eigenphase from them.

In the iterative phase estimation algorithm,

1. We start by finding a quantum circuit that uses the eigenvector of our unitary and an additional control qubit. This circuit applies a controlled variant of the unitary to extract information about the corresponding eigenphase and encode it in the amplitudes of the state of the control qubit. Finally, it measures the control qubit.
2. We run this circuit multiple times, enough to estimate the probabilities of different measurement outcomes. These probabilities depend on the information about the eigenphase that was encoded in the amplitudes of the state.

3 Finally, we estimate the eigenphase from the probabilities of the measurement outcomes we obtained experimentally.

Let's see what the algorithm looks like and what information phase kickback encodes in the state of the control qubit if the eigenphase of the eigenvector is not 0 or 0.5 but an arbitrary real number θ between 0 and 1:

1 As in the previous example, we start with the control qubit in the state $\frac{1}{\sqrt{2}}(|0\rangle + |1\rangle)$ and the target qubit or qubit register in the state $|\psi\rangle$ that is an eigenvector of the unitary U with eigenphase θ:

$$\tfrac{1}{\sqrt{2}}(|0\rangle + |1\rangle) \otimes |\psi\rangle$$

2 We apply the controlled U gate to the qubits, which leads to the eigenvalue $e^{2\pi i \cdot \theta}$ being kicked back as the relative phase of the basis state $|1\rangle$ of the control qubit:

$$\tfrac{1}{\sqrt{2}}|0\rangle |\psi\rangle + \tfrac{1}{\sqrt{2}}|1\rangle U |\psi\rangle = \tfrac{1}{\sqrt{2}}(|0\rangle + e^{2\pi i \cdot \theta}|1\rangle) \otimes |\psi\rangle$$

The target qubits are not entangled with the control qubit after this, so we can safely ignore their state.

3 If we measure the control qubit in the computational basis right now, we'll get 50% chance of each outcome, since the absolute values of both amplitudes are $\frac{1}{\sqrt{2}}$.

Instead, we need to figure out a way to change the state of the control qubit to make the probabilities of the measurement outcomes depend on the value θ. This way, we can determine θ by analyzing the measurement outcomes we get. We can do that by applying a Hadamard gate to the control qubit:

$$H\tfrac{1}{\sqrt{2}}(|0\rangle + e^{2\pi i \cdot \theta}|1\rangle) = \tfrac{1}{\sqrt{2}}\left(\tfrac{1}{\sqrt{2}}(|0\rangle + |1\rangle) + \tfrac{1}{\sqrt{2}}e^{2\pi i \cdot \theta}(|0\rangle - |1\rangle)\right)$$
$$= \tfrac{1}{2}(1 + e^{2\pi i \cdot \theta})|0\rangle + \tfrac{1}{2}(1 - e^{2\pi i \cdot \theta})|1\rangle$$

What is the probability of getting the result 0 when measuring the control qubit now? It's the absolute value of the amplitude of $|0\rangle$, squared, which we can rewrite using Euler's formula $e^{i\gamma} = \cos\gamma + i\sin\gamma$ as follows:

$$P(meas = 0) = \tfrac{1}{4}|1 + e^{2\pi i \cdot \theta}|^2 = \tfrac{1}{4}|1 + \cos 2\pi\theta + i\sin 2\pi\theta|^2$$
$$= \tfrac{1}{4}\left((1 + \cos 2\pi\theta)^2 + (\sin 2\pi\theta)^2\right) = \tfrac{1}{4}\left(1 + 2\cos 2\pi\theta + \cos^2 2\pi\theta + \sin^2 2\pi\theta\right)$$

Now, we rewrite this expression using trigonometric identities $\cos^2\alpha + \sin^2\alpha = 1$ and $1 + \cos 2\alpha = 2\cos^2\alpha$:

$$P(meas = 0) = \tfrac{1}{4}(1 + 2\cos 2\pi\theta + 1) = \tfrac{1}{2}(1 + \cos 2\pi\theta) = \cos^2 \pi\theta$$

4 If we run the described circuit N times and we get the measurement outcome 0 N_0 times of them, we can approximate the probability of measuring 0 as $\frac{N_0}{N}$.

This allows us to estimate the cosine of $\pi\theta$ and, finally, the eigenphase we're looking for:

$$\cos^2 \pi\theta \approx \frac{N_0}{N}$$

$$\theta \approx \frac{1}{\pi} \arccos \sqrt{\frac{N_0}{N}}$$

We can validate this solution by checking it on the two cases we've already seen when exploring the phase kickback trick:

- For the Z gate and its eigenvector $|0\rangle$, the state of the control qubit before and after applying the Hadamard gate is $|+\rangle$ and $|0\rangle$, respectively, so the probability of measuring 0 in the end is 1. The estimated phase we get from this probability is $\frac{1}{\pi} \arccos 1 = 0$, which matches the eigenvalue $+1$ we know this eigenvector to have.
- Similarly, for the Z gate and its eigenvector $|1\rangle$, the state of the control qubit after applying the Hadamard gate is $|1\rangle$, the probability of measuring 0 is 0, the estimated phase is $\frac{1}{\pi} \arccos 0 = 0.5$, which matches the known eigenvalue -1.

The downside of this method is that it doesn't allow us to estimate phases between 0.5 and 1 because the arccosine of a nonnegative value is always between 0 and $\frac{\pi}{2}$. If we know our phase can lie in that interval, we need to estimate its most significant bit differently. I won't spend time modifying this algorithm to account for this scenario, since we have more interesting algorithms ahead of us that will handle this case easily.

5.3.3 Adaptive phase estimation

The next algorithm I'll show you is one of the group of *adaptive phase estimation* algorithms. It takes a different approach, and figure 5.7 shows how to apply it to learn eigenphases with two binary bits of precision, such as 0.25 and 0.75.

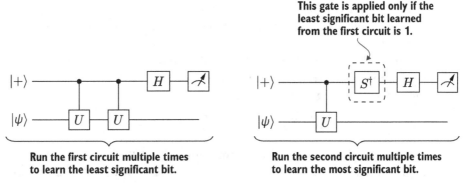

Figure 5.7 In adaptive phase estimation, we learn the phase one binary digit at a time. We start by running a circuit that allows us to learn the least significant binary digit. After this, we use a different circuit, parts of which depend on the information we've discovered so far, to learn the second least significant binary digit. If there are more digits to learn, the process is repeated, with different circuits for each digit.

In the adaptive phase estimation algorithm, we learn the information about the phase in pieces, one binary digit at a time, adjusting the circuit we use for learning the subsequent digits based on the digits we learned previously (thus the name "adaptive"):

1. We start by learning the least significant binary digit by running a fixed circuit multiple times and analyzing the statistics of measurement results.
2. Then, we learn the second least significant digit by running a circuit that depends on the value of the least significant digit.
3. We repeat the process for each digit we need to learn, ending with the most significant digit. For each one, the circuit we use to learn it depends on all the information we learned about the less significant digits.

NOTE This algorithm an example of a broader class of *adaptive quantum algorithms*. These algorithms perform their task by running a series of circuits, learning some information from the results of running each circuit, and modifying the circuits executed afterward based on the information learned so far.

Let's see what the circuits used on each step of adaptive phase estimation algorithm look like. We'll focus on eigenphases that can be represented as a binary fraction with exactly two binary digits, such as the eigenphases of the unitary INC (see table 5.2), to simplify our analysis. In other words, we'll assume that the eigenphase is a multiple of $\frac{1}{4}$.

To start, let's write the eigenphase θ of the unitary U that corresponds to the eigenvector $|\psi\rangle$ as a binary fraction with exactly two binary digits, θ_1 and θ_2:

$$\theta = 0.\overline{\theta_1 \theta_2} = \theta_1 \cdot \tfrac{1}{2} + \theta_2 \cdot \tfrac{1}{4}$$

How can we use phase kickback trick to isolate just the information about the least significant digit θ_2 from the rest of the phase? Let's see what happens if we use phase kickback just like before, starting with the control qubit in the state $\frac{1}{\sqrt{2}}(|0\rangle + |1\rangle)$ and the target qubit(s) in the state $|\psi\rangle$, but apply the controlled U twice instead of just once.

The $|1\rangle$ basis state of the control qubit is multiplied by the eigenvalue each time the controlled U gate is applied. After two applications, it will end up multiplied by the *square* of the eigenvalue $e^{2\pi i \cdot \theta}$:

$$\left(e^{2\pi i \cdot \theta}\right)^2 = e^{4\pi i \cdot \theta} = e^{4\pi i \cdot \left(\theta_1 \cdot \frac{1}{2} + \theta_2 \cdot \frac{1}{4}\right)} = e^{2\pi i \cdot \theta_1} \cdot e^{\pi i \cdot \theta_2}$$

Since θ_1 is a binary digit, 0 or 1, we know that $e^{2\pi i \cdot \theta_1} = 1$, so we can simplify this expression to $e^{\pi i \cdot \theta_2}$. The complete state of the control qubit after applying two controlled U gates will be

$$\tfrac{1}{\sqrt{2}}(|0\rangle + e^{\pi i \cdot \theta_2} |1\rangle)$$

5.3 Finding eigenvalue of the given eigenvector: The phase estimation problem

Now, we can extract information about the value of θ_2 same way we did in the past:
- If $\theta_2 = 0$, the control qubit is in the state $\frac{1}{\sqrt{2}}(|0\rangle + |1\rangle)$.
- If $\theta_2 = 1$, the control qubit is in the state $\frac{1}{\sqrt{2}}(|0\rangle + e^{\pi i}|1\rangle) = \frac{1}{\sqrt{2}}(|0\rangle - |1\rangle)$.
- We can apply a Hadamard gate to the control qubit and then measure it to figure out which of these states it is in.

Now that we know the value of the least significant digit θ_2, we can learn the value of the most significant digit θ_1 accurately. To do that, we use the same phase kickback trick, this time with a single controlled U. This will result in a control qubit in the following state:

$$\frac{1}{\sqrt{2}}(|0\rangle + e^{2\pi i \cdot \theta}|1\rangle) = \frac{1}{\sqrt{2}}\left(|0\rangle + e^{2\pi i \cdot \left(\theta_1 \cdot \frac{1}{2} + \theta_2 \cdot \frac{1}{4}\right)}|1\rangle\right) = \frac{1}{\sqrt{2}}\left(|0\rangle + e^{\pi i \cdot \theta_1} \cdot e^{\frac{1}{2}\pi i \cdot \theta_2}|1\rangle\right)$$

Since we know the value of θ_2, we can eliminate its impact on this state:
- If $\theta_2 = 0$, its contribution to the relative phase of $|1\rangle$ is $e^0 = 1$, and we don't need to do anything to eliminate it.
- If $\theta_2 = 1$, its contribution to the relative phase of $|1\rangle$ is $e^{\frac{1}{2}\pi i} = i$. We can eliminate it by applying the $S^\dagger$ gate. As a reminder,

$$S = \begin{pmatrix} 1 & 0 \\ 0 & i \end{pmatrix}, S^\dagger = \begin{pmatrix} 1 & 0 \\ 0 & -i \end{pmatrix}$$

- We decide whether to apply the $S^\dagger$ gate based on the classical value θ_2 that we learned on the previous step, adjusting our circuit using the information we already have.

With this adjustment used after the application of controlled U gate, we are left with the control qubit in the now familiar state

$$\frac{1}{\sqrt{2}}(|0\rangle + e^{\pi i \cdot \theta_1}|1\rangle)$$

Now, we can learn the value of θ_1 as usual, by applying the Hadamard gate and measuring.

To summarize, the complete adaptive phase estimation algorithm for learning an eigenphase with two bits of precision is

1. Learn the least significant bit of the phase θ_2:
   a) Start in the state $|+\rangle|\psi\rangle$.
   b) Apply controlled U gate twice.
   c) Apply the Hadamard gate to the control qubit.
   d) Measure the control qubit to get the bit θ_2.

2. Learn the most significant bit of the phase θ_1:
   a) Start in the state $|+\rangle|\psi\rangle$.
   b) Apply controlled U gate.
   c) If $\theta_2 = 1$, apply the $S^\dagger$ gate to the control qubit.

d) Apply a Hadamard gate to the control qubit.

e) Measure the control qubit to get the bit θ_1.

How do we modify this algorithm to learn the phase with more binary digits of precision? A similar analysis can show that applying increasing powers of controlled U gates allows us to isolate information about less significant digits: we use controlled U to extract θ_1, controlled U^2—θ_2, controlled U^4—θ_3, controlled U^8—θ_4, and so on. Constructing the circuit for learning the k-th digit follows the same principle: use the appropriate power of controlled U to cancel the contribution from the more significant digits $\theta_1...\theta_{k-1}$ in the relative phase kicked back to the control qubit, and then use phase gates to correct the contribution from the less significant digits $\theta_{k+1}...\theta_n$ to that phase.

5.3.4 Quantum Fourier transform

Before we continue to the third and final phase estimation algorithm of this chapter, we need to learn a useful tool that is an important part of this algorithm. *Quantum Fourier transform* (QFT) is the quantum equivalent of the discrete Fourier transform (DFT). QFT performs DFT on the amplitudes of a quantum state, transforming it into another quantum state with amplitudes that are the DFT of the amplitudes of the initial state.

> **Applications of quantum Fourier transform**
>
> Quantum Fourier transform is commonly used in quantum algorithms that rely on identifying hidden patterns in quantum states, such as periodicity of the amplitudes of the quantum state. This is similar to the way discrete Fourier transform allows us to extract frequency information from a signal.
>
> Discrete Fourier transform works by switching between the *time domain*—the signal sampled at fixed intervals of time—and the *frequency domain*—the distribution of different frequency bands in the signal. Being its quantum equivalent, quantum Fourier transform switches between *amplitude encoding*, in which the information is encoded in the absolute values of the amplitudes of the basis states, and *phase encoding*, in which the information is encoded in the phases of the complex numbers that represent the amplitudes.
>
> However, QFT is not used as a way to speed up the classical computation of the DFT. Encoding the input vectors into a quantum state and then extracting the results of the transformation from the amplitudes of another quantum state introduce too much overhead, so such a use of QFT is less efficient than fast Fourier transform.

In this book, I'll use quantum Fourier transform only as a building block for phase estimation. Following the approach I took for discussing adaptive phase estimation, I'll focus on the one- and two-qubit QFT definition and behavior that are necessary for learning phases with one and two bits of precision we're using as an example, and won't dive into the general form of QFT or its implementation for an arbitrary number of qubits.

5.3 Finding eigenvalue of the given eigenvector: The phase estimation problem

Quantum Fourier transform for one qubit is the Hadamard gate: for a basis state $|x\rangle$,

$$QFT |x\rangle = \tfrac{1}{\sqrt{2}} \sum_{k=0}^{1} (-1)^{kx} |k\rangle = \tfrac{1}{\sqrt{2}} (|0\rangle + (-1)^x |1\rangle)$$

For two qubits, quantum Fourier transform takes a slightly more elaborate form: for a basis state $|x\rangle$,

$$QFT |x\rangle = \tfrac{1}{2} \sum_{k=0}^{3} i^{kx} |k\rangle = \tfrac{1}{2} (|0\rangle + i^x |1\rangle + (-1)^x |2\rangle + (-i)^x |3\rangle)$$

How can we implement the two-qubit QFT? To start, we can rewrite this expression as a tensor product of two single-qubit terms:

$$QFT |x\rangle = \tfrac{1}{\sqrt{2}}(|0\rangle + (-1)^x |1\rangle) \otimes \tfrac{1}{\sqrt{2}}(|0\rangle + i^x |1\rangle)$$

Let's write the basis state x as $\overline{x_1 x_2} = 2x_1 + x_2$, where x_1 and x_2 are the most and the least significant digits of x. We can use this notation to rewrite this expression further, using the facts that $(-1)^x = (-1)^{2x_1+x_2} = (-1)^{x_2}$, $-1 = e^{i\pi}$ and $i = e^{\frac{1}{2}i\pi}$:

$$QFT |x\rangle = \tfrac{1}{\sqrt{2}}(|0\rangle + e^{2\pi i \cdot \frac{1}{2} x_2} |1\rangle) \otimes \tfrac{1}{\sqrt{2}}\left(|0\rangle + e^{2\pi i \cdot (\frac{1}{2} x_1 + \frac{1}{4} x_2)} |1\rangle\right)$$

This expression allows us to implement the two-qubit QFT. Let's walk through the implementation, assuming that it acts on an arbitrary basis state x. Since we'll only use quantum gates and no measurements, this implementation will also act correctly on all superposition states due to the linearity of unitary transformations:

1. Start with a basis state $|x\rangle = |x_1\rangle |x_2\rangle$.
2. Apply a Hadamard gate to the first (most significant) qubit:

$$\tfrac{1}{\sqrt{2}}(|0\rangle + (-1)^{x_1} |1\rangle) \otimes |x_2\rangle = \tfrac{1}{\sqrt{2}}\left(|0\rangle + e^{2\pi i \cdot \frac{1}{2} x_1} |1\rangle\right) \otimes |x_2\rangle$$

3. Apply a controlled S gate with the second qubit as control and the first qubit as target to introduce a relative phase $i^{x_2} = e^{\frac{1}{2}\pi i \cdot x_2}$ to the basis state $|1\rangle$ of the first qubit:

$$\tfrac{1}{\sqrt{2}}\left(|0\rangle + e^{2\pi i \cdot (\frac{1}{2} x_1 + \frac{1}{4} x_2)} |1\rangle\right) \otimes |x_2\rangle$$

4. Apply a Hadamard gate to the second (least significant) qubit:

$$\tfrac{1}{\sqrt{2}}\left(|0\rangle + e^{2\pi i \cdot (\frac{1}{2} x_1 + \frac{1}{4} x_2)} |1\rangle\right) \otimes \tfrac{1}{\sqrt{2}}\left(|0\rangle + e^{2\pi i \cdot \frac{1}{2} x_2} |1\rangle\right)$$

5. This expression is exactly the same as $QFT |x\rangle$, but with the order of bits reversed. To fix that, we apply a SWAP gate to the qubits.

The final expression for the effects of the quantum Fourier transform for a two-qubit basis state might look familiar. Indeed, its terms are very similar to the expressions we saw earlier when discussing the effects of phase kickback when applying controlled U gate one time and two times in adaptive phase estimation. With this in mind, let's see how we can use QFT in our final algorithm in this section—quantum phase estimation.

5.3.5 Quantum phase estimation

Quantum phase estimation algorithm takes an approach that is different from both algorithms we've seen so far. Figure 5.8 shows the outline of quantum phase estimation algorithm used to learn the eigenphase with two bits of binary precision.

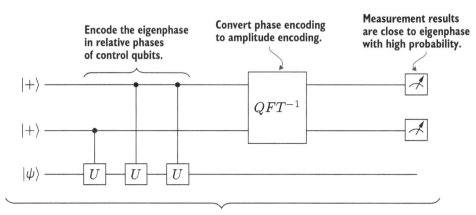

Figure 5.8 In quantum phase estimation algorithm, we use multiple control qubits to encode the information about the eigenphase in phases of their states. Then, we use inverse quantum Fourier transform to convert that information from phase encoding to amplitude encoding, increasing the amplitude of the basis state that encodes the eigenphase compared to the amplitudes of other states. Finally, we measure the control qubits, reading out the bits of the phase as measurement results with high probability.

In the quantum phase estimation algorithm,

1 We use phase kickback to get the information about the eigenphase of the unitary that corresponds to the given eigenvector encoded in the relative phases of the control qubits, similar to the way we did it in other phase estimation algorithms. However, this time we use multiple control qubits, one for every bit of precision we want to get, and encode different information in every control qubit. In this encoding, all basis states of control qubits have equal amplitudes, and the information is stored in the relative phases of the basis states.

2 Next, we convert the information about the eigenphase from phase encoding to amplitude encoding. After this, the basis state that encodes the best approximation of the eigenphase has the largest absolute value in the state of the control qubits, the basis states that encode the next best approximations have smaller absolute values, and so on, with the amplitudes of basis states becoming smaller as they become worse approximations. This can be done using the inverse of quantum Fourier transform.

3   With this encoding in place, reading out the eigenphase from the state of the control qubits becomes easy. We only need to measure them and interpret the measurement results as the notation of a binary fraction—our eigenphase.

Let's see how this process will work out for estimating an eigenphase with exactly two bits of precision. We've already convinced ourselves that the eigenvector of the unitary U remains unchanged when we use it as the target of a controlled U gate, so we'll ignore it when doing the math and focus on the state of the control qubits exclusively. We explored the effect of applying multiple controlled gates to such quantum states in detail when we talked about adaptive phase estimation, so if you need a refresher on that, see section 5.3.3.

The quantum phase estimation algorithm for learning an eigenphase with two bits of precision follows these steps:

   1   Use two additional qubits as the control register, each in the $|+\rangle$ state: $|+\rangle \otimes |+\rangle$.
   2   Apply a controlled U gate with the second qubit as control:

$$|+\rangle \otimes \tfrac{1}{\sqrt{2}} \left(|0\rangle + e^{2\pi i \cdot \left(\theta_1 \cdot \tfrac{1}{2} + \theta_2 \cdot \tfrac{1}{4}\right)} |1\rangle \right)$$

   3   Apply two controlled U gates with the first qubit as control:

$$\tfrac{1}{\sqrt{2}} \left(|0\rangle + e^{2\pi i \cdot \tfrac{1}{2} \theta_2} |1\rangle \right) \otimes \tfrac{1}{\sqrt{2}} \left(|0\rangle + e^{2\pi i \cdot \left(\theta_1 \cdot \tfrac{1}{2} + \theta_2 \cdot \tfrac{1}{4}\right)} |1\rangle \right)$$

   4   The state of these two qubits now is exactly $QFT |\theta\rangle$, so we can apply inverse QFT (the adjoint of the QFT implementation we saw in 5.3.4) to transform it into $|\theta\rangle$.
   5   Measure the state to get the two bits of precision of eigenvalue θ, using big-endian for the notation (first qubit stores the most significant bit).

This is the last of the phase estimation algorithms I wanted to show you in this chapter. Now we can finally write some code to experiment with their implementations!

Comparing phase estimation algorithms

Each of these three algorithms has its pros and cons in terms of efficiency. Iterative phase estimation uses the simplest circuit, so it is the least prone to noise, but it requires a lot of repetitions to estimate the phase with reasonable precision.

Adaptive and quantum phase estimation algorithms also rely on circuit repetition if the eigenphase cannot be represented exactly with the number of bits of precision we chose to work with (or if it can, but we don't know that up front). They require a lot fewer repetitions, though, compared to the iterative algorithm.

Quantum phase estimation requires fewer circuit repetitions compared to adaptive phase estimation, since it seeks the most likely measurement outcome rather than estimates the probabilities of different outcomes. However, the circuit used in quantum phase estimation is much more complicated than the ones used in

(continued)

adaptive phase estimation, with more qubits and much larger circuit depth, so it is a lot more susceptible to noise. In fact, adaptive phase estimation emerged as a way to replace the single run of a large circuit of quantum phase estimation with multiple runs of much smaller circuits, better suited for noisy devices without error correction.

5.3.6 Qiskit

The three algorithms we explored in this section have different mathematical underpinnings, but their implementations end up having a lot in common. To start with, they all solve the same problem based on the same input: the unitary and eigenvector pair and the number of qubits on which this unitary acts. The circuits they use also have similar structure: they all prepare the given eigenvector of the unitary and an additional $|+\rangle$ state on one or two extra qubits and then apply the controlled unitary or several, followed by some extra gates to decode the result and a measurement to read it out.

The complete project code for this section includes implementation of all four phase estimation algorithms we looked at in this section: the one-bit phase estimation algorithm that illustrates the simplest phase kickback and the iterative, adaptive, and quantum phase estimation algorithms. However, they ended up being so similar that I decided to include only one of them in the text as the illustration of our discussion and leave the other three to the GitHub repository.

The following listing shows the Qiskit code that implements the quantum phase estimation algorithm for learning eigenphases with two bits of precision.

Listing 5.5 Qiskit code for the quantum phase estimation algorithm

```
from math import acos, pi, sqrt
from qiskit import QuantumCircuit, transpile
from qiskit.circuit.library.standard_gates import SdgGate
from qiskit_aer import AerSimulator

simulator = AerSimulator(method='statevector')

def two_bit_quantum_phase_estimation(n, eigenvector, u):
    circ = QuantumCircuit(n + 2, 2)
    circ.h(0)                          ◁── The circuit uses two control qubits,
    circ.h(1)                              one per precision digit of the phase.

    eig = range(2, n + 2)
    circ.initialize(eigenvector, eig)  ◁── Prepares the last n qubits in the eigenstate

    circ.append(u.control(1), [1] + list(eig))  ◁── Encodes information about the
    circ.append(u.control(1), [0] + list(eig))      eigenphase in the relative phases
    circ.append(u.control(1), [0] + list(eig))      of control qubits

    circ.swap(0, 1)  ◁── Uses inverse QFT to switch from phase
                         encoding to amplitude encoding
```

5.3 Finding eigenvalue of the given eigenvector: The phase estimation problem

```
    circ.h(1)
    circ.append(SdgGate().control(1), [1, 0])
    circ.h(0)

    circ.measure([0, 1], [0, 1])          ◄─── Measures control qubits
    circ = transpile(circ, backend=simulator)
    res_map = simulator.run(circ).result().get_counts()  ◄──┐ Runs the circuit once
    return int(list(res_map.keys())[0][::-1], 2) / 4        │ and return the result
```

In the Qiskit code, we pass the eigenvector as a list of amplitudes and use the library method `initialize` to prepare the corresponding eigenstate based on these amplitudes. We could've used the methods we developed in chapter 2 instead or designed circuits tailored specifically for the preparation of these states, but this approach leads to shorter and more elegant code.

Each of these algorithms returns a classical value, the eigenphase associated with the given eigenvector, so testing them requires only classical tools. The test for each algorithm needs to select several unitaries and their eigenvectors, run the algorithm on each of them, and compare the results with the eigenvalues calculated mathematically. The unitaries listed in table 5.2 are a good starting point, since they offer examples of phases with different precision. You can, of course, come up with your own test cases as well!

The following listing shows a unit test for the quantum phase estimation for two-bit phases.

Listing 5.6 Qiskit code for testing the quantum phase estimation algorithm

```
def z_gate():            ◄──┐ Defines circuits for the gates
    circ = QuantumCircuit(1) │ used in the test: Z and INC
    circ.z(0)
    return circ

def inc_gate():
    circ = QuantumCircuit(2)
    circ.cx(0, 1)
    circ.x(0)
    return circ.to_gate()

z_eigenvectors = [[1, 0], [0, 1]]   ◄──┐ Defines eigenvectors of these
inc_eigenvectors = [                   │ gates as lists of amplitudes
    [0.5, 0.5, 0.5, 0.5],
    [0.5, -0.5, 0.5, -0.5],
    [0.5, -0.5j, -0.5, 0.5j],
    [0.5, 0.5j, -0.5, -0.5j]
]
                                    ┌─ Defines eigenphases that correspond
z_eigenphases = [0, 0.5]       ◄────┘  to the eigenvectors of these gates
inc_eigenphases = [0.0, 0.5, 0.25, 0.75]

def test_quantum_phase_estimation():
```

```
    for (n_qubits, n_eigenvectors, unitary, eigenvectors, eigenphases) in [
        (1, 2, z_gate(), z_eigenvectors, z_eigenphases),
        (2, 4, inc_gate(), inc_eigenvectors, inc_eigenphases)
    ]:
        for ind in range(n_eigenvectors):
            for _ in range(10):
                est_phase = two_bit_quantum_phase_estimation(
                  n_qubits, eigenvectors[ind], unitary)
                assert est_phase == approx(eigenphases[ind])
```

- `(1, 2, z_gate(), z_eigenvectors, z_eigenphases),` ← Runs the test for each gate
- `for ind in range(n_eigenvectors):` ← Runs the test for each eigenvector of that gate
- `assert est_phase == approx(eigenphases[ind])` ← Checks that the estimated phase matches the actual one

The test code includes the definitions of Z and INC gates, as well as their eigenvectors and eigenphases. These gates are reused by the tests for other algorithms, so it makes sense to define them outside this specific test and to add an extra test to verify that these vectors are indeed eigenvectors of these unitaries with the matching eigenphases.

The complete code for this project, including unit tests for each algorithm, is included in the GitHub repository. Running the project should result in tests passing. You can convert the project from running as a test to running as a Python script to print the phases returned; this can be useful for experimenting with different variants of the algorithms.

5.3.7 Q#

The three algorithms we explored in this section have different mathematical underpinnings, but their implementations end up having a lot in common. To start, they all solve the same problem based on the same input: the unitary and eigenvector pair and the number of qubits on which this unitary acts. The circuits they use also have similar structure: they all prepare the given eigenvector of the unitary and an additional |+⟩ state on one or two extra qubits and then apply the controlled unitary or several, followed by some extra gates to decode the result and a measurement to read it out.

Same as with Qiskit, the complete project code for this section includes implementation of all four phase estimation algorithms we looked at in this section: the one-bit phase estimation algorithm that illustrates the simplest phase kickback and then the iterative, adaptive, and quantum phase estimation algorithms. However, the code for each algorithm ended up being so similar that I decided to include only one of them in the text and leave the rest in the GitHub repository.

The following listing shows the Q# code that implements the quantum phase estimation algorithm for two-bit eigenphases.

Listing 5.7 Q# code for the quantum phase estimation algorithm

```
import Std.Convert.*;
import Std.Math.*;
```

5.3 Finding eigenvalue of the given eigenvector: The phase estimation problem

```
operation TwoBitQuantumPhaseEstimation(
    n : Int,
    eigenstatePrep : Qubit[] => Unit,
    unitary : Qubit[] => Unit is Ctl
) : Double {                                          ⟵ The circuit uses two control qubits,
    use (phase, eig) = (Qubit[2], Qubit[n]);             one per precision digit of the phase.
    ApplyToEach(H, phase);

    eigenstatePrep(eig);      ⟵ Prepares qubits in the eigenstate

    Controlled unitary([phase[1]], eig);    ⟵ Encodes information about eigenphase in
    Controlled unitary([phase[0]], eig);       relative phases of control qubits
    Controlled unitary([phase[0]], eig);
    ResetAll(eigenstate);
                                          ⟵ Uses inverse QFT to switch from
    SWAP(phase[0], phase[1]);                phase encoding to amplitude encoding
    H(phase[1]);
    Controlled Adjoint S([phase[1]], phase[0]);
    H(phase[0]);
    let res = (MResetZ(phase[0]) == One ? 2 | 0) +    ⟵ Measures control qubits
              (MResetZ(phase[1]) == One ? 1 | 0);        and returns the result
    return IntAsDouble(res) / 4.0;
}
```

In the Q# code, we pass the eigenstate of the unitary as an operation that prepares it on an array of qubits, rather than an array of amplitudes. This allows us to choose whether we want to prepare the eigenstates by hand, which we can do easily for the Z gate, or using a library operation, which is more convenient for the INC gate.

Each phase estimation algorithm returns a classical value, the eigenphase associated with the given eigenvector, so testing them requires only classical tools. The test for each algorithm needs to select several unitaries and their eigenvectors, run the algorithm on each of them, and compare the results with the eigenvalues calculated mathematically. The unitaries $Z, INC,$ and T (see table 5.2) are a good starting point, since they offer phases with different number of binary bits. You can, of course, come up with your own test cases as well!

The following listing shows an example of a Q# unit test for one of the algorithms, the quantum phase estimation for two-bit phases.

Listing 5.8   Q# code for testing the quantum phase estimation algorithm

```
operation ZGate(qs : Qubit[]) : Unit is Adj + Ctl {   ⟵ Defines the gates used
    Z(qs[0]);                                            in the test: Z and INC
}

operation IncrementGate(qs : Qubit[]) : Unit is Adj + Ctl {
    CNOT(qs[1], qs[0]);
    X(qs[1]);
}
```

```
operation ZEigenvector(qs : Qubit[], ind : Int) : Unit is Adj {
  if ind == 1 {
    X(qs[0]);
  }
}
```
> Defines eigenstates of these gates as operations that prepare them

```
operation IncrementEigenvector(qs : Qubit[], ind : Int) : Unit is Adj {
  let eigenAmps = [
    [(1., 0.), (1., 0.), (1., 0.), (1., 0.)],
    [(1., 0.), (-1., 0.), (1., 0.), (-1., 0.)],
    [(1., 0.), (0., -1.), (-1., 0.), (0., 1.)],
    [(1., 0.), (0., 1.), (-1., 0.), (0., -1.)]
  ];
  let cp = (a, b) -> ComplexAsComplexPolar(Complex(a, b));
  ApproximatelyPreparePureStateCP(0.0, Mapped(cp, eigenAmps[ind]), qs);
}
operation TestQuantumPhaseEstimation() : Unit {
  for (nQubits, unitary, unitaryStr, eigenstatePrep, eigenphases) in [
    (1, ZGate, "Z", ZEigenvector, [0.0, 0.5]),
    (2, IncrementGate, "INC", IncrementEigenvector, [0.0, 0.5, 0.25, 0.75])
  ] {
    Message($"Running QuantumPhaseEstimation for {unitaryStr}");
    for ind in 0 .. Length(eigenphases) - 1 {
      for _ in 0 .. 10 {
        let estPhase = TwoBitQuantumPhaseEstimation(
          nQubits, eigenstatePrep(_, ind), unitary);
        Fact(AbsD(eigenphases[ind] - estPhase) < 1e-2,
          $"Expected phase {eigenphases[ind]}, got {estPhase}");
      }
    }
  }
}
```
> Runs the test for each gate

> Runs the test for each eigenstate

> Checks that the estimated phase matches the actual one

The test code includes the definitions of Z and INC gates, as well as the operations that prepare their eigenstates. These definitions are reused by the tests for other algorithms, so it makes sense to define them separately and to add a test to verify that the states prepared are indeed eigenstates of these unitaries.

The complete code for this project, including unit tests for each algorithm, is included in the GitHub repository. Running the project should result in tests passing. You can convert the project from running as a test to running as a Q# executable to print the phases returned; this can be useful for experimenting with different algorithms.

5.4 Going beyond

Do you want to spend some more time exploring variations of the problems discussed in this chapter before moving on to the next topic? Here are some additional ideas for simpler examples, similar problems and ways to extend these problems if you want to try your hand at something more challenging:

- In section 5.1, we've considered only three example problems, all of them focused on distinguishing two single-qubit unitaries. Come up with additional examples of similar problems and solve them. For example, you could try distinguishing the Z gate from the S gate, or distinguishing four Pauli gates from each other. You don't have to limit yourself to standard single-qubit gates; analyzing multiqubit gates and arbitrary unitaries can be interesting too!
- Consider unitaries that can not be reliably distinguished in one shot, for example, Ry gate and H gate, or Ry gates with different parameters. Write a program that will distinguish them with high probability.
- In section 5.1, we focused on distinguishing unitary transformations. Think about a similar problem that would aim to figure out which of the list of possible measurements the given operation implements (for example, whether the given operation performs a measurement in the Bell basis or a measurement in the computational basis). How would you solve this problem?
- In section 5.2, we looked at learning the matrix of a single-qubit unitary with real coefficients. How would you generalize this to multiqubit unitaries? Unitaries with complex coefficients?
- Learn about quantum process tomography for noisy processes. How does the description of the process you're learning look like?
- Most phase estimation algorithms we saw in this chapter were designed for estimating the phase with a certain precision. Experiment with running them on inputs with eigenphases that require higher precision to be represented exactly or don't have an exact representation in binary. You can use the existing code for this: try to run one-bit phase estimation on the INC and T gates, and two-bit phase estimation on the T gate. How do different algorithms behave in this scenario?
- Generalize the implementation of the adaptive phase estimation from section 5.3.3 to learn the phase with three or more bits of precision.
- Generalize the implementation of the quantum phase estimation algorithm from section 5.3.5 to learn the phase with three or more bits of precision. (Start with learning the general form of quantum Fourier transform and implementing it to run on an arbitrary number of qubits.)

Summary

- We can use measurements to learn information not only about quantum states but also about quantum operations.
- To learn a property of a given quantum operation, we use it as a part of a larger quantum experiment that chooses and prepares a certain initial state, applies a sequence of operations to it, and measures the result. After we run enough experiments, we analyze their results to extract the information we're looking for.

- Similarly to how we can distinguish quantum states using measurements, we can figure out which of the list of possible gates we are given by applying the given gate to a carefully selected initial state and analyzing the resulting state.
- Quantum process tomography allows us to learn detailed information about an unknown unitary or a noisy process, similar to how quantum state tomography allows us to learn information about an unknown quantum state.
- Phase estimation task focuses on finding the eigenvalue and eigenphase of the given unitary that correspond to its given eigenstate. It is an important building block of many quantum algorithms, most prominently Shor's algorithm for integer factorization, quantum counting algorithm, and HHL algorithm for solving systems of linear equations.
- The phase kickback trick relies on the fact that applying a controlled version of a unitary with the target qubit(s) in a special state can kick a relative phase back to the control qubit(s) instead of changing the state of the target. Phase kickback is broadly used in quantum algorithms, and all phase estimation algorithms rely on it.
- There are multiple ways to approach solving phase estimation task. In this chapter, we considered three solutions that illustrated different classes of algorithms, each of them with their own advantages and disadvantages, depending on whether they will be executed on small noisy devices or on large fault-tolerant ones.
- Iterative phase estimation algorithm constructs a very simple circuit and runs it a lot of times to estimate a function of the eigenphase. It uses the smallest circuit of all phase estimation algorithms but has to run it the most times to get a reasonable precision on the results.
- Adaptive phase estimation algorithms construct a series of different small circuits that each learn a fragment of information we're looking for, and run them one after another, tweaking the later circuits based on the information learned from the previous ones. These algorithms use fewer circuit runs compared to the iterative algorithm, but the circuits themselves are more complicated.
- Quantum Fourier transform is a common primitive in quantum algorithms. It is used to convert information between amplitude encoding, in which the information is encoded in the absolute values of the amplitudes of the basis states, and phase encoding, in which the information is encoded in the phases of the complex numbers that represent the amplitudes.
- Quantum phase estimation algorithm runs a single circuit that encodes the information about the eigenphase in relative phases of multiple control qubits and then applies inverse quantum Fourier transform to make sure that the basis states that are the closest to the binary representation of the eigenphase have the largest amplitudes and the highest probabilities of being measured. Quantum phase estimation uses the fewest circuit runs of all phase estimation algorithms, but it requires the most qubits and the most complicated circuit.

Part 3

Solving a classical problem using a quantum algorithm

By this point of the book, we've covered a lot of building blocks of quantum algorithms and ways to test them. Now, it's time to put them to practice! The third and final part of the book follows the end-to-end process of solving a problem using a quantum algorithm. It includes formulating the problem in quantum terms, coming up with an algorithm to solve it, implementing the solution, testing it, and evaluating its quality.

Chapter 6 covers the first step of the workflow, showing how classical functions can be represented and evaluated as part of quantum computations. Chapter 7 introduces Grover's algorithm for solving search problems—one of the most famous quantum algorithms. In chapter 8, you use Grover's search algorithm to solve the N queens puzzle, learning to apply a theoretical algorithm to a realistic problem. Finally, chapter 9 discusses the performance of quantum programs running on fault-tolerant quantum computers. It dives into comparing quantum solutions with classical ones to figure out whether a quantum algorithm has the potential to show practical quantum advantage for a given problem.

Evaluating classical functions on a quantum computer

This chapter covers

- Implementing classical functions on a quantum computer as reversible computations
- Implementing Boolean logic functions as quantum operations
- Using Q# and Qiskit to implement reversible computations
- Testing reversible computations

The problems we considered in the previous four chapters, versatile as they are, all have something in common. These problems either have no classical analogue (how do you even define an eigenphase of a classical function?) or that analogue is so simple that it doesn't make sense to think of it as a separate problem, such as assigning a value to a variable or reading out the value of the variable.

But ultimately, the goal of quantum computing is to solve problems that are formulated irrespective of whether they are going to be solved on a classical computer or a quantum one. These problems can be classical or quantum in nature, but they have classical inputs and aim to find classical answers. For example, the N queens puzzle that we'll consider in chapter 8 is a purely classical problem, with the puzzle dimensions serving as the input and the queens' placement as the output. Finding the ground state energy of a molecule, on the other hand, is a quantum-mechanical problem, but its input is a set of numbers that describe the molecule structure, and its output is a single number, the ground state energy. The tasks we solved so far were not the problems we aim to solve, but rather the building blocks for algorithms that will solve these problems.

In this chapter and the next three, we will switch gears and discuss solving classical problems on a quantum computer. Figure 6.1 illustrates the general outline of the steps involved in doing that.

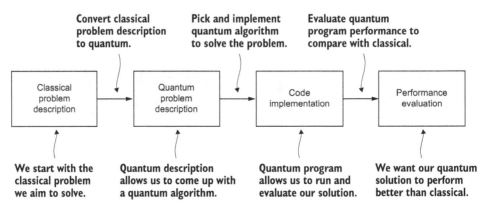

Figure 6.1 To solve a classical problem on a quantum computer, we start by converting the problem to its "quantum" formulation to which we can apply a quantum algorithm. After this, we implement the algorithm itself as a quantum program. Finally, we evaluate the performance of the quantum program and compare it to that of the best classical algorithm for solving the same problem. This way, we can see whether this quantum algorithm offers a practical advantage over the classical approaches.

First, we take the problem we're aiming to solve and convert its classical description into "quantum" terms. This can involve rephrasing it from informal language into formal mathematical definitions or extracting the parts of the problem that can be solved using quantum methods and leaving the other parts to be handled by a classical computer. For example, in Shor's integer factorization algorithm, the task of finding prime factors of the given number is rephrased in terms of finding a period of a classical function that multiplies the number by a constant modulo another constant. Only a small part of the end-to-end solution is quantum. The final answer is obtained using classical postprocessing of the results produced by the quantum component. Some intermediate parts of the solution can also be classical, such as calculating the cosine-sine decomposition we used to implement unitaries in chapter 3.

Next, we implement the algorithm for the quantum formulation of the problem as a quantum program. If some parts of the solution end up being classical, we get a *hybrid program* that will include both quantum and classical code acting together.

Once we've implemented the algorithm, we test it, checking that our code doesn't have bugs and produces the results we're looking for. We might write unit tests that test individual building blocks of the algorithm separately or end-to-end tests that run the whole algorithm and check that its results are correct. We will see examples of both in the next two chapters.

The final step is evaluating the algorithm performance on large problem instances. Since our goal is to find quantum algorithms that offer practical advantage over their classical counterparts, we need to make sure that we can compare the performance of our quantum program to that of the best classical algorithm solving the same problem. We will discuss the performance of quantum algorithms in chapter 9.

The example I will use throughout the next four chapters is the *search problem*—the problem of finding a set of variable values that satisfy a certain set of conditions. The search problem example I'll use in this chapter is *Boolean satisfiability problem*—the problem of finding an assignment of values to the Boolean variables that turns the given Boolean expression true. The search problem is a great getting started task for the topics I'll cover in these chapters for several reasons:

- The classical problem description is simple enough that understanding it does not require specialized knowledge, unlike problems in chemistry and material simulation.
- Solving this problem involves converting classical task descriptions into their quantum representations, which is an extremely important topic in quantum computing (we will discuss it in this chapter).
- The algorithm for solving this problem, Grover's search algorithm, is straightforward to implement, as we will see in chapter 7.
- Finally, Grover's algorithm is a gateway to fascinating discussions of quantum algorithms' performance. This algorithm offers a theoretical advantage over its classical counterpart in the most general case, but it turns out to be unlikely to offer a practical advantage when we take into account all the aspects of its implementation and execution on a quantum computer!

In this chapter, we will focus on the first step of solving a classical problem: converting the problem into quantum terms that can be implemented on a quantum computer. This subdomain of quantum computing is called *reversible computing*. We will start with a definition of what "reversible computing" means in classical and quantum context.

We'll look into implementing some simple example functions next and discuss testing our code. This will be very important later in the chapter, once we start implementing more complicated functions that are more prone to bugs creeping in.

The final project for this chapter will focus on evaluating classical functions described as Boolean expressions—the core of the Boolean satisfiability problem. As I walk you through solving it, you'll learn all the main principles of working with quantum reversible computations that you will need for the problem we consider in the next chapter.

6.1 Reversible computing: Mapping classical computation onto quantum

When we want to run a classical computation on a quantum computer, we start by establishing the rules we'll use for mapping classical variables onto quantum states and classical operations onto quantum gates. Let's consider a classical function $f(x)$

that acts on a classical input x and produces a classical output $f(x)$. The input and the output can be represented in multiple equivalent ways; figure 6.2 shows several simple examples.

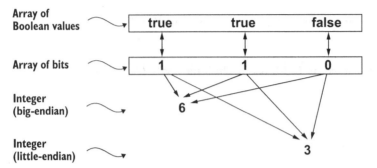

Figure 6.2 The inputs and outputs to any function can be represented in several equivalent ways. An array of Boolean values true and false is the same as an array of bits 0 and 1, which can then be interpreted as a binary notation of an integer. For integers, make sure to track whether the notation you use is big-endian (most significant bit stored first) or little-endian (least significant bit stored first)!

Classical values that serve as input or output for the function might be arrays of Boolean values, arrays of bits 0 or 1, or integers written as their binary notations. (More complicated types such as real numbers or data structures follow the same principles, but we won't need them in this book.) These representations can be easily converted one into another. We usually map Boolean values true and false onto bits 1 and 0, respectively. When mapping an integer onto a bit array, you have to keep track of the endianness used for this: a bit array 110 can represent an integer 6 if interpreted as big-endian (most significant bit written first) or an integer 3 if interpreted as little-endian (least significant bit written first).

How can we implement a quantum algorithm that takes an input x and calculates the value of the classical function $f(x)$? We will use an array of qubits to represent the quantum input to this algorithm, with each qubit corresponding to one bit of the classical input. We map classical bits 0 (false) and 1 (true) onto the basis states $|0\rangle$ and $|1\rangle$, so any classical input x is mapped onto a basis state $|x\rangle$. Any superposition of the basis states is then interpreted as a superposition of several classical inputs. Our ultimate goal is to find a sequence of quantum gates that takes an array of qubits as the input and transforms its state in such a way that the values of the function f for all basis states that were part of the initial state are encoded in the resulting state.

NOTE This phrasing might seem a bit vague. This is intentional! The precise definition of the quantum analogue of a classical computation can depend on the function we want to compute and on the way we plan to use the results later. In this chapter, we'll work through several possible interpretations and see examples of simple functions for which they work and, just as importantly, examples for which they don't.

Before we start looking at examples of functions and figuring out how to implement them, we need to discuss some key differences between classical and quantum computations. Classical computing allows us to do a lot of things that cannot be done in quantum computing or have to be done differently. You might have heard of the *no-cloning theorem*, which shows that you cannot replicate an arbitrary unknown quantum state. Its less known counterpart, the *no-deletion theorem*, shows that you cannot erase arbitrary information from one part of a quantum system using only quantum gates. This means that we need to come up with special tricks to use whenever we need to copy a variable value, erase the old information stored in a variable, use temporary local variables, and in other scenarios that are perfectly commonplace in classical computing.

The key property of quantum systems that causes these limitations is the reversibility of quantum computations. Figure 6.3 illustrates reversible and nonreversible functions.

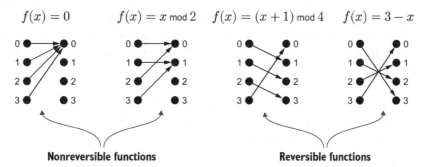

Figure 6.3 A classical function is reversible if it converts each input to exactly one output, and each output is produced by exactly one input. In other words, the input that produced a certain output can be restored from that output.

We call an operation (classical or quantum) *reversible* if the input (or the initial state) can be computed from the output (or the final state), and vice versa. In mathematical terms, reversible operations are known as *bijections* or *one-to-one mappings*: each input is mapped to exactly one output, and each output—to exactly one input.

> **NOTE** We are discussing *logical reversibility*, which deals with the properties of the logic of computation. You might encounter a different kind of reversibility in physics: *physical reversibility* describes physical processes that result in no increase in entropy. Since we discuss only the logic of computation in this book, I use "reversibility" to refer to the first meaning without extra qualifiers.

For example, a classical function on n-bit integers $f(x) = (2^n - 1) - x$ is reversible, since the input x_0 that produced a certain output value f_0 can be recovered easily by applying the same function to the output:

$$f(f_0) = 2^n - 1 - f_0 = 2^n - 1 - f(x_0) = 2^n - 1 - (2^n - 1 - x_0) = x_0$$

A classical function $f(x) = 0$, on the other hand, is not reversible. Any input could have produced the output value 0, and we don't have a way to figure out which input it was.

In quantum computing, all quantum gates are reversible by definition. Remember that all quantum gates are *unitary*; each gate has an adjoint variant that acts as its inverse. If you apply a unitary gate U to an initial state $|\psi\rangle$ and get the final state $|\phi\rangle = U|\psi\rangle$, you can recover the initial state from $|\phi\rangle$ by applying the adjoint of U to that state:

$$U^\dagger |\phi\rangle = U^\dagger U |\psi\rangle = |\psi\rangle$$

Quantum measurements, on the contrary, are not reversible: multiple quantum states can yield the same measurement result, and there's no way to revert the collapse of the quantum state caused by measurement. We do not use measurements to implement reversible classical functions on a quantum computer, since they would make it impossible to carry out the computations on superpositions of basis states.

While the classical function that we want to evaluate on a quantum computer may or may not be reversible, the resulting quantum operations have to be reversible. This limitation makes implementing classical computations on a quantum computer somewhat tricky, but there are techniques that allow us to do that in a standardized manner.

In the rest of this chapter, we'll look at evaluating increasingly complicated classical functions on a quantum computer and learn the key techniques of working with reversible computations in the process.

6.2 Evaluating single-bit functions

To start with, let's look at the simplest possible classical functions: the functions that take one bit input and produce one bit output. There are only four such functions, so let's analyze them in detail. Figure 6.4 shows these functions and the ways they map the input bit to the output bit.

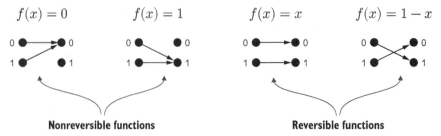

Figure 6.4 Functions $f(x) = 0$ and $f(x) = 1$ are nonreversible: both inputs give the same output. Functions $f(x) = x$ and $f(x) = 1 - x$ are reversible: different inputs are mapped to different outputs, so you can figure out which input produced the given output.

Despite their simplicity, these functions illustrate some important aspects of reversible computations, so they are a great place to start. Let's see how we can compute these functions on a quantum computer, and what challenges we face when implementing functions that are not reversible.

6.2.1 Math

Rather than jump right into the correct way of implementing classical functions on a quantum computer, I'll walk you through several approaches that look more intuitive and show why they don't work or work only for a limited set of functions. This way, you should have an easier time understanding the reasoning behind the final, correct approach.

FIRST ATTEMPT: IN-PLACE COMPUTATION

The functions we're looking at have one-bit input and one-bit output. This means that the easiest thing to try is computing the function in-place: find a transformation that would act on one qubit and have the following effect:

$$|x\rangle \rightarrow |f(x)\rangle$$

And for the two of the functions that are reversible it's actually possible to do that:

- For $f(x) = x$, the in-place transformation is $|x\rangle \rightarrow |f(x)\rangle = |x\rangle$, which corresponds to just applying no gate (or applying the identity gate I).
- For $f(x) = 1 - x$, the in-place transformation is $|x\rangle \rightarrow |f(x)\rangle = |1 - x\rangle = |1 \oplus x\rangle = X|x\rangle$, which can be implemented by applying an X gate. $\oplus$ is addition modulo two, an extremely common operation in reversible computing.

Unfortunately, this idea doesn't work out for nonreversible functions. No quantum gate can perform the transformation $|x\rangle \rightarrow |0\rangle$, since it is not reversible: it maps multiple initial states to the same resulting state and thus cannot have an adjoint defined for it. We need to come up with a different approach that we can use for implementing nonreversible functions and then apply it to the reversible functions too, so that we have a universal approach to implementing all functions regardless of their reversibility.

> **TIP** We will keep the trick of implementing the function $1 - x$ in-place in mind for later. This is the negation function NOT if the input and output are interpreted as Boolean variables, and it is an extremely common building block for other functions.

SECOND ATTEMPT: PRESERVING THE INPUT AS PART OF THE OUTPUT

We just saw a straightforward attempt to implement a function on a quantum computer run into issues because of its nonreversibility. Can we make the classical function reversible first, before mapping it onto a quantum computation?

Following the definition of reversibility, we need to make sure that we can recover the input to the function from its output value. Let's try extending the definition of our single-bit function $f(x)$ to define a new function $F(x, y)$ that acts on two bits instead of one: the first bit x will be used as the input, and the second bit y—as the output. When the new function F acts on these two bits, it leaves the first bit x unchanged and sets the second bit y to the value of the function:

$$F(x, y) = (x, f(x))$$

Now, we can easily find the input x that was used to calculate $f(x)$: it is just the first bit of the two-bit output!

Unfortunately, this approach doesn't bear fruit for any functions, not just the nonreversible ones. It erases the information about the *second bit* of the input y, replacing it with information about $f(x)$. And we need to make sure that our function $F(x)$ is reversible in terms of its complete inputs and outputs; that is, we should be able to recover both bits x and y that were used as its input.

THIRD ATTEMPT: MAKE THE CLASSICAL FUNCTION COMPLETELY REVERSIBLE

It is actually possible to make the classical function reversible before mapping it onto a quantum computation by extending the function to act on two bits. We just need to be a bit more careful about doing that in a way that allows us to recover both bits of the extended input, not just the bit that stores the original input.

Let's modify the definition of the extended function $F(x, y)$ that acts on two bits as follows. When the function F acts on two bits (x, y), it leaves the first bit x unchanged and flips the second bit y if the value of the original function $f(x)$ is 1, leaving it unchanged if $f(x) = 0$. This tweak allows us to preserve the information about the input bit y as well:

$$F(x, y) = (x, y \oplus f(x))$$

Table 6.1 shows the examples of converting single-bit functions to two-bit functions for two of our four functions: $f(x) = 1$ and $f(x) = x$. This conversion works similarly for the other two single-bit functions; I encourage you to try and write it down as an exercise!

Table 6.1 Single-bit functions and their reversible two-bit extensions

Function $f(x)$	Extended function $F(x, y)$	Extended input	Extended output
$f(x) = 1$	$F(x, y) = (x, y \oplus 1)$	(0, 0)	(0, 1)
		(0, 1)	(0, 0)
		(1, 0)	(1, 1)
		(1, 1)	(1, 0)
$f(x) = x$	$F(x, y) = (x, y \oplus x)$	(0, 0)	(0, 0)
		(0, 1)	(0, 1)
		(1, 0)	(1, 1)
		(1, 1)	(1, 0)

Figure 6.5 illustrates the two-bit functions constructed this way and shows that they are reversible even if the original single-bit function was not reversible.

6.2 Evaluating single-bit functions

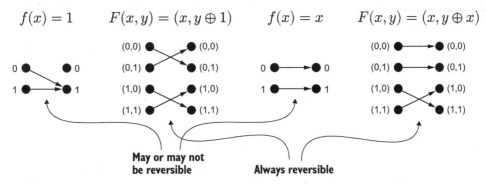

Figure 6.5 The single-bit function can be reversible, like $f(x) = x$, or not, like $f(x) = 1$. Adding an extra bit to the input and output allows us to define the extended function $F(x, y)$ to be reversible regardless of whether the original single-bit function was reversible.

With the updated definition of $F(x, y)$, we can find a quantum transformation that implements it on the two-qubit basis states. Indeed, the effect of the transformation $(x, y) \to (x, y \oplus 1)$ is the same as leaving the first bit alone and changing the second bit to its negation, and we just saw that this can be implemented by applying an X gate to the second qubit. For the second transformation, $(x, y) \to (x, y \oplus x)$, its effect is exactly that of a CNOT gate applied with the first qubit as control and the second qubit as target.

Similarly, we can analyze the remaining two functions $f(x) = 0$ and $f(x) = 1 - x$ to realize that the first one can be implemented by doing nothing and the second one—by applying a controlled-on-zero X gate. This completes the implementation of all single-bit functions we saw earlier in the figure 6.4.

Evaluating classical functions for inputs in superposition

So far, we only talked about mapping classical functions to quantum operations that act on basis states. However, we know that quantum operations have to act on arbitrary quantum states, including superposition states. How can we define the effect of a quantum operation constructed from a classical function on superposition states?

Remember that all quantum gates are linear transformations, and superposition states are linear combinations of basis states. As a result, the effects of a gate U on a superposition input state $\sum_j a_j |j\rangle$ can be defined as a linear combination of the effects of that gate on each basis state:

$$U \sum_j a_j |j\rangle = \sum_j a_j U |j\rangle$$

We can use the linear behavior of quantum operations to derive the effects of an operation U_f constructed from a classical function f. Once we've established that

(continued)

the operation U_f transforms the basis states $|x\rangle|y\rangle \to |x\rangle|y \oplus f(x)\rangle$, we can define its effect on superposition states:

$$U_f \sum_{x,y} a_{x,y} |x\rangle|y\rangle = \sum_{x,y} a_{x,y} U |x\rangle|y\rangle = \sum_{x,y} a_{x,y} |x\rangle|y \oplus f(x)\rangle$$

The final approach we end up with includes two steps:

1. Make the function reversible by preserving its inputs as part of the output and using a separate bit to calculate the function value. This is the key technique of reversible computations!
2. Enumerate all input-output pairs of the reversible variant of the function and guess the quantum gate that performs the necessary transformation on the basis states of a quantum system.

The second step was easy to do with our single-bit functions: their reversible variants act on two qubits, so we needed to analyze only four input-output pairs. However, for more complicated functions we cannot use this approach. The number of input-output pairs grows exponentially with the increase of the number of bits in the function inputs and outputs, so enumerating them becomes a challenge, and guessing the sequence of quantum gates that maps the inputs to the outputs correctly, an impossibility.

Later in this chapter, we'll learn a more structured approach that will allow us to come up with sequences of gates to compute classical functions on quantum computers systematically and even generate quantum programs that do that automatically. But first, let's see the code that implements these single-bit functions and learn to test this kind of programs.

Observing the effects of reversible implementations of classical functions

There are multiple ways to showcase the unitary transformation and its effects. We saw one way to do that in section 3.2, where we used the built-in tools of Qiskit and Q# to get the unitary matrix implemented by a quantum program.

This approach is not ideal for reversible computations, especially once we move on from single-bit functions to functions of multiple arguments. Since each operation we implement corresponds to a classical function, it converts each basis state to another basis state. This means that the unitary matrices of these operations are *sparse*: each row and each column of the matrix has exactly one nonzero element which marks the output state that corresponds to that input basis state. Sparse matrices can be inconvenient to read and interpret, especially for matrices of larger sizes that are extremely common when working with reversible computing.

In this chapter, I use a different way to inspect and later test the effects of quantum operations that is specific to reversible computations. Since each basis state is converted to just one basis state, we can construct a quantum equivalent of a *truth table* for the operation: a table that lists all input basis states and their matching output basis states, similar to the last two columns of table 6.1. We can generate this table by iterating through all possible basis states and printing the basis states to which they are converted by the application of the unitary.

In this section, though, we can simplify this approach further. Since our classical functions only have two inputs, 0 and 1, we can prepare a two-qubit input state $(\alpha |0\rangle + \beta |1\rangle) \otimes |0\rangle$, apply the unitary to it, and print the resulting state. The basis states $|00\rangle$ and $|10\rangle$ will be converted to $|0, f(0)\rangle$ and $|1, f(1)\rangle$. Using different amplitudes α and β for these basis states will allow us to keep track of which basis state was converted to which result.

6.2.2 Qiskit

Functions that implement reversible computations as circuits look just like any other circuit in Qiskit. We saw examples of such functions in chapter 3 and discussed them in detail. Here, I'll focus on the elements that are different when writing the code and observing its results for reversible computations. The following listing shows the Qiskit code that implements the four single-bit functions we discussed in this section as circuits and demonstrates their effects on a simple quantum state.

Listing 6.1 Qiskit: Single-bit functions as quantum operations

```
from math import acos
from qiskit import QuantumCircuit, transpile
from qiskit.circuit.library.standard_gates import XGate
from qiskit_aer import AerSimulator

def quantum_zero():
    return QuantumCircuit(2)      ◁── f(x) = 0; does nothing

def quantum_one():
    circ = QuantumCircuit(2)      ◁── f(x) = 1; applies X gate to the second qubit
    circ.x(1)
    return circ

def quantum_x():
    circ = QuantumCircuit(2)      ◁── f(x) = x; applies CNOT gate
    circ.cx(0, 1)
    return circ

def quantum_one_minus_x():        ◁── f(x) = 1 - x; applies controlled-on-zero X gate
    circ = QuantumCircuit(2)
    circ.append(XGate().control(1, ctrl_state=0), [0, 1])
    return circ

simulator = AerSimulator(method='statevector')
```

```
for (quantum_op, f) in [           ←── Runs the same demo for each function
    (quantum_zero, "f(x) = 0"),
    (quantum_one, "f(x) = 1"),
    (quantum_x, "f(x) = x"),
    (quantum_one_minus_x, "f(x) = 1 - x") ]:
  circ = QuantumCircuit(2)
  circ.ry(2 * acos(0.6), 0)        ←── Prepares input qubit in superposition
  circ.append(quantum_op(), [0, 1]) ←── Applies the reversible operation
  circ.save_statevector()

  circ = transpile(circ, backend=simulator)
  state_vector = simulator.run(circ).result().get_statevector()
  print(f"Applying operation {f} to the state (0.6|0> + 0.8|1>) |0>:")
  print(state_vector.draw(output='latex_source'))
```

The output of this code looks as follows:

```
Applying operation f(x) = 0 to the state (0.6|0> + 0.8|1>) |0>:
\frac{3}{5} |00\rangle+\frac{4}{5} |01\rangle
Applying operation f(x) = 1 to the state (0.6|0> + 0.8|1>) |0>:
\frac{3}{5} |10\rangle+\frac{4}{5} |11\rangle
Applying operation f(x) = x to the state (0.6|0> + 0.8|1>) |0>:
\frac{3}{5} |00\rangle+\frac{4}{5} |11\rangle
Applying operation f(x) = 1 - x to the state (0.6|0> + 0.8|1>) |0>:
\frac{4}{5} |01\rangle+\frac{3}{5} |10\rangle
```

The method `state_vector.draw(output='latex_source')` prints the state vector of the system as the raw ASCII source of its LaTeX representation. The first formula, for example, corresponds to the state $\frac{3}{5}|00\rangle + \frac{4}{5}|01\rangle$. Using this format makes the output a bit easier to read compared to the default format (a list of all amplitudes), since it omits the zero amplitudes and spells out the basis state associated with each amplitude explicitly.

Notice that in this output, Qiskit reverses the order of qubits printed compared to their indices in the code: the first qubit of the circuit is printed last in the state, and the second qubit is printed first. The output produced by the unitary for $f(x) = 0$, $\frac{3}{5}|00\rangle + \frac{4}{5}|01\rangle$, is actually our input state, with the input qubit in the state $0.6|0\rangle + 0.8|1\rangle$ and the output qubit in the state $|0\rangle$, just with the order of qubits reversed.

You can see that the effects of the unitaries are exactly what we would expect them to be: $f(x) = 0$ doesn't change the quantum state, $f(x) = 1$ always flips the state of the output qubit, and the other two functions flip the state of the output qubit conditionally based on the state of the input qubit.

6.2.3 Q#

Operations that implement reversible computations look just like any other operation that implements a unitary transformation in Qiskit. We saw examples of such operations in chapter 3 and discussed them in detail. Here, I'll focus on the elements that are different when writing the code and observing its results for reversible com-

6.2 Evaluating single-bit functions

putations. The following listing shows the Q# code that implements the four single-bit functions we discussed in this section as unitary operations and demonstrates their effects on a simple quantum state.

> Listing 6.2 Q#: Single-bit functions as quantum operations

```
import Std.Diagnostics.DumpMachine;
import Std.Math.ArcCos;

operation QuantumZero(x : Qubit, y : Qubit) : Unit { }     ⟵ f(x) = 0; does nothing

operation QuantumOne(x : Qubit, y : Qubit) : Unit {     ⟵ f(x) = 1; applies X gate to
    X(y);                                                      the second qubit
}

operation QuantumX(x : Qubit, y : Qubit) : Unit {     ⟵ f(x) = x; applies CNOT gate
    CNOT(x, y);
}

operation QuantumOneMinusX(x : Qubit, y : Qubit) : Unit {
    ApplyControlledOnInt(0, X, [x], y);               ⟵ f(x) = 1 - x; applies
}                                                          controlled-on-zero X gate

@EntryPoint()
operation DemoSingleBitFunctions() : Unit {
    for (quantumOp, f) in [                           ⟵ Runs the same demo
        (QuantumZero, "f(x) = 0"),                         for each function
        (QuantumOne, "f(x) = 1"),
        (QuantumX, "f(x) = x"),
        (QuantumOneMinusX, "f(x) = 1 - x")
    ] {
        Message($"Applying operation {f} to the state (0.6|0> + 0.8|1>) |0>:");
        use (x, y) = (Qubit(), Qubit());
        Ry(2.0 * ArcCos(0.6), x);       ⟵ Prepares input qubit in superposition
        quantumOp(x, y);                ⟵ Applies the reversible operation
        DumpMachine();
        ResetAll([x, y]);
    }
}
```

The output of this code looks as follows:

```
Applying operation f(x) = 0 to the state (0.6|0> + 0.8|1>) |0>:

Basis | Amplitude       | Probability | Phase
-----------------------------------------------
 |00> | 0.6000+0.0000i  |   36.0000%  |  0.0000
 |10> | 0.8000+0.0000i  |   64.0000%  |  0.0000

Applying operation f(x) = 1 to the state (0.6|0> + 0.8|1>) |0>:

Basis | Amplitude       | Probability | Phase
```

```
|01> |    0.6000+0.0000i  |      36.0000%  |    0.0000
|11> |    0.8000+0.0000i  |      64.0000%  |    0.0000

Applying operation f(x) = x to the state (0.6|0> + 0.8|1>) |0>:

Basis | Amplitude        | Probability | Phase
--------------------------------------------------
|00> |    0.6000+0.0000i  |      36.0000%  |    0.0000
|11> |    0.8000+0.0000i  |      64.0000%  |    0.0000

Applying operation f(x) = 1 - x to the state (0.6|0> + 0.8|1>) |0>:

Basis | Amplitude        | Probability | Phase
--------------------------------------------------
|01> |    0.6000+0.0000i  |      36.0000%  |    0.0000
|10> |    0.8000+0.0000i  |      64.0000%  |    0.0000
```

The operation DumpMachine we saw in earlier chapters prints the quantum state as a list of basis states and their amplitudes. Unlike in Qiskit, the ordering of qubits in the outputs matches their order in the program.

You can see that the effects of the unitaries are exactly what we would expect them to be: $f(x) = 0$ doesn't change the quantum state, $f(x) = 1$ always flips the state of the output qubit, and the other two functions flip the state of the output qubit conditionally, based on the state of the input qubit.

6.3 Testing reversible computations

How can we test our code that implements classical computations on a quantum computer? These tests should ascertain that the results of the computation done by the quantum program match the expected results calculated classically. We can check this directly using a similar approach to the one we saw in the previous section. Figure 6.6 shows the logic of testing reversible computations by comparing the results of the quantum computation to the results of the classical computation it implements.

These tests rely on listing all possible inputs to the classical function and checking that the quantum computation gives a correct answer for each of these inputs. The sequence of steps for one input x looks as follows:

1. Use the classical function f to calculate the expected output value $f(x)$. We will use this result later to validate the results of the quantum computation.
2. Prepare the basis state that encodes the classical input $|x\rangle$ and the basis state $|0\rangle$ to be used as the inputs to the quantum operation.
3. Apply the quantum operation to the state $|x\rangle |0\rangle$.
4. The state of the system after this should be $|x\rangle |f(x)\rangle$. The test needs to run several checks on the resulting state:
   - Is the resulting state a basis state or a superposition state? The result of applying a properly implemented reversible computation to a basis state

6.3 Testing reversible computations

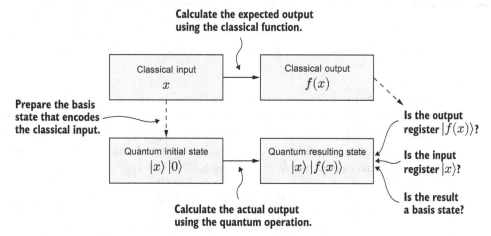

Figure 6.6 To test reversible calculations, we verify that the quantum operation produces the expected results on all basis states. For each input x, we prepare the quantum input in the state $|x\rangle$ and the output in the $|0\rangle$ state and apply the quantum operation. The test then runs a series of checks on the resulting state, using the classically computed value $f(x)$ as part of the verification process.

should be a basis state. However, if you know your code uses only the X gate and its controlled variants, as is typically the case for the code that implements reversible computations, and doesn't use any gates that can introduce superposition, you can skip this check.

- Are the qubits that store the output value indeed in the $|f(x)\rangle$ state? This check uses the classically computed value of the function. Notice that we can skip running a similar check on the input $|x\rangle|1\rangle$ and verifying that the result of the computation is $|x\rangle|1 \oplus f(x)\rangle$. As long as the code doesn't do any weird things like using the output qubit as control for any gates (it shouldn't!), this check would not give us any new information.
- Are the qubits that store the input value still in the $|x\rangle$ state? This check is important, since reversible computations are not supposed to change their inputs. We will see examples of more complicated reversible computations that show the importance of preserving the input state later in this chapter.

Why are these checks sufficient to convince ourselves that our code is correct in all cases, not just when we apply it to the basis states? Remember that we defined the effects of the operation we're implementing based on its effects on the basis states using the linearity of quantum operations. If our code doesn't use any nonlinear operations (measurements) or any gates that can introduce superposition (gates such as H and Ry) or a relative phase (phase gates such as Z, S, and T, or rotation gate Rz), but only the X gate and its controlled variants CNOT, CCNOT, and so on, we can show mathematically that the behavior of the code on superposition states will be correct as long as it behaves correctly on the basis states. Later in this chapter, we'll see that the general method of implementing reversible computations relies only on the X gate and its variants, thus this approach to testing has merit.

170   CHAPTER 6   *Evaluating classical functions on a quantum computer*

The exact way these checks can be implemented depends on the toolkit you're using and the tools it offers. Let's see how to write the tests for the four single-bit functions we implemented in section 6.2 in Qiskit and Q#.

6.3.1 Qiskit

We use the Aer simulator and the method `save_statevector` it adds to the circuit to get the state of the system at the end of the program. If you need a refresher of how it works, see section 2.2 in which we used the same approach to test our state preparation code. The following listing shows the Qiskit test code for the implementations of single-bit classical functions from listing 6.1.

> **Listing 6.3 Qiskit: Testing implementations of single-bit functions**

```
from cmath import isclose
from qiskit import QuantumCircuit, transpile
from qiskit_aer import AerSimulator
import pytest
from .single_bit_functions import *

def f_zero(arg):            ◁─┐ Defines classical functions implemented
    return False               │ by each reversible operation

def f_one(arg):
    return True

def f_x(arg):
    return arg

def f_one_minus_x(arg):
    return not arg

simulator = AerSimulator(method='statevector')
                                              ┌─ Uses matching pairs of classical
@pytest.mark.parametrize("quantum_op,f",      │  functions and quantum
                    [(quantum_zero, f_zero),  ◁┘ operations for tests
                     (quantum_one, f_one),
                     (quantum_x, f_x),
                     (quantum_one_minus_x, f_one_minus_x)])
def test_reversible_computation(quantum_op, f):
    for input in [False, True]:           ◁── Iterates over all classical inputs
        circ = QuantumCircuit(2)
        if input:                ◁── Prepares basis state as quantum input
            circ.x(0)
        circ.append(quantum_op(), [0, 1])   ◁── Applies quantum operation

        expected = f(input)   ◁─┐ Flips the state of the output qubit
        if expected:            │ if classical function value is 1
            circ.x(1)

        if input:       ◁── Uncomputes the input basis state
            circ.x(0)
```

```
circ.save_statevector()
circ = transpile(circ, backend=simulator)      ⬅ If the result is correct, state
res = simulator.run(circ).result()                vector should be |00>.
state_vector = res.get_statevector().data

non_zeros = [not isclose(amp, 0, abs_tol=1e-9) for amp in state_vector]
if any(non_zeros[1:]):                          ⬅ Result is incorrect.
    prefix = f"Error for x={input}:"
    count = non_zeros.count(True)               ⬅ More than one
    if count > 1:                                  basis state present.
        raise Exception(f"{prefix} the state should not be a superposition")
    index = non_zeros.index(True)               ⬅ Output is the most
    if index // 2 > 0:                             significant bit.
        raise Exception(f"{prefix} expected {expected}, got {not expected}")
    else:
        raise Exception(f"{prefix} the state of the input qubit changed")
```

In this code, we aim to end with the qubits in the $|00\rangle$ state if the results of the quantum operation are correct. To do this, we take two additional steps after applying the quantum operation to the input:

1 We flip the state of the output qubit if the value of the classical function is 1 and leave it unchanged if the value is 0. This returns the state of the output qubit to $|0\rangle$ if its state matched the function value and makes it $|1\rangle$ if it didn't.

2 We undo the preparation of the qubit that served as the input by applying an X gate if the input bit was 1. This returns the state of the input qubit to $|0\rangle$ if its state was unchanged by the quantum operation and makes it $|1\rangle$ if it was changed.

The expected result of running the code is four passing tests, one for each function.

6.3.2 Q#

There are multiple ways to write Q# tests for reversible computation. We saw one way to do that in section 2.4, where we used the Python API to get the state of the program after its execution and then analyzed it using Python. Here, I will use a different approach, keeping the test logic in Q# code and using a Python wrapper only to call Q# tests.

Listing 6.4 shows the Q# test code for the implementations of single-bit classical functions from listing 6.2.

Listing 6.4   Q#: Testing implementations of single-bit functions

```
import Std.Diagnostics.CheckAllZero;

function FZero(arg : Bool) : Bool {        ⬅ Defines classical functions
    return false;                             implemented by each
}                                             reversible operation
```

```
function FOne(arg : Bool) : Bool {
  return true;
}
function FX(arg : Bool) : Bool {
  return arg;
}
function FOneMinusX(arg : Bool) : Bool {
  return not arg;
}
operation AssertOperationImplementsFunction(
  op : (Qubit, Qubit) => Unit,
  f : Bool -> Bool
) : Unit {
  use (x, y) = (Qubit(), Qubit());       ◁── Iterates over all
  for input in [false, true] {           ◁── classical inputs
    if input {                           ◁── Prepares basis state
      X(x);                                  as quantum input
    }
    op(x, y);    ◁── Applies quantum operation

    let expected = f(input);    ◁── Flips the state of the output qubit
    if expected {                   if classical function value is 1
      X(y);
    }
    if input {    ◁── Uncomputes the input basis state
      X(x);
    }

    if not CheckAllZero([y]) {
      fail $"Error for x={input}: expected {expected}, got {not expected}";
    }
    if not CheckAllZero([x]) {
      fail $"Error for x={input}: the state of the input qubit changed";
    }
  }
}
```

The logic of this test is the same as the one we just saw in Qiskit code: we aim to end with both qubits in the |0⟩ state if the code was correct. Q# operation `CheckAllZero` returns true if all qubits in the given array are in the |0⟩ state and false otherwise. We can use it to access the internal state of the simulator from Q# code without going through Python.

Listing 6.5 shows the Python test code used to invoke the tests from listing 6.4.

Listing 6.5 Python wrapper for Q# tests for reversible single-bit functions

```
from qsharp import init, eval
import pytest
```

```
@pytest.mark.parametrize("op", ["Zero", "One", "X", "OneMinusX"])
def test_single_bit_function(op):
    init(project_root='.')
    eval("Test.AssertOperationImplementsFunction(" +
        f"ReversibleComputing.Quantum{op}, Test.F{op})")
```

You can see that the only logic implemented in Python is calling the Q# tests for matching pairs of classical functions and their quantum implementations. The expected result of running this code is four passing tests, one for each single-bit function we implemented.

6.4 Evaluating Boolean operations

Now that we have defined how we want to map classical computations onto quantum ones and looked at simple single-bit examples, let's take the next step and think about how we can construct the mappings for more complicated functions. Ideally, we want to do this systematically in a way that can be automated, rather than by coming up with an ad-hoc quantum circuit for every classical function we need to implement.

A similar problem arises in classical computer engineering when a high-level description of the desired circuit behavior needs to be converted into a low-level implementation of logic gates. This step is called *logic synthesis*, and is carried out by tools called *synthesis tools*. Can we borrow some ideas and tools from this classical approach to address our quantum problem? The answer is yes!

Figure 6.7 shows a systematic approach to solving our problem based on classical logic synthesis techniques. In quantum computing literature, it is typically referred to as *synthesis of reversible logic circuits*.

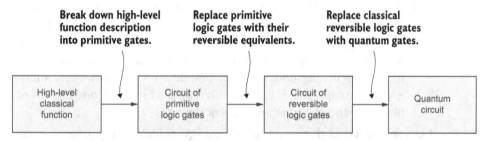

Figure 6.7 To convert a classical function into its quantum implementation, we start by representing it as a sequence of Boolean logic gates. Then, we replace each gate with its classical reversible equivalent. Finally, each classical reversible logic gate is replaced with a quantum gate that implements it.

Synthesis of quantum circuits for reversible computations consists of several steps:

1. A high-level description of the classical function we want to implement is broken down into a sequence of primitive Boolean logic operations, such as AND, OR, and NOT. This can be done automatically using classical synthesis tools!

2 Each Boolean logic operation is replaced with its classical reversible equivalent. This step is similar to what we did to make our single-bit functions reversible before mapping them onto quantum gates.

3 Finally, the classical circuit of reversible Boolean gates is converted into a quantum circuit. This is not as straightforward as just replacing each classical gate with a quantum one (later in this chapter we'll see why), but this can be done systematically.

In the rest of this chapter, we will see how this process works for a specific problem.

We'll start with looking at a small set of primitive Boolean logic operations commonly used in synthesis to see how they can be implemented as quantum circuits. Table 6.2 shows the truth tables of the main Boolean operations that act on one and two bits.

Table 6.2 The truth tables of the main Boolean operations

x_0	x_1	NOT x_0	x_0 AND x_1	x_0 OR x_1	x_0 XOR x_1	x_0 EQUAL x_1
0	0	1	0	0	0	1
0	1	1	0	1	1	0
1	0	0	0	1	1	0
1	1	0	1	1	0	1

This set of operations includes both the basic operations of Boolean algebra and some higher-level operations that we'll use in the remainder of this chapter and the next one:

- AND, OR, and NOT are the basic operations of Boolean algebra.
- Equality and XOR (also known as sum modulo 2) are commonly used *secondary operations*—operations composed of a few basic Boolean operations.
- Two additional operations not shown in the table are the generalizations of the AND and OR operations that act on more than two arguments. The truth tables for these generalizations are both unwieldy and not particularly interesting: the AND of multiple bits is 1 if and only if all the bits are 1, and the OR of multiple bits is 1 if and only if at least one of the bits is 1.

Let's see which of these operations are reversible already, how to make the rest reversible, and how to convert them into quantum operations.

6.4.1 Math

In this section, I'll take a uniform approach to implementing all Boolean operations that matches the last two steps of the more general approach we saw in figure 6.7:

1 Make the Boolean operation reversible.
    We'll use the tricks we came up with for single-bit functions in section 6.2: preserving the input as part of the output and using a separate bit to compute the output. To do this, we will replace a function $f(x)$ with an extended function $F(x, y) = (x, y \oplus f(x))$. Unlike in section 6.2, the input x can consist of several

bits. The output *y* will still be a single bit, since all Boolean operations we'll consider have one-bit outputs.

2 Replace the reversible operation with its quantum implementation.

Some Boolean operations are already reversible and thus allow a different, in-place implementation that doesn't use an extra bit to store the output. I'll note these alternative implementations whenever this happens, since they can be convenient in some cases.

NOT

Classical NOT gate is the only Boolean logic operation that is already reversible. Indeed, NOT 0 = 1 and NOT 1 = 0, and we can recover the input value that produced the given output value by applying the NOT gate to that output value.

This means that for the NOT gate, we can skip the step of making it reversible, and compute it in-place. The effect its quantum implementation on the basis states looks familiar too: a gate that converts $|0\rangle$ to $|1\rangle$ and vice versa is just the X gate!

However, sometimes it can be useful to apply the NOT gate out-of-place, using an extra bit to store the output. For example, evaluating more complicated functions that we'll see in section 6.5 requires calculating several intermediate values based on the input bits and then using these intermediate values to get the final result. If one of these intermediate values is the negation of one of the input bits, we cannot compute it in-place, since this would affect the calculation of the other intermediate values evaluated later.

The extended function that calculates the NOT gate out-of-place is

$$F_{\text{NOT}}(x, y) = (x, y \oplus \text{NOT } x) = (x, y \oplus x \oplus 1)$$

The quantum circuit that evaluates this function consists of two gates:

- A CNOT gate converts the input $|x\rangle |y\rangle$ into $|x\rangle |y \oplus x\rangle$.
- After that, an X gate applied to the second qubit converts $|x\rangle |y \oplus x\rangle$ into $|x\rangle |y \oplus x \oplus 1\rangle$. This X gate can also be applied before the CNOT; these gates *commute*, that is, the order in which they are applied does not change the result.

NOTE You might have noticed that the Boolean function $f(x) = \text{NOT } x$ is the same as the one-bit function $f(x) = 1 - x$ we saw earlier in this chapter, but the circuit we use to calculate it is different. Different sequences of gates can end up performing equivalent transformations! You can check that applying a CNOT gate followed by an X gate on the target qubit is equivalent to a controlled-on-zero X gate.

XOR

Classical XOR gate is not one of the basic Boolean operations, but it's a good starting point for the discussion about implementing two-bit Boolean operations. The XOR gate is not reversible, since each of its outputs is produced by two different inputs.

> **Pigeonhole principle**
>
> More broadly, if an operation has more input bits than output bits, it cannot be reversible, since it's impossible to establish a one-to-one mapping between inputs and outputs. This follows from the *pigeonhole principle*—the observation that if you put n items into $m < n$ containers, at least one container will have more than one item. In our case, the items are inputs and the containers are outputs.
>
> In particular, this means that none of the two-bit Boolean operations are reversible, since each of them has four possible inputs and only two outputs.

However, we can make XOR reversible by preserving only part of its input, rather than the whole input. One possible definition of the extended XOR function is

$$F_{\text{XOR}}(x_0, x_1) = (x_0, x_0 \text{ XOR } x_1) = (x_0, x_0 \oplus x_1)$$

This function is its own inverse, so we can use it to implement the XOR function in-place. Its quantum implementation is familiar again: it's just the CNOT gate!

The extended function that calculates the XOR gate out-of-place acts on three bits (two input bits that we preserve and one bit to calculate the output) and is defined as follows:

$$F_{\text{XOR}}(x_0, x_1, y) = (x_0, x_1, y \oplus x_0 \text{ XOR } x_1) = (x_0, x_1, y \oplus x_0 \oplus x_1)$$

There is no single standard quantum gate that would implement this function. Instead, we can use two CNOT gates, with each of the inputs x_0 and x_1 as control and the output y as the target:

$$(x_0, x_1, y) \xrightarrow{\text{CNOT}_{x_0, y}} (x_0, x_1, y \oplus x_0) \xrightarrow{\text{CNOT}_{x_1, y}} (x_0, x_1, y \oplus x_0 \oplus x_1)$$

EQUALITY

Classical equality function is very similar to XOR and can, in fact, be implemented as a combination of two functions we've seen earlier:

$$x_0 \text{ EQUAL } x_1 = \text{NOT } (x_0 \text{ XOR } x_1)$$

> **TIP** Any time you need to check that two reversible computations are the same, you can do it by writing down their truth tables and comparing them. Remember, quantum computations that don't involve measurements are linear and thus are completely defined by their effects on the basis states, which for reversible computations are the same as the truth tables of classical computations.

Since we've seen that the NOT function can be computed in-place, the out-of-place quantum implementation of the equality function can be done on three qubits (same as XOR) as follows:

1 Implement XOR out-of-place using two CNOT gates, with each of the inputs x_0 and x_1 as control and the output y as the target.

2 Apply in-place NOT to the result stored in the output bit.

This scenario is an excellent example of evaluating the NOT function in-place. Since it's the last step of the computation, and we're negating the final result rather than an input or an intermediate variable, we don't need to use out-of-place evaluation.

AND AND MULTI-BIT AND

The next classical function on the list is AND. It is even "less reversible" than XOR, since it has three different inputs mapped to the same output 0. This means that we cannot implement it in-place, we have to preserve both bits of input to make it reversible.

The extended AND function acts on three bits and can be defined as follows:

$$F_{AND}(x_0, x_1, y) = (x_0, x_1, y \oplus x_0 \text{ AND } x_1)$$

The quantum implementation of this function is just the CCNOT gate, or, in other words, the controlled-NOT gate with two control qubits. Indeed, we need to flip the state of the output qubit if and only if the AND of the two inputs equals 1, that is, when both inputs are 1—and that's exactly the definition of a controlled gate!

The generalization of the AND function that acts on three or more inputs follows the same principle. Since all inputs except one produce the same output 0, we know that we need to preserve all bits of inputs to make the function reversible. We can implement the logic using a controlled-NOT gate with all inputs as controls and the output as a target.

OR AND MULTI-BIT OR

The last classical function in this section is OR. It behaves very similarly to AND: it has three different inputs mapped to the same output 1, so we have to preserve both input bits to make it reversible.

The extended OR function acts on three bits and can be defined as follows:

$$F_{OR}(x_0, x_1, y) = (x_0, x_1, y \oplus x_0 \text{ OR } x_1)$$

However, we don't have a standard quantum operation that would implement this transformation. Instead, we'll represent the OR function as a combination of AND and NOT functions using *De Morgan's laws*:

$$x_0 \text{ OR } x_1 = \text{NOT}\left((\text{NOT } x_0) \text{ AND } (\text{NOT } x_1)\right)$$

This formula allows us to evaluate OR of two bits in the following steps:

1 Evaluate the negations of the input bits NOT x_0 and NOT x_1. We can do this in-place, since each input is used in the computation only once, and modifying them will not accidentally impact a different part of the computation. We'll need to keep in mind that we've modified the input bits for later, though.

2 Evaluate the AND of these two values.

3 Evaluate the negation of the AND to get our OR value. We can do this in-place as well, since this is the final result of the computation.

4 Finally, we need to undo the changes we did to the input bits on the first step, since the overall computation must leave the inputs unchanged.

These steps correspond to the following sequence of quantum gates:

1 Apply X gates to each of the input qubits.
2 Apply a CCNOT gate with two input qubits as controls and the output qubit as the target.
3 Apply an X gate to the output qubit.
4 Apply X gates to each of the input qubits again.

We can swap the last two steps and rewrite them to simplify the quantum program and to express its logic better. Applying a controlled gate with a series of X gates applied to each of the control qubits before and after the controlled gate itself is equivalent to applying the controlled-on-zero variant of the same gate. (Again, you can check this by verifying its effect on all basis states.) Indeed, the effect of the OR function can be described as "0 if all inputs are 0, and 1 otherwise", which is the negation of "1 if all inputs are 0, and 0 otherwise"—and this last function is exactly the effect of the controlled-on-zero X gate.

This gives us the final implementation of the OR function:

1 Apply a controlled-on-zero X gate with two input qubits as controls and the output qubit as the target.
2 Apply an X gate to the output qubit.

The generalization of the OR function that acts on three or more inputs follows the same principle as that of the AND function and uses the same implementation as the two-input OR function, with the controlled-on-zero X gate using all input qubits as controls.

Now, let's see the implementations of these functions in the code.

6.4.2 Qiskit

Listing 6.6 shows the Qiskit code that implements the Boolean operations we discussed in this section as circuits. The code is very similar to that we saw earlier in this chapter and doesn't use any new language features.

Listing 6.6 Qiskit: Implementing Boolean operations as quantum operations

```
from qiskit import QuantumCircuit
from qiskit.circuit.library.standard_gates import XGate

def quantum_not():
  circ = QuantumCircuit(2)
  circ.cx(0, 1)
  circ.x(1)
  return circ

def quantum_xor():
```

```python
    circ = QuantumCircuit(3)
    circ.cx(0, 2)
    circ.cx(1, 2)
    return circ

def quantum_equal():
    circ = QuantumCircuit(3)
    circ.cx(0, 2)
    circ.cx(1, 2)
    circ.x(2)
    return circ

def quantum_and():
    circ = QuantumCircuit(3)
    circ.ccx(0, 1, 2)
    return circ

def quantum_or():
    circ = QuantumCircuit(3)
    circ.append(XGate().control(2, ctrl_state=0), [0, 1, 2])
    circ.x(2)
    return circ

def quantum_multiand(n):
    circ = QuantumCircuit(n + 1)
    circ.append(XGate().control(n), range(n + 1))
    return circ

def quantum_multior(n):
    circ = QuantumCircuit(n + 1)
    circ.append(XGate().control(n, ctrl_state=0), range(n + 1))
    circ.x(n)
    return circ
```

There are multiple ways to show what this code does, for example, use it to print the truth tables of these Boolean operations. The complete code for this section in the GitHub repository includes the tests that verify that these circuits are correct by comparing their effects on the basis states with the results of evaluating the matching Boolean operations classically. The source code of the tests is effectively the same as the code from listing 6.3, so I'm not including it here.

6.4.3 Q#

Listing 6.7 shows the Q# code that implements the Boolean operations we discussed in this section. The code is very similar to that we saw earlier in this chapter and doesn't use any new language features.

> **Listing 6.7 Q#: Implementing Boolean operations as quantum operations**

```
operation Negation(x : Qubit[], y : Qubit) : Unit is Adj + Ctl {
  CNOT(x[0], y);
  X(y);
}
```

```
operation Xor(x : Qubit[], y : Qubit) : Unit is Adj + Ctl {
  CNOT(x[0], y);
  CNOT(x[1], y);
}

operation And(x : Qubit[], y : Qubit) : Unit is Adj + Ctl {
  CCNOT(x[0], x[1], y);
}

operation Or(x : Qubit[], y : Qubit) : Unit is Adj + Ctl {
  ApplyControlledOnInt(0, X, x, y);
  X(y);
}

operation Equality(x : Qubit[], y : Qubit) : Unit is Adj + Ctl {
  CNOT(x[0], y);
  CNOT(x[1], y);
  X(y);
}

operation MultiAnd(x : Qubit[], y : Qubit) : Unit is Adj + Ctl {
  Controlled X(x, y);
}

operation MultiOr(x : Qubit[], y : Qubit) : Unit is Adj + Ctl {
  ApplyControlledOnInt(0, X, x, y);
  X(y);
}
```

There are multiple ways to show what this code does, for example, use it to print the truth tables of these Boolean operations. The complete code for this section in the GitHub repository includes the tests that verify that the implementation of these operations is correct by comparing their effects on the basis states with the results of evaluating the matching Boolean operations classically. The source code of the tests is effectively the same as the code from listing 6.4, so I'm not including it here.

6.5 *Evaluating Boolean expressions*

The last problem of this chapter focuses on evaluating *Boolean expressions*—functions built from Boolean variables, Boolean operators AND, OR, and NOT, and parentheses that define the order in which the expressions should be evaluated.

The Boolean operations x_0 AND x_1, x_0 OR x_1, and NOT x_0 we saw in the previous section are examples of Boolean expressions. However, we already know how to evaluate Boolean expressions that are as simple as that. In this section, we'll look at evaluating slightly more complicated expressions that will allow us to learn more useful tools for implementing reversible computations.

Evaluating a Boolean expression boils down to evaluating several intermediate values and then evaluating the top-level expression using the results of calculations done on the previous steps. This is pretty much how all classical computing works!

Most reversible computations follow this structure as well, combining results of evaluating multiple smaller functions into a single result. Once you learn to implement this pattern on a simple example of Boolean expressions, you'll know how to apply it to more complicated problems.

We'll need a couple of definitions to describe the shape of the expressions we want to evaluate. If you have ever looked at the definition of the Boolean satisfiability problem, you'll find them familiar, but they're worth repeating.

- A *literal* is either a Boolean variable or its negation. Here we only consider variables that are part of the expression input x, not any values obtained from them using other Boolean operators. For example, x_0 and NOT x_1 are literals.
- A *clause* is the result of applying the OR operator to several literals. A clause can also be a single literal. For example, x_0 OR x_1 and NOT x_0 OR NOT x_1 are clauses.
- A *conjunctive normal form* (CNF) of a Boolean expression is a single clause or the result of applying the AND operator to several clauses. For example, the following expression is a Boolean expression in conjunctive normal form:

$$(x_0 \text{ OR } x_1) \text{ AND } (\text{NOT } x_0 \text{ OR NOT } x_1)$$

NOTE Is CNF the only way to describe Boolean expressions, or the simplest one? Neither, actually! Boolean expressions can be written down in many ways. For example, the lengthy expression above is equivalent to the much simpler XOR operator $x_0 \oplus x_1$. However, every Boolean expression has a CNF, so it is a convenient universal way to write them down.

We can now formulate the problem we will consider in this section. We are given a CNF of a Boolean expression with n variables. Our goal is to evaluate this expression on a quantum computer.

This problem is a great getting started project for this topic. It is easy to define and covers all the necessary machinery involved in implementing reversible computations.

6.5.1 Math

The classical computation of a Boolean expression takes two steps:

1. Evaluate each clause as the OR of its arguments and store the results in temporary variables.
2. Evaluate the expression as the AND of the clause evaluation results.

Let's try and replicate this logic in a quantum computation.

We saw earlier in this chapter that both AND and OR operators have to be computed out-of-place, with their inputs separate from their outputs, to make them reversible. This means that we'll need to use extra bits to store the evaluation results of the OR clauses that will be used as inputs to the final AND. This is easy to do in a classical program. We can do something similar in the quantum computation as well, but it will be a little trickier.

In a quantum program, we can allocate extra qubits temporarily, use them in just one part of the computation, and then de-allocate, or release, them. Such qubits are usually referred to as *auxiliary*, to distinguish them from the qubits that serve as the inputs and outputs of our computation and thus remain in use throughout the computation.

Translating the steps of the classical evaluation process into their quantum equivalents naively, we would get the following quantum program:

1. Allocate auxiliary qubits, one per clause, to store the results of their evaluation.
2. Evaluate each clause as the OR of its arguments with the matching auxiliary qubit as the target.
3. Evaluate the expression as the AND of all auxiliary qubits with the output qubit as the target.
4. Release the auxiliary qubits.

This sequence of steps works perfectly, as long as we only ever do quantum computations on basis states. However, the whole point of evaluating classical functions on a quantum computer is to carry out the computations on superposition states. And this is where using the auxiliary qubits starts to become tricky.

In classical computations, we can use any temporary variables and just discard them whenever we don't need them any longer. The same is not as easy to do with the auxiliary qubits once we don't need the information we stored in them. The auxiliary qubits can be entangled with the input and output qubits of our computation, and ignoring this or handling this incorrectly can affect the results of our computation.

Why is leaving auxiliary qubits entangled with the ones we use later in our computation is a bad idea? Remember that entangled qubits cannot be considered in separation, since by definition they form a single system that cannot be represented as a combination of two independent groups of qubits. Auxiliary qubits that are unaccounted for in the theoretical computation can prevent interference in any computation that happens afterward, causing the overall algorithm to produce incorrect results.

> **Example: Entanglement preventing interference**
>
> Let's take a look at a small example of how exactly entanglement can prevent interference from happening properly.
>
> As a reminder, *interference* is the phenomenon of the amplitudes of certain basis states cancelling each other out and the amplitudes of other basis states amplifying each other. The simplest example of interference happens when you apply a Hadamard gate to a qubit to figure out whether it is in the $|+\rangle$ or the $|-\rangle$ state.
>
> If the qubit is in the $|+\rangle$ state, the result of applying a Hadamard gate will be
>
> $$\frac{1}{\sqrt{2}}\left(\frac{1}{\sqrt{2}}(|0\rangle + |1\rangle) + \frac{1}{\sqrt{2}}(|0\rangle - |1\rangle)\right) = |0\rangle$$

6.5 Evaluating Boolean expressions

> In this case, the amplitudes of the basis state $|1\rangle$ in the sum cancelled each other out, and the amplitudes of the basis state $|0\rangle$ amplified each other. Measuring the qubit now will give the result 0 that points to the $|+\rangle$ state. Similarly, if the qubit is in the $|-\rangle$ state, the amplitudes of the $|0\rangle$ state cancel each other out, and measuring the qubit gives the result 1, pointing to $|-\rangle$ state.
>
> However, if the same qubit is entangled with another one, the same action of applying a Hadamard gate and measuring the qubit gives very different results!
>
> For example, let's say that the qubit is the first qubit in the Bell pair, and we want to figure out the relative sign between the two basis states in the pair, that is, to decide whether the state is $\frac{1}{\sqrt{2}}(|00\rangle + |11\rangle)$ or $\frac{1}{\sqrt{2}}(|00\rangle - |11\rangle)$.
>
> Now, applying a Hadamard gate to the first qubit of the two-qubit system transforms it to one of the following states: $\frac{1}{2}(|00\rangle + |01\rangle + |10\rangle - |11\rangle)$ or $\frac{1}{2}(|00\rangle + |01\rangle - |10\rangle + |11\rangle)$. These two states behave identically when the first qubit is measured, giving 0 and 1 results with 50% probability each.
>
> This simple example shows how a single-qubit algorithm stops working if this qubit is entangled with another. The same happens with other, more complicated algorithms.

The next natural thing to try is returning the auxiliary qubits to the $|0\rangle$ state to disentangle them from the main qubits. This is the right approach, as long as it is executed carefully.

We can not, for example, just measure the auxiliary qubits to break the entanglement. Why? Remember that measuring a superposition state collapses it to a basis state that matches the measurement outcome. If we measure only the auxiliary qubits, the state will collapse to a superposition of only those basis states for which the state of the auxiliary qubits matches the measurement outcomes. Sometimes this can be useful, but when working with reversible computations, we need to preserve all the basis states in the input, not just a subset of them, so we can't have any state collapse, even a partial one.

The correct approach to disentangling the auxiliary qubits from the main qubits is called *Bennett's trick*. The general form of Bennett's trick relies on using extra qubits to store an auxiliary copy of the output; its steps are shown in table 6.3.

Table 6.3 The steps of the Bennett's trick

Step	Input	Auxiliary qubits	Auxiliary output	Final output
Initialize	$|x\rangle$	$|0\rangle$	$|0\rangle$	$|y\rangle$
Compute the result and store it in the auxiliary output	$|x\rangle$	$|aux\rangle$	$|f(x)\rangle$	$|y\rangle$
Copy the result to the final output	$|x\rangle$	$|aux\rangle$	$|f(x)\rangle$	$|y \oplus f(x)\rangle$
Uncompute the auxiliary output to return auxiliary qubits to $|0\rangle$	$|x\rangle$	$|0\rangle$	$|0\rangle$	$|y \oplus f(x)\rangle$

Let's walk through these steps in more detail. Note that here we discuss all the transformations as they are applied to the input x, encoded as the basis state $|x\rangle$. In this context, "copy" means "use CNOT gates to copy the basis states" rather than "violate the no-cloning theorem by copying the entire state of the register."

1. We start with four qubit arrays (some of them might consist of just one qubit, depending on the problem definition):
   - The input qubits in the $|x\rangle$ state.
   - Two auxiliary qubit registers: the auxiliary qubits necessary to compute the output, and the temporary output register, both in the $|0\rangle$ state.
   - The output qubits in the $|y\rangle$ state.

   At this point, the state of the system is

   $$|x\rangle \otimes |0\rangle \otimes |0\rangle \otimes |y\rangle$$

2. We run the computation using the first three registers. After this, the state of auxiliary qubits is something we don't care about beyond them being entangled with the rest of the qubits, so we'll denote it $|\text{aux}\rangle$:

   $$|x\rangle \otimes |\text{aux}\rangle \otimes |f(x)\rangle \otimes |y\rangle$$

   For our example problem of evaluating Boolean expressions, we would evaluate the OR clauses and store the results in the auxiliary qubits, then evaluate the final AND expression and store the result in the auxiliary output qubits.

3. We copy the computation result from the auxiliary output qubits to the final output qubits using CNOT gates, one per output bit:

   $$|x\rangle \otimes |\text{aux}\rangle \otimes |f(x)\rangle \otimes |y \oplus f(x)\rangle$$

4. Finally, we *uncompute* both registers of the auxiliary qubits to return them to the $|0\rangle$ state without measurements. To do this, we apply the adjoint of the computation we ran on step 2. By definition, it has the following effect on the system:

   $$|x\rangle \otimes |0\rangle \otimes |0\rangle \otimes |y \oplus f(x)\rangle$$

This sequence of steps can sometimes be simplified, depending on the problem. For example, when evaluating Boolean expressions, we can avoid using the auxiliary output qubit and write the computation result directly to the final output qubit. This will also simplify the uncomputation step. Here is the sequence of steps that is sufficient to evaluate a Boolean expression:

1. Allocate auxiliary qubits, one per expression clause, to store the results of their evaluation. Do not allocate any qubits for auxiliary output.
2. Evaluate each clause as the OR of its arguments with the matching auxiliary qubit as the target. If any literals in the clause are negations of input variables rather than variables themselves, apply an X gate to the corresponding input

qubits to evaluate the negation of the variable before applying the OR operation to the inputs. Remember to apply an X gate to those qubits again afterward to uncompute the changes done to them, same as we did when constructing the OR operation itself.

3 Evaluate the expression as the AND of all auxiliary qubits with the final output qubit as the target.

4 Uncompute the auxiliary qubits using the adjoint of step 2. In this case, the adjoint of the transformation is the same as the transformation itself, so we can just repeat the same steps.

5 Release the auxiliary qubits now that they were returned to the $|0\rangle$ state.

This kind of procedure can be tricky to wrap your head around at a glance. It takes practice and experimentation with different problems to really get the grasp of all the nuances involved. Fortunately, by now you have all the necessary tools at your disposal! Writing the code allows you to can experiment with the solution by varying the input states, exploring the system states at different steps, and so on.

Let's see what the code for our problem looks like.

6.5.2 Qiskit

Listing 6.8 shows the Qiskit code that evaluates a Boolean expression given as its conjunctive normal form. It relies on circuits `quantum_multior` and `quantum_multiand` from listing 6.6 as building blocks.

Listing 6.8 Qiskit: Evaluating a Boolean expression as a quantum operation

```
from qiskit import QuantumCircuit

def evaluate_clause(n, literals):            ◄── Circuit that evaluates one clause
  circ = QuantumCircuit(n + 1)
  if len(literals) == 0:
    return circ

  controls = []                              ┐ Constructs a list of qubits
  for (ind, neg) in literals:                ◄┘ to serve as OR inputs
    controls.append(ind)
    if not neg:                              ┐ Negates inputs that are included
      circ.x(ind)                            ┘ in literals with negations

  circ.append(quantum_multior(len(controls)),   ◄── Applies OR to evaluate the clause
              controls + [n])

  for (ind, neg) in literals:    ◄── Uncomputes negation of inputs
    if not neg:
      circ.x(ind)

  return circ
                                           ┐ Circuit that evaluates
def evaluate_expression(n, expression):    ◄┘ the expression
  n_clauses = len(expression)
```

```
circ = QuantumCircuit(n + n_clauses + 1)       ◁┐ All qubits allocated
if n_clauses == 0:                              │ at the same time
    circ.x(n)
    return circ

for (ind, clause) in enumerate(expression):    ◁┐ Evaluates individual clauses and
    circ.append(evaluate_clause(n, clause),    │ store the result in auxiliary qubits
                list(range(n)) + [n + ind])

circ.append(quantum_multiand(n_clauses),       ◁── Applies AND to evaluate the expression
            range(n, n + n_clauses + 1))

for (ind, clause) in enumerate(expression):    ◁┐ Uncomputes individual clauses
    circ.append(evaluate_clause(n, clause),    │ to free auxiliary qubits
                list(range(n)) + [n + ind])

return circ
```

Notice that in Qiskit, you build circuits that act on a fixed number of qubits, and you need to specify that number upfront, including any auxiliary qubits you'll need to use during the computation. In the circuit produced by evaluate_expression, the first n qubits are inputs, the next n_clauses qubits are auxiliary qubits, and the last qubit is the output. You need to always keep the order of qubits in mind when you're using circuits, whether to interpret the measurement results or to append these circuits to other, larger circuits that carry out more complicated computations.

The logic of the tests is effectively the same as the one we used in listing 6.3, so I'm not including it here. The GitHub repository includes the complete project code with tests for both evaluate_clause and evaluate_expression. The results of code execution should be passing tests.

6.5.3 Q#

Listing 6.9 shows the Q# code that evaluates a Boolean expression given as its conjunctive normal form. It reuses operations MultiAnd and MultiOr from listing 6.7.

Listing 6.9 Q#: Evaluating a Boolean expression as a quantum operation

```
import Std.Arrays.*;

operation EvaluateClause(       ◁── Operation that evaluates one clause
    x : Qubit[],
    y : Qubit,
    literals : (Int, Bool)[]
) : Unit is Adj + Ctl {
    let controlQubits =
        Mapped((ind, _) -> x[ind], literals);    ◁── List of qubits to serve as OR inputs

    let controlPattern =
        Mapped((_, pos) -> pos, literals);       ◁── List of negations in clause literals
    within {
        ApplyPauliFromBitString(PauliX, false,   ◁┐ Negates inputs that are
                                                  │ included in literals with negations
```

6.5 Evaluating Boolean expressions

```
      controlPattern, controlQubits);
  } apply {
    MultiOr(controlQubits, y);    ←— Applies OR to evaluate the clause
  }
}                                 ←┐ Uncomputation done automatically
                                   ┘ by the within-apply construct
operation EvaluateExpression(     ←— Operation that evaluates the expression
  x : Qubit[],
  y : Qubit,
  expression : (Int, Bool)[][]
) : Unit is Adj + Ctl {
  let nClauses = Length(expression);    ┐ Allocates auxiliary qubits
  use clauseResults = Qubit[nClauses]; ←┘ within the operation
  within {
    for (clause, result) in
      Zipped(expression, clauseResults) {  ←┐ Evaluates individual clauses
        EvaluateClause(x, result, clause);   │ and stores the result
    }                                        ┘ in auxiliary qubits
  } apply {
    MultiAnd(clauseResults, y);   ←— Applies AND to evaluate the expression
  }                               ←┐ Uncomputation done automatically
}                                  ┘ by the within-apply construct
```

Q# has several convenient features that let us express this kind of computation neatly. First, the language allows you to allocate extra qubits at any time, thus sparing you the need to keep track of all auxiliary qubits used by the libraries and helper operations you rely on. Here, operation `EvaluateExpression` allocates qubits in addition to those passed to it as the arguments, and no code that calls this operation needs to know about them. The qubits allocated within an operation start in the $|0\rangle$ state and have to be returned to the $|0\rangle$ state by the time they are released at the end of the scope in which they were allocated.

Second, the code uses the within-apply construct called *conjugation*. This is a control flow statement that implements the following pattern:

1. Compute intermediate results using the code in the `within` block.
2. Compute the final results using the code in the `apply` block.
3. Uncompute the intermediate results using the adjoint of the code in the `within` block.

This pattern is common in quantum programs, and having a dedicated language construct that implements it helps keep the code cleaner and eliminate the bugs that would be introduced by writing the uncomputation code by hand every time.

The logic of the tests is effectively the same as the one we used in listing 6.4, so I'm not including it here. The GitHub repository includes the complete project code with tests for both `EvaluateClause` and `EvaluateExpression`. The results of code execution should be passing tests.

6.6 Going beyond

Do you want to spend some more time exploring variations of the problems discussed in this chapter before moving on to the next topic? Here are some additional ideas for simpler examples, similar problems, and ways to extend these problems if you want to try your hand at something more challenging:

- In section 6.5, we looked at just one form of Boolean expressions, the conjunctive normal form. For other problems, it can be useful to consider expressions of similar structure that use different Boolean operations in the clauses. In general, each clause could use a different Boolean operation to combine literals, and the formula could use an operation other than AND to combine the clauses. Modify the code we wrote in this chapter to handle this generalized form of Boolean expressions.
- Consider other examples of classical problems that can be expressed as search problems for a specific function, such as the graph coloring problem. How would you approach implementing the functions that describe them? (We will return to this question in chapter 8.)
- In this chapter, we focused on problems that were formulated in terms of Boolean variables. The other big class of problems are formulated in terms of numbers—integers or fractions. Try to implement some arithmetic operations on integers, such as addition, multiplication, or comparison with an integer constant, as a reversible computation. How do you need to change the test code to accommodate the switch from functions that have single-bit outputs to functions that return multiple bits?

Summary

- Solving a classical problem on a quantum computer starts with converting the classical problem description to a "quantum" formulation, which then is used to implement the quantum algorithm for solving this problem. This is called reversible computing.
- When converting a classical function $f(x)$ to a quantum computation, classical variables are mapped onto qubit arrays, and classical computations are mapped onto unitary transformations. The goal is to find a sequence of quantum gates that mimics the classical function evaluation, transforming the input array in any basis state $|x\rangle$ so that the value of $f(x)$ is encoded in the result.
- A classical function is reversible if it converts each input to exactly one output, and each output is produced by exactly one input.
- The systematic approach to implementing a classical function as a quantum computation starts with writing the process of its evaluation as a sequence of primitive logic gates. Each logic gate is then replaced by its reversible equivalent, and finally, these are replaced with their quantum gate implementations.

- Reversible computing defines the behavior of a quantum operation by specifying its effects on all basis states based on the classical function this operation implements. Its effect on a superposition state is then defined as a linear combination of its effects on individual basis states that are part of that superposition state.
- You can make any nonreversible function reversible by extending its inputs and outputs, keeping the inputs as part of the output and using a separate output bit to calculate the function value.
- You can allocate extra qubits, called auxiliary qubits, to store the values of temporary variables during the computations.
- Uncomputation involves applying adjoint of the parts of the computation you used to get the final result. You need to uncompute any changes you have done to the states of the input qubits and the auxiliary qubits to make sure your computation doesn't introduce any unexpected side effects.

Grover's search algorithm

This chapter covers

- Using Grover's algorithm to solve simple search problems
- Implementing simple classical functions on a quantum computer
- Implementing and testing end-to-end quantum algorithms
- Using Q# and Qiskit to implement Grover's algorithm

As we saw in chapter 6, solving a classical problem on a quantum computer takes several steps (see figure 7.1). It starts with converting the classical problem to its "quantum" formulation that allows us to come up with a quantum algorithm for it. Then, this algorithm has to be implemented as a quantum program. Finally, we need to compare the performance of the quantum solution to that of the best classical solution for the same problem to decide whether using the quantum algorithm for this problem is a good idea.

In chapter 6, we learned the general approach to the first step, converting a classical computation that describes the problem into an equivalent quantum computation. In this chapter, we'll consider the second step and learn an example of a quantum algorithm for solving a classical problem. In the last two chapters, we'll see how to implement this algorithm as an end-to-end solution for a specific problem and to evaluate its performance.

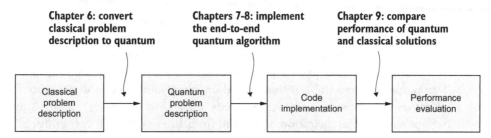

Figure 7.1 Solving a classical problem on a quantum computer involves converting the problem to its "quantum" formulation, implementing the quantum algorithm as code, and evaluating the performance of the quantum solution to compare it to that of the classical algorithms for solving the same problem.

Generally, quantum algorithms are not limited to only quantum computations. Instead, they follow a hybrid quantum-classical structure shown in figure 7.2.

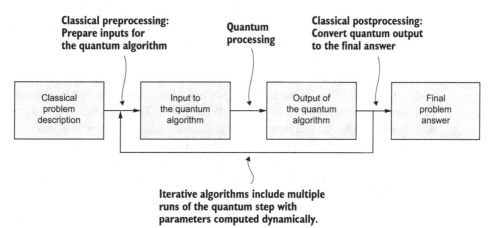

Figure 7.2 A quantum algorithm can combine classical and quantum computations. Typically, it starts with a classical data preprocessing step that prepares input data for the quantum computation and passes it to the quantum subroutine. The results of the quantum computation are then fed into another classical step, postprocessing, that converts them into the final problem solution. Some of these steps can be omitted for simple algorithms or repeated with some variation for iterative algorithms.

In general, a program that solves a classical problem using a quantum algorithm consists of several parts. The first step is classical preprocessing of the data that is used as the input for the quantum algorithm. This step can include getting the classical problem description (for example, reading it from a file or a database or calculating it on the fly using a classical program) and converting it into the format required by the quantum subroutine. For example, a program that calculates the ground state energy of a molecule needs a description of that molecule's structure to work with. The classical preprocessing step will read this description from a file (for example, using the FCIDump file format common for a lot of chemistry software packages) and use that information to calculate the values that will be passed to the quantum algorithm.

Quantum computation is the core of the quantum algorithm. It carries out the computations that are inefficient to do on a classical computer, thus providing the potential quantum speedup over purely classical solutions.

The results of the quantum computation are then fed into classical postprocessing step that converts them into the final problem solution or the decision about the further calculations the program needs to run. For example, the quantum part of Shor's integer factorization algorithm finds the period of a certain function, and the classical postprocessing turns this value into the final answer—the factors of the given number. This step could involve formatting the outputs in a human-readable way, formulating the next iteration of an iterative algorithm, and so on.

The examples of quantum programs you've seen so far in this book didn't always obviously follow this structure, either because the inputs and the outputs of the quantum routines were simple enough to be hardcoded rather than computed, or because the quantum libraries we developed didn't have an "output" beyond the changes they applied to quantum states. Now, we'll finally solve a classical problem that will make the distinction between quantum and classical parts of the solution explicit!

The problem we'll consider in this chapter is called the *unstructured search problem*, and it is defined in the following way. You are given a function f that takes a bit string of n bits as the input and returns a single bit, 0 or 1. This function is guaranteed to be deterministic, that is, to always return the same output for a certain input. However, you do not know anything else about this function! You can only learn something about this function by using the given *oracle*— a tool that allows you to find the value returned by $f(x)$ for any input x you give it but does not expose any information about its internals.

Your goal is to use this oracle to invert the function: to find an input value x_0 for which the value of the function will be 1 or, in other words, to find any solution to the equation $f(x_0) = 1$. You want to do it in as few function evaluations, called *queries*, as possible.

In this formulation of the problem, you cannot analyze the internal structure of the function to figure out how it behaves. For all you know, it could store the mapping of outputs to inputs in a massive lookup table that was generated randomly, so it might not have any meaningful internal structure at all! This way, any algorithm that solves the problem has to stay generic and independent of the specific function given to it.

A lot of classical problems can be either represented as instances of the search problem or solved using this problem as a building block. For example, all constraint satisfaction problems are very straightforward to formulate in terms of the search problem:

- The variables that describe the constraint satisfaction problem are the input x.
- The value of the function f for a specific variable assignment x is defined as follows: if the variable assignment x satisfies all the constraints of the problem, $f(x) = 1$; otherwise, $f(x) = 0$.

- The search problem then looks for any value x_0 for which $f(x_0) = 1$—that is, any variable assignment that satisfies all constraints.

More broadly, most problems can be formulated as search problems: just define the value you're looking for as the input x, and say that $f(x) = 1$ if the value x is the answer to your problem, and $f(x) = 0$ if it's not! However, this approach is not practical for a lot of real-life problems; we'll talk more about this in chapter 9.

To begin the discussion of a quantum solution to the search problem, I'll introduce the concept of *quantum oracles*—the quantum equivalent of the tool used to evaluate the function in the classical search problem. I'll show two types of quantum oracles and their implementation for a simple example problem of looking for a bit string that belongs to the given list.

Next, we'll discuss *Grover's search algorithm*—the quantum algorithm for solving the search problem. I'll walk you through the theory and the basic implementation of the algorithm using the same simple problem to showcase the behavior of the algorithm.

In chapter 8, we'll use Grover's search to solve a more complicated classical problem, the N queens puzzle—a simple constraint satisfaction problem that will allow us to implement and compare different approaches to solving search problems. This will set the scene for chapter 9, in which we'll talk about evaluating the performance of quantum algorithms, comparing different quantum programs in terms of their efficiency and comparing quantum algorithms with their classical counterparts.

7.1 Quantum oracles

In classical computing, an *oracle* is a tool that can solve a certain problem in one operation (called a *query* to the oracle). The concept of oracles is broadly used in complexity theory to study decision problems.

In quantum computing, oracles play a similar role. A *quantum oracle* is a unitary operation that implements a classical function in some way that allows a quantum algorithm to use it to solve a classical problem. The quantum oracle serves as an input to the algorithm, separating the generic logic of the algorithm from the implementation details of the function that describes the specific problem instance.

Grover's search covered in this chapter is probably the most famous quantum algorithm among those that rely on quantum oracles. The quantum oracle used as the input to Grover's algorithm implements the classical function $f(x)$ that describes the search problem—the problem of looking for the value x_0 for which $f(x_0) = 1$. As we'll see later in the book, this function can describe a variety of constraints on the value we search for.

Other well-known examples include Deutsch and Deutsch–Jozsa algorithms that aim to decide whether the given function is constant or balanced, and Bernstein–Vazirani and Simon's algorithms that learn the hidden bit string for the given function of a certain structure. In these cases, the oracle typically implements a simpler classical computation. For example, a function $f(x)$ defined as the sum of bits in the binary notation of x modulo 2 has a very straightforward implementation as a quantum oracle and can be used as an input to both Deutsch–Jozsa and Bernstein–Vazirani algorithms.

To start, let's see how to define and implement two most commonly used types of quantum oracles. In this section, I'll use a very simple classical function: $f(x) = 1$ if x is one of the bit strings on the given list, and 0 otherwise.

Table 7.1 shows an example of a function that acts on three-bit strings and "marks" two of them, 001 and 110. The function returns 1 for each of these two inputs and 0 for the other six possible inputs.

Table 7.1 The function that acts on three-bit strings and "marks" bit strings 001 and 110

x	000	001	010	011	100	101	110	111
$f(x)$	0	1	0	0	0	0	1	0

NOTE Technically, this function takes two parameters: the input x and the list of "marked" bit strings. However, once we specify the problem instance we want to solve, such as the function from table 7.1, the list of bit strings is fixed based on that specification, so that all function evaluations within one run of the algorithm will differ only in the first argument and share the second argument.

7.1.1 Math

There are two main types of quantum oracles used in most quantum algorithms: marking oracles and phase oracles. Both these types encode the n-bit function input x into a state of an n-qubit basis state:

$$x = (x_0, x_1, ..., x_{n-1}) \rightarrow |x\rangle = |x_0\rangle \otimes |x_1\rangle \otimes ... \otimes |x_{n-1}\rangle$$

The two types of quantum oracles differ in how they encode the output of the function $f(x)$ in the effects of the unitary operation that implements the oracle.

PHASE ORACLES

A *phase oracle* is a unitary that acts on n qubits, same as the function f itself, and encodes the return values of the function in the relative phases of the input basis states. Specifically, a phase oracle multiplies the amplitudes of all basis states for which $f(x) = 1$ by a relative phase -1 and leaves the amplitudes of all basis states for which $f(x) = 0$ unchanged. Figure 7.3 shows the effects of the phase oracle for the function described in table 7.1 on a superposition state. You can see that the amplitudes of two "marked" basis states, $|001\rangle$ and $|110\rangle$, are multiplied by -1. All other amplitudes in the superposition are not affected.

7.1 Quantum oracles

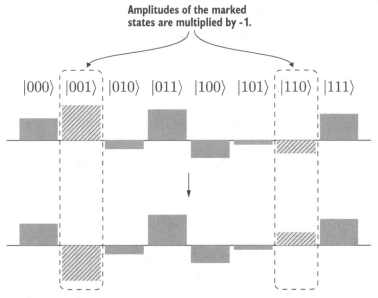

Figure 7.3 The effect of the phase oracle for the function that marks values 001 and 110 on a superposition state with real amplitudes. The amplitudes of the basis states that correspond to the marked values (striped bars) are multiplied by −1. The rest of the amplitudes do not change.

Mathematically, the effect of the phase oracle U_p on the basis state $|x\rangle$ can be expressed as follows:

$$U_p |x\rangle = (-1)^{f(x)} |x\rangle$$

The effect of the phase oracle on a superposition state is defined via its effects on individual basis states and the linearity of unitary transformations:

$$U_p \sum_x a_x |x\rangle = \sum_x (-1)^{f(x)} a_x |x\rangle$$

MARKING ORACLES

By contrast, a *marking oracle* is a unitary that acts on $n+1$ qubits and encodes the return value of the function in the state of that additional qubit (usually called the "target qubit"). When acting on the input qubits in the state $|x\rangle |y\rangle$, where y is a 0 or 1 bit, the marking oracle flips the state of the target qubit for all basis states for which $f(x) = 1$, and leaves it unchanged for all basis states for which $f(x) = 0$. Figure 7.4 shows the effects of the marking oracle for the function described in table 7.1 on a superposition state.

You can see that the amplitudes of the two basis states that correspond to the input value 001, $|001\rangle |0\rangle$ and $|001\rangle |1\rangle$, are swapped, meaning that the state $|001\rangle |0\rangle$ became $|001\rangle |1\rangle$ and vice versa. The same swap happens for the two basis states that correspond to the input value 110. The rest of the basis states are unaffected.

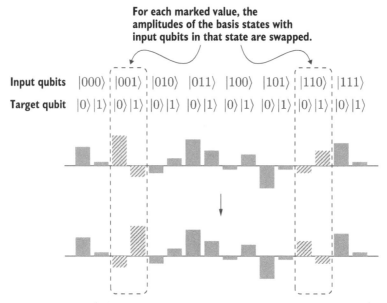

Figure 7.4 The effect of the marking oracle for the function that marks values 001 and 110 on a superposition state with real amplitudes. For each marked value, there are two basis states with the input qubits in the corresponding state (marked with striped bars): for one of them, the target qubit is in the $|0\rangle$ state, and for the other one, it's in the $|1\rangle$ state. The amplitudes of these pairs of basis states are swapped. The rest of the amplitudes do not change.

Mathematically, the effect of the marking oracle U_m on the basis state with the input qubits in the state $|x\rangle$ and the target qubit in the state $|y\rangle$ can be expressed as

$$U_m |x\rangle |y\rangle = |x\rangle |y \oplus f(x)\rangle$$

> **NOTE** This expression should look familiar to you. Indeed, this is exactly the approach to making classical functions reversible and evaluating them on a quantum computer that we saw in chapter 6!

Similarly, to phase oracles and other unitaries, the effect of the marking oracle on a superposition state is defined based on its linearity. Note that both the input qubits and the target qubit can be in superposition in this expression:

$$U_m \sum_{x,y} a_{x,y} |x\rangle |y\rangle = \sum_{x,y} a_{x,y} |x\rangle |y \oplus f(x)\rangle$$

CONVERTING ONE TYPE OF ORACLES INTO ANOTHER

Marking oracles are typically easier to implement, especially once you go beyond the trivial examples and start working with classical functions that rely on general reversible computing techniques in their implementation. We will see examples of such functions in chapter 8 when working on solving the N queens puzzle.

Quantum algorithms, on the other hand, usually rely on a function implementation as a phase oracle. Grover's search is a prominent example of an algorithm that works with a phase oracle, as we'll see in section 7.2.

Conveniently, the two types of oracles can be converted into each other easily. Implementing an algorithm that relies on a phase oracle often starts by implementing a marking oracle for the required function and then converting it into a phase oracle.

How can we implement a phase oracle for a function if we already have the marking oracle for that function implemented? We can use the phase kickback trick similar to the one we saw in chapter 5.

> **TIP** As a reminder, phase kickback refers to the fact that applying a controlled unitary to target qubit(s) in a special state can "kick" a relative phase back to the control qubit(s). We can think of the marking oracle as a controlled X gate that is applied to the target qubit when the control qubits are in one of the basis states that correspond to marked bit strings. With the idea of the oracle reframed this way, phase kickback becomes an obvious trick to try!

Let's see what happens if you apply a marking oracle U_m to a state $|x\rangle|-\rangle$:

$$U_m |x\rangle |-\rangle = U_m |x\rangle \tfrac{1}{\sqrt{2}}(|0\rangle - |1\rangle) = \tfrac{1}{\sqrt{2}}(U_m |x\rangle |0\rangle - U_m |x\rangle |1\rangle)$$

$$= \begin{cases} |x\rangle \tfrac{1}{\sqrt{2}}(|0\rangle - |1\rangle) & \text{if } f(x) = 0 \\ |x\rangle \tfrac{1}{\sqrt{2}}(|1\rangle - |0\rangle) & \text{if } f(x) = 1 \end{cases}$$

$$= \begin{cases} |x\rangle \tfrac{1}{\sqrt{2}}(|0\rangle - |1\rangle) & \text{if } f(x) = 0 \\ -|x\rangle \tfrac{1}{\sqrt{2}}(|0\rangle - |1\rangle) & \text{if } f(x) = 1 \end{cases}$$

You can see that the state of the target qubit $|-\rangle = \tfrac{1}{\sqrt{2}}(|0\rangle - |1\rangle)$ remains unchanged, and the input register x is multiplied by $(-1)^{f(x)}$. That's exactly what we want to happen when we apply a phase oracle to the input register alone! Therefore, to implement a phase oracle for a function, we can temporarily use an extra qubit in the $|-\rangle$ state and apply the marking oracle for the same function to our input register and that extra qubit. The extra qubit can be released afterward, or kept around in the same state for the next time we need to apply the phase kickback trick.

> **Converting a phase oracle into a marking oracle**
>
> Since marking oracles are much easier to implement than phase oracles, the conversion in the other direction, from a phase oracle into a marking oracle, is almost never required. However, it is possible to implement a marking oracle for a function if you only have access to a phase oracle for that function, as long as that phase oracle has a controlled version defined.
>
> How can you do that? The phase kickback trick comes in handy again—that's why you need a controlled version of the phase oracle. Let's start with a basis state $|x\rangle|0\rangle$ and perform the following sequence of steps:

(continued)

1. Apply a Hadamard gate to the target qubit $|0\rangle$:

$$|x\rangle |0\rangle \rightarrow |x\rangle \tfrac{1}{\sqrt{2}}(|0\rangle + |1\rangle)$$

2. Apply a controlled variant of the phase oracle U_p with the target qubit as the control and the input qubits $|x\rangle$ as the target. The term $|x\rangle |0\rangle$ of the superposition remains unchanged, since the control qubit in it is in the $|0\rangle$ state. The term $|x\rangle |1\rangle$, however, becomes $(U_p |x\rangle)|1\rangle$, and this expression depends on the value of $f(x)$: if $f(x) = 0$, $U_p |x\rangle = |x\rangle$, and the term remains unchanged, but if $f(x) = 1$, $U_p |x\rangle = -|x\rangle$, and the term acquires the relative phase of -1.

   Put together, the effect of the controlled phase oracle on the state is

$$|x\rangle \tfrac{1}{\sqrt{2}}(|0\rangle + |1\rangle) \rightarrow \begin{cases} |x\rangle \tfrac{1}{\sqrt{2}}(|0\rangle + |1\rangle) & \text{if } f(x) = 0 \\ |x\rangle \tfrac{1}{\sqrt{2}}(|0\rangle - |1\rangle) & \text{if } f(x) = 1 \end{cases}$$

3. Apply a Hadamard gate to the target qubit again. This does not affect $|x\rangle$, and the state of the target qubit becomes

$$\begin{cases} \tfrac{1}{\sqrt{2}}(|0\rangle + |1\rangle) & \text{if } f(x) = 0 \\ \tfrac{1}{\sqrt{2}}(|0\rangle - |1\rangle) & \text{if } f(x) = 1 \end{cases} \rightarrow \begin{cases} |0\rangle & \text{if } f(x) = 0 \\ |1\rangle & \text{if } f(x) = 1 \end{cases}$$

You can analyze the scenario in which the target qubit starts in the $|1\rangle$ state in the same way, and the result will be the same: the state of the target qubit remains unchanged if $f(x) = 0$, and it is flipped if $f(x) = 1$. And this is exactly the behavior of the marking oracle for this function!

With these definitions of marking and phase oracles in mind, let's implement both kinds of oracles for the example we'll be using in the first part of this chapter: the function $f(x) = 1$ if x is one of the bit strings on the given list, and 0 otherwise.

The marking oracle for this function is a unitary that acts on the input qubit register and the target qubit. It should flip the state of the target qubit if the input qubit register is in one of the basis states from the given lis and leave the target qubit unchanged for all other basis states.

We have actually encountered a quantum gate with a similar effect earlier in the book when implementing a CS unitary in section 3.9. We applied a series of controlled single-qubit gates for that, with each gate using multiple control qubits and a control pattern that corresponded to a binary notation of an integer. This is exactly the kind of gate we need here as well, since we need to apply a state flip (an X gate) to the target qubit if the control register is in a basis state from the given list.

The implementation of the marking oracle ends up being very straightforward: for each state on the given list, apply a controlled gate with the input register as control and the target qubit as the target, using that state as the control pattern. For the earlier example of the list [001, 110], the marking oracle will use two controlled X gates with control patterns $|001\rangle$ and $|110\rangle$.

> **NOTE** In the code, it can be more convenient to represent the list entries as integers rather than as bit strings. If you do this, you need to keep an eye on the endianness of the encoding you use to map integers onto bit strings and qubit arrays to keep it consistent throughout the program.

We won't try and implement the phase oracle for this function by hand. Instead, the phase kickback trick we just discussed will give us the phase oracle automatically!

Before we move on to the code for these two oracles, let's take a moment to consider our plan for testing it. Fortunately, we don't need to reinvent the wheel! We spent a fair amount of time in previous chapters learning to test different kinds of unitaries, so we can just reuse our learnings from earlier. For phase oracles, we can take the same approach we introduced in section 3.3: use the built-in language tools to extract the matrix of the unitary and compare it with the expected matrix.

The matrix of a phase oracle

What does the matrix of a phase oracle look like? Remember that the columns of a unitary matrix U describe the results of applying this unitary to each of the basis states: the first column of U is the vector $U|0\rangle$, the second column is $U|1\rangle$, and so on, and the last column is $U|2^n - 1\rangle$. We can construct the matrix of a transformation if we know its effect on each basis state.

When a phase oracle is applied to a basis state, it doesn't change the state, other than possibly multiplying it by -1. For any basis state $|x\rangle$, the vector $U|x\rangle$ is either $|x\rangle$ itself or $-|x\rangle$, depending on the value of the function $f(x)$.

This means that the matrix of any phase oracle has a very simple shape: it is a diagonal matrix with each element on the main diagonal either 1 or -1. We can figure out which elements are 1 and which ones are -1 by calculating the function f for each basis state.

We could use a similar approach for testing marking oracles as well, but their matrix representations are slightly more tricky to spell out. Instead, it is more convenient to use the approach to testing reversible computations from section 6.3: compare the results produced by the oracle with those returned by classical function evaluation. Now, let's see how to convert those ideas for oracles and tests for them into code.

7.1.2 Qiskit

The following listing shows the Qiskit code that implements the marking oracle for the function that marks the states from the given list and the phase kickback trick that allows to apply it as a phase oracle.

Listing 7.1 Qiskit code for the marking oracle and the phase kickback trick

```
from qiskit import QuantumCircuit
from qiskit.circuit.library.standard_gates import XGate
```

```
def mark_states(n, marked_states):
    circ = QuantumCircuit(n + 1)
    for state in marked_states:
        stateBE = (f"{{:0>{n}b}}".format(state))[::-1]      ◁──┐ Reverses control bit
        circ.append(XGate().control(n, ctrl_state=stateBE),     │ string since controls
            range(n + 1))                                       │ use little-endian
    return circ

def phase_oracle(n, marking_oracle):
    circ = QuantumCircuit(n + 1)         ◁──┐ Uses an extra qubit in the minus state
    circ.h(n)                               │ that remains a part of the circuit
    circ.z(n)
    circ.append(marking_oracle, range(n + 1))
    circ.z(n)
    circ.h(n)
    return circ
```

The function that constructs the circuit for the marking oracle, mark_states, is similar to those we saw in chapter 6. It takes two classical parameters, the number of input qubits and the list of the states to be marked, and returns the circuit built from this information.

Phase kickback trick is implemented as the function phase_oracle. It takes two arguments, the number of input qubits n and the circuit implementing the marking oracle, and constructs a circuit that acts on $n + 1$ qubits. Notice that here, unlike in the Q# code you'll see next, the auxiliary qubit used to implement the phase kickback trick cannot be released immediately after use. Any auxiliary qubits you need in Qiskit subcircuits have to remain a part of the whole circuit, although they can be reused in the later subcircuits.

The persistence of the phase kickback qubit affects the way we have to write the unit tests for Qiskit code. When we get the matrix of the unitary implemented by the circuit returned by phase_oracle, its dimensions will be $2^{n+1} \times 2^{n+1}$ instead of $2^n \times 2^n$ like one would expect from the phase oracle acting on n qubits. What will this matrix look like, taking into account that the rightmost qubit of the register (the qubit with index n) is the phase kickback qubit?

In Qiskit, the rightmost qubit corresponds to the most significant bit of the matrix indices (for a refresher on the matrix indices and their endianness, see our discussion in section 3.5). The sequence of gates applied in the phase kickback implementation leaves the state of the qubit unchanged: whether it was $|0\rangle$ or $|1\rangle$, it will return to that state and remain unentangled with the input qubits. This means that the resulting matrix will still be diagonal, with 1 or −1 elements on the main diagonal and 0 elements everywhere else.

However, −1 elements will only be found in the top left block of the matrix, which corresponds to the phase kickback qubit starting in $|0\rangle$ state. Indeed, phase kickback only changes the input qubits if the target qubit is in the $|-\rangle$ state. If it is in the $|+\rangle$ state, applying the marking oracle doesn't have a −1 phase to kick back into the state of the input qubits, so their state will remain unchanged. The bottom-right block of the matrix will be just an identity. Overall, the matrix will look as follows, where U_p is the matrix of the phase oracle we're looking to implement:

$$\begin{pmatrix} U_p & 0 \\ 0 & I \end{pmatrix}$$

You can find the complete code for this project, including tests for the marking oracle and the phase oracle implemented using it, in the GitHub repo.

7.1.3 Q#

The following listing shows the Q# code that implements the marking oracle for the function that marks the states from the given list and the phase kickback trick that allows to apply it as a phase oracle.

> **Listing 7.2 Q# code for the marking oracle and the phase kickback trick**

```
import Std.Arrays.Reversed;

operation MarkStates(x : Qubit[], y : Qubit, markedStates : Int[]) : Unit {
  for state in markedStates {
    ApplyControlledOnInt(state, X, Reversed(x), y);    ◄── Reverse order of qubits to
  }                                                         use big-endian notation
}

operation ApplyPhaseOracle(
  x : Qubit[], markingOracle : (Qubit[], Qubit) => Unit
) : Unit {
  use aux = Qubit();
  within {
    H(aux);        ◄── Uses an extra qubit
    Z(aux);            in the minus state
  } apply {
    markingOracle(x, aux);
  }
}
```

The signature of the operation implementing the marking oracle, `MarkStates`, is similar to those of the operations implementing reversible computations we saw in chapter 6. This operation acts on a register of input qubits and a target qubit and takes additional classical parameters—in this case the list of marked states.

Phase kickback trick is implemented as the operation `ApplyPhaseOracle`. It takes two arguments, the input qubit register and the marking oracle, allocates an auxiliary qubit in the $|-\rangle$ state, and applies the marking oracle to that input register and the auxiliary qubit. Taken together, the ultimate effect of using `ApplyPhaseOracle` is that of applying a phase oracle that matches the given marking oracle to the input register. Since the auxiliary qubit ends up not entangled with the input qubits, it can be uncomputed, its state returned to $|0\rangle$, and released.

With these two operations implemented, you don't need to write the code for the phase oracle for this function separately. Instead, you can apply this phase oracle using a combination of these operations:

```
operation Main() : Unit {
  use x = Qubit[3];
  ApplyToEach(H, x);
  let markingOracle = MarkStates(_, _, [1, 6]);
  ApplyPhaseOracle(x, markingOracle);
  DumpMachine();
}
```

The output of this code looks as follows:

```
Basis  | Amplitude        | Probability | Phase
---------------------------------------------------
|000>  |  0.3536+0.0000i  |   12.5000%  |   0.0000
|001>  | -0.3536+0.0000i  |   12.5000%  |  -3.1416
|010>  |  0.3536+0.0000i  |   12.5000%  |   0.0000
|011>  |  0.3536+0.0000i  |   12.5000%  |   0.0000
|100>  |  0.3536+0.0000i  |   12.5000%  |   0.0000
|101>  |  0.3536+0.0000i  |   12.5000%  |   0.0000
|110>  | -0.3536+0.0000i  |   12.5000%  |  -3.1416
|111>  |  0.3536+0.0000i  |   12.5000%  |   0.0000
```

You can see that two of the basis states, |001⟩ and |110⟩, acquired a relative phase of −1, which is the expected effect of the phase oracle. You can find the complete code for this project, including tests for the marking oracle and the phase oracle implemented using it, in the GitHub repo.

Note that the marking oracle in this listing is very specific to the problem we're solving, although not the instance of that problem. If we have a different problem to solve—for example, the N queens puzzle we'll consider in chapter 8—we'll need to implement the marking oracle for it from scratch. However, the phase kickback trick implementation is universal: we can use it to convert any marking oracle to a phase oracle regardless of the specific function implemented by this oracle.

7.2 Grover's search algorithm

Now that we're familiar with quantum oracles and their implementation, we're ready to discuss the quantum algorithm for solving the unstructured search problem—Grover's search algorithm. The formulation of the search problem for the quantum algorithm is very similar to that for the classical algorithm. You are given a deterministic classical function f that converts a bit string of n bits into a single bit, 0 or 1. Your goal is the same, find any bit string x_0 for which $f(x_0) = 1$.

However, this time the way you can access the function is different: instead of using a classical oracle that allows you to calculate $f(x)$ for any single bit string x, you are given a quantum oracle that implements this function. The algorithm relies on a

7.2 Grover's search algorithm

phase oracle—a unitary U_f that acts on n qubits in superposition and encodes the values of the function in the relative phases of the basis states in that superposition:

$$U_f |x\rangle = (-1)^{f(x)} |x\rangle$$

TIP Sometimes you'll see a description of the search problem that provides a marking oracle that implements the function $f(x)$ instead of a phase oracle. In this case, you can use the phase kickback trick we discussed in the previous section to convert the marking oracle to a phase oracle.

Just like any algorithms that rely on oracles, classical or quantum, Grover's search algorithm is generic and doesn't depend on the specific problem we're solving. I'll discuss the algorithm in abstract terms and implement it in a way that takes the quantum oracle as the code argument, emphasizing this generic approach. However, once we get to testing our code and exploring its behavior, we will need an example problem to use. For now, I'll use the oracle that marks a fixed set of bit strings, the one we discussed and implemented in section 7.1.

NOTE Searching for one bit string from a list is not a particularly interesting problem. It literally takes a list of problem solutions as the input, so it feels like an overkill to use a quantum algorithm to solve it! This is very true, but this will allow us to test our generic algorithm implementation on a simple problem with a well-understood set of solutions. In the next chapter, we'll work with a more interesting problem that is a much better illustration of using Grover's search to solve a problem end to end.

7.2.1 Definitions

Before we discuss Grover's algorithm itself, let's introduce several definitions of the quantum states and operations it uses. Figure 7.5 shows the main quantum states we'll use in our discussion of the algorithm and its steps. This visualization is very useful because it allows us to derive Grover's algorithm without using lengthy trigonometric formulas, so I'll use it throughout this section.

The quantum states used in the algorithm are *equal superpositions* (superpositions in which all nonzero amplitudes have the same value) of basis states that correspond to groups of input bit strings with certain properties. The first group of bit strings is the *search space* of the algorithm (all bit strings that might be solutions to the problem). The size of the search space (the number of bit strings in it) is commonly denoted as N. The corresponding quantum state is a superposition of matching basis states, each with amplitude $\frac{1}{\sqrt{N}}$. It is called the *mean*:

$$|\text{mean}\rangle = \frac{1}{\sqrt{N}} \sum_x |x\rangle$$

The mean does not only serve to describe the search space; it plays an important role in Grover's algorithm itself! We'll see this in just a few pages, once we define the rest of the states involved in it.

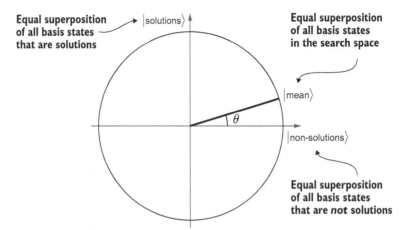

Figure 7.5 The main states used in Grover's search algorithm. $|\text{mean}\rangle$ is the superposition of all basis states in the search space (that is, states that correspond to bit strings that are potential solutions to the problem). These bit strings can be split in two groups: the ones that are solutions (included in the superposition $|\text{solutions}\rangle$) and the ones that are not ($|\text{non-solutions}\rangle$). The angle θ is defined by the number of problem solutions and the size of the search space.

Very often, we don't know anything about the structure of the search space, so we define it simply as all possible bit strings of length n. In this case, the size of the search space is $N = 2^n$, and the mean is just an equal superposition of all n-qubit basis states.

However, if the problem we're solving has some structure, we can exploit that when defining the search space for the algorithm. We will see how modifying the search space can reduce its size, simplify the quantum oracle implementation, and improve the algorithm runtime later, once we go through the basic structure of the algorithm and apply it to a realistic problem in chapter 8; we explore this topic further in chapter 9.

The next kind of bit strings we're interested in is all bit strings that are solutions to our problem—all x for which $f(x) = 1$. The number of problem solutions is denoted as M and is assumed to be nonzero. The corresponding quantum state is

$$|\text{solutions}\rangle = \frac{1}{\sqrt{M}} \sum_{x:f(x)=1} |x\rangle$$

The last kind of bit strings is all bit strings that are in the search space but are *not* solutions to our problem—all x for which $f(x) = 0$. This is the complement of the set of solutions, so it has $N - M$ bit strings in it, and the corresponding quantum state is

$$|\text{non-solutions}\rangle = \frac{1}{\sqrt{N-M}} \sum_{x:f(x)=0} |x\rangle$$

The states $|\text{solutions}\rangle$ and $|\text{non-solutions}\rangle$ are orthogonal, since each basis state is part of one or the other, never both at once. This allows us to use the visualization from figure 7.5 with these states acting as orthogonal axes. It turns out that all the steps of the algorithm will treat all solutions to the problem in the same way and all non-solutions in the same way, so all the other states we'll see during the algorithm can be expressed as linear combinations of |solutions⟩ and |non-solutions⟩.

These definitions let us plot the state |mean⟩ on figure 7.5. Indeed, this state can be represented as the following linear combination:

$$|\text{mean}\rangle = \frac{1}{\sqrt{N}} \sum_{x:f(x)=1} |x\rangle + \frac{1}{\sqrt{N}} \sum_{x:f(x)=0} |x\rangle$$

$$= \frac{\sqrt{M}}{\sqrt{N}} \frac{1}{\sqrt{M}} \sum_{x:f(x)=1} |x\rangle + \frac{\sqrt{N-M}}{\sqrt{N}} \frac{1}{\sqrt{N-M}} \sum_{x:f(x)=0} |x\rangle$$

$$= \sqrt{\frac{M}{N}} |\text{solutions}\rangle + \sqrt{\frac{N-M}{N}} |\text{non-solutions}\rangle$$

We can then represent $\sqrt{\frac{M}{N}}$ and $\sqrt{\frac{N-M}{N}}$ as sine and cosine of some angle θ, respectively, since their squares add up to 1:

$$\sqrt{\frac{M}{N}} = \sin\theta, \quad \sqrt{\frac{N-M}{N}} = \cos\theta$$

On the circle plot shown in figure 7.5, θ is the angle between the horizontal axis (the non-solutions) and the mean. You can see that these two states are shown to be close to each other. Grover's search is used for problems in which there are relatively few solutions, so most of the states in the search space are non-solutions, and the mean of them is close to the mean of all non-solutions.

What if the problem has a lot of solutions?

What happens if the assumption about the small number of solutions doesn't hold? Can Grover's search be applied if problem solutions make up a large portion of the search space?

In this case, you don't need a complicated quantum algorithm at all! Just pick a value x at random and check whether it is a solution to your problem. Repeating this a few times will give you the answer with high probability. This kind of algorithm is called *Monte Carlo methods*.

Indeed, let's say 25% of the search space are solutions:

1. The first value you pick will be a solution with 25% probability.
2. In the 75% of the cases that your first pick is not a solution, you pick a second value that will be a solution with 25% probability as well. This means that the probability of getting a solution in at most two tries is $0.25 + 0.75 * 0.25 \approx 0.44$.
3. The third value you pick will bring your success probability to $0.25 + 0.75 * (0.25 + 0.75 * 0.25) \approx 0.58$, and so on.

Generally, if the ratio of the number of solutions M to the search space size N is $\frac{M}{N} = p$, the probability of getting a correct answer after trying K values at random is $1 - (1-p)^K$. The higher p is, the faster this probability grows with the increase of K, and the fewer attempts you need to get a reasonable success probability.

(continued)

This simple classical approach will also be much faster than any quantum algorithm you can come up with for this scenario. We will discuss the performance of quantum algorithms in chapter 9, but for now it's enough to say that a single call to a quantum oracle is going to be orders of magnitude slower than a single computation of the same function on a classical computer. Therefore, you want to use quantum algorithms only in cases when the asymptotic speedup they offer is very significant.

With these definitions in mind, we're ready to discuss the algorithm itself. Figure 7.6 shows the effects of two operations that are the core of the algorithm.

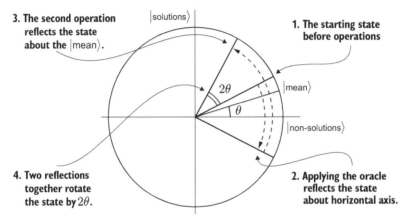

Figure 7.6 The main operations used in Grover's search algorithm. Applying the phase oracle reflects the system state about the horizontal axis, the average of all non-solutions. "Reflection about the mean" reflects the system state about the mean state, the average of all states in the search space. Together, these two operations rotate the state of the system counterclockwise by a fixed angle.

The first operation we use in Grover's algorithm is the phase oracle itself. To plot the effect of the phase oracle on a state in our visualization, let's see what happens when we apply the oracle to a linear combination of states |solutions⟩ and |non-solutions⟩.

For each basis state $|x\rangle$ that is part of |non-solutions⟩, $f(x) = 0$, so the phase oracle doesn't change it. On the other hand, for each basis state $|x\rangle$ that is part of |solutions⟩, $f(x) = 1$, so the phase oracle multiples this basis state by -1. Overall, we can see that

$$U_f(\alpha \,|\text{solutions}\rangle + \beta \,|\text{non-solutions}\rangle) = -\alpha \,|\text{solutions}\rangle + \beta \,|\text{non-solutions}\rangle$$

On the plot, the effect of the phase oracle is a reflection about the horizontal axis, the state |non-solutions⟩.

The second operation we use is called "reflection about the mean," and it is exactly what the name says: reflection of the state about the axis defined by the state |mean⟩. As figure 7.6 shows, this operation leaves the component of the state that is parallel to |mean⟩ unchanged, and multiplies the component orthogonal to |mean⟩ by -1.

These two operations are the only ones used in Grover's search algorithm.

Implementing reflection about the mean

How can we implement reflection of a quantum state $|\phi\rangle$ about a fixed quantum state $|\psi\rangle$ as a quantum operation? Mathematically, you can describe reflection about a state using ket-bra notation:

$$|\psi\rangle\langle\psi| + (-1) \cdot (I - |\psi\rangle\langle\psi|)$$

The first term in this expression describes taking the component of the state $|\phi\rangle$ that is parallel to $|\psi\rangle$ and leaving it unchanged. The second term corresponds to taking the remainder of the state $|\phi\rangle$ (that is, the component of this state that is orthogonal to $|\psi\rangle$) and multiplying it by -1.

The easiest way to implement this transformation relies on knowing how to prepare the state $|\psi\rangle$ from some simple initial state—for example, $|0\rangle$. Let's say you can implement a unitary transformation V that converts the state $|0\rangle$ into the state $|\psi\rangle$: $V|0\rangle = |\psi\rangle$. Then, you can rewrite the reflection unitary as follows:

$$|\psi\rangle\langle\psi| + (-1) \cdot (I - |\psi\rangle\langle\psi|) = 2|\psi\rangle\langle\psi| - I = 2V|0\rangle\langle 0|V^\dagger - I$$

Since V is a unitary, you know that $VV^\dagger = I$, and you can rewrite this as follows:

$$2V|0\rangle\langle 0|V^\dagger - I = 2V|0\rangle\langle 0|V^\dagger - VV^\dagger = V(2|0\rangle\langle 0| - I)V^\dagger$$

This gives you the sequence of steps that implements the reflection unitary:

1. Apply the unitary $V^\dagger$ (remember that the rightmost unitary in product expressions gets applied to the quantum state first!).
2. Apply the unitary $2|0\rangle\langle 0| - I$.
3. Apply the unitary V.

The unitary $2|0\rangle\langle 0| - I$ is the reflection about the $|0\rangle$ state, which flips the signs of all basis states except $|0\rangle$. It is the same as flipping the sign of only the $|0\rangle$ state and then applying a global phase -1. Grover's search algorithm is not sensitive to the global phase (although some of its derivatives, such as the quantum counting algorithm, are!), so you can ignore the global phase and implement this unitary as follows:

1. Apply an X gate to each qubit to convert the $|0...0\rangle$ state to the $|1...1\rangle$ state.
2. Use a controlled Z gate to flip the sign of only the $|1...1\rangle$ state.
3. Apply an X gate to each qubit again to uncompute the initial changes, converting the $|1...1\rangle$ state back to $|0...0\rangle$.

The exact implementation of the reflection about the mean will thus depend on the structure of the search space in the problem. If the search space is all bit strings of length n, the state $|\text{mean}\rangle$ is an equal superposition of all basis states on n bits, and it is really easy to prepare: just apply a Hadamard gate to each qubit!

7.2.2 Math

The overall structure of Grover's algorithm is shown in figure 7.7:

1. You start by preparing the initial state of the algorithm, |mean⟩.
2. You apply several iterations, each one consisting of two steps shown in figure 7.6. On each iteration, you apply the phase oracle and then the reflection about the mean.
3. Finally, you measure the state of the system to get the algorithm results. If you chose the right number of iterations (more on that later), the measurement will produce a correct answer—one of the M solutions to the problem—with high probability.

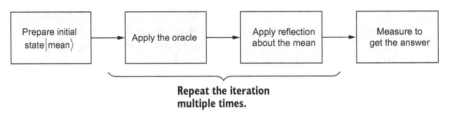

Figure 7.7 The overall structure of Grover's search algorithm. You start by preparing the system in the mean state, the average of all states in the search space. Then you apply several iterations, each composed of applying the phase oracle followed by a reflection about the mean. Finally, you measure the system and check whether the result is an answer to the problem.

Why does this algorithm work? If you look at the figure 7.6, you'll notice that the two operations that compose the iteration are both reflections about different axes. Taken together, their effects amount to a counterclockwise rotation by the angle 2θ. Figure 7.8 shows how the state of the system evolves with each iteration of Grover's algorithm.

The initial state of the system will be close to the horizontal axis, the |non-solutions⟩ state. With each rotation, the state will move counterclockwise by a fixed angle, further away from |non-solutions⟩ and closer to |solutions⟩. The closer the state is to |solutions⟩, the larger the amplitudes of all the basis states that correspond to problem solutions are, and the higher the probability of the measurement returning one of those basis states is.

> **TIP** Grover's search is a probabilistic algorithm. In most cases, there is a nonzero probability of getting an incorrect answer after the final measurement, even if it is a very small one. To account for this, make sure to verify the algorithm result by calculating the value of the function for it.

You'll notice that the success probability of the algorithm doesn't plateau. If you keep applying iterations after the state of the system is vertical (or as close to vertical as possible), the state will keep rotating counterclockwise, now reducing the success probability with each iteration. Eventually, once the state is nearly horizontal and

7.2 Grover's search algorithm

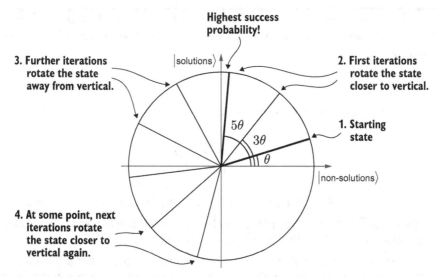

Figure 7.8 Each iteration of Grover's algorithm rotates the state of the system in counterclockwise direction by the angle 2θ. Up to a certain point, each iteration rotates the state closer to the vertical axis, the $|\text{solutions}\rangle$ state. The closer the state is to $|\text{solutions}\rangle$, the higher the probability of the measurement yielding a correct answer is. If you apply too many iterations (in this case, three or more), the state will go beyond vertical, and further iterations will decrease success probability.

success probability becomes minimal, subsequent iterations will increase success probability again, and so on. The probability of getting the correct answer oscillates, starting with low and then increasing and decreasing in turns.

How can we figure out the number of iterations we should use when running Grover's algorithm? It turns out that the strategy of choosing the optimal number of iterations depends on how much you know about the problem and its solutions.

If you know the number of problem solutions M, you can simply calculate the optimal number of iterations—the number that gives the best success probability.

Looking at the figure 7.8, you can see that the angle between the initial state of the system and the horizontal axis is θ, and each iteration increases it by 2θ. After K iterations, the angle will be $(2K+1)\theta$. Your goal is to get to the point where the state of the system is close to vertical axis—that is, the angle between it and the horizontal axis is close to $\frac{\pi}{2}$. This gives you the following equation for the number of iterations:

$$(2K+1)\theta \approx \frac{\pi}{2}$$

Recall that we defined θ so that $\sin\theta = \sqrt{\frac{M}{N}}$. Usually, we assume that the solutions are a very small portion of the search space, so the angle θ is very small. This allows us to make some simplifications. For small angles, $\sin\theta \approx \theta$, so we can use the approximation

$$\theta = \sqrt{\frac{M}{N}}$$

If each iteration rotates the state of the system by only a small angle, we'll need a lot of iterations, so $K \gg 1$. We can then discard the +1 term in $2K + 1$ to get the final equation:

$$2K\sqrt{\frac{M}{N}} \approx \frac{\pi}{2}$$

The optimal number of iterations is thus

$$K \approx \frac{\pi}{4}\sqrt{\frac{N}{M}}$$

> **What if I don't know the number of solutions up front?**
>
> When you're setting out to solve a problem, you often don't know the exact number of solutions to it. Fortunately, you don't need to!
>
> First, you'll notice that while there is only one number of iterations that yields the highest success probability, there are multiple values for which the success probability is *high enough*. Often, doing several iterations fewer or more will change the success probability from 99% to maybe 95%, which is still pretty good. If you can estimate the number of solutions to the problem approximately, you can use that approximation to get the rough number of iterations that will likely still be useful.
>
> Second, if you cannot estimate the number of solutions at all, you can try and get the answer using a simple heuristic. Run a sequence of searches with increasing number of iterations: 1, 2, 4, and so on, until one of the runs gives you the correct answer. It is possible to show that this approach introduces only a small overhead in terms of the number of iterations compared to the optimal number of iterations.

In comparison, the best classical algorithm that runs under the same assumptions involves picking a random bit string from the search space and checking whether it is a solution to the problem using the classical oracle. This algorithm would take an average of $\frac{N}{M}$ queries to produce an answer. We say that Grover's search algorithm offers a *quadratic asymptotic speedup* over the classical algorithm, since it takes approximately $\sqrt{\frac{N}{M}}$ queries.

> **NOTE** We'll discuss whether this asymptotic speedup translates to a potential practical advantage in chapter 9!

Before we move on to writing the code, let's consider how we are going to test it. There are two main approaches to testing larger quantum algorithms that solve classical problems:

- Testing individual building blocks of the implementation.
- Testing the end-to-end algorithm by checking that it produces correct results.

In the case of Grover's search, the first approach means testing the quantum oracle for the classical function and the operation V that prepares the state $|\text{mean}\rangle$ used to implement reflection about the mean. In practice, it makes a lot of sense to test the oracle implementation using the techniques we learned in chapter 6. However, the state preparation operation is usually either trivial, such as in the case of the search space of all n-bit strings, or done using a state preparation library operation, so writing separate tests for it is usually not worth the trouble. Any problems in the implementation of the simpler components of the algorithm are likely to show up in the distribution of the end-to-end algorithm results.

Checking the results of probabilistic algorithms can be a bit tricky: since the results are not deterministic, some portion of runs is expected to produce incorrect results. Conveniently, there are some instances of problems for which Grover's algorithm is deterministic! For example, if the number of solutions M is exactly a quarter of the size of the search space N, running the algorithm with exactly one iteration gives us a 100% success rate.

To see this, recall the equation $\sin \theta = \sqrt{\frac{M}{N}}$. If $\frac{M}{N} = \frac{1}{4}$, $\sin \theta = \frac{1}{2}$, and $\theta = \frac{\pi}{6}$. One iteration will bring the angle between the state of the system and the horizontal axis to $3\theta = \frac{\pi}{2}$, which means that this state will be exactly |solutions⟩, and measuring it is guaranteed to give a correct answer.

Consequently, for a two-qubit search space, we need to use oracles that mark exactly one basis state out of four; for a three-qubit search space, two basis states out of eight; and so on. We also need to make sure the tests validate that our solution has the right endianness, so the test cases must include integers that have asymmetric binary representation. For example, if a test uses a two-qubit oracle that marks only the |00⟩ state (a symmetric bit string) or a three-qubit oracle that marks the pair of states |001⟩ and |100⟩ (bit strings that are mirror images of each other), it won't detect a bug in the solution that accidentally reverses the order of bits in the returned bit string. Now, let's see how to implement Grover's algorithm as a quantum program.

7.2.3 Qiskit

The following listing shows the Qiskit code that implements generic Grover's search algorithm. Qiskit offers a library implementation of Grover's iteration called `GroverOperator`, but for the purposes of this chapter, let's write all the code by hand.

Listing 7.3 Qiskit code for Grover's search algorithm

```
def grovers_search(n_bits, marking_oracle, prepare_mean, n_iterations):
    iter = QuantumCircuit(n_bits + 1)          ⟵ Defines circuit for Grover's iteration

    phase_or = phase_oracle(n_bits, marking_oracle)   ⟵ Converts marking oracle to phase oracle

    iter.append(phase_or, range(n_bits + 1))   ⟵ Applies the phase oracle

    iter.append(prepare_mean.inverse(), range(n_bits))
    iter.x(range(n_bits))
    iter.append(ZGate().control(n_bits - 1),            Applies reflection
                range(n_bits))                          about the mean
    iter.x(range(n_bits))
    iter.append(prepare_mean, range(n_bits))
```

```
circ = QuantumCircuit(n_bits + 1, n_bits)           ◀── The complete algorithm circuit
circ.append(prepare_mean, range(n_bits))            ◀── Prepares the mean
circ.append(iter.to_gate().power(n_iterations),     ◀── Applies multiple iterations
        range(n_bits + 1))
circ.measure(range(n_bits), range(n_bits))          ◀── Measures to get the results

return circ
```

This code creates the circuit for Grover's search algorithm, given the parameters of the problem it solves:

- The integer `n_bits` gives the number of qubits used to encode the input x.
- The gate `marking_oracle` implements the marking oracle for the function $f(x)$. (The conversion from a marking oracle to a phase oracle is handled within the algorithm itself.)
- The gate `prepare_mean`, when applied to the state $|0\rangle$, prepares the state $|\text{mean}\rangle$. It is used both to prepare the initial state of the algorithm and to implement reflection about the mean.
- The integer `n_iterations` defines the number of Grover's iterations to be applied before the final measurement. This algorithm implementation leaves the choice of the iteration number to the user, allowing you to experiment with different strategies.

The code is mostly based on the same language constructs you've seen earlier in the book. The two new elements are the methods of Qiskit `Gate` class that allow us to construct more complex circuits easily: the method `inverse()` returns the adjoint of the gate, and the method `power(n)` returns the n-th power of the gate.

The tests for this code are built similarly to those you've seen in chapter 4. Since this circuit ultimately produces a classical value—an array of measurement results—the process of verification is similar to that of verifying a much simpler circuit in section 4.1 that measures a basis state. The tests need to run the circuit multiple times and check that each time the result is one of the marked states.

The complete project includes the marking oracle and the phase kickback trick from listing 7.1, as well as the testing code. It can be found in the GitHub repository.

7.2.4 Q#

The following listing shows the Q# code that implements generic Grover's search algorithm.

Listing 7.4 Q# code for Grover's search algorithm

```
import Std.Arrays.*;

operation RunGroversSearch(
    nBits : Int,
    markingOracle : (Qubit[], Qubit) => Unit,
    prepareMeanOp : Qubit[] => Unit is Adj,
```

```
        nIterations : Int                            Converts marking oracle
) : Bool[] {                                         to phase oracle
    let phaseOracle = ApplyPhaseOracle(_, markingOracle);

    use qs = Qubit[nBits];
    prepareMeanOp(qs);       ←—— Prepares the mean

    for _ in 1 .. nIterations {
      phaseOracle(qs);       ←—— Applies the phase oracle
      within {
        Adjoint prepareMeanOp(qs);
        ApplyToEachA(X, qs);              Applies reflection
      } apply {                           about the mean
        Controlled Z(qs[1...], qs[0]);
      }
    }

    let meas = MResetEachZ(qs);       ←—— Measures to get the results
    return Mapped(m -> m == One, meas);  ←—— Converts Result variables to Booleans
}
```

The code relies on the same language constructs you've seen earlier in the book, including the use of partial application to define the phase oracle based on a marking oracle and passing operations as arguments to other operations.

The tests for this code are built similarly to those you've seen in chapter 4. Since this program returns a classical value (an array of Boolean values that encode the measurement results) the process of verification is similar to that of verifying a much simpler program in section 4.1 that measures a basis state. The tests need to run the program multiple times and check that each time the result is one of the marked states.

The complete project includes the marking oracle and the phase kickback trick from listing 7.2, as well as the testing code. It can be found in the GitHub repository.

7.3 Going beyond

Do you want to spend some more time exploring variations of the problem discussed in this chapter before moving on to a more advanced example of a problem solved using Grover's search? Here are some additional ideas for topics to explore:

- Modify the code that runs the end-to-end Grover's algorithm (section 7.2) to include problem instances that do not have a 100% success rate. Calculate and print success rate of the algorithm depending on the number of iterations chosen. Does the algorithm behave the way you expected it to behave?
- Consider other simple problems you could solve using Grover's algorithm and try implementing them using the techniques you've learned in chapter 6.
- Quantum counting is an algorithm for estimating the number of solutions for a given search problem. As we saw in figure 7.6, Grover's iteration is effectively a rotation by the angle 2θ that depends on the search space size N and the

number of solutions in it M. The properties of rotation matrices suggest that the unitary that implements Grover's iteration has two eigenvalues, $e^{i \cdot 2\theta}$ and $e^{-i \cdot 2\theta}$. Quantum counting applies phase estimation to Grover's iteration to estimate its eigenvalues and to derive the number of solutions from that estimate. Try to implement quantum counting algorithm and explore its behavior on different problem instances.

Summary

- Programs that utilize quantum algorithms are often hybrid: they combine quantum computations with classical preprocessing for preparing the inputs to the quantum subroutine and post-processing for interpreting its outputs and producing the final answer or making decisions about the next computation to run.
- Unstructured search problem gives you a deterministic function that converts an input bit string into a single bit 0 or 1. Your goal is to find an input x_0 for which the value of the function $f(x_0) = 1$.
- An oracle is a tool that allows you to calculate the function for any given input but does not expose any information about the internal implementation of that function. Oracles are used in both classical and quantum computing to discuss generic algorithms that do not depend on the specific problem instance.
- Phase oracles encode the values of the functions in the signs of amplitudes of the input basis states.
- Marking oracles encode the values of the functions in the state of an additional qubit.
- You can convert a marking oracle into a phase oracle and vice versa using variants of the phase kickback trick.
- Grover's search algorithm can solve the unstructured search problem for a function given as a quantum oracle. It offers a quadratic speedup in the number of queries to the quantum oracle compared to the "brute force" classical algorithm that has access to the function only via a classical oracle.
- Grover's algorithm is a probabilistic algorithm; it produces the correct result with high probability, but not in 100% of cases. You need to validate the answer x_0 it gives you by calculating the value $f(x_0)$ using a classical computation and checking that it is indeed 1.

Solving N queens puzzle using Grover's algorithm

This chapter covers
- Applying Grover's algorithm to a nontrivial search problem
- Implementing search problem constraints on a quantum computer
- Implementing and testing quantum algorithms end to end
- Using Q# and Qiskit to write hybrid programs

In chapter 7, we learned to use Grover's algorithm for solving search problems—problems that, given a black box implementation of a function that returns 0 or 1, aim to find a function input x for which $f(x) = 1$. There are plenty of problems that can be formulated as a search problem, since pretty much any task can be phrased as a "yes/no" problem: "Is the value x a solution to the problem I'm looking at? $f(x) = 1$ if it is, and 0 if it's not."

The problem we used to test our implementation of Grover's algorithm was a very simple one: looking for elements of the given list. This example allowed us to experiment with the algorithm without putting a lot of effort into implementing the oracle that describes the problem, so it was a good starting point. Its downside, however, is that the algorithm looks for one of the values from a predefined list that is literally hardcoded into the solution. We know the answer up front before we can start looking for it!

In this chapter, we'll continue discussing search problems and Grover's algorithm. This time, however, we'll work through a more complicated problem example that is a much better illustration of the workflow of developing a quantum solution to a classical problem. Figure 8.1 shows the steps to solve a search problem using Grover's algorithm.

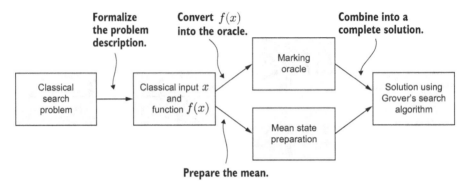

Figure 8.1 Solving a search problem using Grover's algorithm starts with deciding on the representation of the function input x and the way to calculate the function $f(x)$ based on it. Then, we implement the marking oracle for this function and the operation that prepares the state $|\text{mean}\rangle$ based on that decision. Finally, these building blocks are used in Grover's search to get the end-to-end solution.

1. First, we decide how to represent the problem description as the function input x and how to calculate the function $f(x)$ classically based on that input.
2. Then, we use the techniques from chapter 6 to convert the classical function calculation into an equivalent reversible computation and implement a marking oracle.
3. Additionally, we need to represent the search space of all possible inputs x as the operation that prepares the state $|\text{mean}\rangle$. This operation does not depend on how we decide to calculate the function $f(x)$, only on which inputs we're going to search through and how we decided to represent them. To implement it, we might use the state preparation library from chapter 2, the language library tools, or develop a custom state preparation routine tailored to a specific problem.
4. Finally, we use Grover's search as described in chapter 7 with the marking oracle and the state preparation operation as the building blocks to solve the problem.

In the example used in chapter 7, these steps were trivial. The problem looked for a bit string of certain length, so it was natural to use bit strings of that length as function inputs. The function $f(x)$ was defined as "is this bit string on the list of answers?" so we didn't need to get creative with calculating it either.

For this chapter, I picked the *N queens puzzle*—a well-known constraint satisfaction problem that is often used to illustrate various programming techniques. Here, it will let me showcase several important techniques used in solving search problems and optimizing the solutions and make the steps of the workflow much more pronounced.

The N queens puzzle seeks to place N queens on an $N \times N$ chessboard in such a way that no two queens attack each other. Consequently, no two queens can occupy the same row, column, or diagonal. Figure 8.2 shows several placements of four queens on a 4×4 chessboard, both valid and invalid ones.

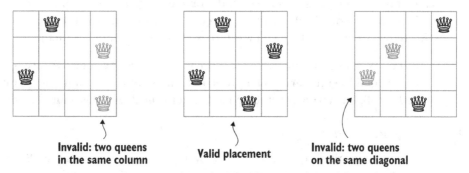

Figure 8.2 Valid and invalid placements of queens on a 4×4 chessboard. The middle placement is valid: all queens are in different rows, columns, and diagonals. The left placement has two queens in the same column, and the right placement has two queens on the same diagonal, so they are invalid.

The valid queen placement shown in figure 8.2 and the placement that mirrors it vertically or horizontally (the resulting placement is the same either way) are the only two problem solutions for four queens. As the problem size grows, though, the number of solutions grows as well, and finding them becomes more challenging.

The key difference between the example we considered in chapter 7 and this problem is the way they are formulated. The example from the previous chapter was described in terms of the problem solutions right away: we know that the function f returns value 1 for inputs from this list, so let's find one of these inputs. The N queens puzzle, on the contrary, focuses on the properties the solution must have: we don't know up front where exactly the queens should be placed on the board, but we know the constraints on their placement. This kind of formulation, in which the problem describes the constraints that the solution should satisfy rather than the solution itself, is much more typical for search problems and makes a lot more sense!

We'll start with the naive solution to the N queens puzzle. This approach, though straightforward, will turn out to be impossible to run on a quantum simulator even with minor tweaks (more on that later!), so we will not spend time implementing it in code. Instead, we'll move on to discussing two optimized solutions that take different approaches to encoding the queens' placement and checking whether it satisfies all the constraints of the puzzle. Later, in chapter 9, we'll use these two solutions to illustrate how we think about the performance of quantum algorithms and comparing their efficiency.

The problem instance we'll use throughout the chapter will be the 4×4 puzzle shown in figure 8.2. The N queens puzzle doesn't have any solutions for $N = 2$ or 3, and it's not particularly interesting to try and place a single queen on a 1×1 board; $N = 4$ is the smallest nontrivial problem instance that has solutions. It will also allow us to run our code on a quantum simulator to get the results for the two optimized solutions. Unfortunately, even the optimized solutions become prohibitively large to simulate for larger problem instances.

I cannot emphasize enough the importance of writing tests for your code. In this case, it is extremely important to test the oracle you write for the puzzle constraints. This puzzle is nontrivial, and the correctness of the end-to-end solution can be affected by so many factors, you want to exclude at least some of them.

> **NOTE** When writing the code for this chapter, I initially got a 0% success rate for the end-to-end search. The problem turned out to be not in the quantum code at all, but a typo in Python code I used to check that the result was correct.

8.1 Naive solution

Let's try to solve the N queens puzzle following the flow shown in figure 8.1, starting with formalizing the problem. What is the most straightforward thing you can do to encode the placement of the queens on an $N \times N$ board? We can use the encoding shown in figure 8.3.

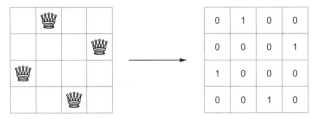

Figure 8.3 The naive input encoding uses one bit per board cell. This bit is 1 if there is a queen in this cell and 0 if the cell is empty.

In this encoding, we represent each cell of the board with one bit that indicates whether there is a queen placed there (bit set to 1) or not (0). For an $N \times N$ board, we need N^2 bits to represent the queens' positions on it.

Since this encoding doesn't impose any constraints on the queens' placement, the function $f(x)$ will need to check all constraints required by the puzzle.

One way to do this is to find all pairs of board cells that are in the same row, column, or diagonal, and check that none of the pairs have queens in both of the cells at once. How many such pairs are there?

- If we have M cells on the same line (whether this line is horizontal, vertical, or diagonal), there are $\frac{M(M-1)}{2}$ different pairs on it.
- Rows and columns are lines with N cells each, so the number of pairs on the same horizontal and vertical lines of cells is $2N \cdot \frac{N(N-1)}{2} = N^2(N-1)$.
- The number of pairs of cells on the same diagonal is $\frac{N(N-1)(2N-1)}{6}$ for each direction of diagonals. This gives a total of $\frac{N(N-1)(2N-1)}{3}$ pairs of cells on the same diagonal.

NOTE You can prove this by induction: calculate the value explicitly for $n = 2$ and then see how many extra pairs appear with the move from an $(N-1) \times (N-1)$ board to an $N \times N$ one. Alternatively, you can write a script to compute the number of pairs for the first few values of N and find the matching sequence in The On-Line Encyclopedia of Integer Sequences (https://oeis.org/)!

When we convert a classical computation to a reversible one, we usually need to add extra bits to store the intermediate steps of the computation (we saw an example in section 6.5). A good rule of thumb to estimate the number of extra bits is "one bit per constraint you want to check," although the exact number can vary depending on the implementation.

TIP To reduce the number of qubits used by your solution, you could evaluate the row constraints first, use an extra qubit to check whether all row constraints are satisfied and uncompute them, thus freeing these qubits for reuse when evaluating the column constraints. The downside of this approach is that it makes the computation longer, since you need to do more rounds of computation and uncomputation.

How many bits would we need to check whether all constraints hold using this encoding for our smallest example with $N = 4$? If we add up the bits used to store the input, the output, and all the constraints, we'll get $16 + 1 + 48 + 28 = 93$ bits. What does this mean for our solution and our goal to run it on a simulator?

Simulating quantum programs

Is it possible to run Grover's search for a function that takes about a hundred bits to calculate on a quantum simulator? Each bit used in the computation of a classical reversible function is mapped to a qubit, so the quantum program for this algorithm will use about a hundred qubits total. Remember that a state of N qubits is described using 2^N complex numbers, so just storing the amplitudes of a state for $N = 30$ takes several gigabytes of memory! Generally, quantum simulators work perfectly well for arbitrary programs that use under 30 qubits; they might be able to run certain programs that use up to 40 qubits, but they balk shortly after that.

If the program that needs to be simulated has a special structure, these limits can be stretched. For example, *sparse simulators* store only the nonzero amplitudes and the associated basis states of the superposition state rather than all amplitudes. If a program acts on *sparse states*—that is, uses a lot of qubits but relatively few basis states—sparse simulators will be much better at handling it than regular simulators and will manage to run larger problem instances.

Reversible computations are a particularly good candidate for sparse simulation, since the computation they implement is often sparse. They allocate extra qubits to store the intermediate computation results, but the way these qubits are used does not increase the number of basis states in the computation. We can take advantage of this, for example, to test reversible computations on basis states the way we did in section 6.3.

(continued)

The bulk of the computation in Grover's search happens within the oracle that implements the function $f(x)$ as a reversible computation. Thus, Grover's algorithm is well-suited for sparse simulation too.

The search space for the problem encoding we chose includes all bit strings of length N^2, so the quantum program will manipulate approximately $2^{N^2} = 2^{16} = 65536$ basis states. (This number will be temporarily doubled whenever phase kickback is in action, since the qubit used for it is in a superposition state.)

Another factor to consider is the number of iterations necessary to run Grover's algorithm for this problem. With the search space size 2^{16} and only 2 valid queen placements, the optimal number of iterations is $\frac{\pi}{4}\sqrt{\frac{2^{16}}{2}} \approx 142$. Even if the sparse simulator can handle that many terms in the superposition, this number of iterations will take a while to run.

We can estimate that this solution is not going to allow us to solve the small problem instance on a simulator. Since this is our goal for this chapter, it doesn't make much sense to try to implement it as quantum code, unless we can optimize it to run much faster. Can we do that? One way to optimize this solution is to find a more efficient way to evaluate the constraints in the marking oracle, shown in figure 8.4.

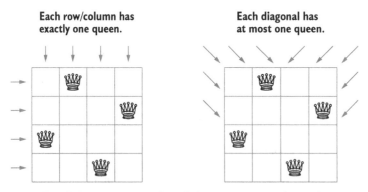

Figure 8.4 To improve on our naïve solution, we can count the number of queens in each row and each column and check that there is exactly one. We can do the same for the diagonals, checking that the number of queens in each diagonal is zero or one.

Consider a single row of the board. Instead of looking at all pairs of cells in it and checking that no pair contains two queens, we can count the number of cells that contain queens and check that this number is exactly one. Indeed, if we need to place N queens on a board with N rows without having two queens in one row, the only way to do this is to place one queen per row. This tweak takes some extra bits to count the queens in the row, but it reduces the number of constraints we need to check from $\frac{N(N-1)}{2}$ to just one!

We can apply the same optimization to check that no queens share a column. The check that no queens share a diagonal can be done similarly, as long as we check that the number of queens on each diagonal is zero or one rather than exactly one. Indeed, unlike rows and columns, it is possible to have diagonals with no queens on them in a valid placement.

These optimizations reduce the number of qubits used in the marking oracle significantly. However, tweaking the oracle implementation in this manner doesn't reduce the size of the search space, so we're still looking at 65,536 basis states to search through and over a hundred iterations to do that. With this in mind, I'll skip the code for this solution and move on to the next topic: coming up with a more efficient solution.

8.2 Encoding constraints in the search space

Can we change the way we describe the problem inputs x and the function $f(x)$ to make the solution faster? In this section, we'll explore a way to do just that by reducing the size of the search space. This will allow us to reduce the number of iterations and simplify the calculations done in a single iteration.

8.2.1 Math

The search space is the set of all inputs that can possibly be the solutions for our problem. If we can rule out some of the inputs that are definitely not the solutions, we'll make the search space smaller while not losing any of the inputs that are actually solutions.

To do this, we need to analyze the structure of the problem we're solving and see if there is an easy way to identify some non-solutions. This will effectively encode part of the constraints imposed by the problem into the structure of the search space.

N queens puzzle is a very well-structured problem, so it is very easy to find inputs that are not solutions:

- Let's keep the input representation the same for now: use one bit per the board cell to indicate whether there is a queen placed there.
- We're looking to place N queens on the board, so we know that any inputs that have more than N or less than N bits set to 1 cannot be valid solutions.
- Furthermore, we know that each row has to have exactly one queen in it. This means that any inputs that have no queens or two or more queens in one of the rows cannot be valid solutions either.

This gives us a way to reduce the search space: we need to limit our search only to the inputs that have exactly one bit set to 1 in each row.

The |mean⟩ state that describes this search space looks differently from the one we used in the previous section. Instead of an equal superposition of all basis states of length N^2, it will be a tensor product of N special N-qubit states, known as the *W states*, each representing one row of the board. The W state on N qubits is an equal superposition of N basis states, each consisting of $N - 1$ 0 bits and one 1 bit:

$$|W_N\rangle = \frac{1}{\sqrt{N}}\left(|10...0\rangle + |010...0\rangle + ... + |0...01\rangle\right)$$

How does this additional restriction on the possible inputs affect the oracle implementation? It turns out that it allows us to simplify the oracle quite a bit.

To start, we don't need to check that no two queens share a row any longer. Since this constraint is built into the structure of the search space, any basis states that don't satisfy it will never be included in the superposition state Grover's search acts on, so the oracle doesn't need to handle them.

We still need to check the other two constraints, but we can simplify that too. Figure 8.5 shows how to check that no two queens share a column.

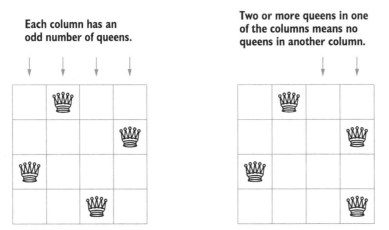

Figure 8.5 Check that each column has exactly one queen, knowing that each row has exactly one queen. We can count the parity of the number of queens in each column and check that it's odd. Any placement for which this constraint is not satisfied will have at least one empty column with even parity.

Instead of counting queens in each column and checking that the number is one, we can count the parity of the number of queens (the number modulo 2) using a sequence of XOR gates. For a placement in which every column has exactly one queen, all parities will be odd. However, if one of the columns has two or more queens, at least one other column will have no queens and even parity. Notice that this way we can't detect columns with an odd number of queens greater than one in them. We don't need to, though: the goal of the oracle is to figure out that the set of constraints as a whole is not satisfied, not to find each constraint that is not satisfied, and we can do this using just the empty columns.

We can also skip checking the number of queens in the last column. If the column constraints are not satisfied, either there is a column with two queens and another column with no queens, or there is a column with three or more queens and two or more columns with no queens. In either case, there are at least two columns for which the queen count is even, so we can skip any single column and still detect the problem.

We cannot use the parity trick to replace counting the queens on each diagonal, since a diagonal can have zero or one queens on it without making the placement invalid. Instead, let's see how to reorganize this check to improve it. Figure 8.6 shows how to check that no two queens share a diagonal by focusing on pairs of rows.

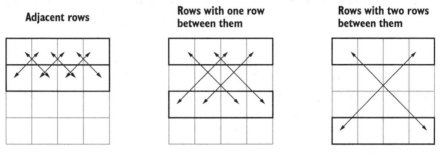

Figure 8.6 To check that no two queens share a diagonal, we check each pair of rows separately. For each pair of rows, we go through all pairs of cells within them that are on the same diagonal. Since each row has exactly one queen, at most one of these pairs of cells will have two queens in them at once, so we can combine the results of all checks for a pair of rows in the same bit using XOR.

If we look at two rows of the board that have d rows between them, we need to check all pairs of cells that have d columns between them. If any of these pairs has queens in both cells, the placement is invalid. The fact that each row has exactly one queen means that at most one pair of cells can have queens in both cells, so we don't need to use complicated logic to combine the results of individual pair checks. Instead, we can use just one bit per a pair of rows and use a sequence of CCNOT gates to compute XOR of checks for each pair of cells within these rows.

How do these optimizations impact the number of bits used by the solution and the size of the search space? For an $N \times N$ board,

- We still use N^2 bits to store the problem input and 1 bit to store the output of the marking oracle.
- We need $N - 1$ extra bits for the column checks (and none for the row checks!).
- Checking the diagonals needs one bit per a pair of rows, for a total of $\frac{N(N-1)}{2}$ bits.
- The total number of bits is $\frac{3N^2+N}{2}$.

The search space consists of all bit strings of length N^2 for which the first N bits contain exactly one 1 bit, the second N bits contain exactly one 1 bit, and so on. Each of the N-bit chunks of the bit string can take one of the N possible values, so the search space has a total of N^N bit strings. (Compare this with $2^{N^2} = (2^N)^N$ bit strings that the naive solution has to search through!)

For our smallest example with $N = 4$, the number of bits used by the solution is 26, the search space size is $4^4 = 256$, and the optimal number of iterations is only $\frac{\pi}{4}\sqrt{\frac{256}{2}} \approx 9$. This is much better than the naive solution! A simulator can run this program easily now. With these estimates in mind, let's see what the code looks like for this puzzle.

8.2.2 Qiskit

Listing 8.1 shows the Qiskit code that prepares the |mean⟩ state for the N queens puzzle solution that we discussed in this section. This approach uses one qubit to represent each cell of the board and indicates whether there is a queen placed there. However, we optimize the search by only considering inputs that have exactly one queen in each row and encoding this constraint in the |mean⟩ state preparation routine.

Listing 8.1 Qiskit: Solving N queens puzzle—state preparation

```
from math import sqrt
from qiskit import QuantumCircuit
from qiskit.circuit.library import StatePreparation

def prep_mean_bits(n):
    wstate_amps = [0] * (2 ** n)          ◄─── Calculates the amplitudes
    for i in range(n):                          of the W state on n qubits
        wstate_amps[1 << i] = 1 / sqrt(n)

    wstateprep = StatePreparation(wstate_amps)
    circ = QuantumCircuit(n * n)                  Prepares the W state on
    for r in range(n):                       ◄─── each row of n qubits
        circ.append(wstateprep, range(r * n, (r + 1) * n))
    return circ.to_gate()
```

This code uses the library class `StatePreparation` that prepares the quantum state with the given amplitudes.

The following listing shows the Qiskit code that implements the marking oracle for this approach.

Listing 8.2 Qiskit: Solving N queens puzzle—the marking oracle

```
from qiskit import QuantumCircuit, QuantumRegister
from qiskit.circuit.library.standard_gates import XGate

def oracle_bits(n):                            The presence of a queen in row r and
    x = QuantumRegister(n * n)       ◄─────── column c is described with x[r * n + c].
    y = QuantumRegister(1)
                                                          Qubits for
    valid_column = QuantumRegister(n - 1)    ◄─────────── column constraints
    invalid_rowpair = QuantumRegister(n * (n - 1) // 2)

    circ = QuantumCircuit(x, valid_column, invalid_rowpair, y)

    def one_queen_per_column():
        for c in range(n - 1):                    Computes XOR of all
            for r in range(n):             ◄───── qubits in this column
                circ.cx(x[r * n + c], valid_column[c])
                                     ◄─── All valid_column qubits should be 1.
```

Qubits for diagonal constraints → `invalid_rowpair`

Evaluates column constraints → `def one_queen_per_column()`

```
def one_queen_per_diagonal():
    ind = 0
    for r1 in range(n):                    ◁──┤ Evaluates diagonal constraints
        for r2 in range(r1 + 1, n):           │ for each pair of rows
            for c1 in range(n):
                for c2 in [c1 + (r2 - r1),  ◁──┤ Computes AND of each qubit pair on
                           c1 - (r2 - r1)]:   │ the same diagonal in these two rows
                    if c2 >= 0 and c2 < n:
                        circ.ccx(x[r1 * n + c1],  ◁──┤ Computes XOR of all ANDs because,
                                 x[r2 * n + c2],     │ at most, one of them will be 1
                                 invalid_rowpair[ind])
                        ind += 1
    circ.x(invalid_rowpair)   ◁──┤ All invalid_rowpair qubits should be 0;
                                 │ switch them to 1s using X gates.

one_queen_per_column()      ◁── Evaluates all constraints
one_queen_per_diagonal()                              ┌── Checks that all constraints
circ.append(XGate().control(len(valid_column) +   ◁──┤   are satisfied
                            len(invalid_rowpair)),
            valid_column[:] + invalid_rowpair[:] + y[:])
one_queen_per_column()                  ◁── Uncomputes the constraints
one_queen_per_diagonal()

return circ
```

Since the constraint on the number of queens in each row is handled by the state preparation, the marking oracle focuses on the other two constraints: each column must have exactly one queen, and each diagonal must have at most one queen. The code allocates extra qubits to store the results of validating the constraints for each column and each pair of rows and then evaluates these constraints.

> **Are reversible computations their own adjoints?**
>
> Notice that this code uncomputes the evaluation of the constraints by calling the same code that was used to evaluate them rather than its adjoint. Is there a property of reversible computations that allows us to take this shortcut?
>
> Turns out that the adjoint of a reversible computation that evaluates a classical function is the same as the computation itself! Indeed, recall section 6.2: to make a function $f(x)$ reversible, we define another function $F(x, y)$ as follows:
>
> $$F(x, y) = (x, y \oplus f(x))$$
>
> What happens if we apply the function $F(x, y)$ twice in a row?
>
> $$F(F(x, y)) = F(x, y \oplus f(x)) = (x, y \oplus f(x) \oplus f(x)) = (x, y)$$
>
> This means that the reversible function $F(x, y)$ is its own inverse. This property transfers to its implementation as a quantum operation too!

(continued)

For the N queens puzzle, each of the individual constraints checks is done independently: we don't use the results of constraint evaluation to check other constraints, only to get the final answer. As a result, we can uncompute them in any order and use the same code we used to compute them for uncomputation.

In general, if you're computing several reversible functions and some of them use the results of evaluating others as inputs, you cannot use the same shortcut for uncomputation. Instead, you have to reverse the order of computation the way adjoint does: start by uncomputing the functions that were evaluated last.

Let's say you compute $h(x) = g(f(x))$ using the reversible implementations F and G of the functions f and g, with the implementation of G relying on an auxiliary variable y that acts as the input to g:

$$F(x, y) = (x, y \oplus f(x))$$
$$G(x, y, z) = (x, y, z \oplus g(y))$$

The reversible function $H(x, y, z)$ will not be its own inverse:

$$H(x, y, z) = G(F(x, y), z) = G(x, y \oplus f(x), z) = (x, y \oplus f(x), z \oplus g(y \oplus f(x)))$$

$$H(H(x, y, z)) = H(x, y \oplus f(x), z \oplus g(y \oplus f(x)))$$
$$= (x, y \oplus f(x) \oplus f(x), z \oplus g(y \oplus f(x)) \oplus g(y \oplus f(x) \oplus f(x)))$$
$$= (x, y, z \oplus g(y \oplus f(x)) \oplus g(y)) \neq (x, y, z)$$

The second expression corresponds to uncomputing the auxiliary variables first and then attempting to uncompute g using incorrect inputs for it.

For N queens problem, Grover's search doesn't offer a deterministic solution, so it is easier to test parts of the implementation rather than the end-to-end algorithm. We'll test the marking oracle implementation and skip tests for Grover's search implementation and mean state preparation, since those are standard components at this point.

The tests for this marking oracle implementation are very similar to those you've seen in section 6.3, so I do not include them in the text. They apply the oracle to multiple basis states and check that the result matches the classically computed function value for each input. For Grover's algorithm, we only care about the behavior of the oracle on the basis states from the search space, since the oracle is never applied to any other basis states. So, we can speed up the tests by running them on just these basis states instead of all basis states on N^2 qubits.

In addition to tests, we'll want to run the end-to-end solution to explore its success probability. Listing 8.3 shows Python code for checking that the classical answer produced by the solution—the placement of N queens on the board—is correct. This code is used in both Qiskit and Q# projects that run the solution end to end.

8.2 Encoding constraints in the search space

Listing 8.3 Python: Validating the answer for N queens puzzle

```
def check_placement_bits(n, bits):         ◄─── Validates queens
  board = [bits[n * row:n * (row + 1)]           placement classically
           for row in range(n)]
  for r in range(n):                       ◄─── Checks that one queen
    n_q = 0                                     is placed in each row
    for c in range(n):
      if board[r][c] == '1':
        n_q += 1
    if n_q != 1:
      return False
  indices = [row.index('1') for row in board]
  return check_one_queen_per_column_diagonal(n, indices)

def check_one_queen_per_column_diagonal(n, indices):
  for r1 in range(n):
    for r2 in range(r1 + 1, n):            ◄─── Checks that at most one
      diff = indices[r1] - indices[r2]          queen is placed in each
      if diff == 0 or abs(diff) == r2 - r1:     column and each diagonal
        return False
  return True
```

Finally, listing 8.4 shows the code that runs an end-to-end Grover's search for the N queens puzzle and gets its results. To make things more interesting, the code runs Grover's search multiple times with different numbers of iterations and gathers statistics on the way the number of iterations affects the success rate of the algorithm.

Listing 8.4 Python: Evaluating Qiskit solution for N queens puzzle

```
from time import time
from qiskit import transpile
from qiskit_aer import AerSimulator
from n_queens import *

n_rows = 4
print(f"Running for board size {n_rows}, mode = Bits")
simulator = AerSimulator(method='statevector')
n_runs = 100

for n_iter in range(1, 18):                ◄─── Tries different numbers of iterations
  circ = grovers_search(n_rows, n_iter)
  circ = transpile(circ, backend=simulator).decomposed()
  start_time = time()
  res_map = simulator.run(circ, shots=n_runs).result().get_counts()
  end_time = time()

  n_correct = 0                            ┐ Calculates the success rate
  for (bitstring, num) in res_map.items(): ◄┘ of the quantum algorithm
    if check_placement_bits(n_rows, bitstring):
      n_correct += num
```

```
print(f"{n_iter} iterations - success rate {n_correct / n_runs * 100}%" +
    f" ({round(end_time - start_time)} sec)")
```

For this encoding, ignore the fact that Qiskit measurement results are returned in reversed order compared to the order of qubits in the code. Reversing the encoding rotates the queens' placement by 180 degrees. Since N queens placement is a symmetric problem, the rotated placement is valid if and only if the intended placement is valid.

The output of this code will look something like this:

```
Running for board size 4, mode = Bits
1 iterations - success rate 7.0% (15 sec)
2 iterations - success rate 19.0% (30 sec)
3 iterations - success rate 33.0% (45 sec)
4 iterations - success rate 61.0% (57 sec)
5 iterations - success rate 77.0% (71 sec)
6 iterations - success rate 82.0% (90 sec)
7 iterations - success rate 92.0% (108 sec)
8 iterations - success rate 98.0% (127 sec)
9 iterations - success rate 97.0% (137 sec)
10 iterations - success rate 89.0% (150 sec)
11 iterations - success rate 78.0% (165 sec)
12 iterations - success rate 63.0% (180 sec)
13 iterations - success rate 52.0% (194 sec)
14 iterations - success rate 33.0% (209 sec)
15 iterations - success rate 15.0% (225 sec)
16 iterations - success rate 5.0% (239 sec)
17 iterations - success rate 0.0% (254 sec)
```

The output matches the expected behavior of Grover's search algorithm: as the number of iterations increases, the success probability grows up to the optimal number of iterations (8-9 in this case). After the number of iterations surpasses the optimal number, the success probability starts to decrease until it drops to near zero. You can experiment with the code to increase the number of iterations further to observe the full periodic behavior of success probability.

The complete project for this section consists of the following components:

- Problem-specific code (listings 8.1 and 8.2)
- Generic Grover's search implementation (listing 7.3)
- The code that runs the end-to-end problem solution and calculates its success rate (listings 8.3 and 8.4)
- The test code (not included here)

You can find the complete project code in the GitHub repository.

8.2.3 Q#

Listing 8.5 shows the Q# code that implements the operation that prepares the |mean⟩ state for the described approach to solving the N queens puzzle.

As a reminder, this approach uses the straightforward input representation: each qubit represents one cell of the board and indicates whether there is a queen placed there. However, we only consider inputs that have exactly one queen in each row, and we encode this constraint in the |mean⟩ state.

Listing 8.5 Q#: Solving N queens puzzle—state preparation

```
import Std.Arrays.Chunks;
import Std.Convert.IntAsDouble;
import Std.Math.Sqrt;
import Microsoft.Quantum.Unstable.StatePreparation.PreparePureStateD;

function GetWStateAmps(n : Int) : Double[] {        ⟵ Calculates the amplitudes
  mutable amps = [0.0, size = 2 ^ n];                 of the W state on n qubits
  for i in 0 .. n - 1 {
    set amps w/= (1 <<< i) <- Sqrt(1.0 / IntAsDouble(n));
  }
  return amps;
}
                                                    Operation that prepares the
                                                    mean state on n × n board
operation PrepareMean_Bits(      ⟵
  n : Int,
  qs : Qubit[]
) : Unit is Adj {
  let wstateAmps = GetWStateAmps(n);              Prepares the W state on
  for row in Chunks(n, qs) {        ⟵            each row of n qubits separately
    PreparePureStateD(wstateAmps, row);
  }
}
```

Notice that the logic of calculating the amplitudes of the W state for a given number of qubits is implemented as a separate function, rather than as a part of the operation `PrepareMean_Bits`. Why is this necessary?

We'll need the adjoint of the state preparation operation to implement reflection about the mean in the Grover's iteration, so the operation `PrepareMean_Bits` has to have its adjoint variant defined. The easiest way to ensure that is to implement the operation in a way that allows the Q# compiler to generate its adjoint automatically.

However, Q# compiler cannot generate adjoint of operations that use mutable variables in the code. Instead, we move the classical computation out of the operation and into a separate function. Q# functions are deterministic and cannot have side effects, so calling the function `GetWStateAmps` with the same parameter `n` in the operation and in its adjoint variant is guaranteed to produce the same return value. This makes it safe to use when generating the adjoint of an operation.

The following listing shows the Q# code that implements the marking oracle for this approach.

Listing 8.6 Q#: Solving N queens puzzle—the marking oracle

```
function GetRowPairInd(              ← Function that converts the pair of
    n : Int,                            rows (row1, row2) into an Integer Index
    row1 : Int, row2 : Int
) : Int {                            ← Iterates through all pairs in order of row1
    mutable ind = 0;                    Increasing and then row2 Increasing
    for r1 in 0 .. n - 1 {
        for r2 in r1 + 1 .. n - 1 {
            if r1 == row1 and r2 == row2 {   ← Returns the Index of the pair
                return ind;                      that matches the Input
            }
            set ind += 1;
        }
    }
    return -1;
}

operation Oracle_Bits(              ← The marking oracle
    n : Int,                        ← The presence of a queen in row r and
    x : Qubit[],                        column c is described with x[r * n + c].
    y : Qubit
) : Unit {
    use validColumn = Qubit[n - 1];              ← Qubits for column constraints
    use invalidRowPair = Qubit[n * (n - 1) / 2]; ← Qubits for diagonal constraints
    within {
        for c in 0 .. n - 2 {          ← Evaluates column constraints
            for r in 0 .. n - 1 {      ← Computes XOR of all qubits in this column
                CNOT(x[r * n + c], validColumn[c]);
            }
        }  ← All qubits in validColumn should be 1.

        for r1 in 0 .. n - 1 {         ← Evaluates diagonal constraints for each pair of rows
            for r2 in r1 + 1 .. n - 1 {
                let rowPairInd = GetRowPairInd(n, r1, r2);
                for c1 in 0 .. n - 1 {
                    for c2 in [c1 + (r2 - r1),       ← Computes AND of each qubit pair on
                               c1 - (r2 - r1)] {       the same diagonal in these two rows
                        if c2 >= 0 and c2 < n {   ← Computes XOR of all ANDs since,
                            CCNOT(x[r1 * n + c1],     at most, one of them will be 1
                                  x[r2 * n + c2],
                                  invalidRowPair[rowPairInd]);
                        }
                    }
                }
            }
        }  ← All qubits in invalidRowPair should be 0.
        ApplyToEachA(X, invalidRowPair);  ← Switches them to 1s using X gates
    } apply {
        Controlled X(validColumn + invalidRowPair, y);  ← Checks that all
    }                                                      constraints are satisfied
}
```

8.2 Encoding constraints in the search space

Since one of the constraints is handled by the state preparation, the marking oracle has to check only the other two constraints: each column must have exactly one queen and each diagonal must have at most one queen. The code allocates extra qubits to store the results of validating the constraints for each column and each pair of rows and then evaluates these constraints.

Notice that the code uses the within-apply construct to evaluate the constraints, calculate the final value of the function based on those results, and then uncompute the constraints' evaluation automatically. We've used this construct earlier, starting with chapter 6. Here, you can see that it grows more and more convenient as the computations that need to be uncomputed become more complicated.

For N queens puzzle, Grover's search doesn't offer a deterministic solution, so it makes sense to separate the tests from the end-to-end algorithm execution. The key component that requires testing is the marking oracle implementation. Grover's search implementation and mean state preparation are standard components at this point, so we can skip writing the tests for them.

The tests for this marking oracle implementation are very similar to those you've seen in section 6.3, so I'm not including them in the text. They apply the oracle to multiple basis states and check that the result matched the classically computed function value every time. Note that for Grover's algorithm, we only care about the behavior of the oracle on the basis states that belong to the search space—the oracle is never applied to any other basis states. As a result, we can speed up the tests by limiting them to just these basis states, not all basis states on N^2 qubits. However, we do need to write Python code to run the algorithm end-to-end, since we want to see it solve the actual N queens puzzle!

Listing 8.7 shows the Python host code that calls the Q# implementation of Grover's search for the N queens puzzle. To make things more interesting, the code runs Grover's search multiple times with different numbers of iterations and gathers statistics on the way the number of iterations affects the success rate of the algorithm.

Listing 8.7 Python: Evaluating Q# solution for N queens puzzle

```
from qsharp import init, eval
from time import time

n_rows = 4
oracle = f"NQueens.Oracle_Bits({n_rows}, _, _)"
prep_mean = f"NQueens.PrepareMean_Bits({n_rows}, _)"

print(f"Running for board size {n_rows}, mode = Bits")
init(project_root='.')
for n_iter in range(1, 18):      ◁── Tries different numbers of iterations
    n_runs = 100
    n_correct = 0
    start_time = time()                       Calculates the success
    for _ in range(n_runs):               ◁── rate of the quantum algorithm
        res_bits = eval("GroversSearch.RunGroversSearch(" +
            f"{n_rows ** 2}, {oracle}, {prep_mean}, {n_iter})")
```

```
    if check_placement_bits(n_rows, res_bits):
        n_correct += 1
end_time = time()
print(f"{n_iter} iterations - success rate {n_correct / n_runs * 100}%" +
    f" ({round(end_time - start_time)} sec)")
```

As a reminder, `check_placement_bits` is the function from listing 8.3 that checks whether the queens placement is valid.

The output of this code will look something like this:

```
Running for board size 4, mode = Bits
1 iterations - success rate 7.0% (2 sec)
2 iterations - success rate 22.0% (4 sec)
3 iterations - success rate 36.0% (6 sec)
4 iterations - success rate 49.0% (8 sec)
5 iterations - success rate 65.0% (10 sec)
6 iterations - success rate 89.0% (11 sec)
7 iterations - success rate 89.0% (13 sec)
8 iterations - success rate 100.0% (15 sec)
9 iterations - success rate 100.0% (16 sec)
10 iterations - success rate 94.0% (19 sec)
11 iterations - success rate 79.0% (20 sec)
12 iterations - success rate 65.0% (22 sec)
13 iterations - success rate 49.0% (25 sec)
14 iterations - success rate 32.0% (27 sec)
15 iterations - success rate 20.0% (29 sec)
16 iterations - success rate 1.0% (31 sec)
17 iterations - success rate 1.0% (34 sec)
```

You see that the output shows the expected behavior of Grover's search algorithm: as the number of iterations increases, the success probability grows at first. After the number of iterations surpasses the optimal number, the success probability starts to decrease until it drops to near zero. You can experiment with the code to increase the number of iterations further to observe the full periodic behavior of success probability.

The complete project for this section consists of the following components:

- Problem-specific Q# code (listings 8.5 and 8.6)
- Generic Grover's search implementation in Q# (listing 7.4)
- The Python code that runs the end-to-end problem solution and calculates its success rate (listings 8.3 and 8.7)
- The test code (not included here)

You can find the complete project code in the GitHub repository.

8.3 Changing problem encoding

We just saw how using the naive solution can be improved by tweaking the search space to encode part of the problem constraints in its structure. Can we take this approach one step further and change the input representation to reflect part of the problem constraints?

8.3.1 Math

In the previous section, we noticed that any viable solutions to the N queens puzzle will always have exactly one queen in each row. This observation, while very simple, is key to significantly reducing the search space size and simplifying the logic of the oracle.

We can use the same observation to change the input encoding. Since we know up front that each row has only one queen, we don't need to use N bits to represent the individual cells of the row. Instead, we can encode the queen's position in a row as the integer index of the column it occupies. Figure 8.7 shows an example of this encoding for $N = 4$.

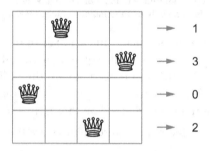

Figure 8.7 The new input encoding relies on the fact that only inputs in which each row has exactly one queen can be solutions to the puzzle. We represent each row of the board as just one integer, the column index of the queen in that row.

This encoding uses only $\lceil \log_2 N \rceil$ bits for each row. For our example of $N = 4$, the possible column indices we need to represent are 0, 1, 2, 3, and we need just 2 bits to store the binary representation of these numbers.

The new encoding does not reduce the search space size of the problem; we're still looking at all inputs that have one queen in each row, for a total of N^N possible inputs. But the inputs are now encoded more compactly, with $N \lceil \log_2 N \rceil$ bits needed to represent the input instead of N^2 we had in the previous approach.

The $|\text{mean}\rangle$ state has to change to reflect the new representation. Since we encode each row independently, the $|\text{mean}\rangle$ state remains a tensor product of N identical states that describe each row. But each of the per-row states will now use $\lceil \log_2 N \rceil$ qubits, and the superposition that describes a row will include the N basis states that correspond to integers from 0 to $N - 1$, inclusive:

$$|E_N\rangle = \frac{1}{\sqrt{N}} (\,|0\rangle + |1\rangle + |2\rangle + \ldots + |N-1\rangle\,)$$

For the case of $N = 4$, this state will be simply an equal superposition of all basis states on two qubits.

Now, let's see how the encoding change modifies the oracle implementation. Same as with the previous approach, we don't need to check that no two queens share a row. This is handled by the encoding itself, since it explicitly uses only one number to represent the queen's position in the row.

The other two types of constraints, exactly one queen in each column and, at most, one queen on each diagonal, look very different now. Figure 8.8 shows how to evaluate these constraints with the new encoding.

Since we already know the indices of the queens' positions in each row, we don't need to check all possible pairs of cells that might have queens in the same column or on the same diagonal any longer. Instead, we can iterate over all pairs of rows and

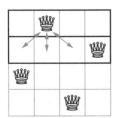 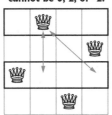 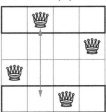

Figure 8.8 To check that no two queens share a column or a diagonal, we need to check each pair of rows separately. For each pair of rows, we calculate the difference of the indices of queens within them. This difference cannot be equal to zero or to the difference between the indices of these rows.

calculate the difference between the indices of the queens in each pair of rows. This difference cannot be 0, since this would mean that these two queens are in the same column. It also cannot be Δ or $-\Delta$, where Δ is the difference between the indices of the two rows, since this would mean that these two queens are on the same diagonal.

How many bits we need for a solution implemented based on this input encoding?

- We need $N\lceil \log_2 N \rceil$ bits to store the problem input and 1 bit to store the output of the marking oracle.
- The column and the diagonals checks need one bit for each pair of rows, for a total of $\frac{N(N-1)}{2}$ bits.
- We might need a couple more auxiliary qubits to implement the computations themselves. The main part of the constraints check is calculating the difference of two integers, which, depending on the implementation, can take several additional bits to act as carry bits. The Qiskit code will need 2 extra qubits for this, and the Q# code—1, so we'll use 2 as the number of auxiliary qubits. However, these bits are used only temporarily when subtracting two integers, and thus they can be reused in the next subtraction.
- The total number of bits is $N\lceil \log_2 N \rceil + \frac{N(N-1)}{2} + 3$.

For our small example, $N = 4$, and the number of bits used by the solution is 17, which means that the quantum simulator will use less memory to run this program compared to the solution we've seen in the previous section. The search space size is still $4^4 = 256$, though, so the optimal number of iterations is still 9.

> **Can we improve the solution further?**
>
> The input description that relies on queens' indices in their respective rows allows us to reduce the search space size even further. We only need to consider the potential solutions in which all indices of queens' positions in their rows are distinct. In other words, the search space can consist of only the inputs which are permutations of all integers from 0 to $N-1$, inclusive. We can prepare the $|\text{mean}\rangle$ state as an equal superposition of basis states that are such permutations and drop the check for queens being in the same column from the oracle.

> With this improvement, the search space size goes down from N^N to $N!$, which for $N = 4$ means the reduction from 256 to 24. The optimal number of iterations goes from 9 to 3, which is a significant improvement, especially for such a small test case. On the other hand, each iteration is likely to become more complicated due to the $|\text{mean}\rangle$ state becoming harder to prepare.

You can see that even for a problem as simple as this puzzle, there are multiple ways to approach the solution and multiple decisions to make when implementing the chosen approach. Making the right choice can mean the difference between getting the problem solution in minutes, in hours, or even not getting it at all.

How can we compare the different solutions to the same problem and decide which implementation choices are the best? That's exactly what we'll talk about in chapter 9! Meanwhile, let's see how to implement the solution that uses the new input encoding.

8.3.2 Qiskit

Listing 8.8 shows the Qiskit code that prepares the $|\text{mean}\rangle$ state for the N queens puzzle solution described in this section. With the new representation, the position of a queen in each row is represented as an integer, stored in an array of $\lceil \log_2 N \rceil$ qubits. The state preparation needs to split the board representation into N chunks, one per row, and prepare the state $|E_N\rangle$ (the equal superposition of basis states from $|0\rangle$ to $|N-1\rangle$) on each of them.

Listing 8.8 Qiskit: Solving N queens puzzle—state preparation

```
from math import sqrt
from qiskit import QuantumCircuit
from qiskit.circuit.library import StatePreparation

def bits_per_row(n):                    # Calculates the number of bits
    return (n - 1).bit_length()         # in binary representation of n

def prep_mean_indices(n):
    bitsize = bits_per_row(n)
    mean_amps = [1 / sqrt(n)] * n + [0] * (2 ** bitsize - n)
    meanstateprep = StatePreparation(mean_amps)
    circ = QuantumCircuit(n * bitsize)
    for r in range(n):                           # Prepares the equal superposition
        circ.append(meanstateprep,               # on each row of bitsize qubits
                    range(r * bitsize, (r + 1) * bitsize))
    return circ.to_gate()
```

The following listing shows the Qiskit code that implements the marking oracle for this approach.

Listing 8.9 Qiskit: Solving N queens puzzle—the marking oracle

```python
from qiskit import QuantumCircuit, QuantumRegister
from qiskit.circuit.library import CDKMRippleCarryAdder
from qiskit.circuit.library.standard_gates import XGate

def oracle_indices(n):
  bitsize = bits_per_row(n)                              # Uses library adder
                                                         # for integers of
  adder = CDKMRippleCarryAdder(bitsize).to_gate()        # the given bit size

  x = QuantumRegister(n * bitsize)
  y = QuantumRegister(1)
  invalid_rowpair = QuantumRegister(n * (n - 1) // 2)
  carryin = QuantumRegister(1)
  carryout = QuantumRegister(1)

  circ = QuantumCircuit(x, invalid_rowpair, carryin, carryout, y)
  circ.x(carryout)           # Carryout in state |1> used to keep
                             # subtraction from overflowing

  def one_queen_per_column_diagonal():    # Evaluates column and diagonal
    ind = 0                               # constraints for each pair of rows
    for r1 in range(n):
      for r2 in range(r1 + 1, n):         # Arguments to subtract column
        diff_inds = carryin[:] + \        # indices of queens in rows r1 and r2
          x[bitsize * r2:bitsize * (r2+1)] + \
          x[bitsize * r1:bitsize * (r1+1)] + \    # Subtraction and addition done in
          carryout[:]                             # place, with the result stored in
                                                  # the input register r1
        circ.append(adder.inverse(), diff_inds)   # Subtracts two indices
        for diff in [0,              # Checks that the difference of indices
                     r1 - r2,        # is not equal to 0, r1-r2, or r2-r1
                     r2 - r1]:

          circ.append(XGate().control(bitsize + 1,
                      ctrl_state=diff + (2 ** bitsize)),   # If equal to 0, r1-r2,
                      x[bitsize * r1:bitsize * (r1+1)] +   # or r2-r1, marks the row
                      carryout[:] +                        # pair as invalid
                      [invalid_rowpair[ind]])
        circ.append(adder, diff_inds)     # Uncomputes subtraction

        ind += 1
  one_queen_per_column_diagonal()
  circ.append(XGate().control(len(invalid_rowpair),    # Checks that all
                  ctrl_state=0),                       # row pairs are valid
            invalid_rowpair[:] + y[:])
  one_queen_per_column_diagonal()

  circ.x(carryout)
  return circ
```

As in section 8.2, the constraint on the number of queens in each row is handled by the state preparation, so the marking oracle only needs to check that no two queens are in the same column or diagonal. To do this, it calculates the difference of the queens' column indices in each pair of rows and checks that it is different from zero and the difference between the row indices.

Subtraction is done as an adjoint of the library adder `CDKMRippleCarryAdder` that performs in-place addition of two integers with carry-in and carry-out bits. The carry-out bit starts as 1 before subtraction to make sure the difference between the two indices never ends up negative. We can handle all three checks for the difference in the same way, using a controlled X gate, without considering representation of negative integers.

The structure of the code that runs end-to-end Grover's search and calculates its success rate is very similar to the code we saw in section 8.2, since the only difference between these two implementations is in the encoding of the queens' placement; the high-level logic of the solution is similar.

The output of this code will look something like this:

```
Running for board size 4, mode = Indices
1 iterations - success rate 9.0%(0 sec)
2 iterations - success rate 27.0%(0 sec)
3 iterations - success rate 31.0%(0 sec)
4 iterations - success rate 56.0%(0 sec)
5 iterations - success rate 75.0%(0 sec)
6 iterations - success rate 85.0%(0 sec)
7 iterations - success rate 93.0%(0 sec)
8 iterations - success rate 98.0%(0 sec)
9 iterations - success rate 99.0%(0 sec)
10 iterations - success rate 89.0%(0 sec)
11 iterations - success rate 82.0%(1 sec)
12 iterations - success rate 58%(1 sec)
```

You can find the complete code of this project in the GitHub repository.

8.3.3 Q#

Listing 8.10 shows the Q# code that implements the operation that prepares the $|\text{mean}\rangle$ state for the approach to solving the N queens puzzle described in this section. With the new representation, the position of a queen in each row is represented as an integer, stored in an array of $\lceil \log_2 N \rceil$ qubits. So, the state preparation operation needs to split the board representation into N chunks, one per row, and prepare the state $|E_N\rangle$ (the equal superposition of basis states from $|0\rangle$ to $|N-1\rangle$) on each of them.

Listing 8.10   Q#: Solving N queens puzzle—state preparation

```
import Std.Arrays.Chunks;
import Std.Convert.IntAsDouble;
import Std.Math.*;
import Microsoft.Quantum.Unstable.StatePreparation.PreparePureStateD;
```

```
operation PrepareMean_Indices(n : Int, qs : Qubit[]) : Unit is Adj {
  let meanAmps = [1.0 / Sqrt(IntAsDouble(n)), size = n];
  for row in Chunks(BitSizeI(n - 1), qs) {
    PreparePureStateD(meanAmps, row);
  }
}
```

The amplitudes of the state $|E_N\rangle$ in this code are straightforward to define, so we don't need a separate function to calculate them like we did in listing 8.5.

Listing 8.11 shows the Q# code that implements the marking oracle for this approach. It reuses the function GetRowPairInd from listing 8.6 that maps pairs of rows to unique indices.

Listing 8.11 Q#: Solving N queens puzzle—the marking oracle

```
import Microsoft.Quantum.Unstable.Arithmetic.*;

operation Oracle_Indices(n : Int, x : Qubit[], y : Qubit) : Unit {
  let bitSize = BitSizeI(n - 1);
  let indices = Chunks(bitSize, x);            ◄── The column of a queen in row r
                                                    is indices[r] in big-endian encoding.
  use invalidRowPair = Qubit[n * (n - 1) / 2];
  within {
    use aux = Qubit();                         ◄── Extra |1> qubit used as the most significant
    X(aux);                                         bit to keep subtraction from overflowing
    for r1 in 0 .. n - 1 {
      for r2 in r1 + 1 .. n - 1 {              ◄── Reverses column
        let rowPairInd = GetRowPairInd(n, r1, r2);   indices to make
        let ind1 = Reversed([aux] + indices[r1]); ◄── them little-endian
        let ind2 = Reversed(indices[r2]);
        within {                               ◄── Calculates ind1 - ind2
          Adjoint IncByLE(ind2, ind1);              and stores in ind1
        } apply {                              ◄── Checks that the difference of indices
          for diff in [0L,                         is not equal to 0, r1-r2, or r2-r1
                       IntAsBigInt(r1 - r2),
                       IntAsBigInt(r2 - r1)] {
            ApplyIfEqualL(X, diff + (1L <<< bitSize),  ◄── If equal to 0, r1-r2,
                ind1, invalidRowPair[rowPairInd]);        or r2-r1, marks the
          }                                              row pair as invalid.
        }
      }
    }
    X(aux);
  } apply {                                    ◄── Checks that all
    ApplyControlledOnInt(0, X, invalidRowPair, y);   row pairs are valid
  }
}
```

As in section 8.2, the constraint on the number of queens in each row is handled by the state preparation, so the marking oracle has to check only that no two queens are in the same column or diagonal. However, the new approach combines these two checks into one, iterating over all pairs of rows and checking that the queens' placement in them does not violate either constraint. Consequently, the code doesn't need to allocate a separate qubit register for columns checks like the oracle from listing 8.6 did.

For each pair of rows, the oracle needs to find the difference between the column indices of the two queens in it. This can be done using a library operation IncByLE, which adds its first argument to its second argument. Since subtraction is the inverse of addition, adjoint of this library operation will subtract the first argument from the second argument. Padding the second argument with a most significant bit equal to 1 makes sure that subtraction result remains positive; this simplifies our check. (This is the same trick we used in Qiskit by setting the carry-out bit to 1.)

Finally, the difference between the column indices is compared with 0 and with the differences between the row indices. These are classical values, so the comparison can be done using another library operation ApplyIfEqualL. This operation is effectively a controlled gate: it applies the given gate (in this case, X) if the given quantum integer equals the given classical integer.

The structure of the Python code that runs end-to-end Grover's search based on this encoding and calculates its success rate is very similar to the code we saw in section 8.2, since the only difference between these two solutions to the N queens puzzle is in the representation of the queens' placement.

The output of the complete code will look something like this:

```
Running for board size 4, mode = Indices
1 iterations - success rate 8.0% (1 sec)
2 iterations - success rate 18.0% (2 sec)
3 iterations - success rate 31.0% (4 sec)
4 iterations - success rate 48.0% (6 sec)
5 iterations - success rate 68.0% (8 sec)
6 iterations - success rate 85.0% (10 sec)
7 iterations - success rate 97.0% (13 sec)
8 iterations - success rate 100.0% (16 sec)
9 iterations - success rate 99.0% (20 sec)
10 iterations - success rate 94.0% (24 sec)
11 iterations - success rate 80.0% (29 sec)
12 iterations - success rate 56% (35 sec)
```

You can find the complete code of this project in the GitHub repository.

8.4 Going beyond

Do you want to spend some more time exploring variations of the problem discussed in this chapter before moving on to the next topic? Here are some additional ideas for similar problems if you want to try your hand at something more challenging:

- In the oracle we implemented in section 8.3, we merged the checks for columns with the checks for diagonals, since their implementations were very similar. Try to do the same for the oracle from section 8.2.

- Consider boards of different shapes, for example, a rectangular $N \times M$ board or a square $N \times N$ board with a square area cut out from the middle. How do you need to modify the solution in this case? Which of the tricks you learned can still be used?
- The *domination number* of an $N \times N$ board is the minimum number of queens necessary for each cell to be either occupied by a queen or under attack from one. This number is typically less than N, for example, for the standard chess board with $N = 8$ the domination number is 5. How would you search for a placement of queens that achieves domination on an $N \times N$ board?
- A lot of other logic puzzles focused on filling squares of a grid with values that satisfy certain constraints allow you to explore Grover's search. Here are a few examples:
  - In Latin squares, the goal is to fill the cells of an $N \times N$ square with digits 1 through N in such a way that each row and each column includes all N digits.
  - In Kakuro puzzles, grid cells have to be filled with numbers that should add up to the given row and column sums.
  - In Sudoku puzzles, the goal is to fill the squares with numbers so that each row, column, and subsquare have no duplicate numbers.
  - In Takuzu puzzles, grid cells have to be filled with 0s and 1s so that each row and column has equal numbers of 0s and 1s and no row or column has three copies of the same digit next to each other.

Summary

- A search problem usually has multiple ways to describe it as the input x and the function $f(x)$. Different descriptions can lead to solutions of different efficiency.
- The best way to speed up the solution to a search problem is reducing the search space size by analyzing the constraints and encoding part of them in the search space representation. This can lead to both simpler oracle implementation and fewer algorithm iterations necessary.
- If reducing search space size is not practical, it might be possible to change the encoding of the inputs within the search space to allow for simpler function evaluation and more efficient oracle implementation.
- When you implement a quantum algorithm to run on a quantum simulator, it is important to consider the total number of qubits used in the program, the length of the program, and, if running on a sparse simulator, the number of basis states in superposition states that are manipulated during the program execution.
- Sparse simulators are more efficient compared to full-state simulators for programs that act on a large number of qubits but only use a small subset of all basis states.

Evaluating the performance of quantum algorithms

This chapter covers
- Comparing quantum algorithms with classical algorithms for the same problem
- Factors that affect performance of quantum algorithms
- Using Azure Quantum Resource Estimator to estimate performance of quantum programs on future quantum computers

In chapter 8, we came up with two quantum algorithms for solving the N queens puzzle—variants of Grover's search that relied on different problem encoding and oracle implementation. How can we compare these two algorithms to decide which of them is better? And how can we figure out whether either of these algorithms can beat the classical solution to the N queens puzzle for large boards?

These questions arise whenever somebody comes up with a quantum algorithm to solve a problem. Comparing quantum solutions with each other and with classical ones is a critical part of quantum algorithm development. After all, we're building quantum computers to achieve practical quantum advantage—to solve useful problems that classical computers cannot handle. Understanding what kinds of problems these can be and what the quantum solutions to them look like gives us important information for making decisions about the architecture of the future quantum computers as we build them.

Before we start looking for answers for these questions, let's pause and think about the root question: How can we define the "quality" of a problem solution? You probably spend more time considering quality of classical solutions, but the same fundamental principles apply to quantum ones.

There is no single metric to define the quality of a software solution. Instead, it is usually defined as a combination of several metrics, illustrated in figure 9.1.

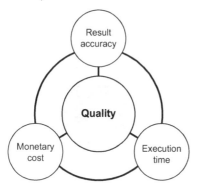

Figure 9.1 The key metrics that describe the quality of a problem solution are the accuracy of the result and the time and cost required to get it. We can often trade off these metrics by using different algorithms or implementations.

The first metric is the *accuracy of the result*. The search problem is not the best example to illustrate this metric, since it doesn't define approximate solutions: a value is either a valid answer or not. For other problems, such as the phase estimation problem we saw in section 5.3 or the problem of evaluating the energy of the ground state of a molecule in quantum chemistry, the answer is a number—an estimate of the true value of the eigenphase or the energy, respectively. The closer to the true value this estimate is, the better the solution.

The second metric is *time to get the solution*. For the solution to be useful in practice, it has to yield the result in hours or days, not in years or decades. A solution that returns the answer in minutes is better than another that produces the same result but takes days.

The third, less commonly discussed metric, is *monetary cost*. Let's say you have two algorithms that produce the answer with the same accuracy in the same time, but one of them runs on your laptop and the other one requires a supercomputer or a whole cluster of virtual machines from your favorite cloud provider. The first algorithm is clearly the winner, since it's so much easier and cheaper to run.

We can often choose which of these metrics we want to optimize by choosing the algorithm we use to solve the problem or tweaking its hyperparameters. Sometimes, it is possible for one solution to beat another one across all metrics; in other cases, we need to choose which ones are important for us and which ones we're willing to sacrifice.

In this chapter, we'll talk about the performance of quantum algorithms and the ways we compare them with each other and with classical algorithms. The discussion will follow the flow shown in figure 9.2.

We'll start with a purely classical question: How to choose the classical solution that we will compare with the quantum one. Establishing a fair baseline is extremely important for making the comparison candid, even if it ends up unfavorable for the quantum algorithm!

Then, we'll talk about the high-level principles of comparing the performance of algorithms. As with classical algorithms, asymptotic complexity is not the only consideration when comparing algorithms. Here, you will learn about the factors that affect the complexity of a quantum solution even before it makes it to the actual quantum computer.

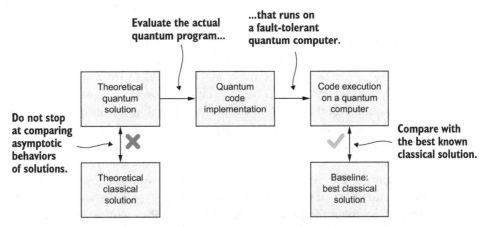

Figure 9.2 To understand performance of a quantum algorithm, you need to take into account not only its asymptotic complexity but also its practical behavior. The performance estimates are affected by the overheads introduced by the algorithm implementation and then by its execution on a fault-tolerant quantum computer. You also need to choose the best known classical algorithm as the baseline for comparison.

Next, we'll dig deeper into the factors that affect the performance of a quantum solution when it is executed on a real quantum computer. Most of this discussion assumes using fault-tolerant quantum computers running error correction. The quantum computing community agrees that we will need fault-tolerant quantum computers to achieve practical quantum advantage, so it makes sense to focus on the effect their architecture will have on the performance of quantum algorithms running on them.

Lastly, I'll introduce an example of a tool that estimates performance of quantum programs assuming their execution on fault-tolerant quantum computers, Azure Quantum Resource Estimator, and show you how to get and to interpret the resource estimates it does. This will finally allow us to discuss our solutions to the N queens puzzle and compare them to the classical solutions to this problem.

I'll use the N queens puzzle as the example problem in the bulk of this chapter. The two algorithms from chapter 8 will act as the example quantum algorithms whenever I talk about comparing performance of specific algorithms.

> **NOTE** Grover's search is my favorite algorithm for teaching quantum computing. While it is unlikely to offer a practical advantage, it makes for a fantastic illustration of the many reasons why a quantum algorithm can be less efficient in practice than on paper!

9.1 Choosing the classical solution for comparison

In chapter 7, we discussed Grover's algorithm and compared it with the classical search algorithm. For the purposes of that chapter, we represented our problem as *unstructured search problem*, which assumed that we don't have any information about the internal structure of the problem that would help us solve it. Under this assumption, we developed a generic quantum algorithm suitable for solving any search problems—a quantum equivalent of a brute-force classical algorithm.

However, once we start solving a specific problem instead of a generic search problem, this assumption becomes too limiting. Grover's algorithm indeed uses no information about the problem structure, other than the information used in the oracle implementation and mean state preparation. But is this the case for all classical algorithms as well?

In chapter 8, we solved the N queens puzzle by representing it as a search problem, implementing the quantum oracle for it, and running Grover's search based on that oracle. But even for this quantum algorithm, you have seen firsthand how the information about the problem structure affects the solution: encoding part of the constraints in the search space allows us to both reduce the search space size and simplify the oracle implementation and thus speeds up the algorithm significantly.

The same thing happens with classical solutions, although the effects are even more pronounced. The problems we want to solve often have an internal structure, and the solutions that exploit it are much more efficient than the naive brute-force approaches.

Let's consider the N queens puzzle again. There are plenty of classical approaches to this problem that rely on the structure of the puzzle; figure 9.3 shows just a few examples.

- Brute-force algorithms consider all possible placements of N queens on the board that satisfy a certain subset of constraints and then check whether each placement satisfies the rest of constraints. There are a lot of variants of brute-force solutions that vary in their definitions of "possible placements":
  - The most straightforward solution places N queens independently, with N^2 possible cells for each queen, for a total of $(N^2)^N$ possible placements.
  - The slightly optimized variant places one queen in each of N rows (N^N placements total).
  - An even better algorithm generates $N!$ permutations of numbers from 1 to N and places the queens in the corresponding columns in each row, guaranteeing that all queens are in different columns.

  Either way, each placement is considered as a whole, and invalid placements are not used to inform the next steps.
- Backtracking algorithms try to place queens one by one, eliminating a lot of non-solutions without needing to complete them.

9.1 Choosing the classical solution for comparison

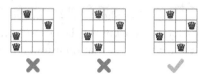

Brute force: try every placement; if invalid, retry a different one.

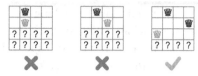

Backtracking: place queens one by one; if a conflict is found, backtrack; otherwise, try placing the next one.

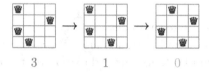

3   1   0

Local search: pick random placement and move queens one at a time to minimize the number of conflicts.

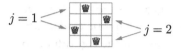

Explicit construction: for $j = 1, 2$ place queens at $(j, 2j)$ and $(n/2 + j, 2j - 1)$.

Figure 9.3 The classical solutions to the N queens puzzle range from brute-force solutions similar to those we considered as the equivalent to Grover's search to methods that exploit all the available information about the problem to construct the solution mathematically.

- Local search algorithms start with a random initial placement and tweak it by moving one or two queens at a time to reduce the number of attacks on the board.
- Finally, a mathematical formula allows us to build a solution (although not all possible solutions) for an arbitrary board size without using a computer at all! (B. Bernhardsson, "Explicit Solutions to the N-queens Problem for All N," https://dl.acm.org/doi/10.1145/122319.122322)

When we look to show a practical quantum advantage for a given problem, our goal is not to find a quantum algorithm that is better than *some* classical solution for it. Rather, we want the quantum algorithm to be better than *all* classical solutions, including the best ones designed specifically for this problem with full understanding of its structure.

Is Grover's algorithm going to speed up database search?

If you've heard about Grover's algorithm before, you've probably heard that it's going to speed up all search applications we have, including database search. In the light of our discussion in this chapter, does this sound plausible?

Databases are collections of data designed specifically to facilitate efficient storage and retrieval of information. I have yet to see a database that runs queries by picking a random entry and checking whether it fits the search criteria. Instead, they use techniques such as indexing to allow locating the relevant entries faster. Additionally, database queries aim to find all entries that satisfy the search criteria rather than just a single one, which makes them even worse applications for Grover's search.

In practice, we're looking to apply quantum computing algorithms to problems that do not have efficient classical solutions. If a problem has a known classical solution that is efficient enough for practical purposes, it's very unlikely that quantum computing will offer us an improvement over it.

9.2 Performance comparisons: Asymptotic vs. practical

Algorithms, quantum and classical both, are often described in terms of their *asymptotic complexity*—the rate at which the amount of resources required to solve a problem grows as the problem size increases.

Asymptotic complexity can be expressed in terms of any resources that are important for the algorithm. For example, classical multiplication algorithms are analyzed in terms of the number of single-digit multiplications required to multiply two n-digit numbers; for sorting algorithms, we typically consider the numbers of comparisons and swaps and the amount of additional memory required to sort an array of n numbers, and so on.

When we discussed the performance of Grover's algorithm and its classical counterpart in chapter 7, we focused on the asymptotic complexity of these algorithms, expressed in terms of the number of oracle queries. We compared the average asymptotic number of oracle calls necessary to get the solution and concluded that Grover's search offered us a quadratic speedup compared to the classical brute-force algorithm.

Asymptotic complexity is a useful tool for getting the big picture of algorithm behavior and the relative performance of two algorithms. If one algorithm has a linear complexity (the resources it uses grow at most as fast as cn for some constant c and input size n) and another algorithm has a quadratic complexity (dn^2 for some other constant d), we know that the first algorithm will perform better than the second one for problems larger than a certain threshold. This threshold is called the *crossover point*—the problem size for which the two algorithms offer similar performance. For smaller problems, one algorithm is better, and for larger problems, the other algorithm is better.

However, asymptotic behavior is not the only thing we need to consider. It is an abstraction that hides away a lot of implementation complexity of the algorithms. We need to do a more thorough analysis to figure out where the crossover point of the two algorithms is and where the problems of sizes we care about are located relative to that point. This idea is illustrated in figure 9.4.

The fact that an algorithm has a better asymptotic complexity than the other one doesn't mean it's always better. For example, the Karatsuba algorithm is a multiplication algorithm that is asymptotically faster than the traditional multiplication: it uses $O(n^{1.58})$ single-digit multiplications to multiply n-digit numbers, while the traditional algorithm uses n^2. However, in practice, it is less efficient for numbers commonly used in most computations and is used only for very specialized applications that rely on multiplication of very large numbers, such as cryptography.

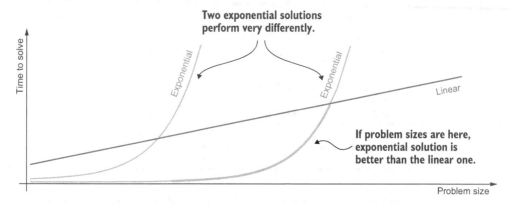

Figure 9.4 When comparing the performance of algorithms, it's important to consider not only their asymptotic behavior but also the details. Algorithms can have the same asymptotic behavior but vastly different growth rates once you take into account all the factors. The solution with worse asymptotic behavior can be better in practice if the problem sizes are smaller than the crossover point—the problem size for which two algorithms have similar performance.

When we consider algorithms that involve oracles, the difference between the costs of an oracle call in the quantum and classical implementations can be very significant.

Quantum oracles implement classical computations in a way we saw in chapter 6, by breaking them down into primitive logical operations, making each operation reversible, and then replacing reversible operations with their quantum equivalents. This procedure introduces a considerable overhead in terms of the number of quantum gates used to implement a quantum oracle compared to the number of logical operations used to compute the same function on a classical computer. As a result, a computation that is trivial to do on a classical computer, such as multiplication, can take noticeable amount of time on a quantum computer.

To summarize, it is very important to not stop the discussion of quantum and classical algorithms at the comparison of their asymptotic behavior. Instead, we need to implement the quantum algorithm we have in mind and to estimate its performance on problems of practical sizes to compare it to the real performance of a classical algorithm.

9.3 Estimating performance of a quantum solution

Let's say that you have already implemented the quantum algorithm you have in mind. How can you estimate its performance and compare it to that of another algorithm, quantum or classical? The naive measure of a quantum program performance is the time it takes to run this program on a quantum simulator. This approach is misleading for several reasons.

First, different quantum simulators can be better for simulating different kinds of programs. For example, let's take a look at the two quantum solutions to the N queens puzzle from chapter 8 that we implemented in Q# and Qiskit. Their run time on a simulator depends not only on the algorithm, but also on the implementation language and the simulator used for that language. Table 9.1 shows the simulation time for Q# and Qiskit implementations of each algorithm, running for the optimal number of iterations (9) and repeated a hundred times.

Table 9.1 Simulation times for different solutions to the N queens puzzle

Algorithm	Qiskit run time	Q# run time
Section 8.2	137 sec	16 sec
Section 8.3	< 1 sec	20 sec

If we compare the execution time of Qiskit implementations, the second algorithm (section 8.3) is much faster: it completes a hundred runs in under a second, while the first algorithm (section 8.2) takes over two minutes to do the same. But if we look at the run times of Q# programs, the first algorithm will turn out to be slightly faster: 16 seconds versus 20 seconds for the second algorithm.

> NOTE This discrepancy comes from the fact that Qiskit simulator is full state, in which case the time of simulation is heavily influenced by the number of qubits allocated by the program. The Q# simulator is sparse, and the time of simulation depends primarily on the number of the basis states manipulated by the program, which is the same for both algorithms.

More importantly, the time it takes to run a program on a quantum simulator is not really a good indicator of the time it will take it to run on a quantum computer. Remember that quantum simulators are classical programs themselves and run on classical computers. So, they need to put in a lot of extra work into pretending to be quantum computers by maintaining the state of the program as a vector of complex numbers and simulating the effects of the gates and measurements by updating this vector. Something as simple as applying a gate to one qubit might require updating all elements of the vector representing the quantum state of the system, and the size of this vector can grow exponentially with the number of allocated qubits. At the same time, on a quantum computer, applying a gate is a physical process that acts on just a few qubits regardless of the total number of qubits used by the program.

Our ultimate goal is to run quantum algorithms on fault-tolerant quantum computers, so we need to take that into account when estimating the performance of our programs. We also need to keep in mind that quantum computers are not mature enough yet to be fault-tolerant, so we cannot just grab a computer, run our algorithm on it, and measure how long it took! Instead, we need to make an informed prediction about the possible architecture of the future fault-tolerant quantum computers and estimate the resources required to run our program on them based on this prediction.

> WARNING This section and the next one are based on the current assumptions about how future fault-tolerant quantum computers might work. There are still a lot of open scientific and engineering problems to solve before we get there,

so while the main principles are most likely to stay unchanged, the details are almost certain to change.

How does the architecture of a fault-tolerant quantum computer affect the performance of quantum algorithms running on it? Figure 9.5 shows the main factors we need to take into account.

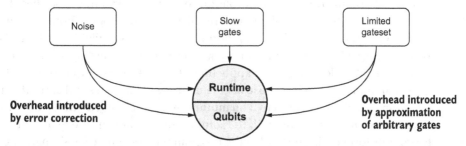

Figure 9.5 Physical qubits are noisy, they support a limited set of gates, and these gates are slow. We have to use error correction to enable reliable computation on noisy qubits. We also have to use a special process to implement arbitrary logical gates on logical qubits. These factors affect both the run time of algorithms on the quantum computers and the numbers of qubits required to run them.

First, applying gates and measurements to the physical systems we use as qubits—photons, or atoms, or small manufactured devices that behave according to the laws of quantum mechanics—is slower than applying classical logical gates to bits used in a classical computer. Depending on the physical implementation of qubits, a single gate or measurement can take from tens of nanoseconds to microseconds to apply. In contrast, classical logical gates take nanoseconds or less. Even if the quantum program used the exact same number of gates as the classical one, it would take longer to run.

Second, the physical qubits are all inherently noisy due to their physical nature. The error rates for gates and measurements are projected to reach 10^{-4} or 10^{-6} in optimistic scenarios. This means that it is impossible to carry out a long computation using physical qubits directly: the noise will ruin it really fast, effectively rendering the results random.

> **NOTE** For example, consider a program that uses Grover's search to find one value out of 16 or 32—a very short computation that uses less than 10 qubits. When you run it several times, on a simulator you will get the correct answer in the majority of the runs, and just a few incorrect answers. However, if you run it on the current NISQ devices (or on noisy simulators that imitate them), you will get all possible results with roughly equal probability.

Instead, fault-tolerant computers will use *error correction*, a technique that enables reliable computation using unreliable (noisy) qubits. It encodes logical qubits—qubits used in the quantum programs—in states of multiple physical qubits and represents logical gates—gates the quantum programs apply to qubits—as sequences of gates and measurements applied to those physical qubits. Error correction does not make the computation completely noise-free, but it allows us to reduce the error rates to values as low as we need.

Error correction is one of the major sources of overhead when running quantum programs on fault-tolerant quantum computers. Since each logical gate can take dozens or even hundreds of physical gates and measurements to implement, it takes a lot longer to apply a single logical gate than a physical gate.

Logical architecture of a fault-tolerant quantum computer describes the error correction code used, logical qubit connectivity (the way logical qubits are arranged and can interact with each other), and the operations available for logical qubits. You can use arbitrary gates in your quantum program, including arbitrary rotations and multicontrolled gates, and apply them to any subsets of qubits. But while the quantum simulator can just construct the matrices of any gates and apply them to the quantum state directly, the actual quantum computer cannot do that—this operation is just not available to it. Instead, the software stack that runs the quantum program has to transform each gate used in the program into a sequence of simpler operations that can be applied to logical qubits.

Depending on the logical architecture, logical qubits are likely to have limited connectivity: it might only be possible to apply a gate to two qubits if they are right next to each other. If your program needs to apply a gate to two qubits that are placed far from each other, it cannot do that directly. Instead, this gate needs to be replaced by a sequence of gates, each of them applied to pairs of adjacent qubits.

To facilitate this, the software stack will typically use auxiliary qubits in addition to the *data qubits*—the qubits used to carry out the main computation. For example, the data qubits can be arranged in rows that are separated by rows of auxiliary qubits. The only goal of those auxiliary qubits is to enable applying multi-qubit gates to distant data qubits; they are not used in the main computation.

The other factor to consider is that you can apply only a very limited set of operations directly to logical qubits. If your program uses other gates—for example, arbitrary rotation gates such as Ry—these gates need to be constructed from the available operations.

To extend the set of gates that can be used on a quantum computer, we use so-called *magic gates* and their companion *magic states*. Magic gates are not supported by the logical architecture directly. Instead, we prepare rough approximations of magic states and refine them through a process called *magic state distillation*. Finally, we use these magic states to apply magic gates in the sequences of operations that approximate arbitrary gates.

Magic gate: The T gate

A typical example of a magic gate is the T gate and its matching T state:

$$T = \begin{pmatrix} 1 & 0 \\ 0 & e^{i\pi/4} \end{pmatrix}, \ |T\rangle = T\,|+\rangle = \tfrac{1}{\sqrt{2}}(|0\rangle + e^{i\pi/4}\,|1\rangle)$$

> Together with some simple gates that are supported by a typical logical architecture, the T gate allows us to approximate any single-qubit gate as precisely as we want.

Currently, we assume that magic state distillation is necessary for fault-tolerant quantum computation. This process runs in parallel with the "main" computation in a separate area of the quantum computer, and its only goal is to supply magic gates to the main computation. Depending on your program and the gates you use in it, producing magic states can be a major contributor to the overall resource requirements of running the program.

This is a very high-level overview of the things that you need to account for when estimating the run time of your program on a fault-tolerant quantum computer. It mentions just a few main factors that have significant effect, but even they are a lot to keep in mind! Doing all these calculations for every program you write can seem daunting.

Fortunately, we don't need to do these estimations by hand. Specialized software tools can do quantum resource estimation automatically based on the program you have and a few numeric parameters. Let's take a look at one such tool.

9.4 Azure Quantum Resource Estimator: An overview

Multiple software tools for programmatic quantum resource estimation emerged in the past few years. They work with different algorithm descriptions as inputs and use different assumptions about the architecture of quantum computers the algorithms will run on. I will not offer an overview of all these tools here, since their list is growing and their capabilities are changing very fast.

In this section, I'll show you one example of a software tool for resource estimation—Azure Quantum Resource Estimator (AQRE), part of Azure Quantum Development Kit. Conveniently, AQRE can estimate the resources required to run programs written in both Qiskit and Q#, which makes it perfect for this book.

> ### Using Azure Quantum Resource Estimator with Qiskit and Q#
>
> The exact way of invoking AQRE for the given quantum program and getting the results depends on the language. As of November 2024,
>
> - You can run resource estimation for Q# programs locally, via the Azure Quantum Development Kit extension for VS Code or via the Python package `qsharp`.
> - To run AQRE for Qiskit programs, you need to use Azure Quantum cloud service.
>
> The resource estimates done by AQRE do not depend on the language of the input program but rather on what the program does. For simplicity, I will use the estimates done for Q# programs from chapter 8. Qiskit estimates will have the same structure and very similar numeric values.

(continued)

Creating an Azure account and using Azure Quantum workspace to run programs on quantum hardware or cloud simulators, including AQRE, is out of scope for this book, so I will not discuss the details of running AQRE for Qiskit programs. If you want to reproduce this chapter's estimates for Qiskit programs from chapter 8 or to use AQRE with your own Qiskit programs, I encourage you to refer to the Azure Quantum documentation on setting up an Azure Quantum workspace (https://mng.bz/W244) and running AQRE for Qiskit programs from it (https://mng.bz/8OeZ).

You can run Azure Quantum Resource Estimator for a Q# operation that doesn't have inputs, such as an operation marked as @EntryPoint(), directly from Visual Studio Code using Azure Quantum Development Kit extension. Our N queens code from sections 8.2 and 8.3 doesn't have an entry point defined for it yet, since we called it from the Python host code. We can add an entry point operation to the Q# code from section 8.2 as shown in listing 9.1.

Listing 9.1 Q# entry point example for N queens puzzle

```
@EntryPoint()
operation Main() : Bool[] {
  let nRows = 4;
  let nIter = 9;
  let nBits = nRows ^ 2;
  return RunGroversSearch(nBits, Oracle_Bits(nRows, _, _),
    PrepareMean_Bits(nRows, _), nIter);
}
```

This code does the same thing as the Python wrapper from listing 8.7. It defines the values that describe the specific puzzle instance and the oracle/state preparation operations that we want to use and calls generic Grover's search with these parameters.

The list of code actions provided by the Azure Quantum Development Kit extension for this operation includes the Estimate command that runs resource estimation for this operation. Once you click on it, the extension will prompt you for several parameters; leave all of them set to default values. After you enter the last parameter, you'll get the resource estimates for this code that will look similar to figure 9.6.

The resource estimates overview consists of two parts. The Results section shows the resources required to achieve the fastest estimated run time. The space-time diagram shows the possible tradeoffs between the two metrics, run time and the number of physical qubits.

> **NOTE** In this chapter, we've been focusing on execution time and monetary cost as the quality metrics. You can think of the number of qubits as a contributor of the cost metric: the more qubits the algorithm needs, the more expensive it is to run it—and to build a quantum computer that can do that!

9.4 Azure Quantum Resource Estimator: An overview

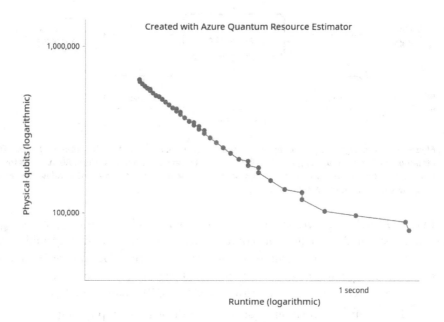

Figure 9.6 An example of resource estimates produced by Azure Quantum Resource Estimator

The main information you can gain from the plot is the ballpark estimates of how fast you can execute the program and how many physical qubits a fault-tolerant quantum computer will need to do that. For the example in figure 9.6, you need a computer with about a hundred thousand physical qubits, and it will be able to run the program in about a second. A larger computer will be able to run the program faster.

How does AQRE get these estimates? The high-level scheme is shown on figure 9.7.

AQRE takes multiple inputs that can be grouped as follows:

- The quantum program in Qiskit or Q# that we want to estimate
- The error budget, which is the maximum allowed probability of the algorithm failure
- The parameters of the assumed fault-tolerant quantum computer architecture:
  - Physical qubit parameters: their error rates and operation times

- The error correction scheme and its parameters
- The magic state distillation protocol and its parameters

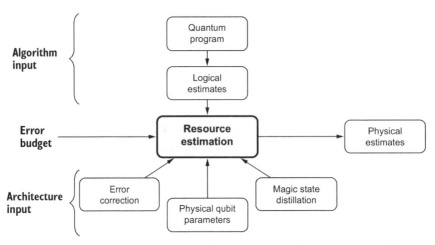

Figure 9.7 The high-level inputs and processing logic of Azure Quantum Resource Estimator. The first step reduces the quantum program to a set of logical resource estimates. Then, AQRE looks for the parameters of the different architectural components of the quantum computer that allow to execute the program within the given error budget.

In our example, we used one of the default configurations that roughly corresponds to a realistic model of a quantum computer based on superconducting qubits running *surface code*, a commonly assumed error correction code. You can choose a different default configuration or tweak the individual parameters separately.

The resource estimation algorithm used by AQRE takes several steps:

1. The resource estimation algorithm goes through the input program and collects *logical estimates*, the information about the logical resources it uses. This step tracks several numeric values: the number of logical qubits allocated by the program, the numbers of certain types of gates and measurements, and the number of steps in the program execution (the circuit depth).
2. The logical estimates are converted into lower-level parameters to account for the layout and connectivity of logical qubits and the decomposition of the logical gates into sequences of magic gates and gates supported by the logical architecture.
3. The resource estimation algorithm searches for the numeric parameters of the error correction code and magic state distillation process that allow to execute the program with desired level of reliability.

This overview should give you an idea of what is going on when we use AQRE to estimate the resources used by our programs. This is sufficient for the purposes of this chapter, so I will not go into more details here. If you want to dig deeper into the internals of AQRE, check out its documentation (https://mng.bz/EaNo).

9.5 Solutions' performance for the N queens puzzle

Now that we've discussed the basic ideas that you need to take into account when evaluating performance of quantum solutions, it's finally time to return to the original questions we posed in this chapter:

1. Which quantum algorithm is better, the one from section 8.2 or from 8.3?
2. Is either of these algorithms better than the best classical solution?

Let's do a comparison using a slightly larger problem instance than we used in chapter 8, with $N = 10$ queens. It is large enough that we cannot run our code on a simulator, so resource estimation is the only way for us to get information about its performance.

The 10 queens problem has 724 different solutions. With the search space size $N^N = 10^{10}$, both quantum solutions will need approximately a hundred iterations (109, to be precise) to return one of the correct answers with high probability.

To start, let's run resource estimation for these parameters and compare the results based on the slowest of the estimates we get on the run-time/qubit number plot.

> **NOTE** Remember that sometimes you can trade off fewer physical qubits required to run the algorithm for longer run time. Waiting for 30 minutes instead of 1 minute makes a lot of sense if this means you can run your algorithm on a computer with $700k$ qubits instead of $3.5M$.

If you run resource estimation for both quantum algorithms with these inputs and the default resource estimation parameters, you'll get the following results:

- A solution that encodes each board cell with one bit (section 8.2): 37 minutes, $670k$ physical qubits
- A solution that encodes each queen with its column index (section 8.3): 3 minutes, $340k$ physical qubits

The solution that uses a more efficient encoding turns out to be better not only in the number of physical qubits used but also in the run time.

We could push this comparison further to analyze larger problem instances, but it is more interesting to switch to the second question: How do quantum solutions compare with the classical ones? Unfortunately, the results are unfavorable for our quantum algorithms:

- The simplest brute-force algorithm without any optimizations written in Python solves the 10 queens problem in under 0.1 second on my laptop. Additionally, it finds all valid placements instead of a single one like the quantum solutions do.
- More sophisticated algorithms such as local search can solve the problem for $N = 1,000,000$ in minutes, if not seconds. The 1992 paper "Minimizing Conflicts" by Minton et al. (https://ntrs.nasa.gov/citations/19930006097) showed the heuristic solution that solved it in under 4 minutes. A modern classical computer would take seconds to do the same.

- Finally, the explicit construction solution solves the problem as fast as it can print out the result!

This exercise shows us the importance of approaching the analysis of quantum algorithms' performance with care, both in accounting for all factors that affect the run time and execution cost of quantum programs and in comparing it with the classical solutions.

9.6 Further reading

Here is a short list of references that are good starting points if you want to learn more about estimating the performance of quantum algorithms and comparing it to the classical algorithms:

- Hoefler, T., Haener, T., & Troyer, M. (2023). Disentangling hype from practicality: On realistically achieving quantum advantage. https://arxiv.org/abs/2307.00523
- Viamontes, G. F., Markov, I. L., & Hayes, J. P. (2005). Is quantum search practical? https://arxiv.org/abs/quant-ph/0405001
- Beverland, M. E., Murali, P., Troyer, M., et al. (2022). Assessing requirements to scale to practical quantum advantage. https://arxiv.org/abs/2211.07629

9.7 Going beyond

Do you want to spend some more time digging deeper into the topics discussed in this chapter? Here are a couple of project ideas you can tackle if you want to try your hand at something more challenging:

- In this chapter, we analyzed the performance of Grover's search for the N queens puzzle. Consider other classical problems that can be solved using Grover's search and compare the estimated performance of their quantum solution to the best classical solutions.
- Comparing performance of different algorithms that solve the same problem is a common application of quantum resource estimation. Think of other quantum algorithms you could implement and compare. You can start with the quantum state preparation algorithm from chapter 2 and compare it with the Qiskit and Q# library operations, or the unitary implementation algorithm from chapter 3 and compare it with the Qiskit library operation.

Summary

- The quality of a problem solution is a combination of the accuracy of the answer it gives and the time and the expense needed to produce that answer. When comparing quantum and classical solutions, it is important to use these practical metrics rather than more abstract properties such as the asymptotic behavior of the algorithms.
- When we look for practical quantum advantage for a classical problem, we have to compare the quantum solution with the *best* known classical solution of all.

Such a solution will typically be designed specifically for this problem and take advantage of all information about the problem structure.
- If a problem has an efficient classical solution, quantum computing is unlikely to offer an improvement over it. The search for practical quantum advantage focuses on problems that don't have a known efficient classical solution.
- Quantum algorithms aim to run on future fault-tolerant quantum computers, so any estimates of the algorithms' performance have to take into account the overhead introduced by the architecture of these computers.
- Error correction is a technique that enables reliable computation using noisy qubits. It encodes logical qubits and gates—the ones used in quantum programs—as multiple physical qubits and gates on an actual quantum device.
- Magic gates are gates that are not supported by the quantum computer directly but have to be generated using a separate process. These gates allow us to approximate any gate the program needs with required accuracy.
- Error correction and magic state distillation are several of the key factors that affect the resource requirements of quantum algorithms. The other factors include execution time of quantum gates and measurements and the limitations on the qubit connectivity.
- You have to take into account a lot of information about the logical architecture of quantum computers to make realistic estimates of your algorithm's performance. Specialized software tools such as Azure Quantum Resource Estimator allow you to make these estimates automatically based on your quantum program.

appendix A
Setting up your environment

The first step of starting a software project is setting up the development environment for it. If you're already familiar with the language you've chosen to use for the projects in this book, feel free to skip the setup step and dive right in! In case you're new to quantum programming or are comfortable with one of the languages and looking to add the other one to your toolbox, this appendix includes brief instructions for setting up the development environment for both Qiskit and Q#.

Multiple environments support Q# and Qiskit. Jupyter Notebook, for example, provides a great environment for getting started and learning the basic concepts, since it supports a broad variety of visualization tools. Azure Quantum offers Jupyter Notebook-based cloud programming environment for Q#, and several cloud development platforms do the same for Qiskit, allowing you to start coding without any local setup.

For larger projects, however, especially multifile projects that involve unit tests like the ones discussed in this book, you'll want to set up a local environment and use your preferred IDE and/or command line for building and running these projects. I recommend using Visual Studio Code to work with Q#. You can use any IDE that supports Python to develop Qiskit projects; I use Visual Studio Code for Qiskit as well.

Both Qiskit and Q# distributions include Python packages. It is recommended to set up different Python-dependent programming tools as separate virtual environments to simplify their management and isolate their dependencies. I use Miniconda, a minimal installer of Conda package manager (https://docs.conda.io/en/latest/miniconda.html), to manage Python environments.

A.1 Qiskit

Qiskit is a Python library developed by IBM and currently the most popular circuit-level quantum programming language.

A.1.1 Running Qiskit online

You can run Qiskit code online using one of the cloud platforms from the list of recommended notebook environments for Qiskit (see "Explore Newly Recommended Notebook Environments for Qiskit," https://mng.bz/BX40).

A.1.2 Installing Qiskit locally

Qiskit is distributed as a set of Python packages, so you only need to install these Python packages to get started with Qiskit. I used Python 3.12, Qiskit 1.3.1, and qiskit-aer 0.15.1 to develop the Qiskit code for this book. Once you have a Python environment set up, you can install the latest version of Qiskit using pip or conda:

```
pip install qiskit qiskit-aer
```

Now, you can run files containing Qiskit code just like regular Python files, by navigating to the folder containing the project and using

```
python qiskit_example.py
```

If you run into any problems setting up your Qiskit environment, check the latest documentation (https://docs.quantum.ibm.com/start/install) to see any changes to the installation instructions that occurred since this book has been released. Note that you don't need to install Qiskit Runtime because this book doesn't require you to run your code on quantum hardware.

A.2 Q#

Q# is a domain-specific language developed by Microsoft that focuses on high-level quantum algorithm design. It can be integrated with Python.

A.2.1 Running Q# online

You can run small Q# code snippets using Code with Azure Quantum (https://mng.bz/dX5N). This tool will run your code and show you the results of its execution on a simulator. However, it does not support multifile projects, Python integration, or unit tests.

Alternatively, you can use Azure Quantum to run Q# code as Jupyter Notebooks (https://mng.bz/rKOB). This environment supports Python integration but not multifile projects or unit tests. It also allows you to run your code on quantum hardware, but this is not necessary for this book.

A.2.2 Installing Q# locally

To access all Q# functionality you'll need for running this book's samples, I recommend setting it up in Visual Studio Code. Azure Quantum Development Kit extension for Visual Studio Code (https://mng.bz/VVNP) provides language support in the editor: running code on the simulator and debugging, as well as convenient IntelliSense features such as syntax highlighting, autocompletion, and error checking.

There are three ways to run standalone Q# code snippets (for example, the code in the first two sections of chapter 2) after you install this extension:

- Use the Run Q# File command under the Play icon dropdown in the top-right of the editor window.
- Use the Run code action from the list of code actions shown next to the operation that serves as the entry point to the code.
- Press Ctrl+F5.

The output produced by the Q# code will appear in the debug console.

Q# unit tests and examples of hybrid quantum-classical processing are implemented via Python integration, so you will need to set it up to work with the majority of the code in this book. I used Python 3.12 and Q# 1.11.1 to develop the Q# code for this book. You can install the latest version of Q# using pip or conda:

```
pip install qsharp
```

Now, you can run Python projects that include Q# projects just like regular Python projects by navigating to the folder containing the project and using

```
python classical_host.py
```

If you run into any problems setting up your Q# environment, check the latest documentation (see "Set Up the Quantum Development Kit Extension," https://mng.bz/xK9W) to see any changes to the installation instructions that occurred since this book has been released.

A.3 pytest

Unit tests in this book are Python-based and use the pytest testing framework. Once you have a Python environment set up, you can install the latest version of pytest using pip or conda:

```
pip install pytest
```

Now, you can run the tests for Qiskit projects and Python-based tests for Q# projects just like regular Python tests by navigating to the folder containing the tests and running pytest. If you used separate virtual environments for Q# and for Qiskit, you'll need to install pytest in both of them separately.

A.4 Getting the code

The code for the projects developed in this book is available in a GitHub repository located at https://github.com/tcNickolas/quantum-programming-in-depth. You can get a local copy of the code by cloning this repository using the standard GitHub tools.

The repository contains folders for each chapter of the book and subfolders for each section of the chapter. Each chapter folder contains complete code developed in each section of that chapter, both in Qiskit and in Q#. Follow the instructions in the repository's README file to run the samples.

index

A

adjoint variant 37, 55, 104, 122, 160, 229
algorithms *See* classical vs. quantum algorithms, Deutsch–Jozsa algorithm, Grover's search algorithm, Harrow–Hassidim–Lloyd (HHL) algorithm, phase estimation algorithms, quantum algorithms, Shor's algorithm
amplitude 29–30, 33, 67, 92, 131–132, 138, 142, 144, 203
ansatz 20
asymptotic complexity 246–247
Azure Quantum Development Kit xvi, 25–26, 251–252, 261
Azure Quantum Resource Estimator (AQRE)
    architecture input factors 253–254
    configuration options 254
    error budget usage 253
    input program requirements 252
    logical vs. physical resource estimates 254
    overview of 251–254
    space-time tradeoff visualization 252–253
    using with Qiskit and Q# 252

B

basis states
    behavior on single-bit basis inputs 162–163
    conversion from measurement outcomes 93
    correctness checks using |0⟩ and |1⟩ 168–171
    description of 29–33, 36–38
    determining parity state 113–118
    measurement outcome probabilities 91–93
    using in superposition discrimination 98–99
Benioff, Paul 5

big-O notation 3
bit strings
    big-endian vs. little-endian 30
    basis state indexing 30–31
    defining 203–204
    See also Boolean operators and operations
block-diagonal unitary, implementing 66–70, 75–79
Boolean operators and operations
    AND and multi-bit AND 177
    clause evaluation logic 181
    CNF (conjunctive normal form) 181
    EQUALITY implementation 176
    NOT implementation options 175
    OR and multi-bit OR 177–178
    XOR as CNOT 175
    See also bit strings

C

circuit synthesis
    classical synthesis tool use 173–174
    logic synthesis overview 173
    quantum circuit conversion 174–175
    reversible logic gate mapping 173
classical computing
    classical algorithms and 156–157, 202, 210, 214, 243–244, 247
    comparison with quantum computing 2, 4
    computational limits 4
classical vs. quantum algorithms
    accuracy, time, and cost metrics 242
    asymptotic vs. practical performance 246–247
    choosing the best classical algorithm as the comparison baseline 243

INDEX

classical vs. quantum algorithms *(continued)*
   crossover point illustration 4, 247
   impact of implementation overhead 248
   oracle execution cost 247
   practical vs. asymptotic behavior 243
   See also Deutsch-Jozsa algorithm, Grover's search algorithm, Harrow–Hassidim–Lloyd (HHL) algorithm, phase estimation algorithms, quantum algorithms, Shor's algorithm
computational complexity theory
   asymptotic behavior 243
   quadratic speedup 5–6, 210
controlled gates
   CCNOT for AND 177
   CNOT for XOR 175
   CNOT gate for parity 115
   controlled gates in matrix notation 66
   controlled-on-zero variant of a gate 32
   controlled-on-zero X gate 178
   CR_y gate 32
   definition and usage 31–32
   matrix forms 67–68
   Q# implementation 74–75
   Qiskit implementation 74
   See also Hadamard gate, quantum gates
cosine-sine decomposition
   CS matrix implementation 71–72
   CS unitary 64, 71–72, 74, 80–83
   definition and usage 64–65
   matrix multiplication verification 74
   SciPy library implementation 65
crossover point 4, 246

D

Deutsch-Jozsa algorithm 7, 193
   See also classical vs. quantum algorithms, quantum algorithms
development environments
   cloud-based Q# and Qiskit 259–260
   GitHub repository structure 262
   Jupyter Notebook compatibility 259
   multifile project considerations 259
   README usage and folder contents 262
   using Miniconda to manage Python environments 259
   using Visual Studio Code with Q# and Qiskit 259
   See also Python language, Q# language, Qiskit language
Dirac notation
   basis state representation 91
   controlled gates in 31
   using for multiqubit states 43–44
dump_operation
   matrix retrieval for Q# operations 61
   partial application in Q# 61

E

eigenphases
   definition and examples 133–134
   eigenvalues 133–134, 147, 149, 214
   eigenvectors 133–135, 147–149
   mathematical representation of 133
   phase estimation problem 134
   relationship to eigenvalues 133
   using in quantum algorithms 134
entanglement, preventing interference with 182–183
equal superpositions, definition of 203

F

fault-tolerant quantum computers 7–8, 54, 153, 243, 248–251, 253
Feynman, Richard 5
function reversibility
   definition and properties 159
   irreversibility of quantum measurement 160
   logical vs. physical reversibility 159
function testing
   input-output verification steps 168–170
   Q# CheckAllZero 171–172
   Qiskit testing implementations of single-bit functions 170–171
   testing reversible computations 167–172

G

ground state energy, calculating 20, 156, 191, 242
Grover's search algorithm 190–214
   algorithm overview 202–203
   comparison of iteration success rates 231–232
   end-to-end validation approach 227, 232
   implementing reflection about the mean 206–208
   iteration structure 208–209
   practical limitations of 6, 210–211, 256
   solving a search problem using 216
   suitability for sparse simulation 220
   superposition initialization 204–205
   unit tests for 213
   unstructured search use case 202
   working with multiple solutions 210
   See also classical vs. quantum algorithms, quantum algorithms

H

Hadamard gate 103–105, 123, 125, 138–139, 141, 143, 182–183, 198, 207
   See also controlled gates, quantum gates

hardware
  major milestones in 7–8
  noisy intermediate-scale quantum (NISQ) era 7
  quantum supremacy demonstrations 8
Harrow–Hassidim–Lloyd (HHL) algorithm 20, 122, 134, 152
  See also classical vs. quantum algorithms, quantum algorithms
hybrid quantum-classical processing 11, 191, 261

I

IBM Quantum 10
IDE setup
  Azure Quantum Development Kit extension for Visual Studio Code 261
  IntelliSense features 261
initial state preparation
  common algorithms using equal superpositions 20
  importance of, when working with quantum algorithms 19–21
  simple vs. arbitrary states 20–21
input encoding
  big-endian vs. little-endian 158
  integer vs. bit array representation 158

J

joint measurements
  auxiliary qubit role 114–115
  implementing joint/parity measurements 113–117
  preserving superposition state 113–115

M

Manin, Yuri 5
marking oracle implementation
  uncomputing constraint checks 226, 231
matrix decomposition
  CS unitary decomposition 66
  CS unitary math background 72
  two-qubit decomposition strategy 64–66
matrix reconstruction
  column sign determination 131
  diagonal vs antidiagonal test 131
  estimating coefficients 130
  unitary matrix structures 130
mean state preparation 216, 226, 231, 244
measurement testing and verification
  basis state preparation 95–96
  classical interpretation 93
  classical register use in Qiskit 93–94
  compare against input state 96
  computational basis 92
  deterministic outcomes for basis states 92
  Hadamard basis 104
  measurement in Qiskit and Q# 94–97
  multiple trial statistics 109
  noncomputational basis 104–105
  oracle behavior verification 197–199
  Q# test logic and conversion 96–97
  Qiskit test automation 94–95
  Result in Q# 96
  result interpretation logic 100–101
  unit testing strategy in Q# and Qiskit 213
  See also testing and verification
middle-layer software 10
Miniconda, managing Python environments with 259
multiplexers 75
multiqubit state
  Dirac notation 43–44
  n-qubit state expansion 43
  recursive preparation 44
  state vector representation 43

N

N queens puzzle
  constraint satisfaction formulation 217–218
  diagonal conflict detection 223–224
  encoding strategies comparison 255
  Grover's search implementation 215–239
  physical qubit and runtime estimates 255
  quantum algorithm shortcomings 255–256
  row/column constraints 217, 221–222
  solution space complexity 220–221, 234–235
  success rate with different encodings 228, 232
N queens puzzle and Azure Quantum Resource Estimator (AQRE)
  code parameterization example 252
  resource plot interpretation 253
  simulation vs. AQRE comparison 248
N queens puzzle, classical solutions
  backtracking approach 245
  brute-force variants 244–245
  explicit construction method 246
  local search heuristics 245
  performance at large N 255–256
National Quantum Initiative Act 12
noisy intermediate-scale quantum (NISQ) era 7
nuclear magnetic resonance 7

O

oracle design
  black-box definition 193
  Q# operation for oracles 201–202

266 INDEX

oracle design *(continued)*
   Qiskit circuits for oracles 199–200
   search condition encoding 194–196
   unitary construction for oracles 196–197
   verification of oracle correctness 197–199

P

partial application
   usage in Q# 61
   use case with dump_operation 61
partial information extraction
   joint measurements 114–116
   parity without collapsing state 113–114
   qubit entanglement and auxiliary qubit 115
Pauli gates 123, 151
phase estimation algorithms
   adaptive algorithm 140–142
   comparison of techniques 145–146
   iterative algorithm 138–139
   quantum Fourier transform 143–144
   quantum phase estimation algorithm 144–145
   use of controlled unitaries 135–136
phase kickback
   control qubit phase alteration 136–137
   principle overview 135–136
   usage in oracle design 195–196
Python language
   developing tests for Q# with Python 42–43
   pytest parameterization 171
   pytest, installing 261
   Q# and Python integration 60–61
   Q# test invocation from Python 173
   qsharp package 98, 251
   SciPy library 65, 83
   unit testing with pytest 62–63
   using Miniconda to manage Python environments 259
   See also development environments, Q# language, Qiskit language

Q

Q# installation
   Azure Quantum Development Kit extension 261
   development versions used by author 261
   online execution with Azure Quantum 260
   pip and conda installation methods 261
   running and debugging code 261
Q# language
   ApplyControlledOnInt function 70, 73
   ApplyToEachA ifunction 231
   cloud-based environment 259–260
   Controlled and Adjoint keywords 201
   controlled-on-zero syntax 37–38, 167, 180
   developing tests with Python 42–43
   DumpMachine function 29–30, 38
   DumpOperation function vs. Python tools 62
   Fact assertion 97
      IncByLE operation 238–239
   measurement 95–97
   Message function 96
   operation specializations 37
   partial application syntax 61
      PreparePureStateD function 21, 229, 238
   Python integration 60–61
   releasing qubits 26
   Result data type 96
   Q# vs. Qiskit code structure 24–25
   test invocation from Python 173
   test logic and conversion 96–97
   qubit ordering conventions 67
   syntax differences in Q# and Qiskit 58
   unit testing strategy in Q# and Qiskit 213
   using Visual Studio Code with Q# and Qiskit 259
   See also development environments, Python language, Qiskit language
Qiskit installation
   development versions used by author 260
   local installation via pip or conda 260
   online execution platforms 260
   Qiskit Runtime not required 260
Qiskit language
   cloud-based environment 2260
   control and ctrl_state usage 69, 166, 179
   controlled unitary 128
   custom gates 35–36
   developing tests 40–41
   initialize method 21, 146-147
   measurement 94–95
   pytest parameterization 171
   Q# vs. Qiskit code structure 24–25
   save_statevector method 28–29
   simulation 28, 94–95, 112
   StatePreparation library 224
   syntax differences in Q# and Qiskit 58
   test architecture 147
   test automation 94–95
   to_gate method 34
   transpilation 36
   quantum_info Operator 60
   unit testing strategy in Q# and Qiskit 213
   unitary matrix retrieval methods 59–60
   unitary_simulator usage 59
   using Visual Studio Code with Q# and Qiskit 259
   See also development environments, Python language, Q# language
quantum algorithms
   adiabatic model 5
   algorithm optimization 11–12

computational complexity of 6
evaluating the performance of 241-257
gate-based model 5
hybrid algorithms 11
measurement-based model 5
practicality considerations 5–6
quantum counting algorithm 122, 134
small-data big-compute problems 4–5
See also classical vs. quantum algorithms, Deutsch-Jozsa algorithm, Grover's search algorithm, Harrow–Hassidim–Lloyd (HHL) algorithm, phase estimation algorithms, Shor's algorithm

quantum circuits
measurement integration 93–94
Qiskit transpilation 36
simulator backends 94–95, 112

quantum Fourier transform (QFT)
definition and application 142–143
QFT of one- and two-qubit states 143
two-qubit implementation 143–144

quantum gates
CCNOT gate 2
CNOT gate 2
Hadamard gate H 2
Pauli gates X, Y, and Z 2, 123, 151
phase shift gates S and T 2
rotation gate Ry 2
See also controlled gates, Hadamard gate

Quantum Katas 3, 49
Quantum Open Source Foundation 14
quantum oracles 52–53, 127, 193–206, 244, 247
quantum random access memory (qRAM) 20
quantum simulators 10
advantages for debugging 27–28
limitations and memory constraints 28
state introspection 28–29

quantum state discrimination
basis-to-state mapping 98–100
Bell states 102–106
minimum error approach 106–108
nonorthogonal state discrimination 106–109
orthogonal overlapping states 102–105
orthogonality constraints 99
probabilistic logic 100–101
superpositions with distinct basis states 98–101

quantum state tomography
amplitude estimation 110–111
relative phase estimation 111–112
test accuracy of reconstruction 112–113

quantum computing's technologies, applications, and initiatives
comparison with classical computing 1–2
conditions for practical advantage 4
error correction demonstrations 8

exponential speedup 5
government initiatives 12
hardware and software components of 5
hype versus practical application 4
industry involvement 13
job opportunities 13
main technologies under development 7
master's degree programs 13
milestones achieved 7–8
performance evaluation 12
practical applications 5
Quantum Flagship 12
quantum software development workflow 14
quantum software stack 9–10
quantum supremacy, demonstrations and refutations 8
quantum system simulation 4–5
testing and debugging 11
See also classical vs. quantum algorithms, quantum algorithms

qubits
auxiliary qubit role 114–115
basis states for control qubits 136–137
control qubit phase alteration 136–137
implementing a single-qubit unitary 58
memory and qubit savings 235
n-qubit state expansion 43
physical qubit and runtime estimates 255
Q# qubit reset enforcement 26
qubit connectivity 250
qubit error rates and gate speed 249
qubit ordering conventions 67
releasing qubits in Q# 26
using Dirac notation for multiqubit states 43–44

R

reflection about the mean operation 20–21, 52–54, 206
resource estimation
fault-tolerant computer assumptions 248–250
logical architecture factors 249–250
magic state distillation 250–251
qubit connectivity 250
qubit error rates and gate speed 249
simulator limitations 247–248
reversible computation
design constraints for quantum systems 159–160
evaluating single-bit functions 160–164
formulating classical logic in quantum terms 157–158
reversibility constraints and strategies 159–161
reversible computing 157–160

reversible computation *(continued)*
  reversible operation definitions 166–167, 179–180
  testing reversible computations 158–161

S

search space
  binary encoding of items 194
  initial superposition coverage 204–205
  reflection step impact 206–208
  solution probability estimation 209–210
Shor's algorithm 5–6, 122, 134, 152
  See also classical vs. quantum algorithms, quantum algorithms
state preparation
  phase estimation circuits and 135–136
  recursive algorithm 21-48
  state evolution and 20–21
  superposition testing state 165
supercomputers 1–2, 4
superposition states
  discrimination via measurement 98–100
  overlapping basis state cases 102–104
  preservation during parity test 113–114
  See also state preparation

T

tensor product 143, 221, 233
testing and verification
  case selection for testing 40
  corner cases (diagonal/antidiagonal matrices) 63–64
  developing tests for Q# with Python 42–43
  developing tests for Qiskit 40–41
  enumeration of classical inputs 167–169
  implementation vs. theory 246
  oracle behavior verification 197–199, 227, 231
  problem-specific performance metrics 242
  pytest parameterization for Qiskit 171
  Q# test invocation from Python 173
  random matrix generation 63
  realistic simulation expectations 248
  search space-restricted testing 231
  test parameter coverage 41–42
  testing quantum software 39–41
  truth table equivalence in quantum circuits 176
  unit test vs. integration test 41
  unit testing strategy in Q# and Qiskit 213
  unit testing with pytest 62–63

U

unitaries, distinguishing
  controlled gate comparisons 126–127
  math strategy and initial state selection 124
  phase kickback 126–127
  testing solutions 127–129
  using orthogonal state mapping 123–125
unitary matrices and operations
  antisymmetric structure 56–57
  applying Ry and Z gates 57
  definition and properties 55–56
  eigenvector multiplication 133
  input validation 58
  matrix representation options 130
  phase alteration detection 126
  reconstruction via experiments 130–131
  special cases and tolerances 58
  symmetric vs. antisymmetric branches 56–57
  syntax differences in Q# and Qiskit 58
  testing against known gates 57